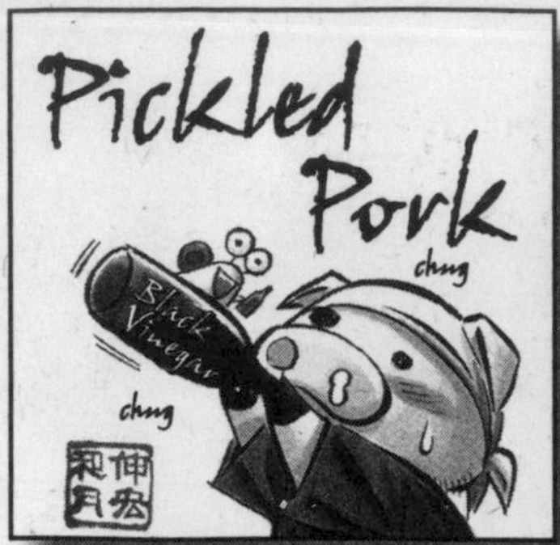
Pickled
Pork
chug
Black Vinegar
chug
伸宏
和月

"If I could be a manga artist, I wouldn't mind dying at 30."
That's what I thought when I was 20, but now I'm over 30 and I've been making a living as a manga artist for 10 years, and there are still so many things that I want to draw. The truth is, it would be really inconvenient for me to die now. I'm just not ready to go yet. (It was bad enough having to deal with the disappointment of being canceled mid-series.) Consequently, I've become more health conscious. I've even started drinking black vinegar. As you can see in the illustration, it might be a good thing to do.

—Nobuhiro Watsuki

Nobuhiro Watsuki earned international accolades for his first major manga series, **Rurouni Kenshin**, about a wandering swordsman in Meiji Era Japan. Serialized in Japan's *Weekly Shonen Jump* from 1994 to 1999, **Rurouni Kenshin**, available in North America from VIZ Media, quickly became a worldwide sensation, inspiring a spin-off short story ("Yahiko no Sakabatô"), an animated TV show and a series of novels. Watsuki's latest hit, **Buso Renkin**, began publication in *Weekly Shonen Jump* in June 2003.

BUSO RENKIN
VOL. 5
The SHONEN JUMP ADVANCED
Manga Edition

STORY AND ART BY
NOBUHIRO WATSUKI

English Adaptation/Lance Caselman
Translation/Toshifumi Yoshida
Touch-up Art & Lettering/James Gaubatz
Design/Yukiko Whitley
Editor/Urian Brown

Managing Editor/Frances E. Wall
Editorial Director/Elizabeth Kawasaki
VP & Editor in Chief/Yumi Hoashi
Sr. Director of Acquisitions/Rika Inouye
Sr. VP of Marketing/Liza Coppola
Exec. VP of Sales & Marketing/John Easum
Publisher/Hyoe Narita

Printed in the U.S.A.

Published by VIZ Media, LLC
P.O. Box 77010
San Francisco, CA 94107

SHONEN JUMP ADVANCED Manga Edition
10 9 8 7 6 5 4 3 2 1
First printing, April 2006

THE WORLD'S MOST
CUTTING-EDGE MANGA
SHONEN JUMP ADVANCED
www.shonenjump.com

www.viz.com

RATED
T+
FOR OLDER TEEN

PARENTAL ADVISORY
BUSO RENKIN is rated T+ for Older Teen and is recommended
for ages 16 and up. This volume contains fantasy violence.

SHONEN JUMP ADVANCED MANGA EDITION

STORY & ART BY
NOBUHIRO WATSUKI

Vol. 5
A Friend of Everyone

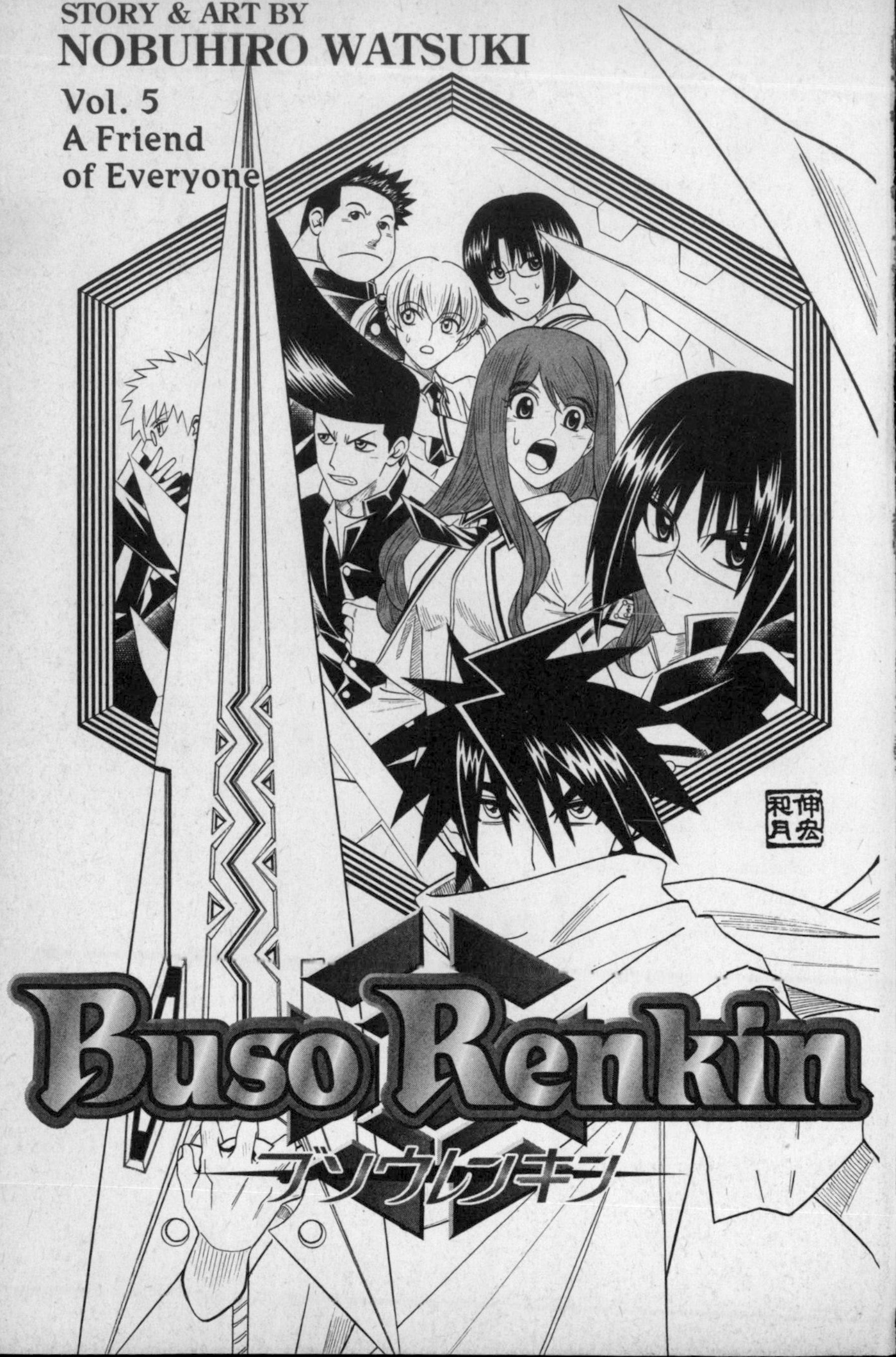
伸宏
和月
Buso Renkin
ブソウレンキン

Alchemy
Alchemy is an early proto-science combining elements of various disciplines that swept through Europe over the millennia. Its goals were the transmutation of base metals into gold and the creation of an Elixir of Immortality, neither of which succeeded. But unknown to the world at large, alchemy achieved two earthshaking supernatural successes–the homunculi and the kakugane.

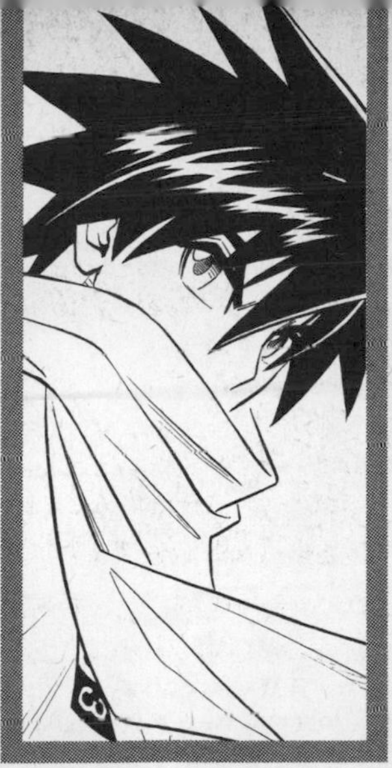

Kazuki Muto

Kazuki was once killed by a homunculus but was restored to life by Tokiko, who replaced his heart with a magical talisman called a kakugane. Kazuki is 16 years old, a year older than his sister Mahiro. His Buso Renkin is a lance called "Sunlight Heart."

武装錬金 CHARACTERS

Homunculus
An artificial being created by alchemy. The form and powers of the homunculus differ depending on the organism it was based on. Homunculi feed on human flesh, and can only be destroyed by the power of alchemy.

Kakugane
The kakugane are forged from a magical alchemic alloy. They are activated by the deepest parts of the human psyche, the basic instincts. Each kakugane can materialize a unique weapon called a Buso Renkin.

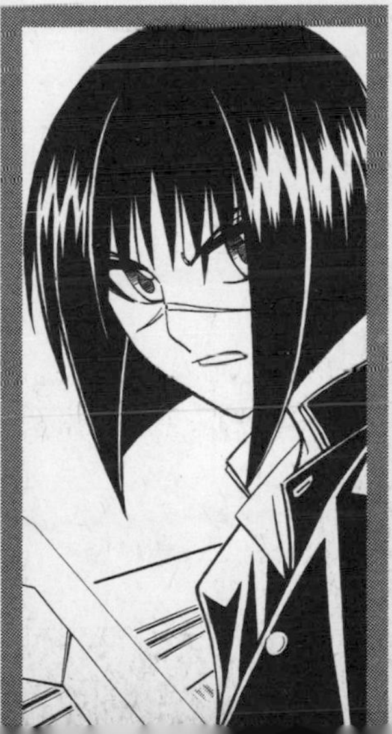

Tokiko Tsumura

A girl chosen to be an Alchemist Warrior, an expert of Buso Renkin. Her Buso Renkin is a Death Scythe called the "Valkyrie Skirt."

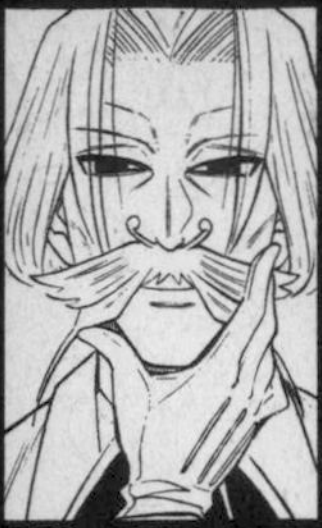

Dr. Butterfly (Bakushaku Chouno)

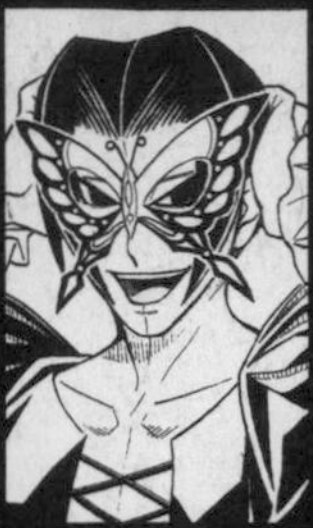

Papillon (Koushaku Chouno)

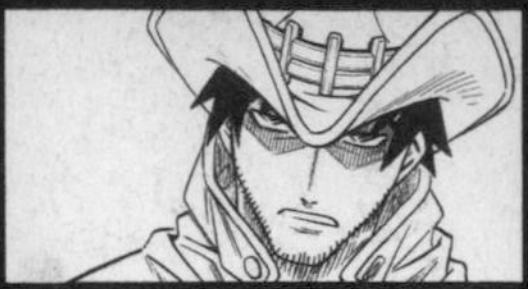

Captain Bravo (Warrior Chief)

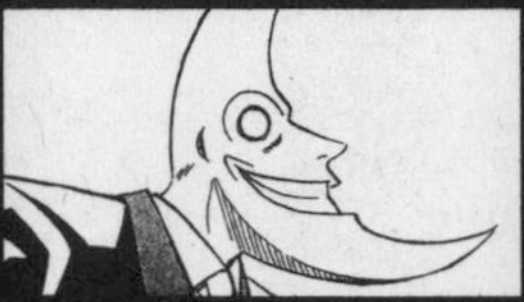

Moonface

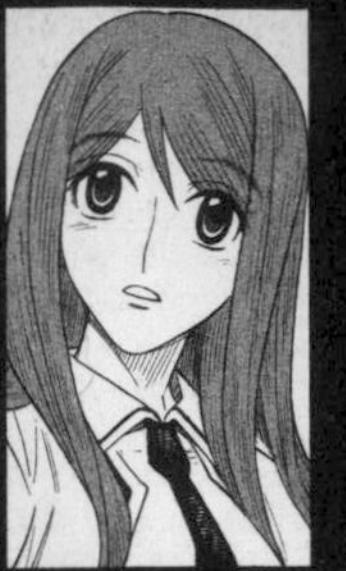

Mahiro Muto

STORY

Alchemist Warrior Tokiko comes to Ginsei City and uses herself as bait for the homunculi, artificial life forms that lurk in the darkness to devour unsuspecting humans. But Kazuki Muto, a high school student, unaware of Tokiko's intentions, tries to save her and is killed. Tokiko restores Kazuki's life with an alchemic talisman called a kakugane, and he fights at Tokiko's side to save his friends.

After Tokiko and Kazuki defeat Papillon's homunculi, Captain Bravo decides to train Kazuki to be an Alchemist Warrior. Meanwhile, Dr. Butterfly sends the homunculi Kinjo and Jinnai to eliminate Kazuki and the Warriors. The kakugane-armed homunculi are defeated, but soon a new threat arises--Kazuki and Tokiko's schoolmates Ouka and Shusui Hayasaka are sent to destroy them. In the battle that follows, the twins are revealed to be Familiars, human vassals of the homunculi. But when Tokiko goes in for the kill, Kazuki stays her hand, and the Hayasaka are placed under the protection of the Alchemist Warriors.

From Ouka, the Warriors learn the secret location of the L.X.E. hideout, which they then assault. There they encounter only Moonface, who has been left behind to delay them. To their horror they discover that Dr. Butterfly has taken the Warrior Traitor to complete his recovery by feeding on their fellow students!

Hideyuki Okakura

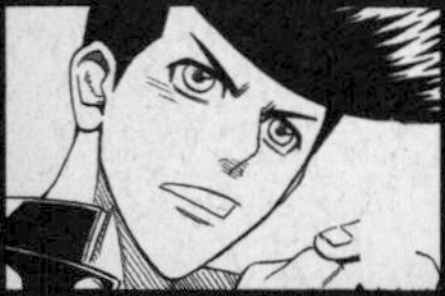

Masashi Daihama

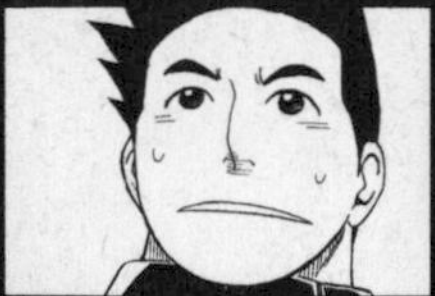

Koji Rokumasu

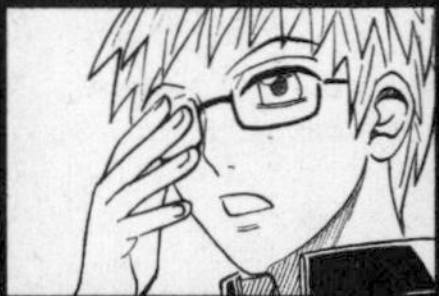

Chii-chin (Chisato Wakamiya)

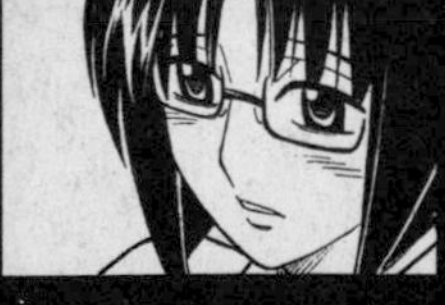

Angel Gozen

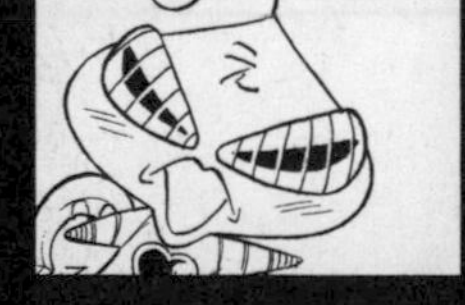

Saa-chan (Saori Kawai)

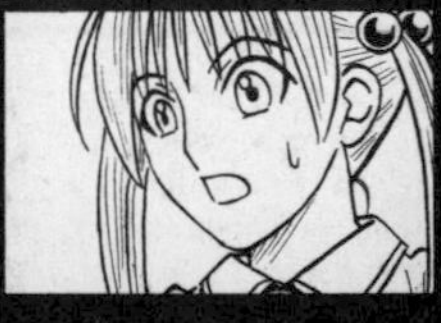

BUSO RENKIN
Volume 5: A Friend of Everyone

CONTENTS

Chapter 37: In the Same Category   7

Chapter 38: A Friend of Everybody   27

Chapter 39: Overflowing Power   47

Chapter 40: A Sign of Death   67

Chapter 41: Papillon vs. Butterfly, Part I   87

Chapter 42: Papillon vs. Butterfly, Part II   107

Chapter 43: Who Are You?   125

Chapter 44: The Pulse Quickens   145

Chapter 45: A Spring Night Two Months Past   165

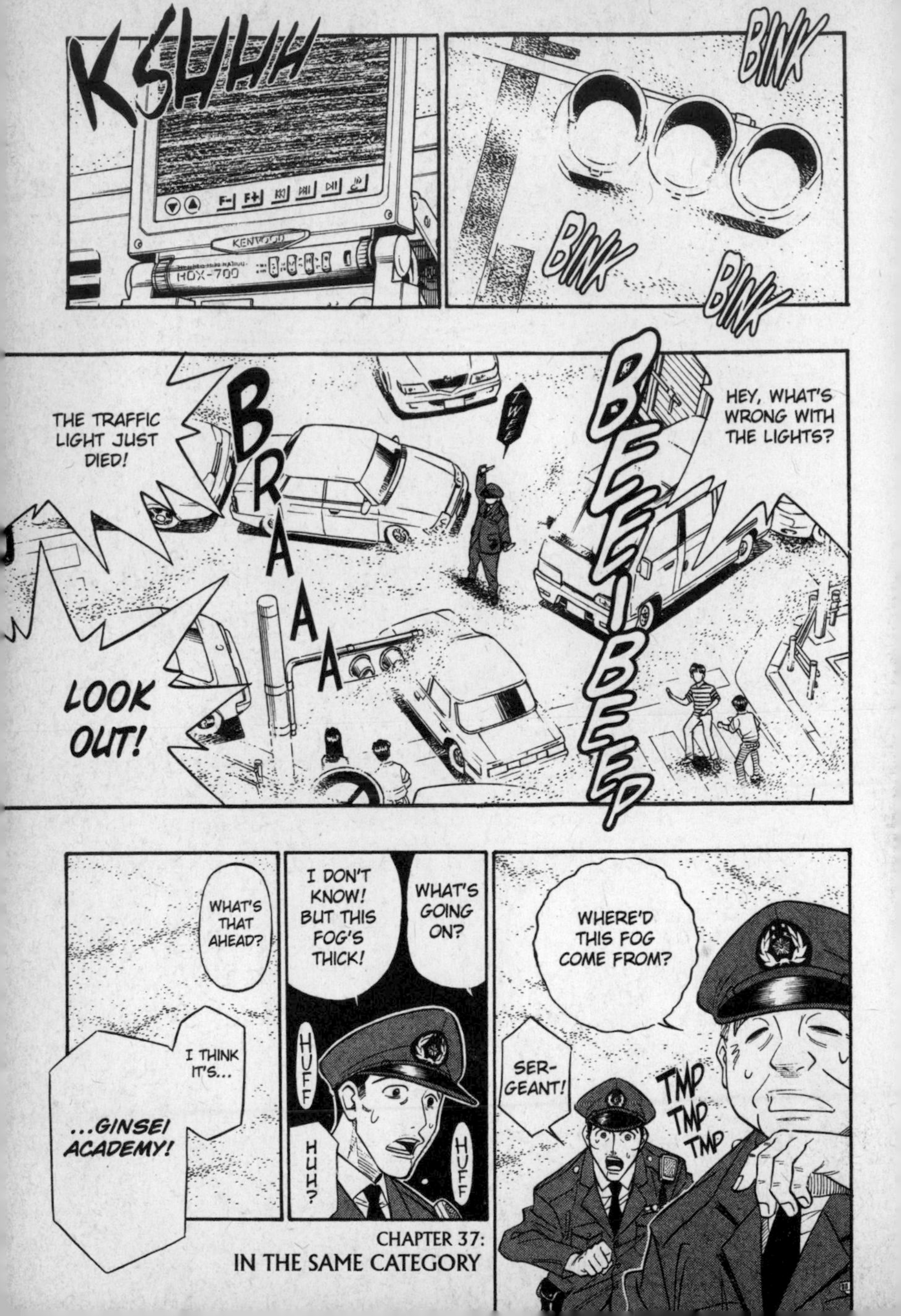
BINK
BINK
BINK
KSHHH
KENWOOD
HDX-700
HEY, WHAT'S WRONG WITH THE LIGHTS?
BEEBEEP
TWEE
BRAAAA
THE TRAFFIC LIGHT JUST DIED!
LOOK OUT!
WHERE'D THIS FOG COME FROM?
SER-GEANT!
TMP TMP TMP
WHAT'S GOING ON?
I DON'T KNOW! BUT THIS FOG'S THICK!
HUFF
HUFF
HUH?
WHAT'S THAT AHEAD?
I THINK IT'S...
...GINSEI ACADEMY!

CHAPTER 37: IN THE SAME CATEGORY

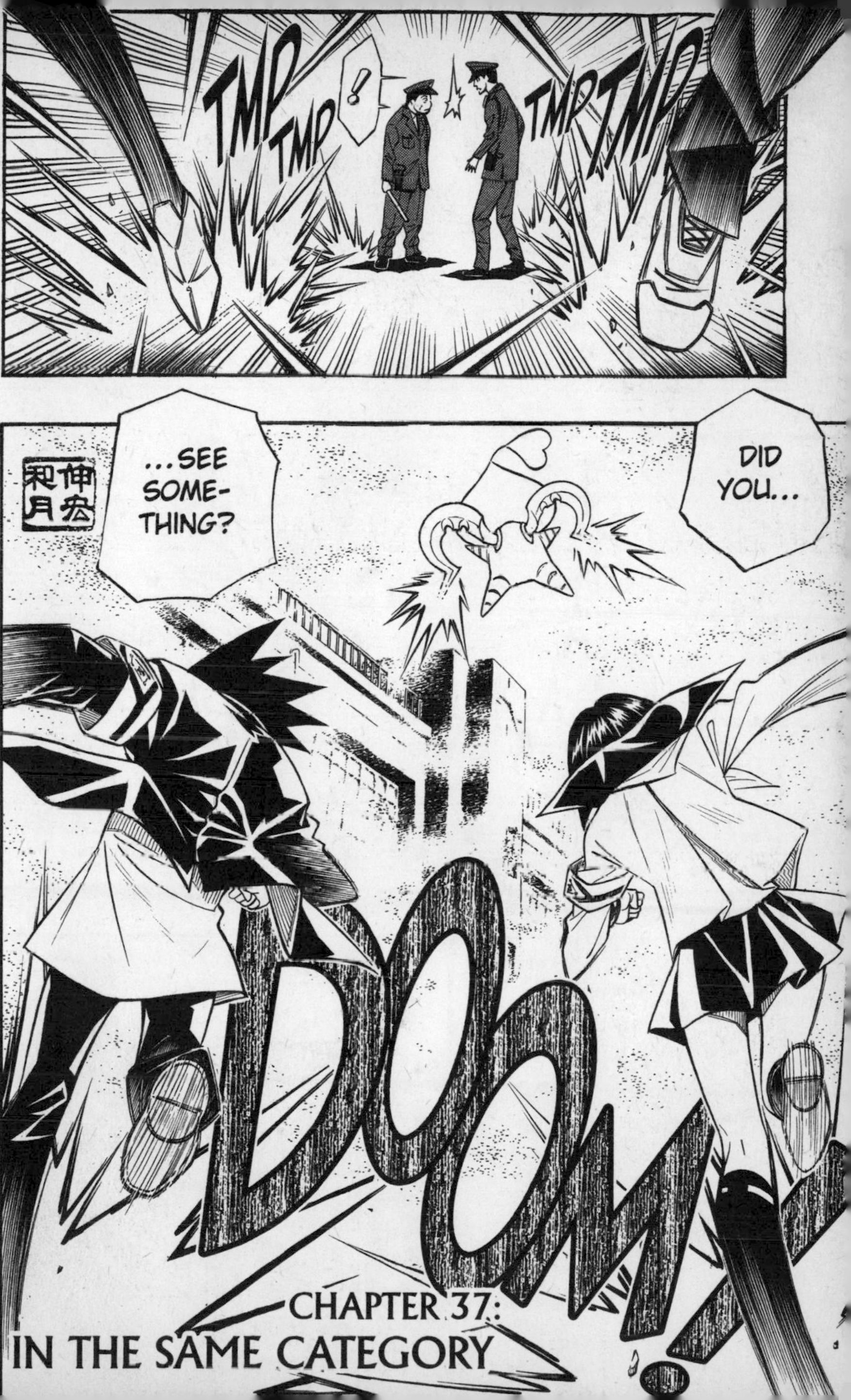
TMP TMP
!
TMP TMP
DID YOU...
...SEE SOME-THING?
伸宏和月
DOOM!

CHAPTER 37: IN THE SAME CATEGORY

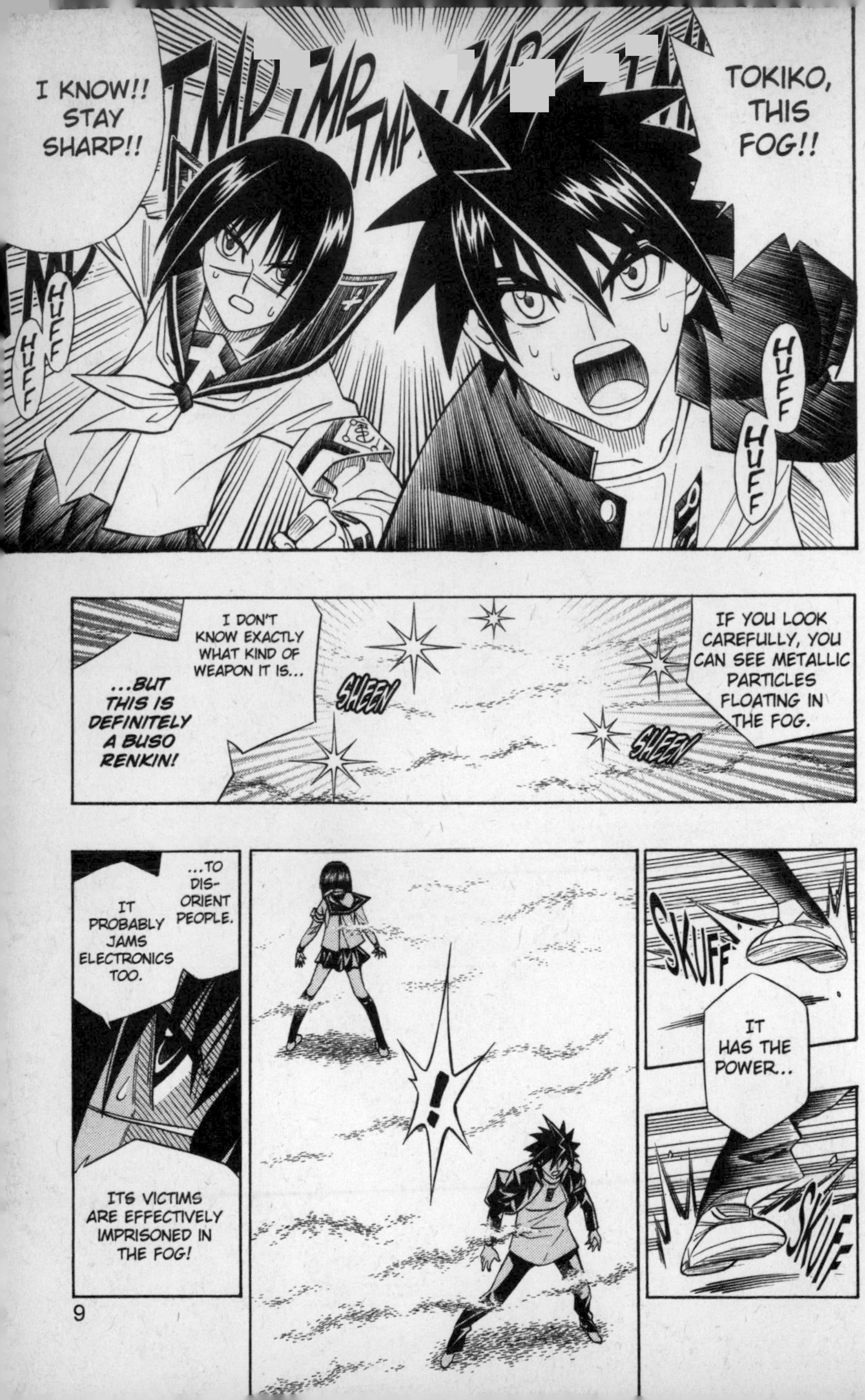
TOKIKO, THIS FOG!!
TMP TMP TMP
I KNOW!! STAY SHARP!!
HUFF HUFF
HUFF HUFF
IF YOU LOOK CAREFULLY, YOU CAN SEE METALLIC PARTICLES FLOATING IN THE FOG.
SHEEN
SHEEN
I DON'T KNOW EXACTLY WHAT KIND OF WEAPON IT IS...
...BUT THIS IS DEFINITELY A BUSO RENKIN!
SKUFF
IT HAS THE POWER...
SKUFF
!
...TO DIS-ORIENT PEOPLE.
IT PROBABLY JAMS ELECTRONICS TOO.
ITS VICTIMS ARE EFFECTIVELY IMPRISONED IN THE FOG!

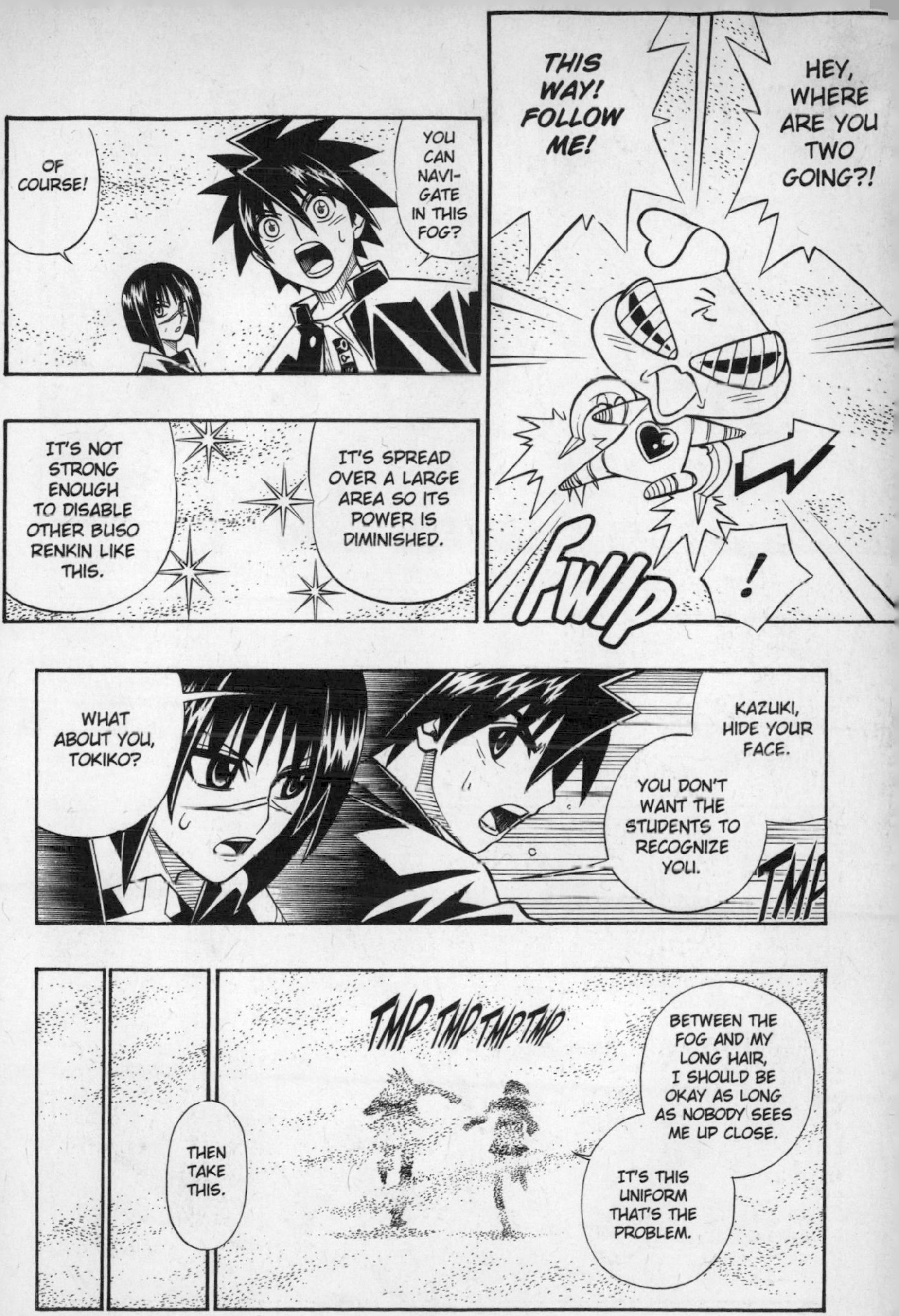
HEY, WHERE ARE YOU TWO GOING?!
THIS WAY! FOLLOW ME!
FWIP
!
YOU CAN NAVI-GATE IN THIS FOG?
OF COURSE!
IT'S SPREAD OVER A LARGE AREA SO ITS POWER IS DIMINISHED.
IT'S NOT STRONG ENOUGH TO DISABLE OTHER BUSO RENKIN LIKE THIS.
KAZUKI, HIDE YOUR FACE.
YOU DON'T WANT THE STUDENTS TO RECOGNIZE YOU.
TMP
WHAT ABOUT YOU, TOKIKO?
TMP TMP TMP TMP
BETWEEN THE FOG AND MY LONG HAIR, I SHOULD BE OKAY AS LONG AS NOBODY SEES ME UP CLOSE.
IT'S THIS UNIFORM THAT'S THE PROBLEM.
THEN TAKE THIS.

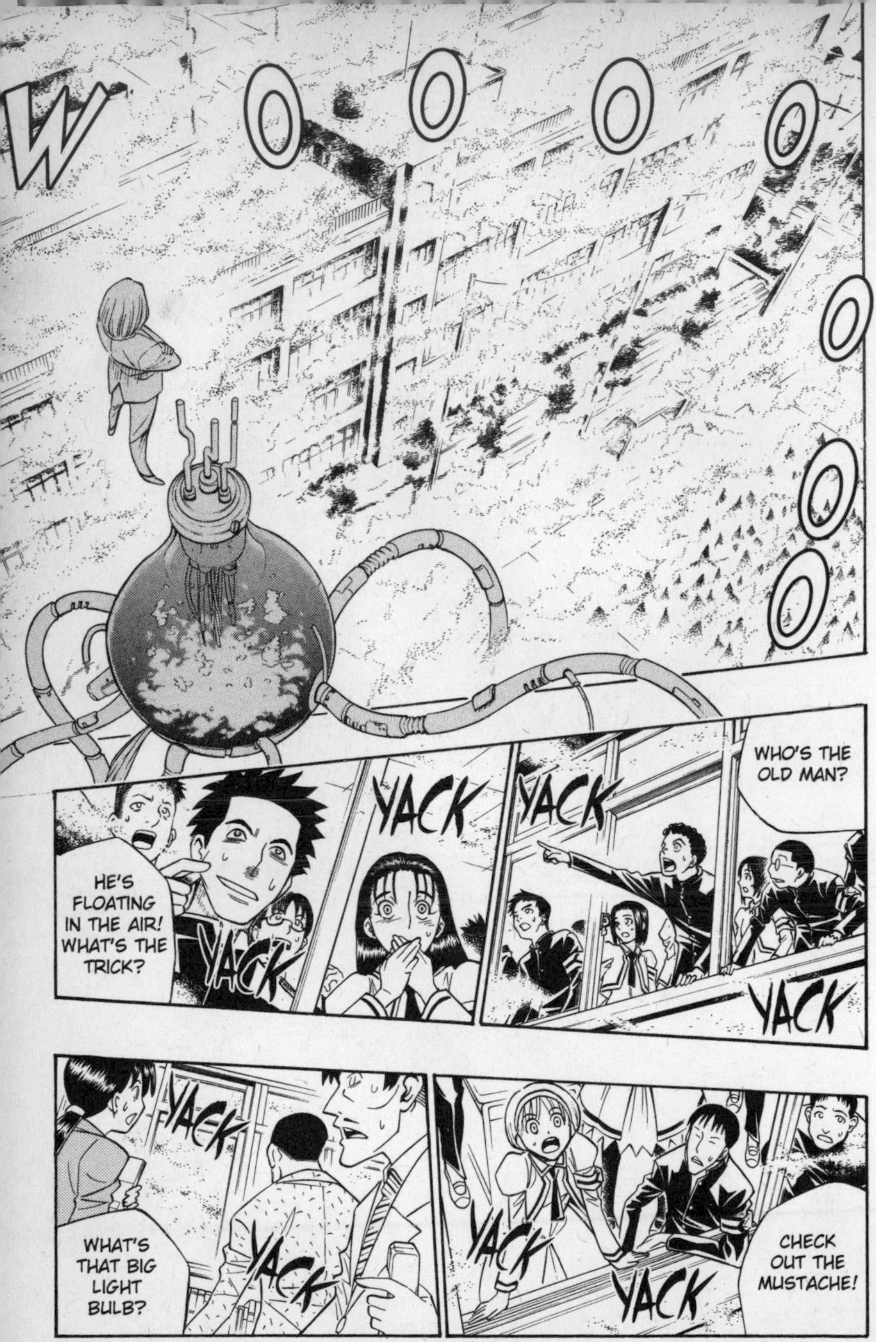
WOOOOOOO
YACK
WHO'S THE OLD MAN?
YACK
YACK
YACK
HE'S FLOATING IN THE AIR! WHAT'S THE TRICK?
YACK
CHECK OUT THE MUSTACHE!
YACK
YACK
YACK
WHAT'S THAT BIG LIGHT BULB?
YACK

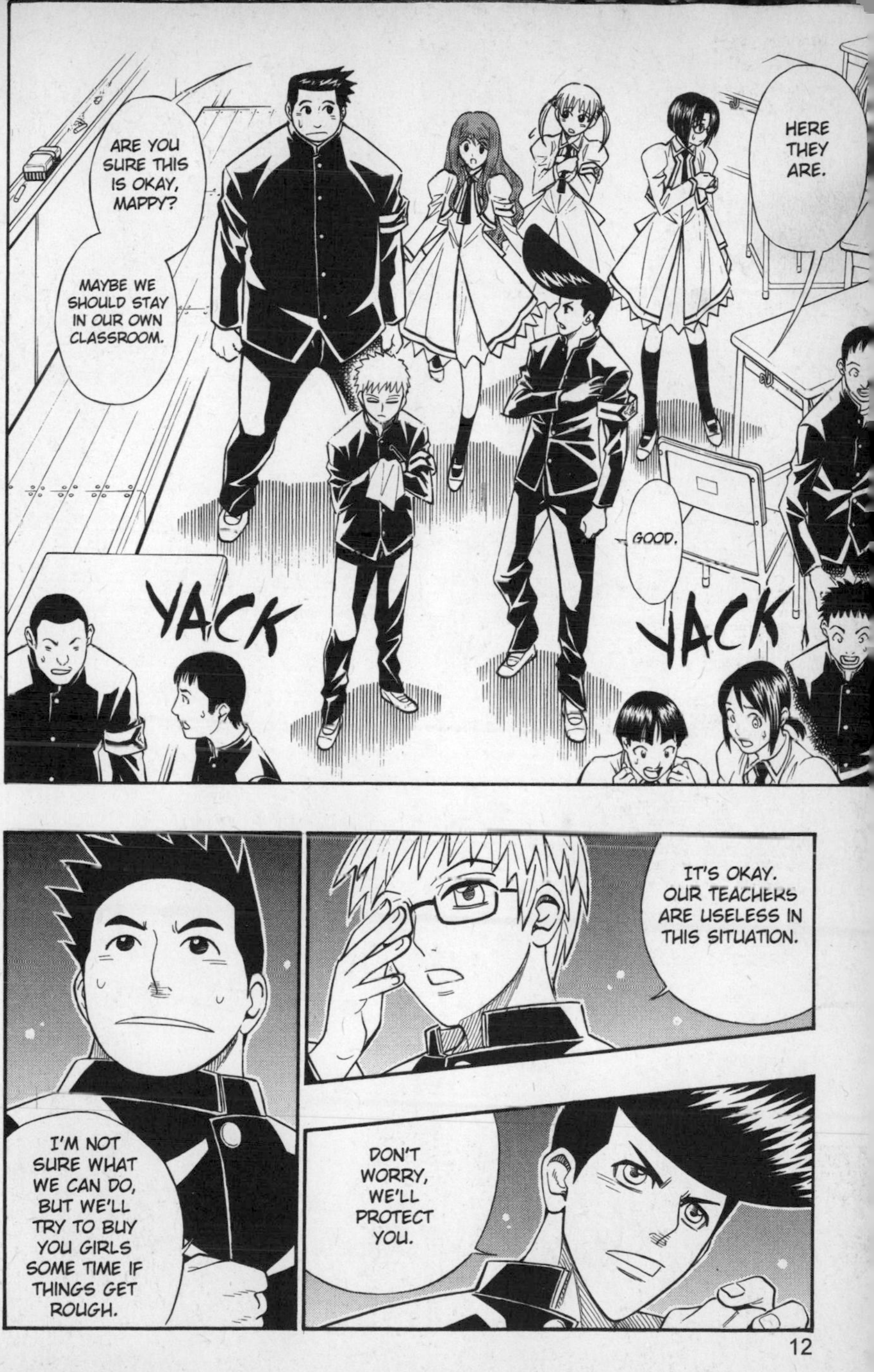
HERE THEY ARE.
YACK
GOOD.
ARE YOU SURE THIS IS OKAY, MAPPY?
MAYBE WE SHOULD STAY IN OUR OWN CLASSROOM.
YACK
IT'S OKAY. OUR TEACHERS ARE USELESS IN THIS SITUATION.
DON'T WORRY, WE'LL PROTECT YOU.
I'M NOT SURE WHAT WE CAN DO, BUT WE'LL TRY TO BUY YOU GIRLS SOME TIME IF THINGS GET ROUGH.

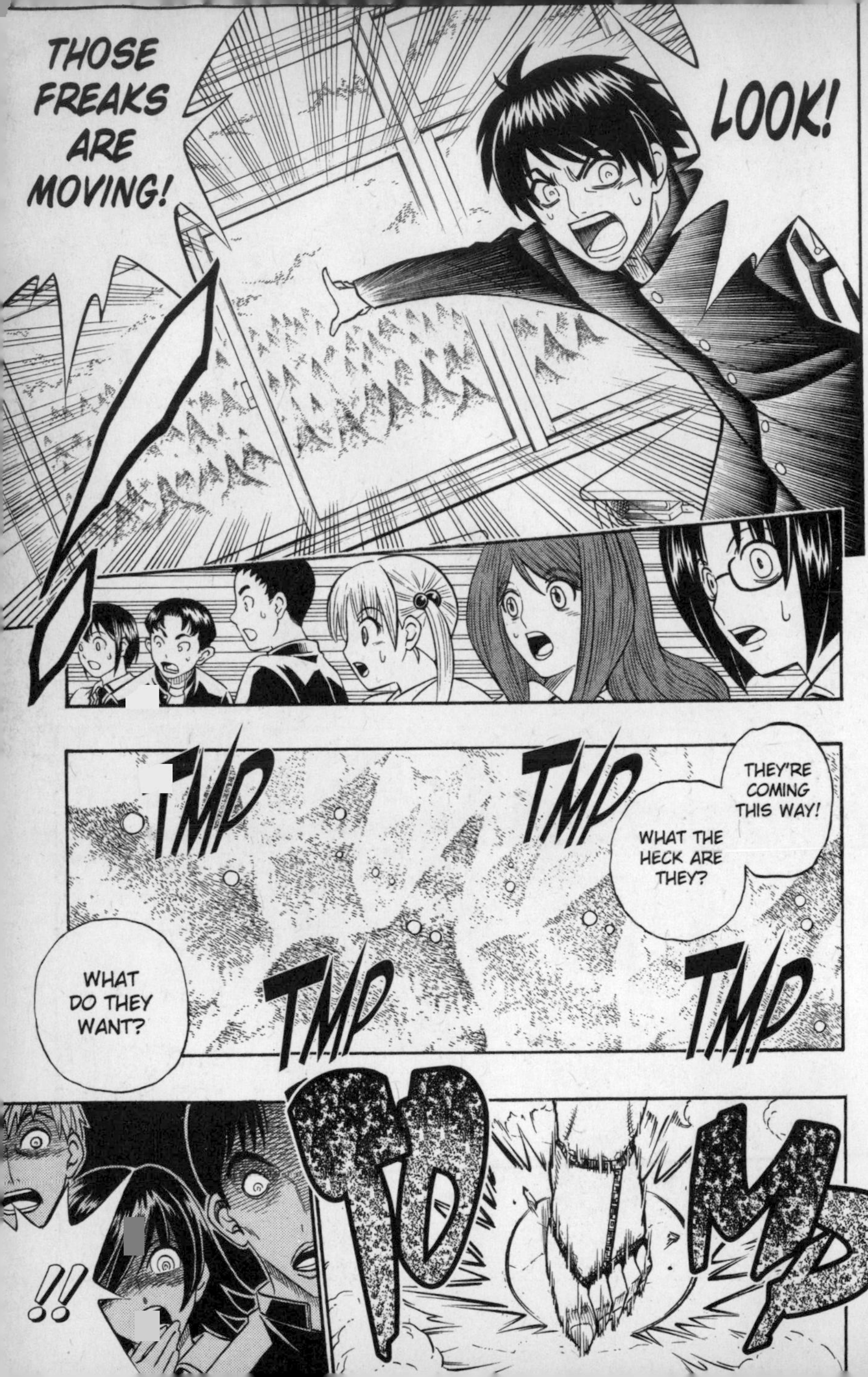
LOOK!
THOSE FREAKS ARE MOVING!
THEY'RE COMING THIS WAY!
TMP
TMP
WHAT THE HECK ARE THEY?
TMP
TMP
WHAT DO THEY WANT?
!!

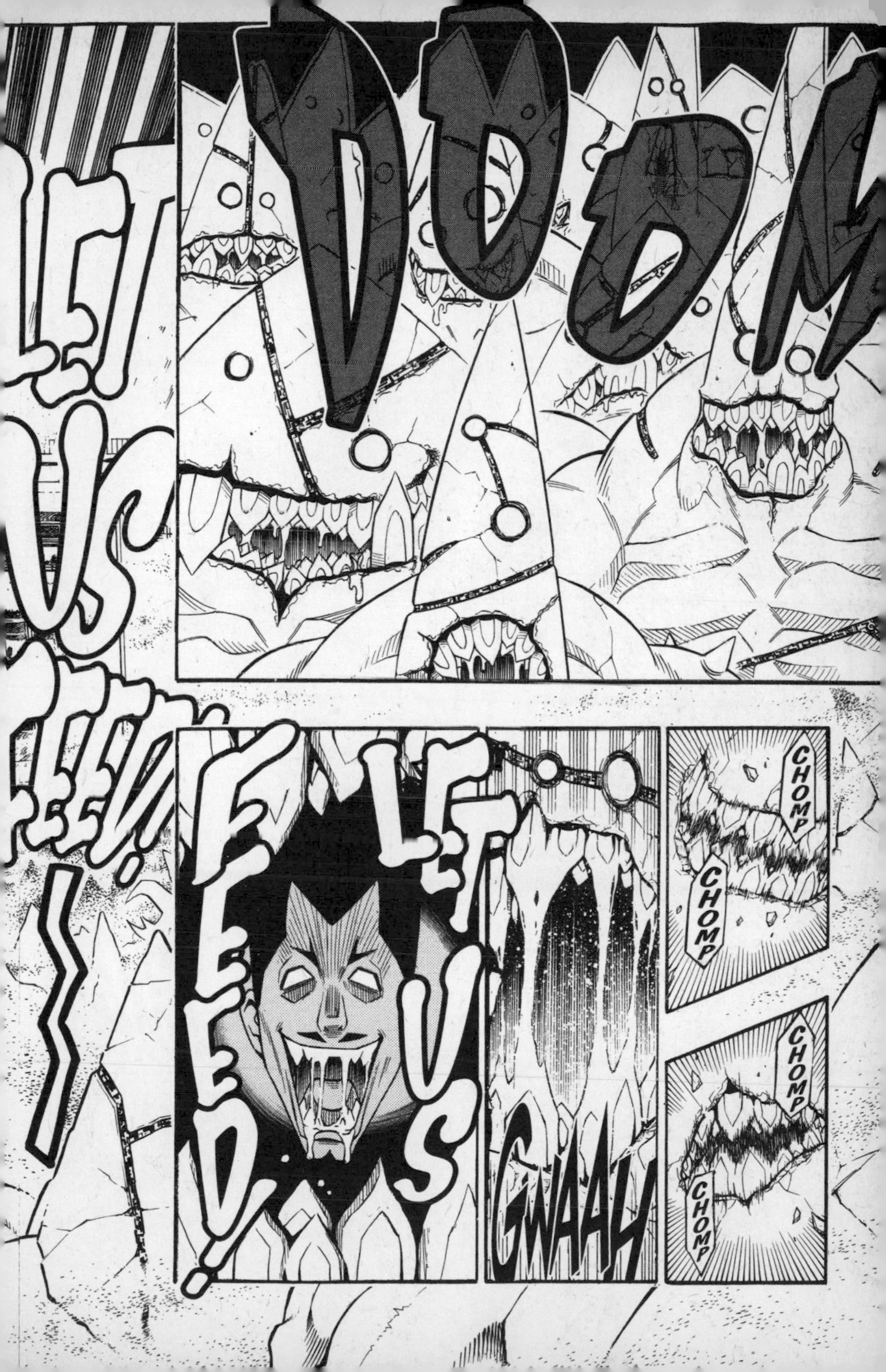
CHOMP CHOMP
CHOMP CHOMP
GWAAH
LET US FEED!
LET US

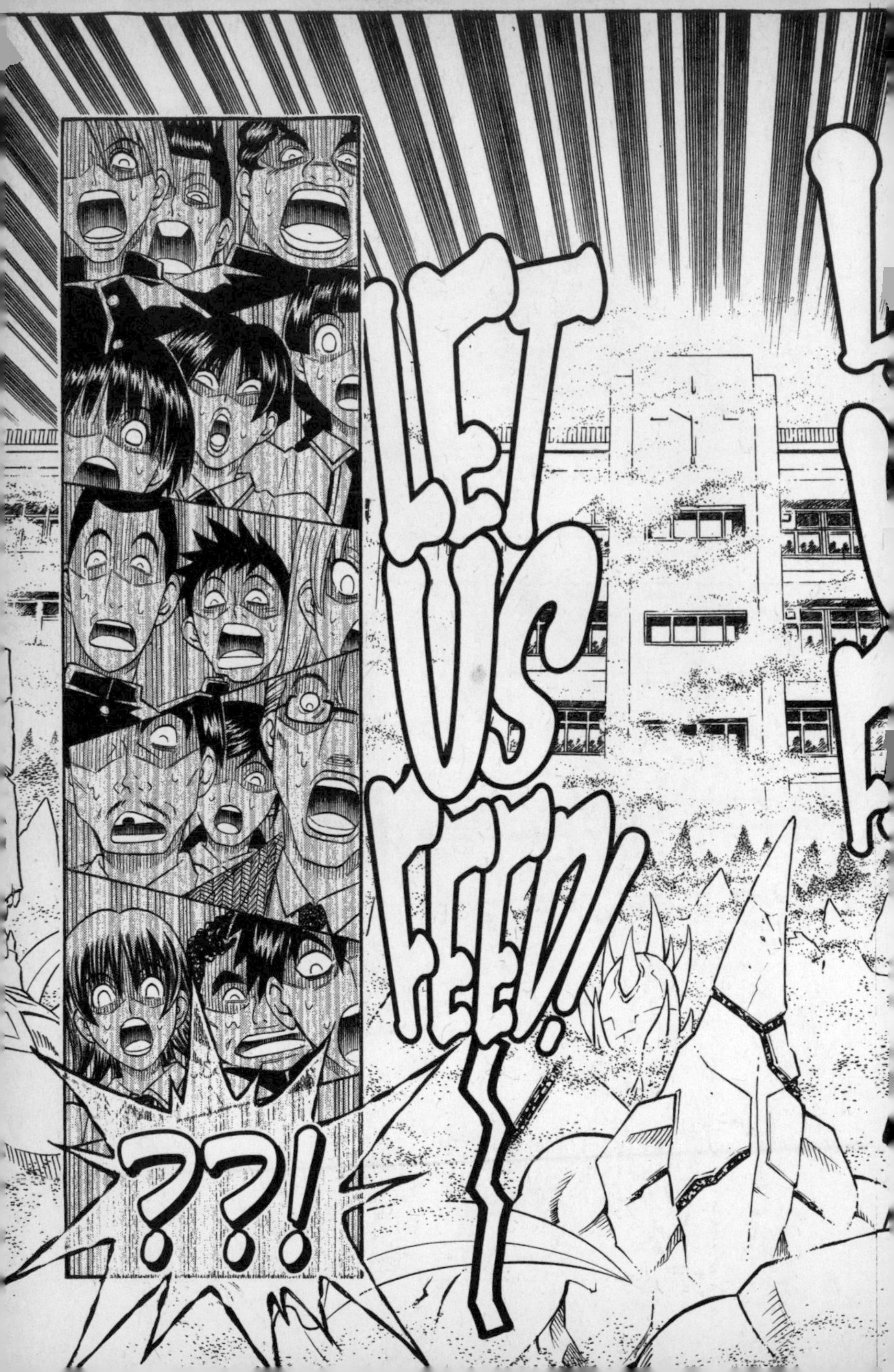

LET US FEED!!
??!

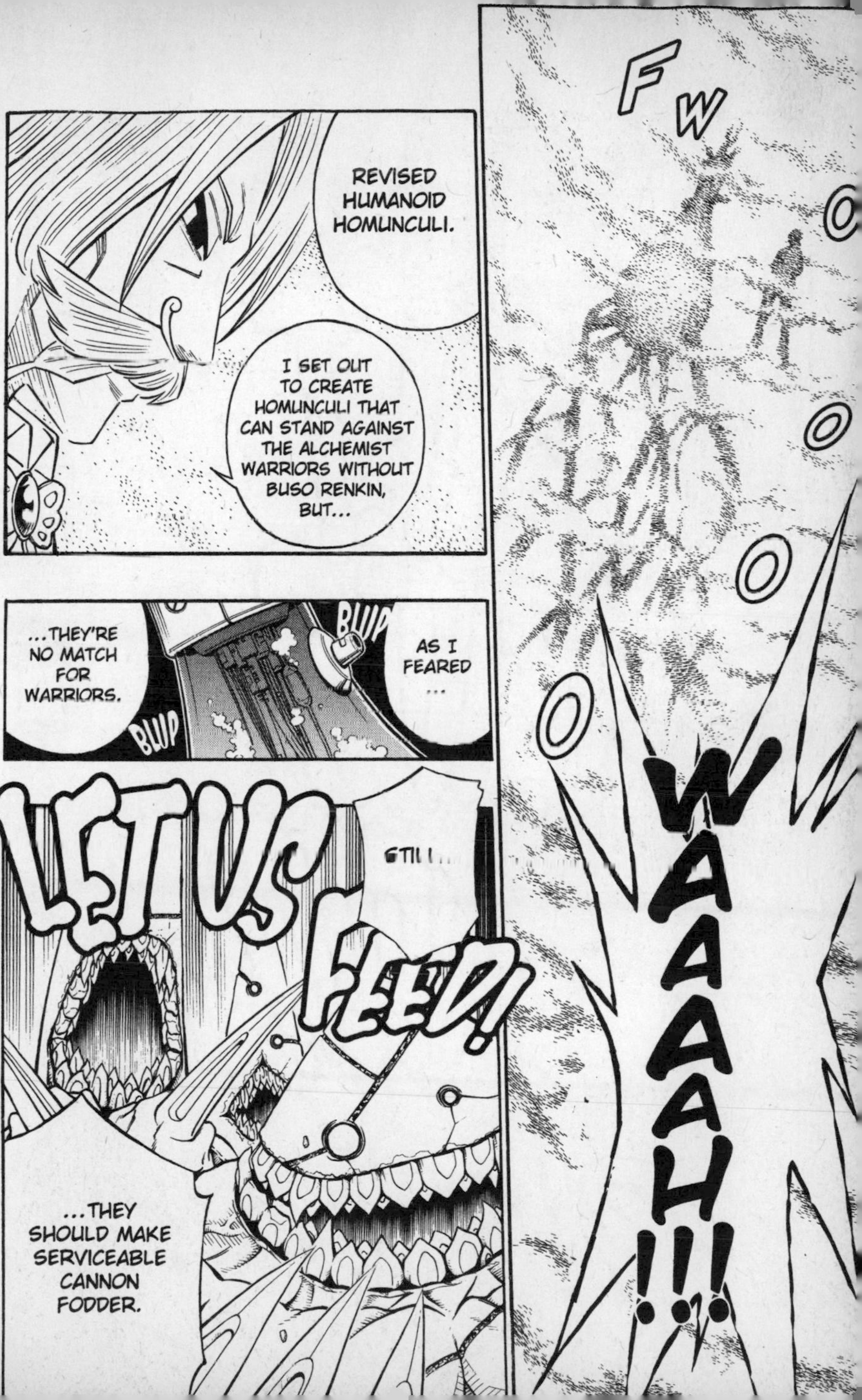
FWOOOO
WAAAAH!!!
REVISED HUMANOID HOMUNCULI.
I SET OUT TO CREATE HOMUNCULI THAT CAN STAND AGAINST THE ALCHEMIST WARRIORS WITHOUT BUSO RENKIN, BUT...
BLUP
AS I FEARED...
...THEY'RE NO MATCH FOR WARRIORS.
BLUP
STILL...
LET US FEED!
...THEY SHOULD MAKE SERVICEABLE CANNON FODDER.

READ THIS WAY

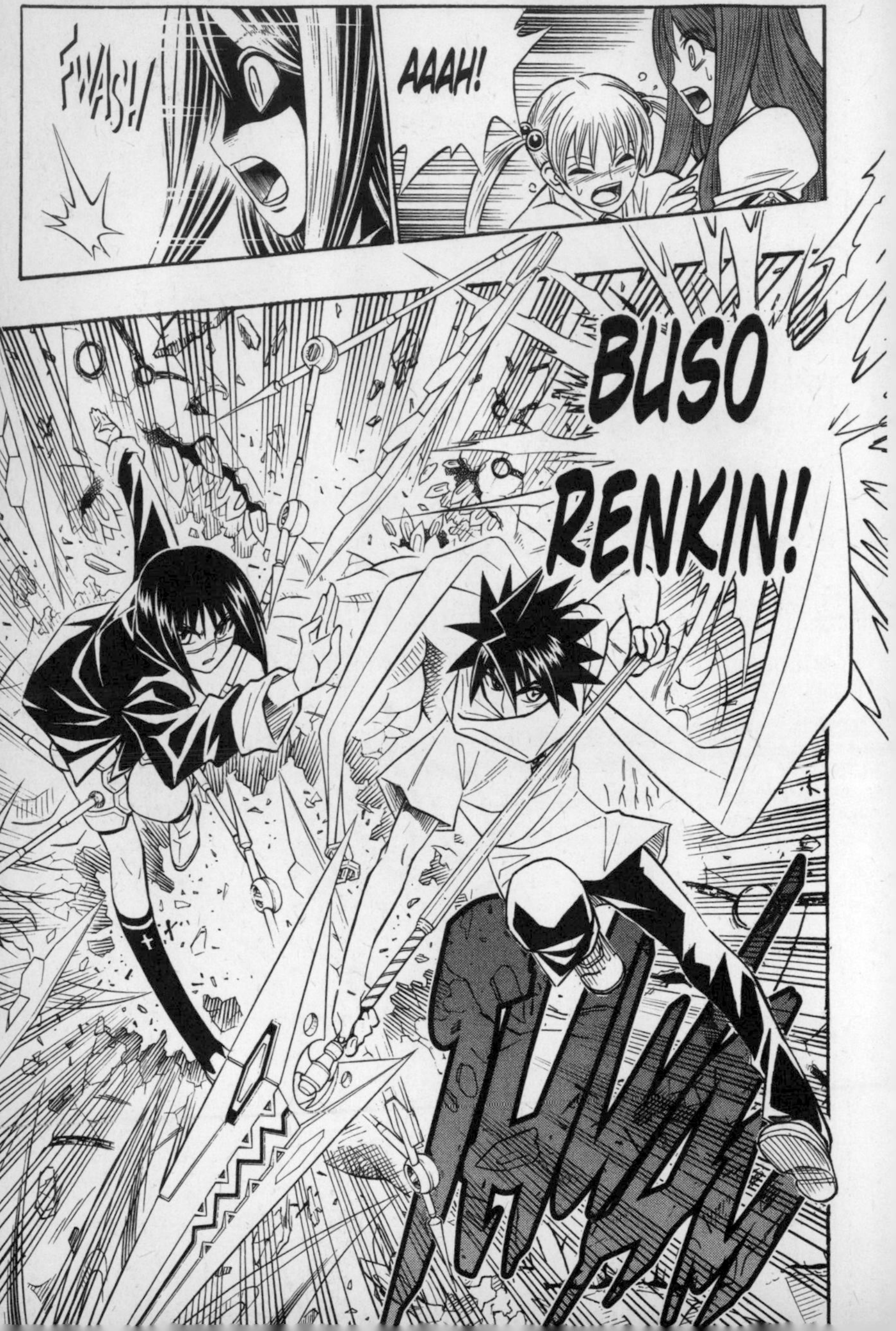
AAAH!
FWASH!
BUSO RENKIN!

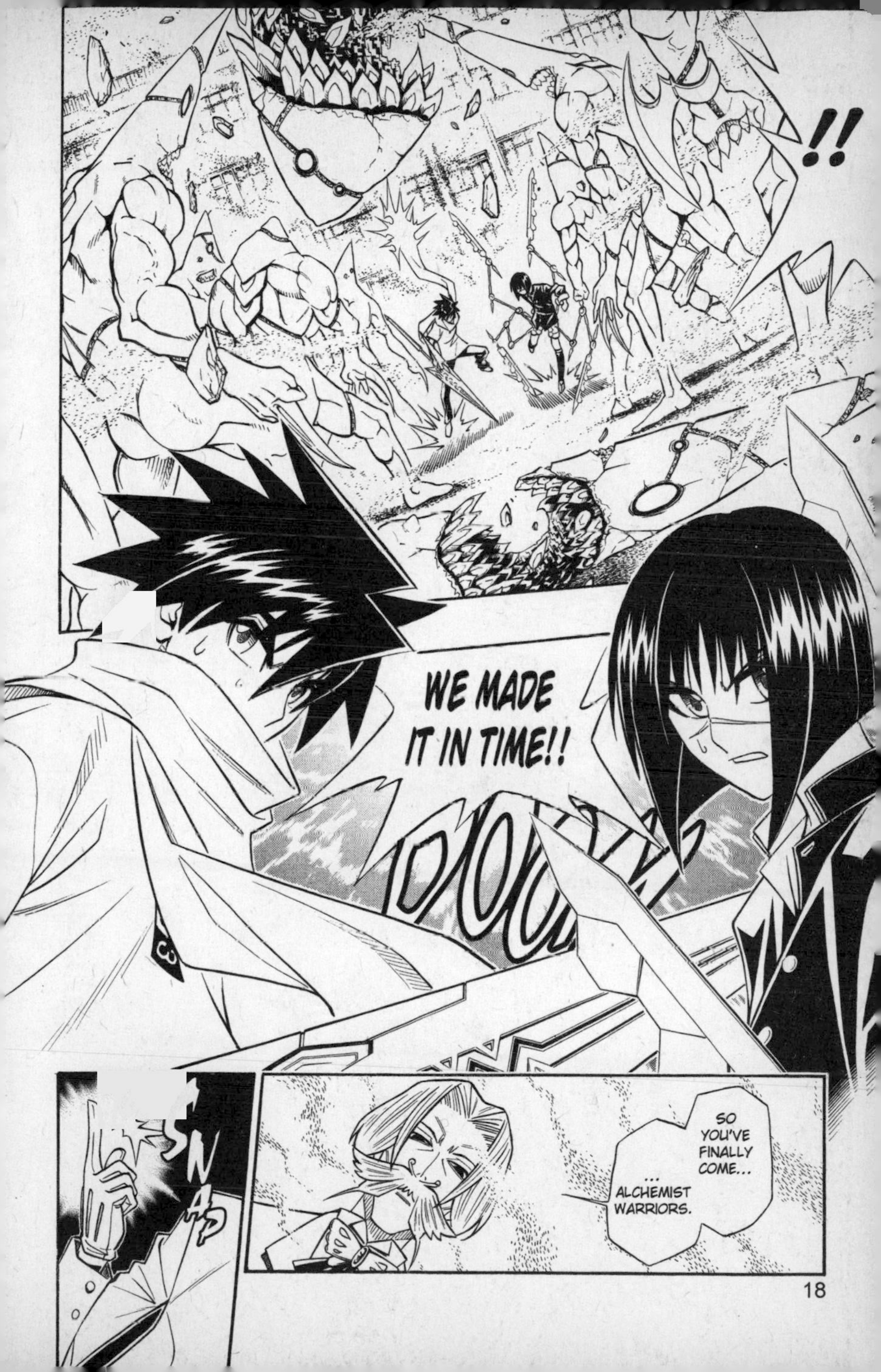
!!
WE MADE IT IN TIME!!
SO YOU'VE FINALLY COME...
...ALCHEMIST WARRIORS.
SNAP

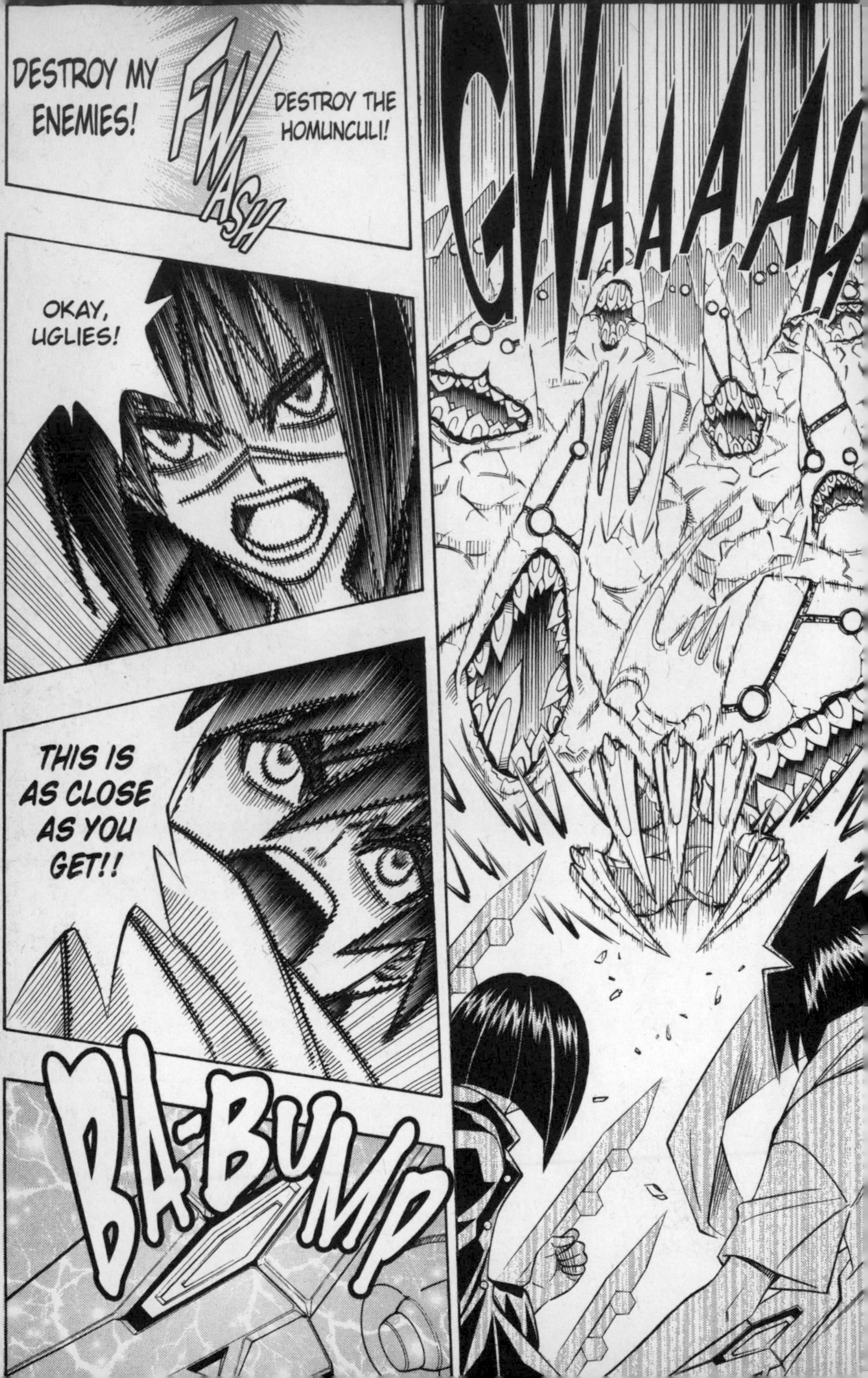
GWAAAAH
DESTROY THE HOMUNCULI!
FWASH
DESTROY MY ENEMIES!
OKAY, UGLIES!
THIS IS AS CLOSE AS YOU GET!!
BA-BUMP

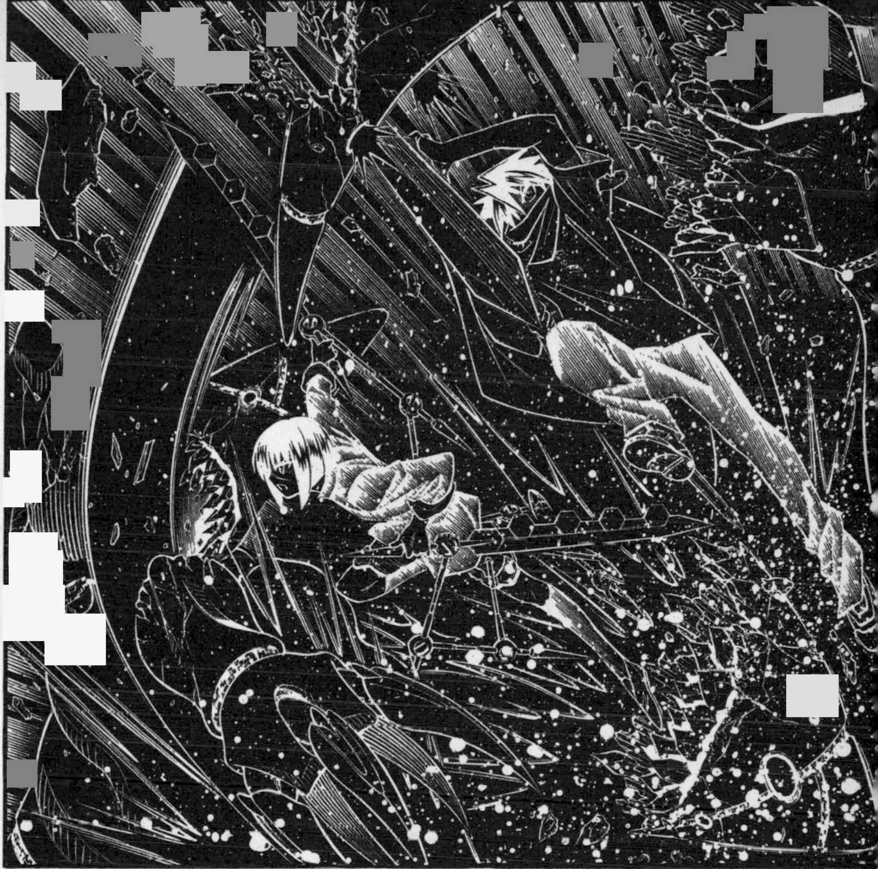

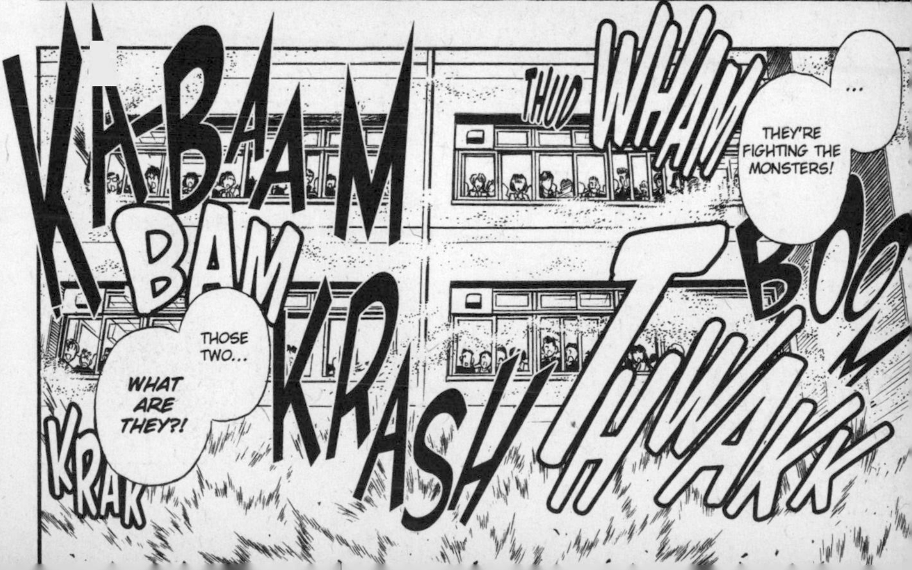
...
THEY'RE FIGHTING THE MONSTERS!
WHAM
THUD
BOOM
THWAKK
KRASH
THOSE TWO...
WHAT ARE THEY?!
BAM
KA-BAM
KRAK

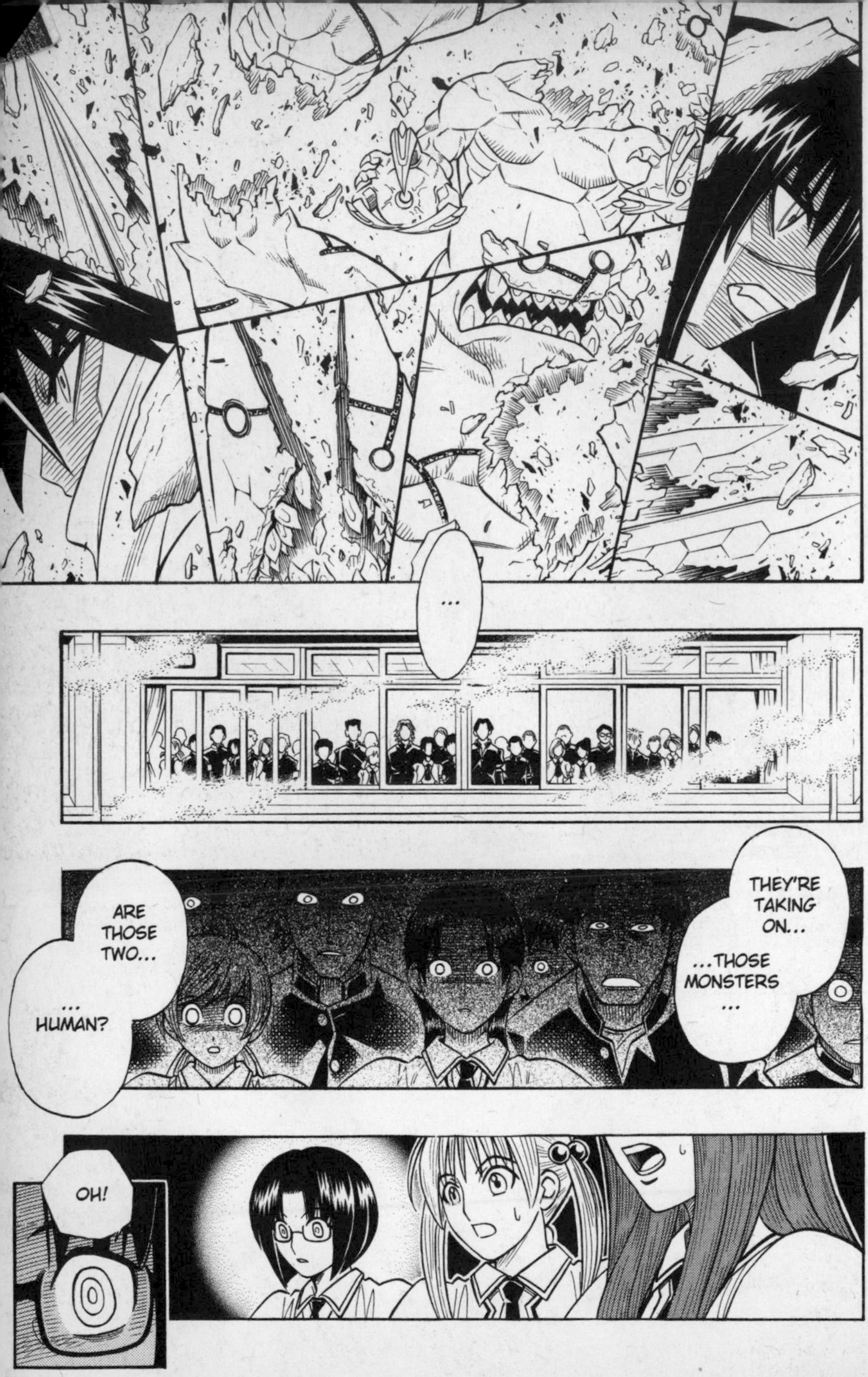
...
THEY'RE TAKING ON...
...THOSE MONSTERS...
ARE THOSE TWO...
...HUMAN?
OH!

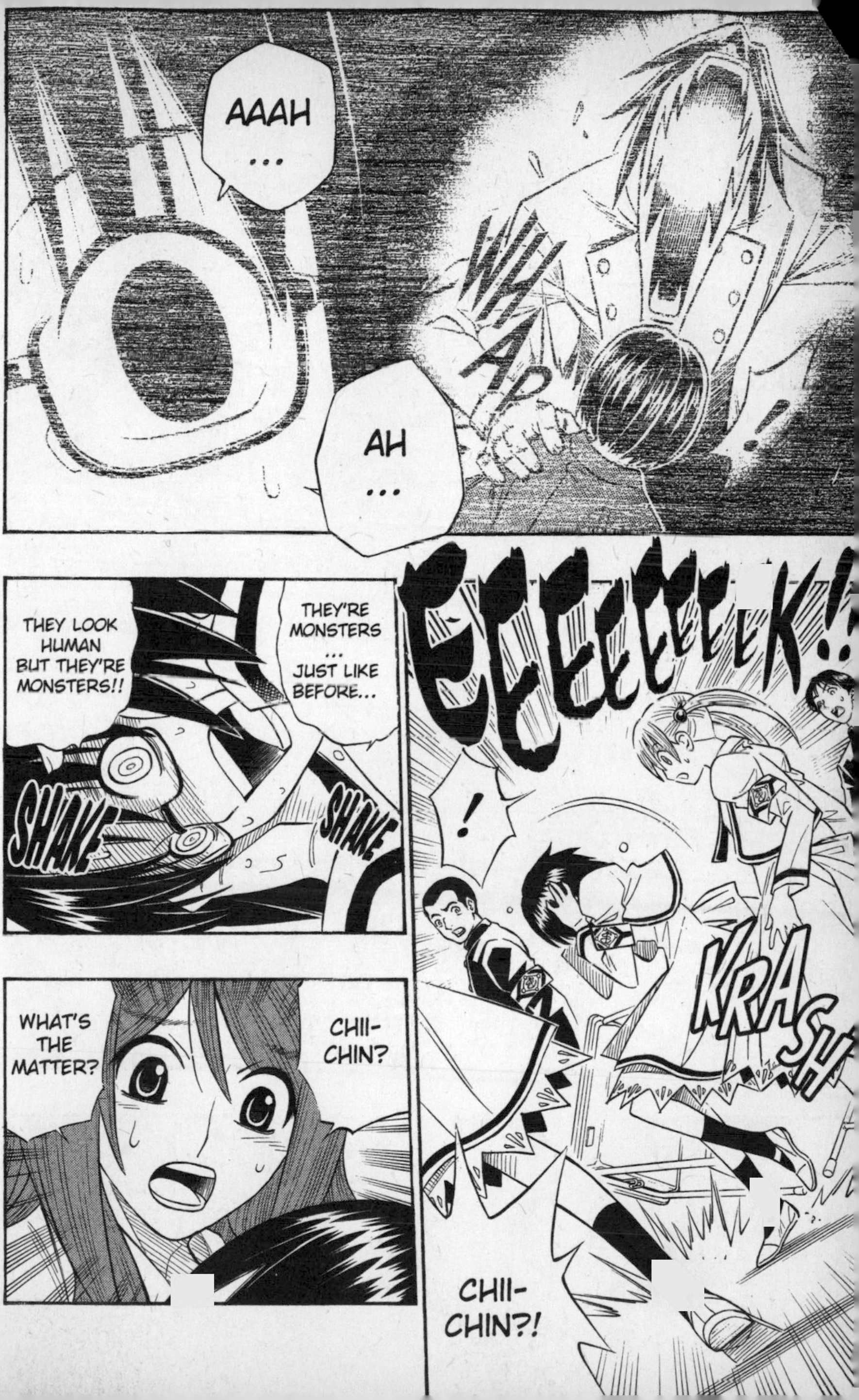
AAAH ...
WHAP
!
AH ...
EEEEEEEEK!!
!
KRASH
CHII-CHIN?!
THEY'RE MONSTERS ... JUST LIKE BEFORE...
THEY LOOK HUMAN BUT THEY'RE MONSTERS!!
SHAKE
SHAKE
CHII-CHIN?
WHAT'S THE MATTER?

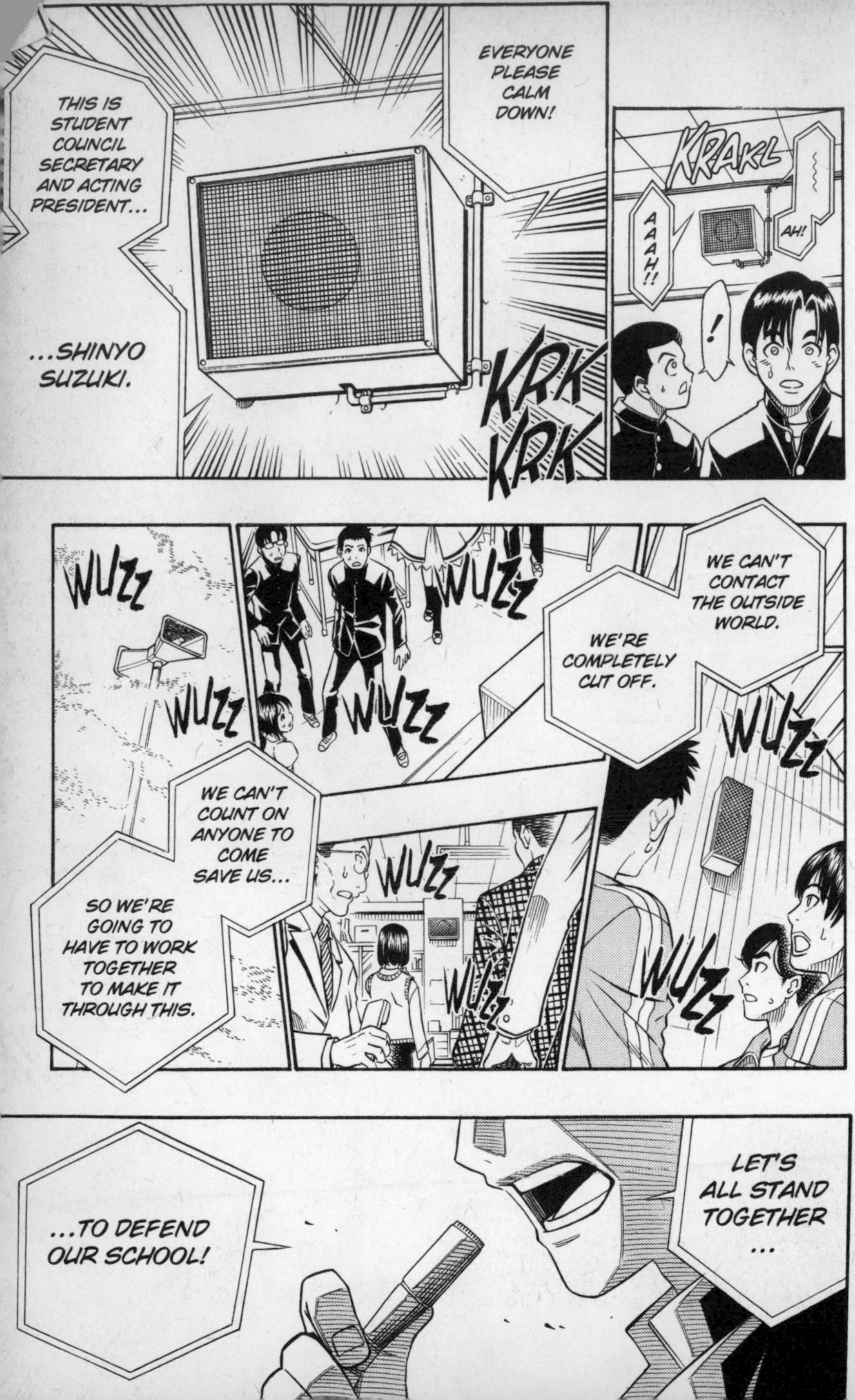
EVERYONE PLEASE CALM DOWN!
KRAKL
AAAAH!!
AH!
!
THIS IS STUDENT COUNCIL SECRETARY AND ACTING PRESIDENT...
...SHINYO SUZUKI.
KRK KRK
WE CAN'T CONTACT THE OUTSIDE WORLD.
WE'RE COMPLETELY CUT OFF.
WUZZ
WUZZ
WUZZ
WUZZ
WUZZ
WUZZ
WE CAN'T COUNT ON ANYONE TO COME SAVE US...
SO WE'RE GOING TO HAVE TO WORK TOGETHER TO MAKE IT THROUGH THIS.
WUZZ
WUZZ
LET'S ALL STAND TOGETHER ...
...TO DEFEND OUR SCHOOL!

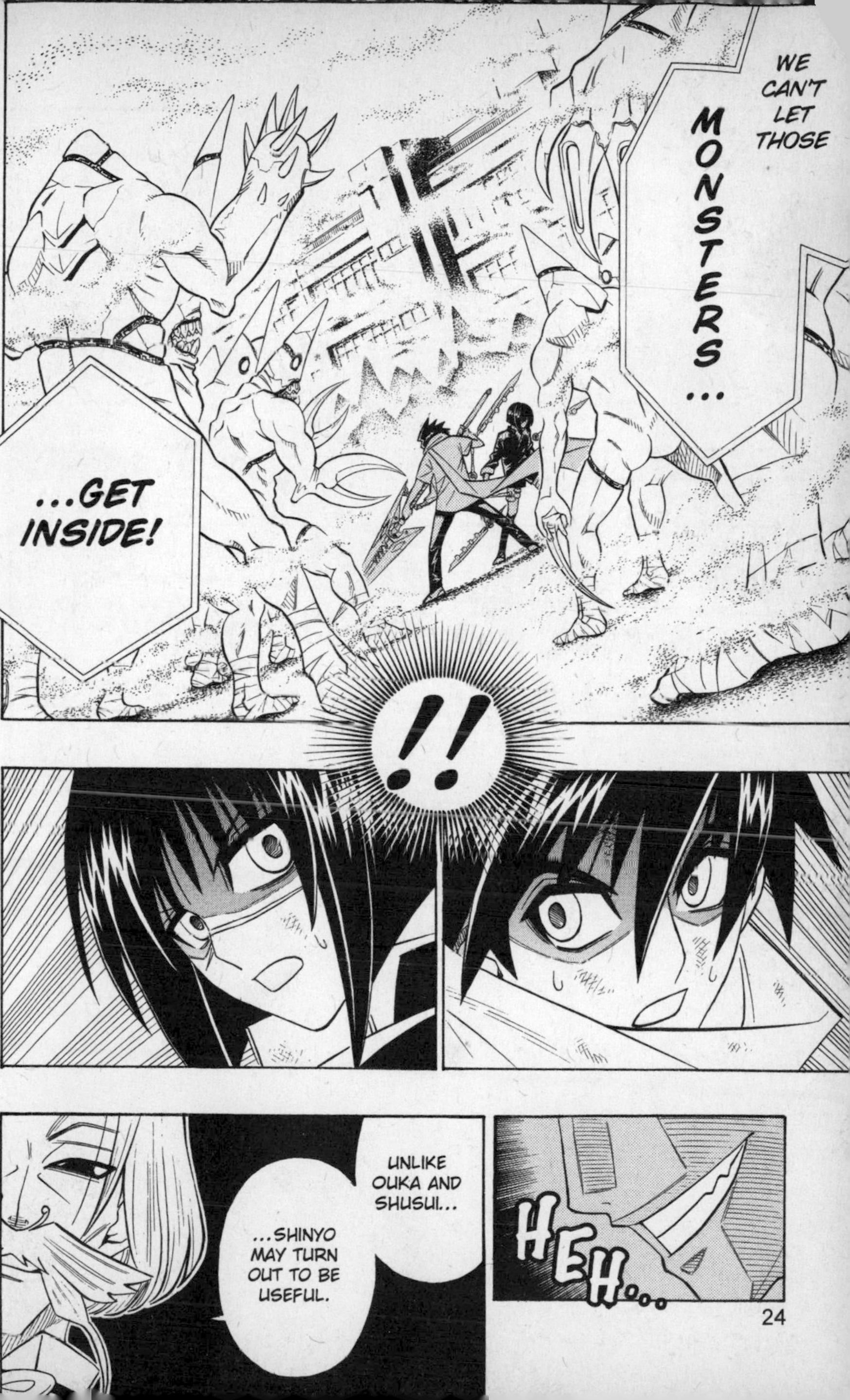
WE CAN'T LET THOSE
MONSTERS...
...GET INSIDE!
!!
HEH...
UNLIKE OUKA AND SHUSUI...
...SHINYO MAY TURN OUT TO BE USEFUL.

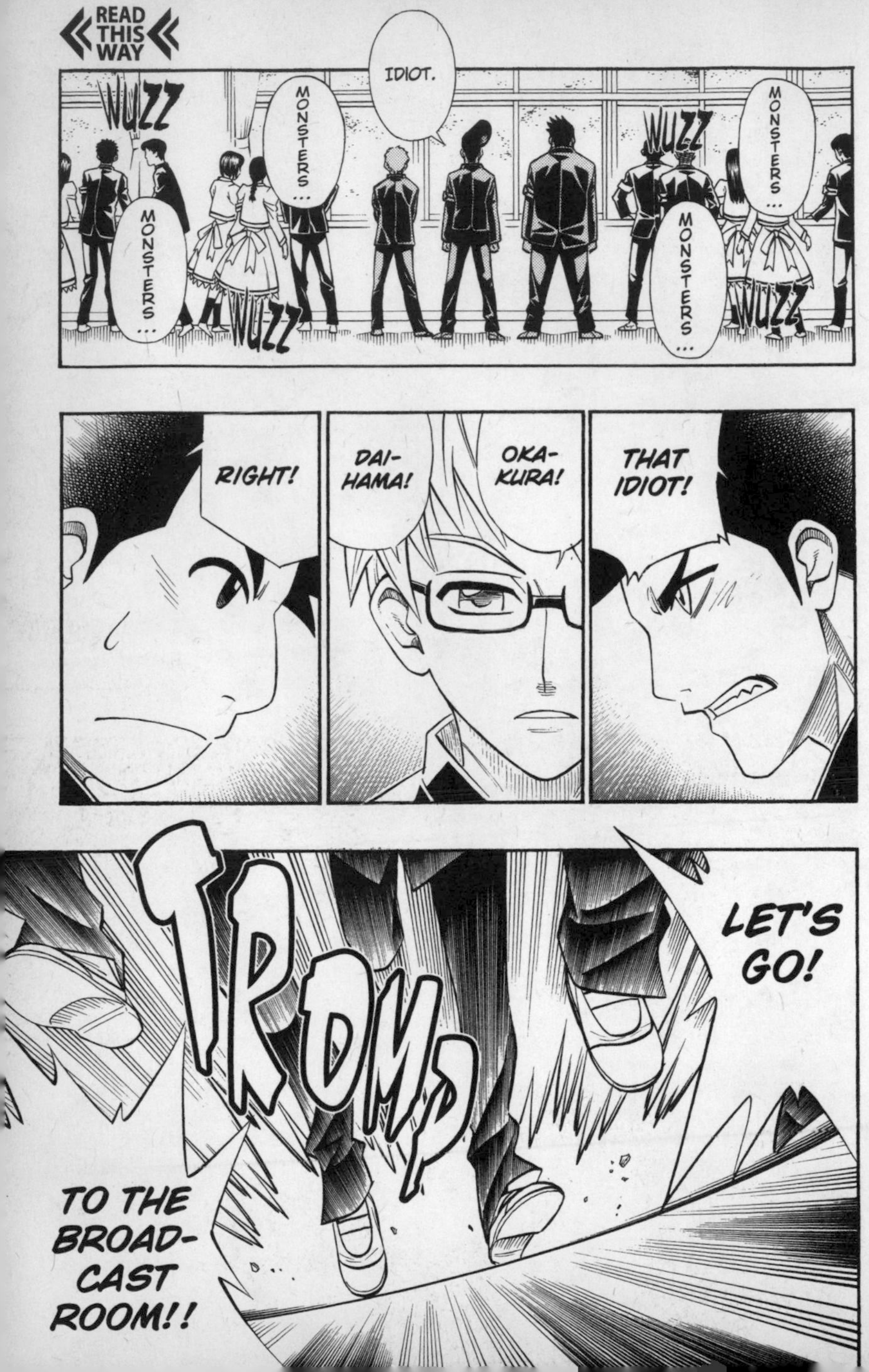
READ THIS WAY
WUZZ
MONSTERS...
MONSTERS...
WUZZ
IDIOT.
MONSTERS...
MONSTERS...
WUZZ
WUZZ
THAT IDIOT!
OKA-KURA!
DAI-HAMA!
RIGHT!
LET'S GO!
TROMP
TO THE BROAD-CAST ROOM!!

- Height: 158cm; Weight: 44kg
- Measurements: 83-57-85
- Born: April 28; Aries; Blood Type: A; Age: 16
- Likes: Mahiro, Saori, Japanese confections
- Dislikes: Ghosts, spirits, and monsters
- Hobby: Searching for new sweets (especially Japanese)
- Special Ability: Pulling all-nighters (record is 2 1/2 days)
- Affiliations: Ginsei Academy Year 1 Classroom A,
               Dorm resident

Character File No. 20

CHISATO WAKAMIYA

Author's Notes
- Originally created as a background character in the first episode.
- Then I thought, "even if Mahiro is close to Kazuki, having only her brother for a friend is a little weird." So she was upgraded to supporting character.
- I named her after the older of my two nieces. Now I regret having made her hair so much like Tokiko's because I'm afraid I'll mix them up when I get tired.
- She's smarter and more straightforward than most of the other characters. She's the most practical one in Mahiro's circle of friends. Because of that, she's not as well equipped to deal with bizarre situations. You probably won't see it in these pages, but she helps Mahiro and Saori prepare for tests. Chisato is meant to be more normal than the others.

CHAPTER 38:

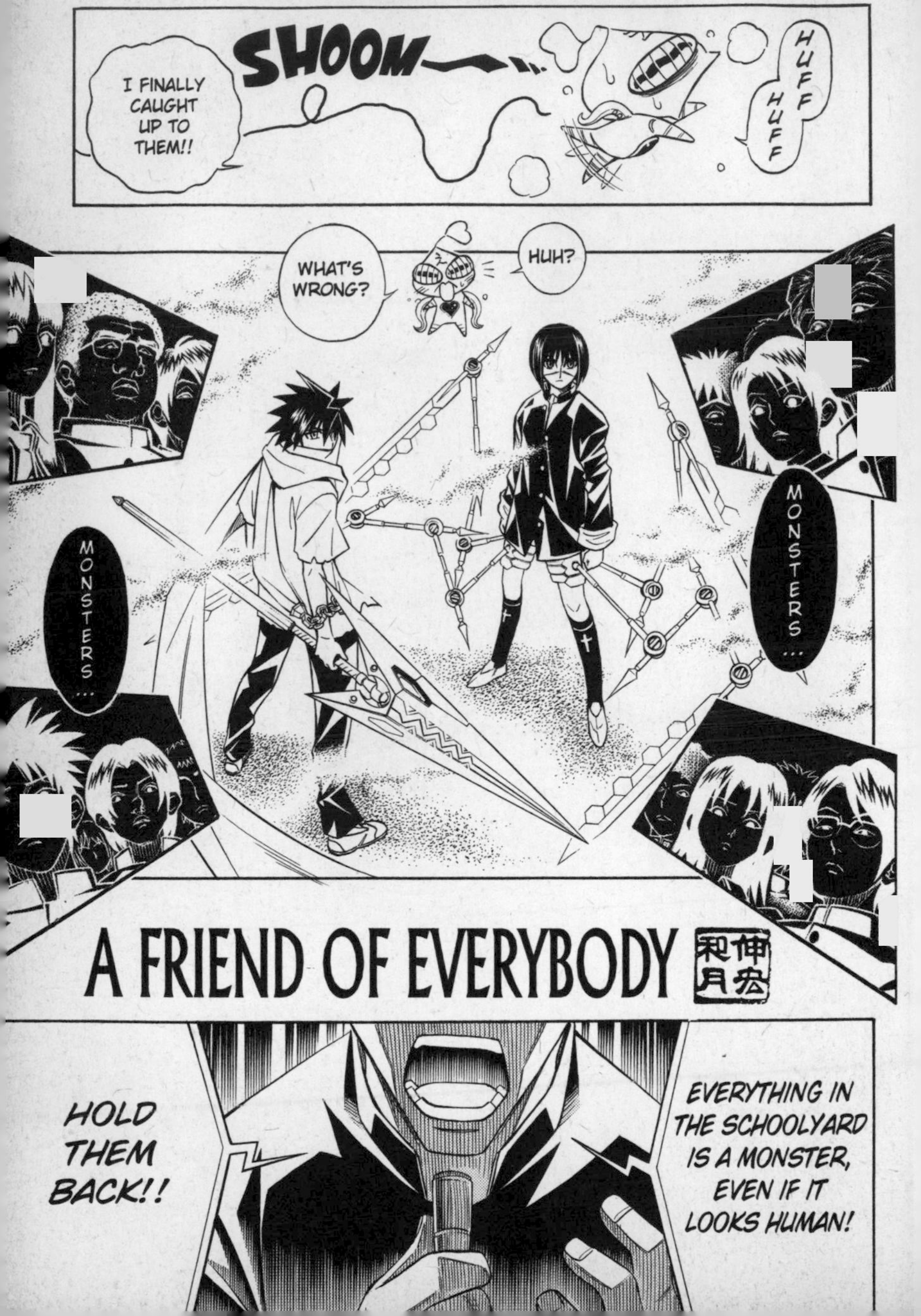
HUFF HUFF
SHOOM
I FINALLY CAUGHT UP TO THEM!!
HUH?
WHAT'S WRONG?
MONSTERS...
MONSTERS...
EVERYTHING IN THE SCHOOLYARD IS A MONSTER, EVEN IF IT LOOKS HUMAN!
HOLD THEM BACK!!

A FRIEND OF EVERYBODY

伸宏和月

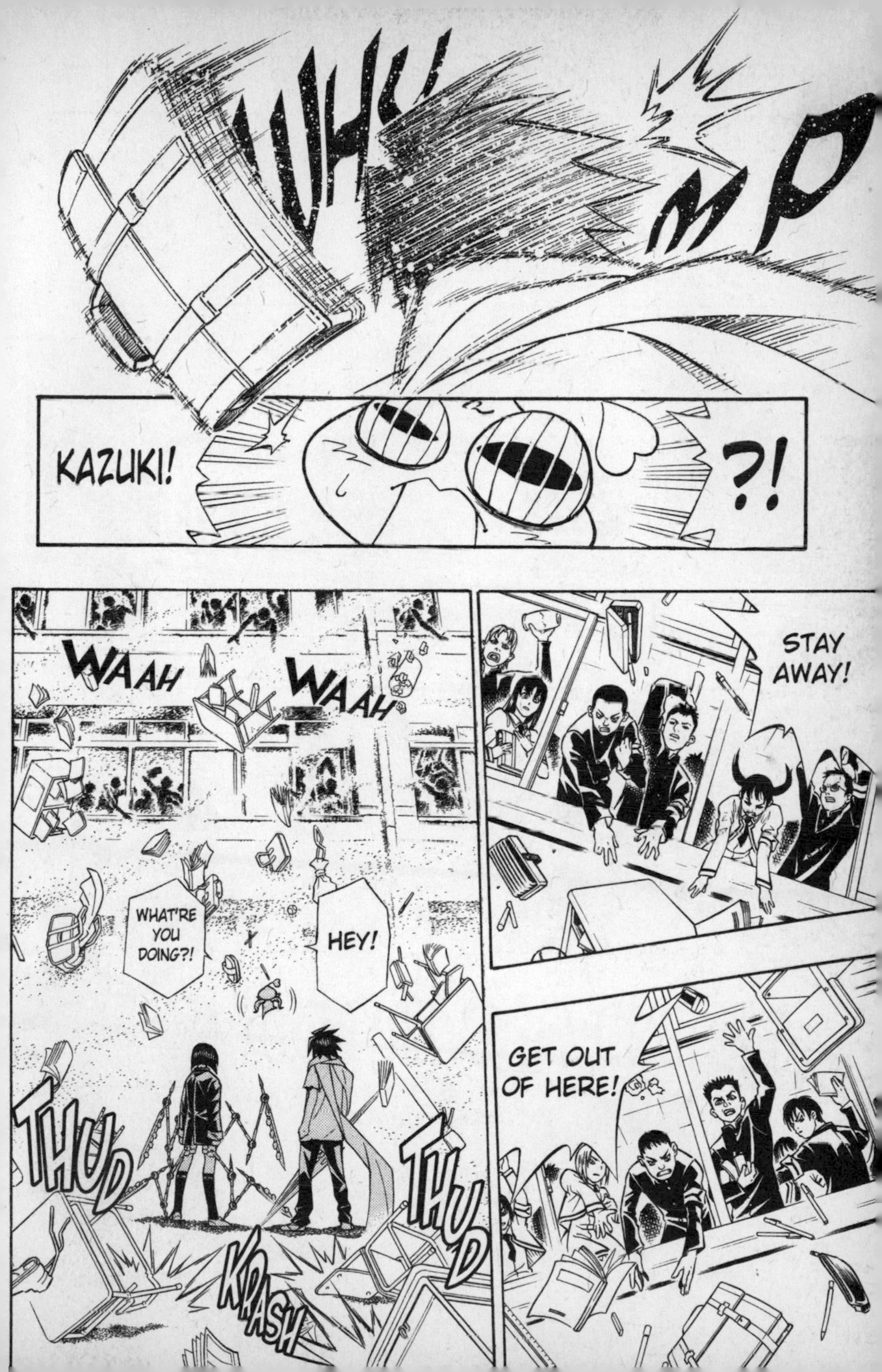
WHUMP
?!
KAZUKI!
STAY AWAY!
GET OUT OF HERE!
WAAH
WAAH
HEY!
WHAT'RE YOU DOING?!
THUD
THUD
KRASH

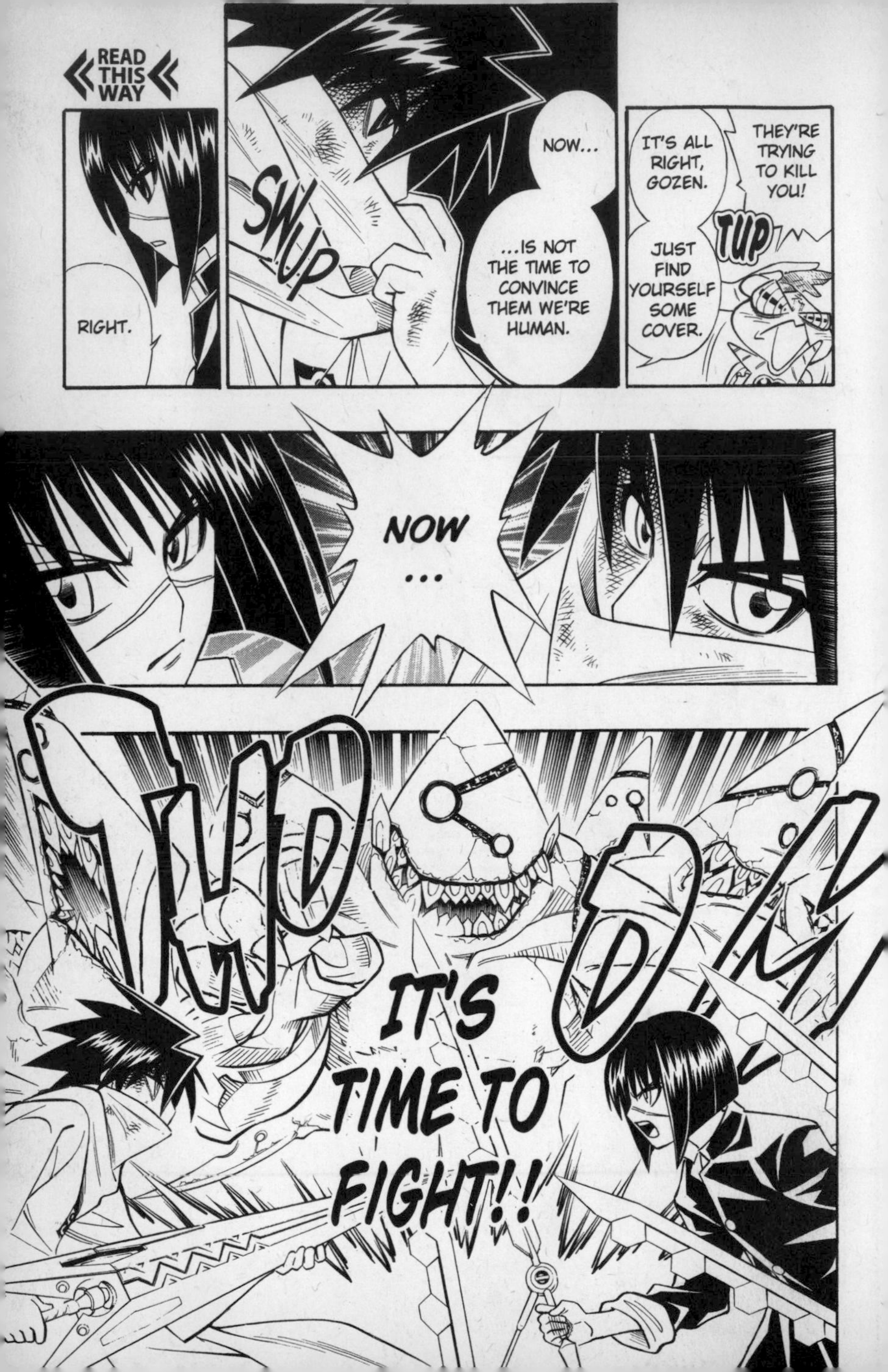
READ THIS WAY
THEY'RE TRYING TO KILL YOU!
TUP
IT'S ALL RIGHT, GOZEN.
JUST FIND YOURSELF SOME COVER.
NOW...
...IS NOT THE TIME TO CONVINCE THEM WE'RE HUMAN.
SWUP
RIGHT.
NOW ...
IT'S TIME TO FIGHT!!

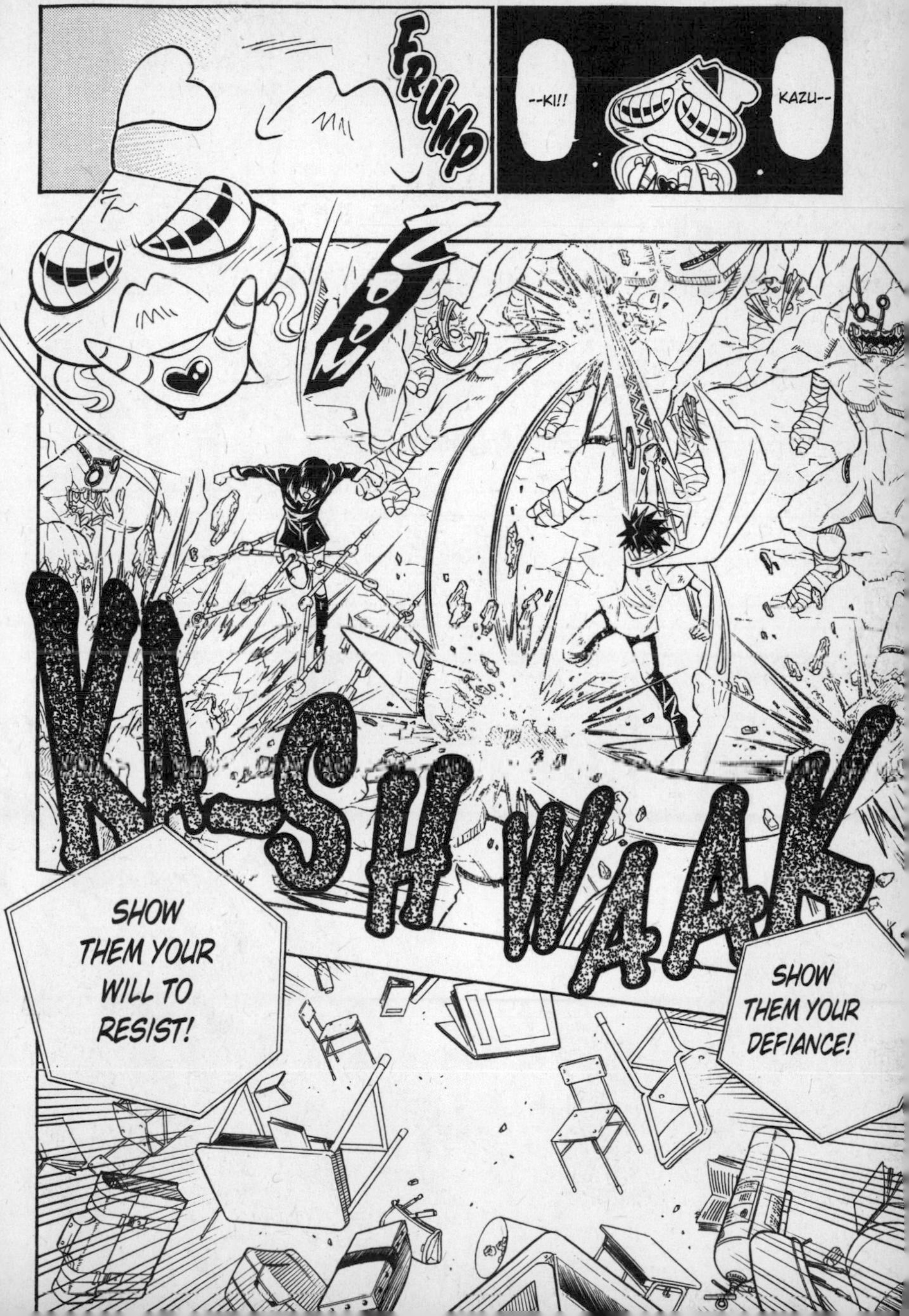
KAZU--
--KI!!
FRUMP
ZOOM
KA-SHWAAK
SHOW THEM YOUR DEFIANCE!
SHOW THEM YOUR WILL TO RESIST!

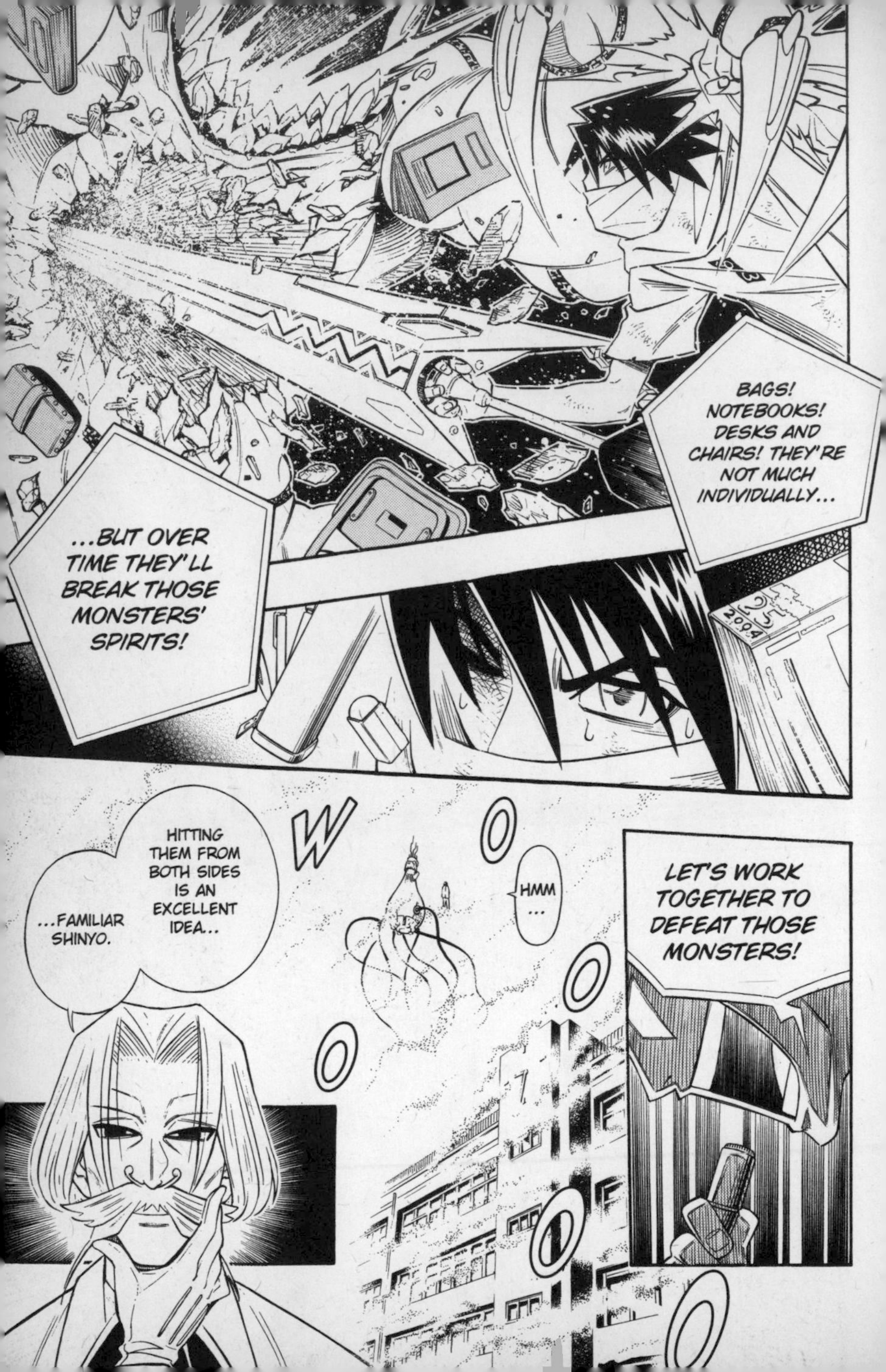
BAGS! NOTEBOOKS! DESKS AND CHAIRS! THEY'RE NOT MUCH INDIVIDUALLY...
...BUT OVER TIME THEY'LL BREAK THOSE MONSTERS' SPIRITS!
LET'S WORK TOGETHER TO DEFEAT THOSE MONSTERS!
WOOOOO
HMM ...
HITTING THEM FROM BOTH SIDES IS AN EXCELLENT IDEA...
...FAMILIAR SHINYO.

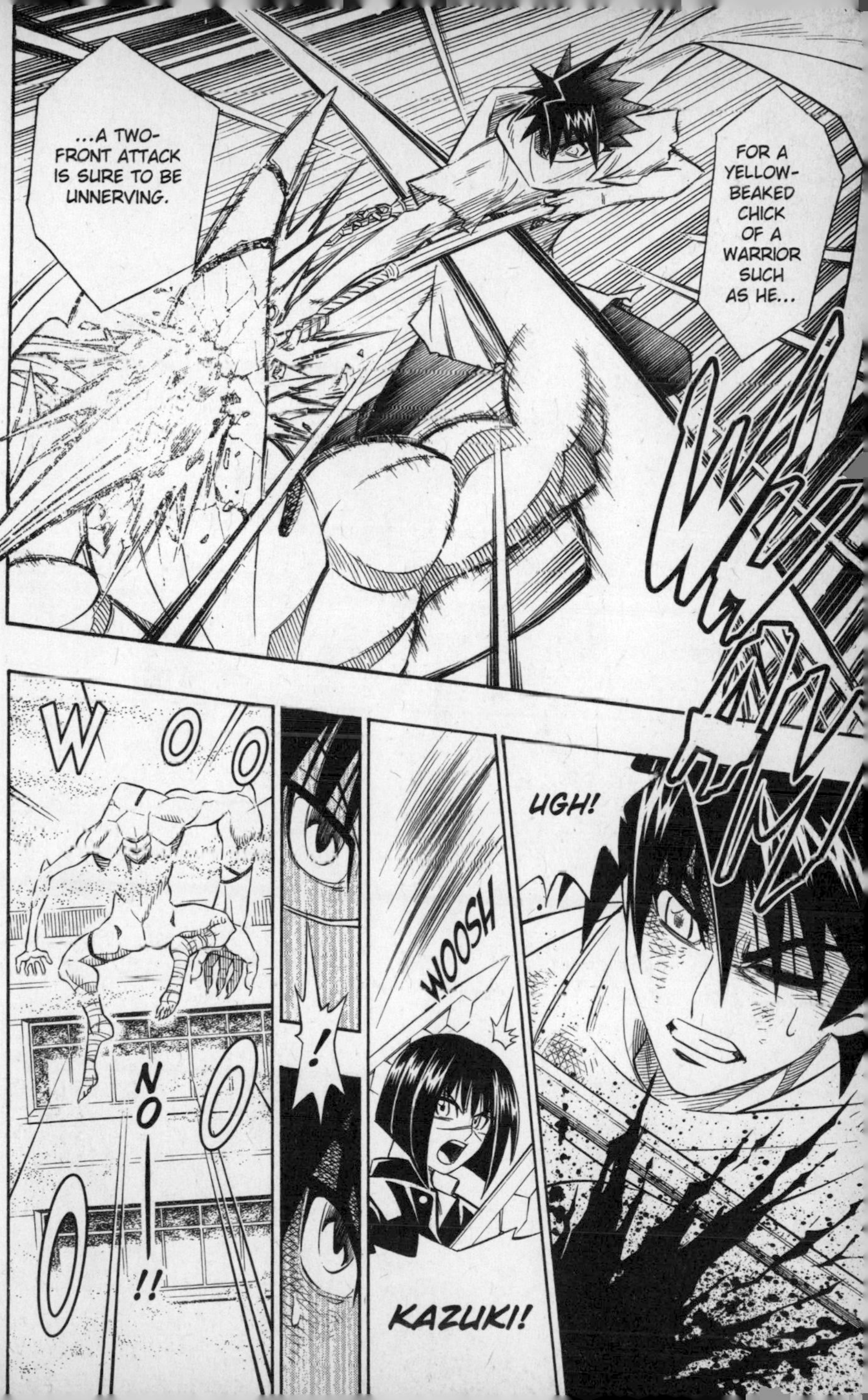
FOR A YELLOW-BEAKED CHICK OF A WARRIOR SUCH AS HE...
...A TWO-FRONT ATTACK IS SURE TO BE UNNERVING.
UGH!
WOOSH
KAZUKI!
!
WOOO
NO—!!

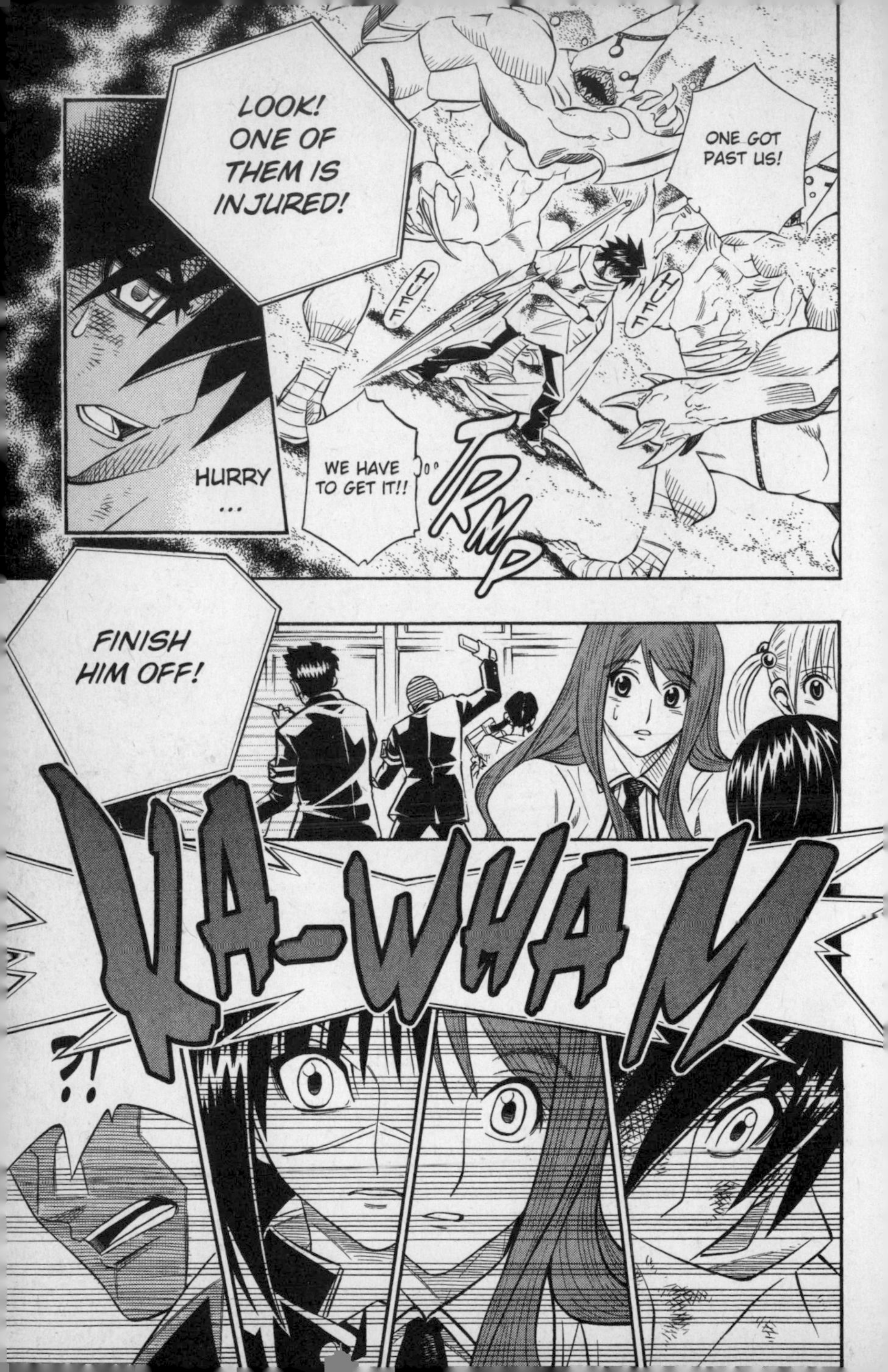

ONE GOT PAST US!
LOOK! ONE OF THEM IS INJURED!
HUFF
HUFF
WE HAVE TO GET IT!!
TRMP
HURRY ...
FINISH HIM OFF!
KA-WHAM
?!

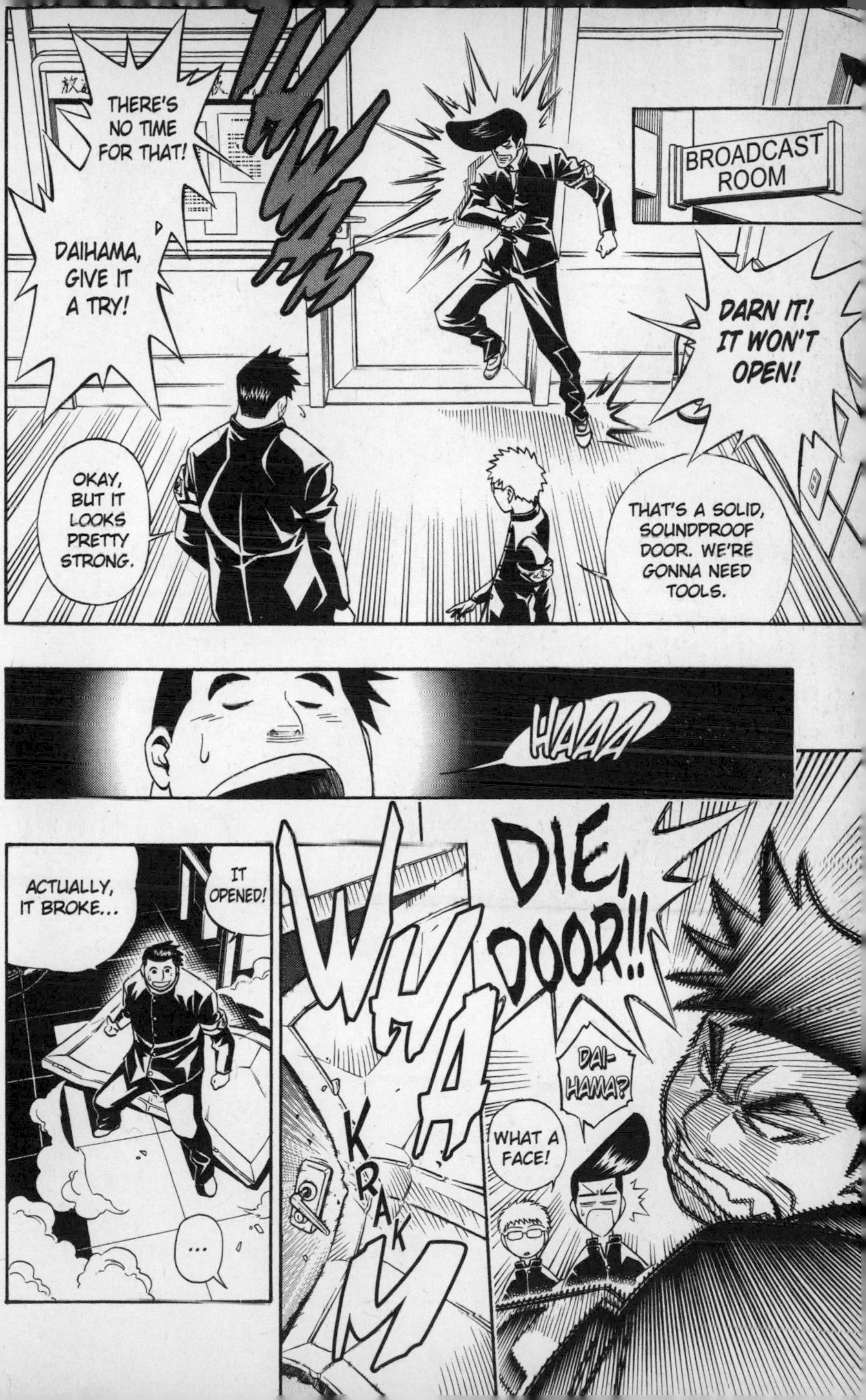

BROADCAST ROOM
WHAM
DARN IT! IT WON'T OPEN!
THAT'S A SOLID, SOUNDPROOF DOOR. WE'RE GONNA NEED TOOLS.
THERE'S NO TIME FOR THAT!
DAIHAMA, GIVE IT A TRY!
OKAY, BUT IT LOOKS PRETTY STRONG.
HAAA
DIE, DOOR!!
WHAM
KRAK
DAI-HAMA?
WHAT A FACE!
IT OPENED!
ACTUALLY, IT BROKE...
...

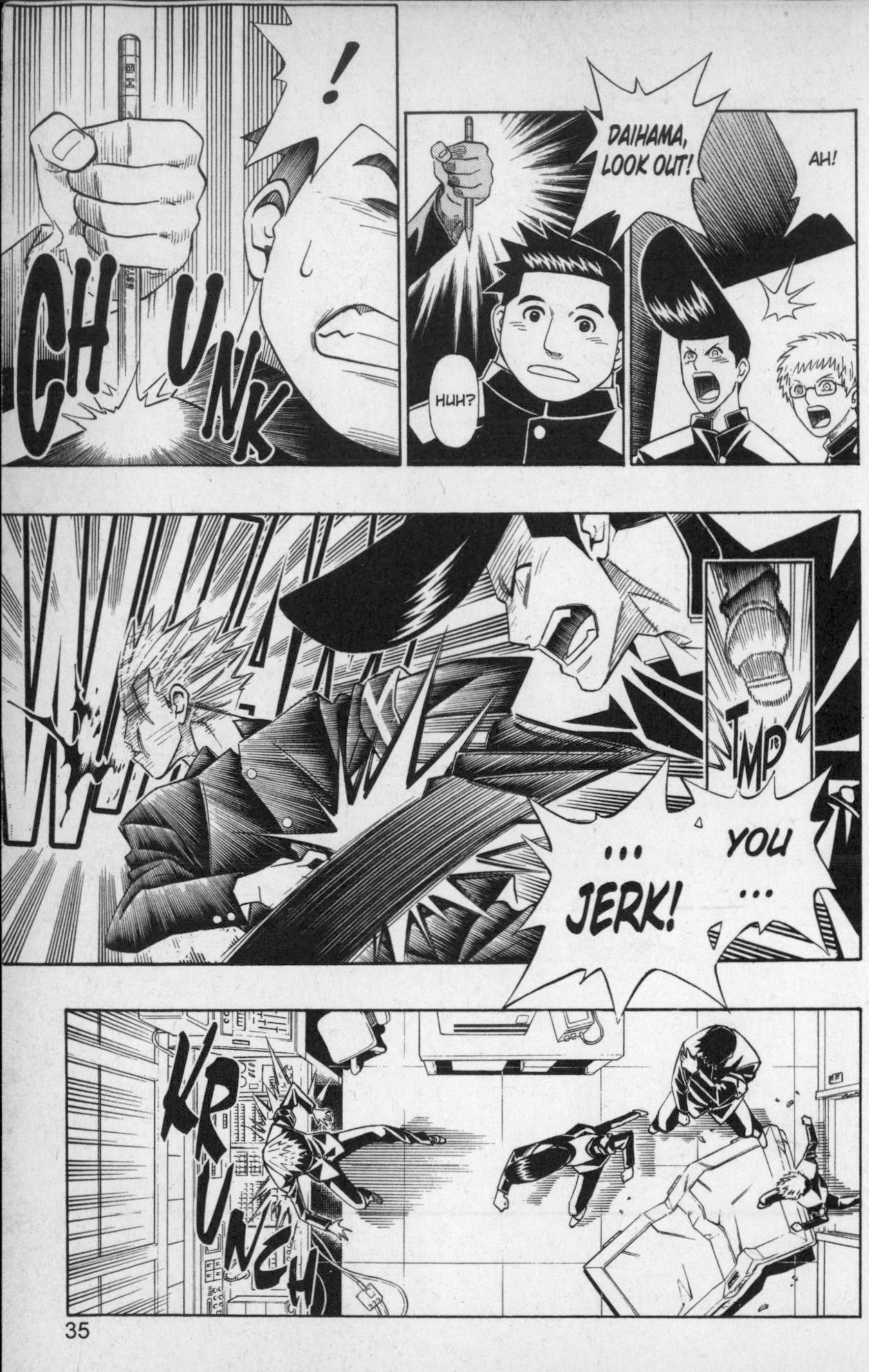
DAIHAMA, LOOK OUT!
AH!
HUH?
!
CHUNK
TMP
YOU ... ... JERK!
KRUNCH

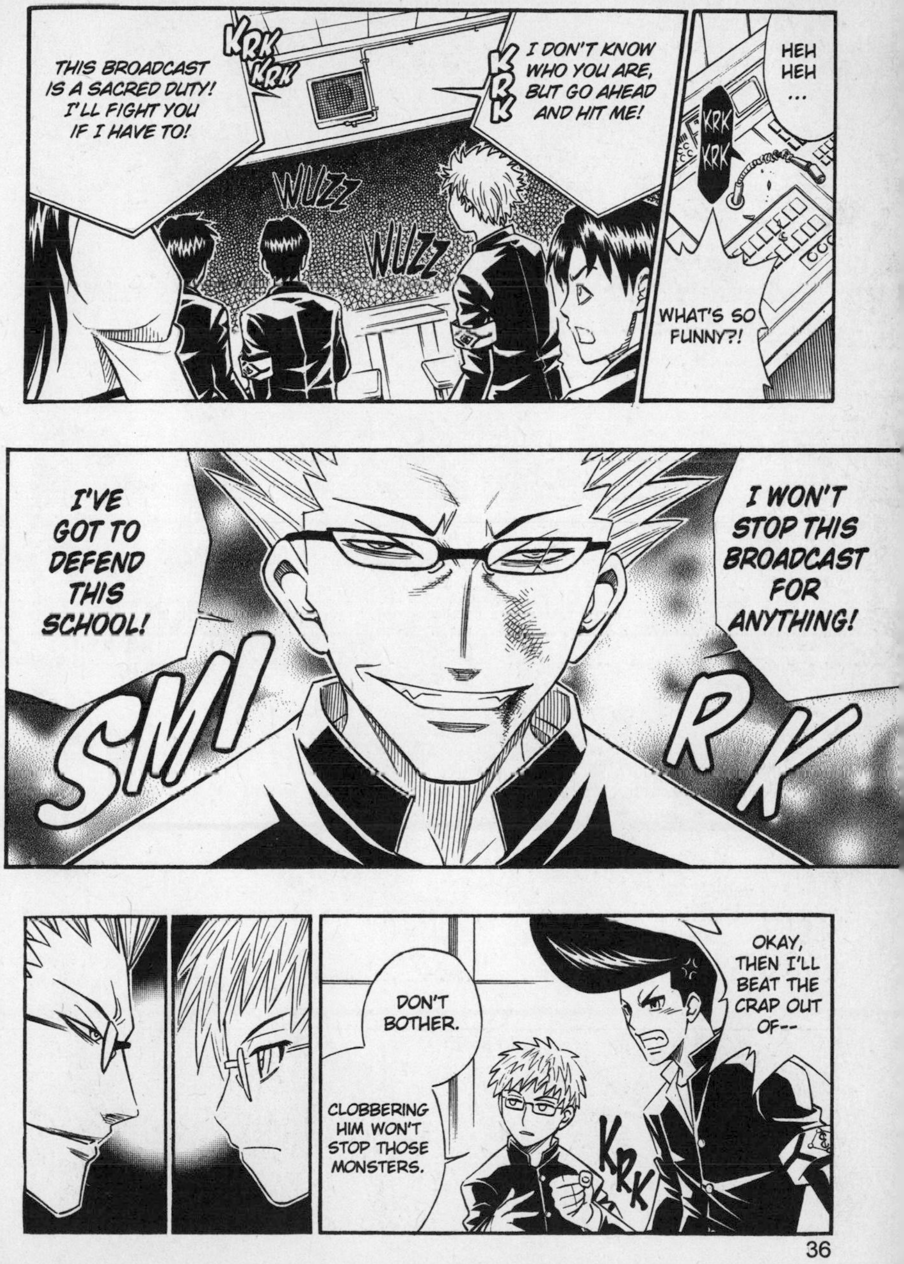
HEH HEH ...
KRK KRK
WHAT'S SO FUNNY?!
I DON'T KNOW WHO YOU ARE, BUT GO AHEAD AND HIT ME!
KRK
KRK KRK
THIS BROADCAST IS A SACRED DUTY! I'LL FIGHT YOU IF I HAVE TO!
WUZZ
WUZZ
I WON'T STOP THIS BROADCAST FOR ANYTHING!
I'VE GOT TO DEFEND THIS SCHOOL!
SMI RK
OKAY, THEN I'LL BEAT THE CRAP OUT OF--
DON'T BOTHER.
CLOBBERING HIM WON'T STOP THOSE MONSTERS.
KRK

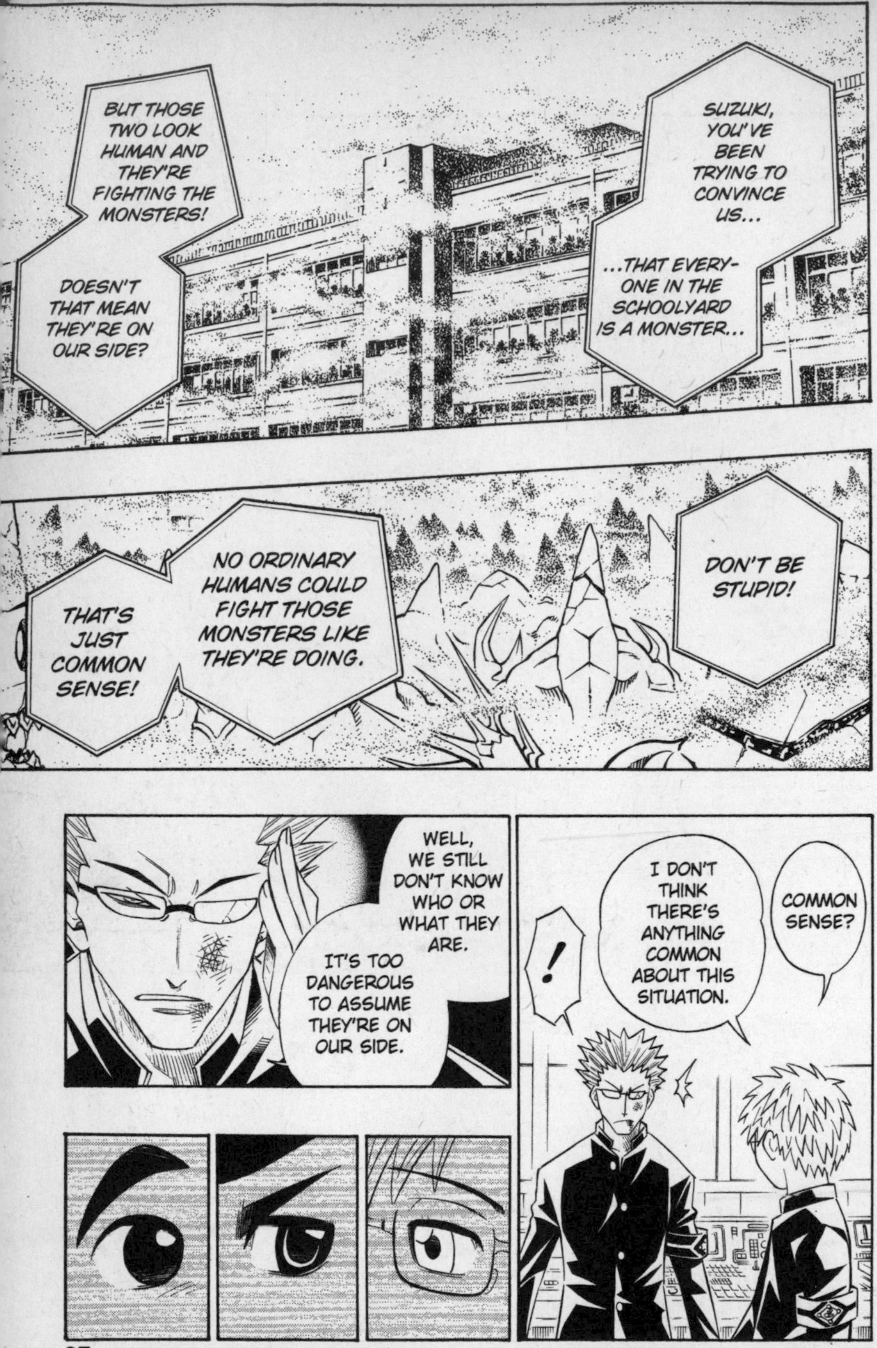
SUZUKI, YOU'VE BEEN TRYING TO CONVINCE US...
...THAT EVERY-ONE IN THE SCHOOLYARD IS A MONSTER...
BUT THOSE TWO LOOK HUMAN AND THEY'RE FIGHTING THE MONSTERS!
DOESN'T THAT MEAN THEY'RE ON OUR SIDE?
DON'T BE STUPID!
NO ORDINARY HUMANS COULD FIGHT THOSE MONSTERS LIKE THEY'RE DOING.
THAT'S JUST COMMON SENSE!
COMMON SENSE?
I DON'T THINK THERE'S ANYTHING COMMON ABOUT THIS SITUATION.
!
WELL, WE STILL DON'T KNOW WHO OR WHAT THEY ARE.
IT'S TOO DANGEROUS TO ASSUME THEY'RE ON OUR SIDE.

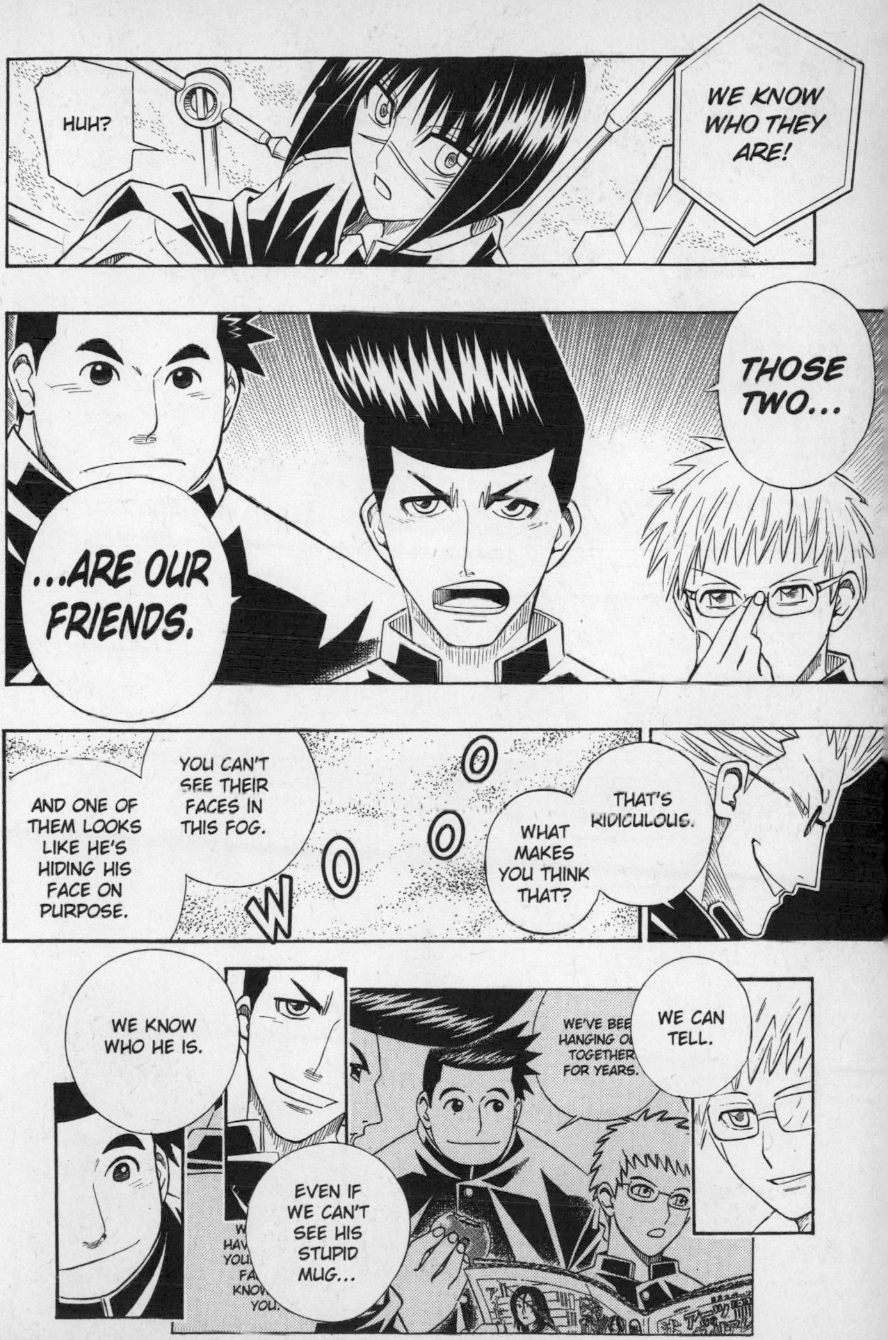
WE KNOW WHO THEY ARE!
HUH?
THOSE TWO...
...ARE OUR FRIENDS.
THAT'S RIDICULOUS.
WHAT MAKES YOU THINK THAT?
YOU CAN'T SEE THEIR FACES IN THIS FOG.
AND ONE OF THEM LOOKS LIKE HE'S HIDING HIS FACE ON PURPOSE.
WOOO
WE CAN TELL.
WE'VE BEE HANGING O TOGETHER FOR YEARS.
WE KNOW WHO HE IS.
EVEN IF WE CAN'T SEE HIS STUPID MUG...

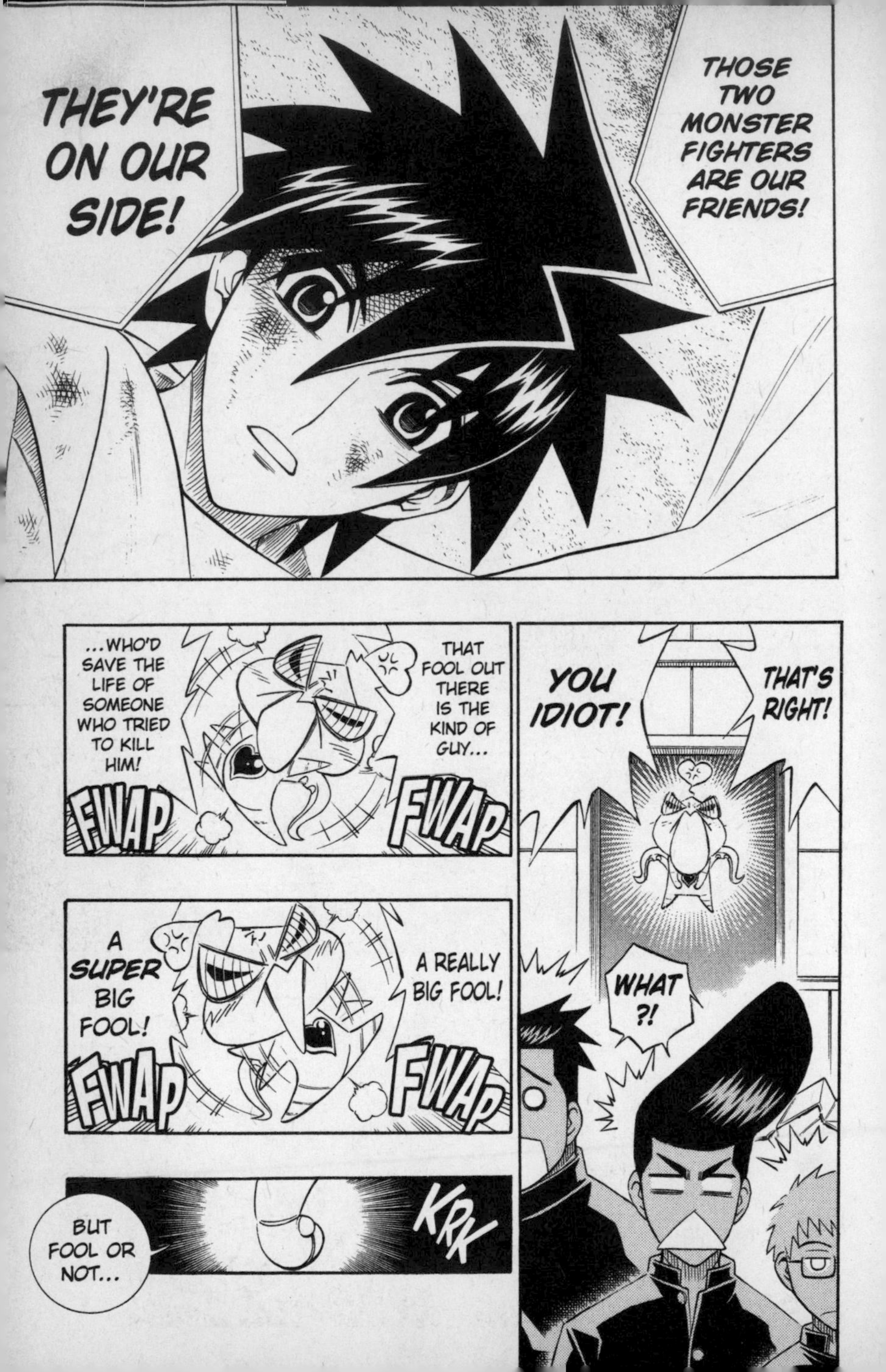
THOSE TWO MONSTER FIGHTERS ARE OUR FRIENDS!
THEY'RE ON OUR SIDE!
THAT'S RIGHT!
YOU IDIOT!
WHAT?!
THAT FOOL OUT THERE IS THE KIND OF GUY...
...WHO'D SAVE THE LIFE OF SOMEONE WHO TRIED TO KILL HIM!
FWAP
FWAP
A REALLY BIG FOOL!
A SUPER BIG FOOL!
FWAP
FWAP
KRK
BUT FOOL OR NOT...

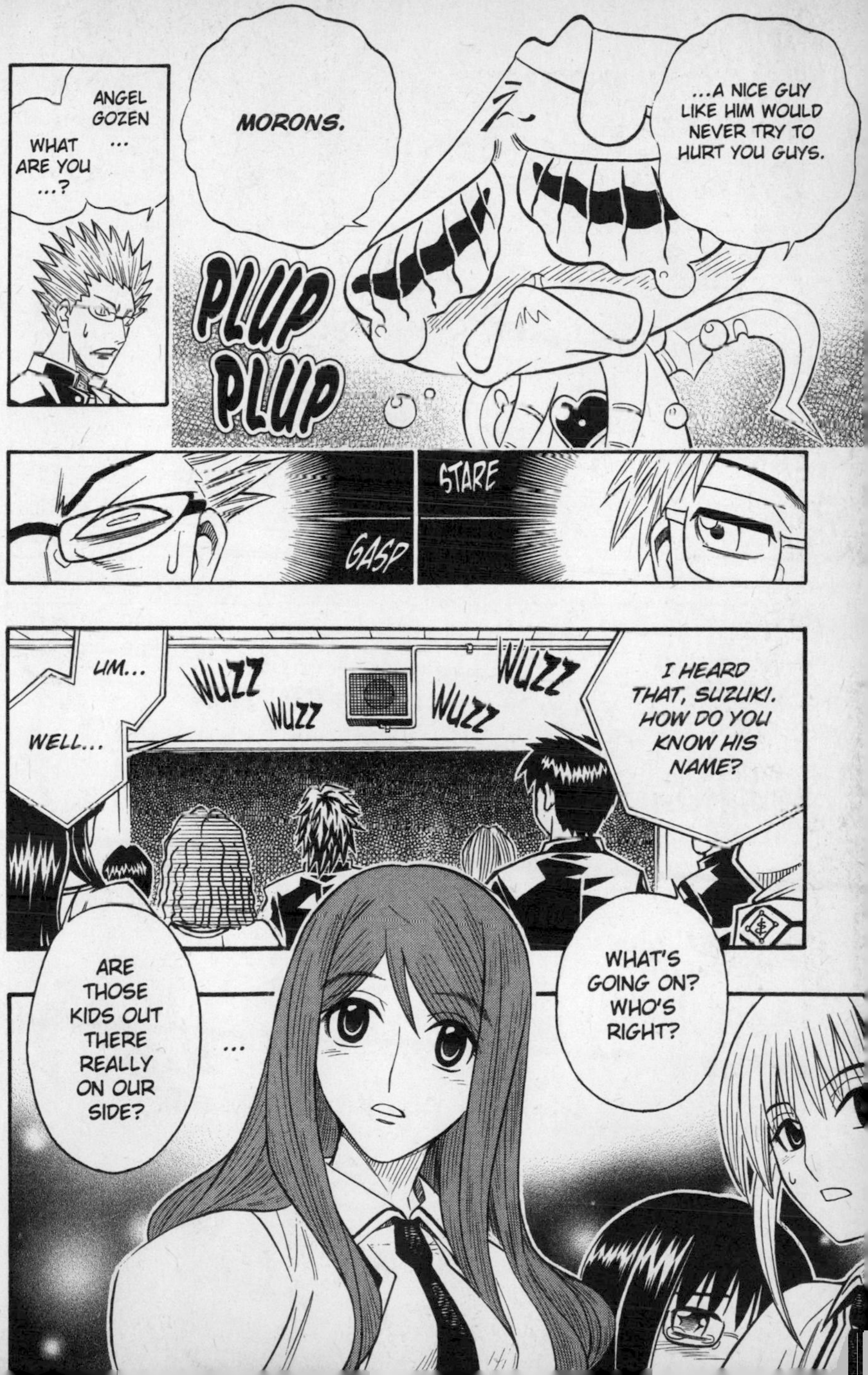
...A NICE GUY LIKE HIM WOULD NEVER TRY TO HURT YOU GUYS.
MORONS.
PLUP PLUP
ANGEL GOZEN ...
WHAT ARE YOU ...?
STARE
GASP
I HEARD THAT, SUZUKI. HOW DO YOU KNOW HIS NAME?
WUZZ
WUZZ
WUZZ
WUZZ
UM...
WELL...
WHAT'S GOING ON? WHO'S RIGHT?
...
ARE THOSE KIDS OUT THERE REALLY ON OUR SIDE?

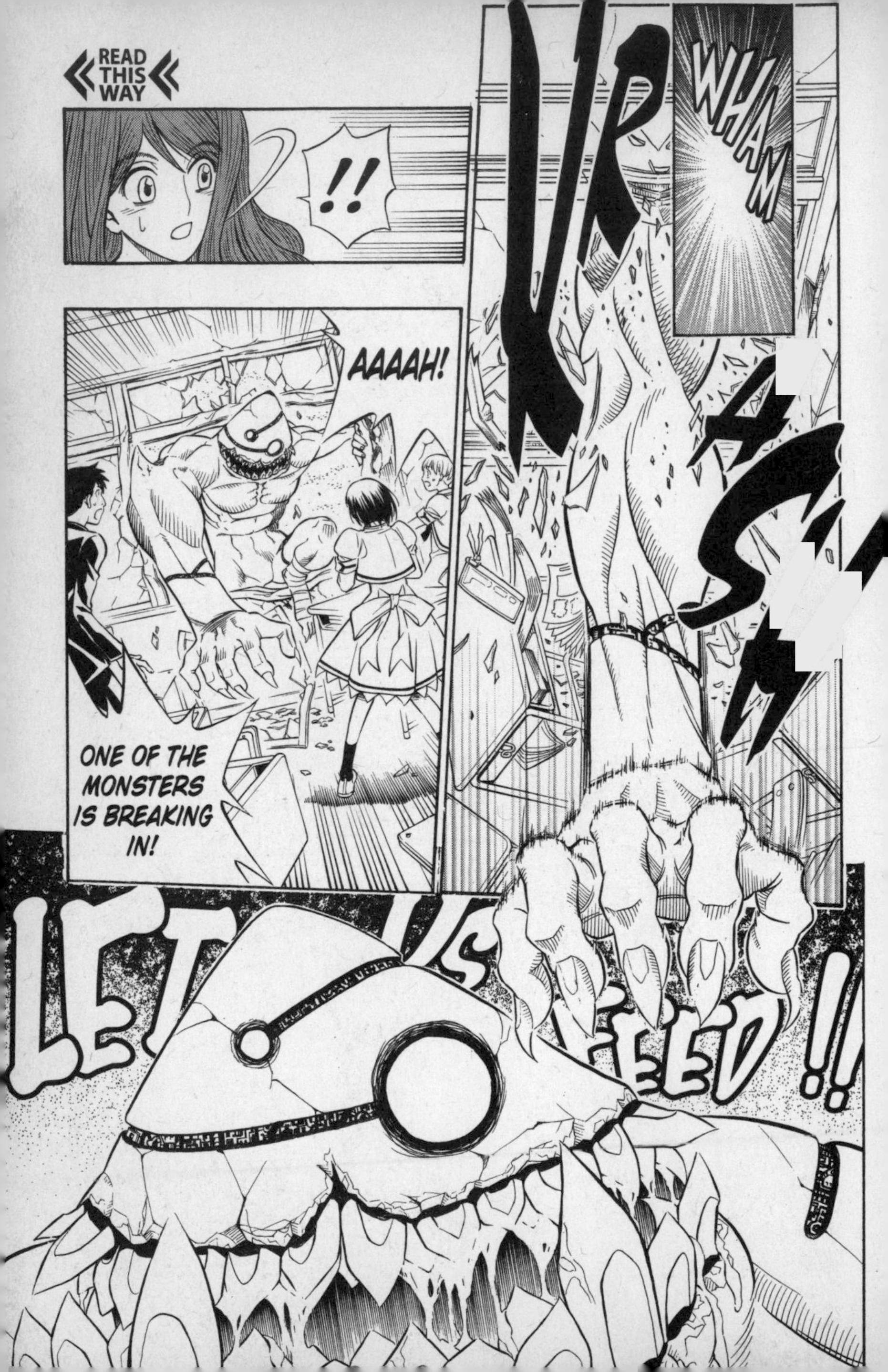
READ THIS WAY
WHAM
!!
AAAAH!
ONE OF THE MONSTERS IS BREAKING IN!
LET US FEED!!

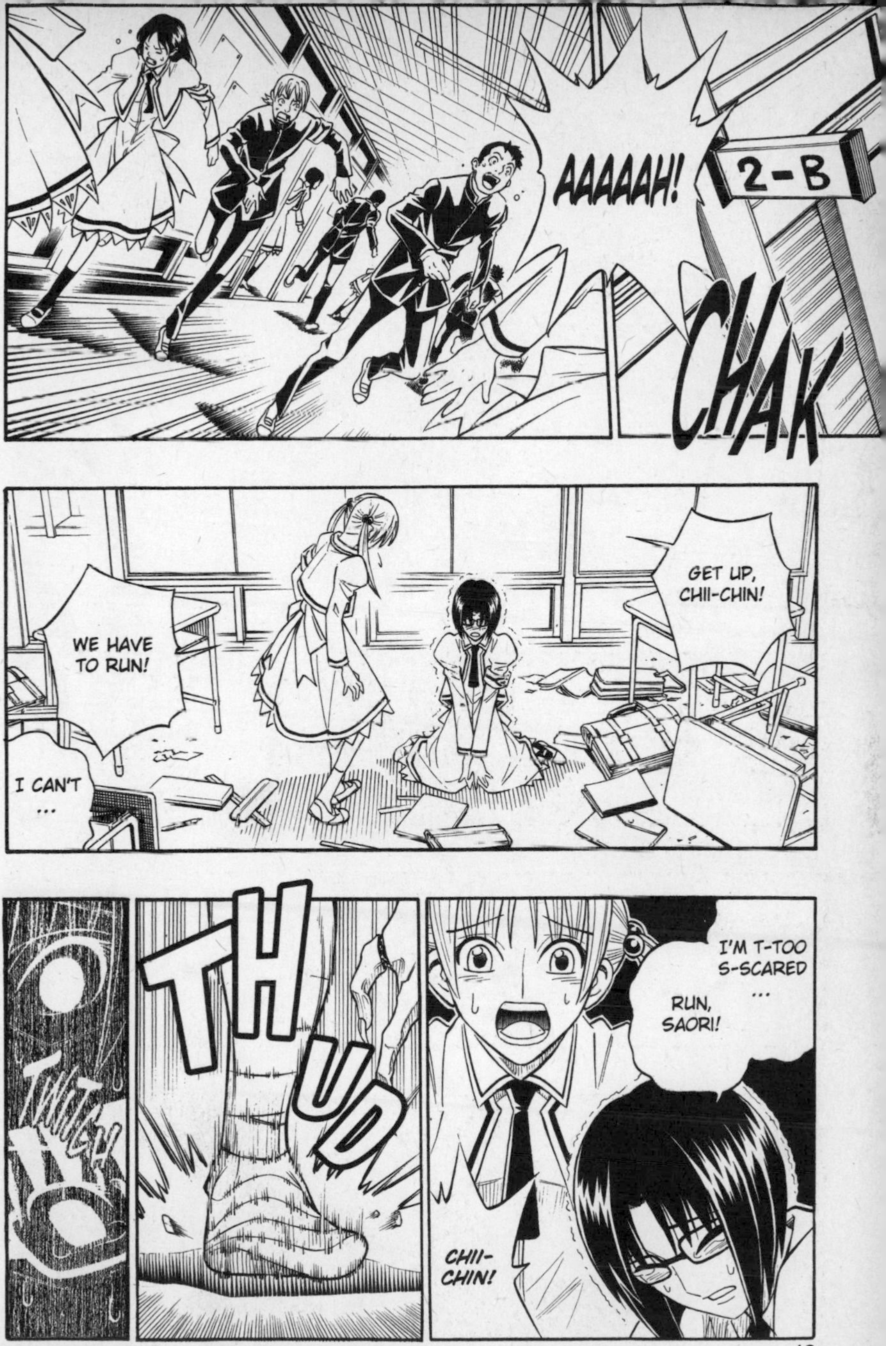
2-B
AAAAAH!
CHAK
GET UP, CHII-CHIN!
WE HAVE TO RUN!
I CAN'T ...
I'M T-TOO S-SCARED ...
RUN, SAORI!
CHII-CHIN!
THUD
TWITCH

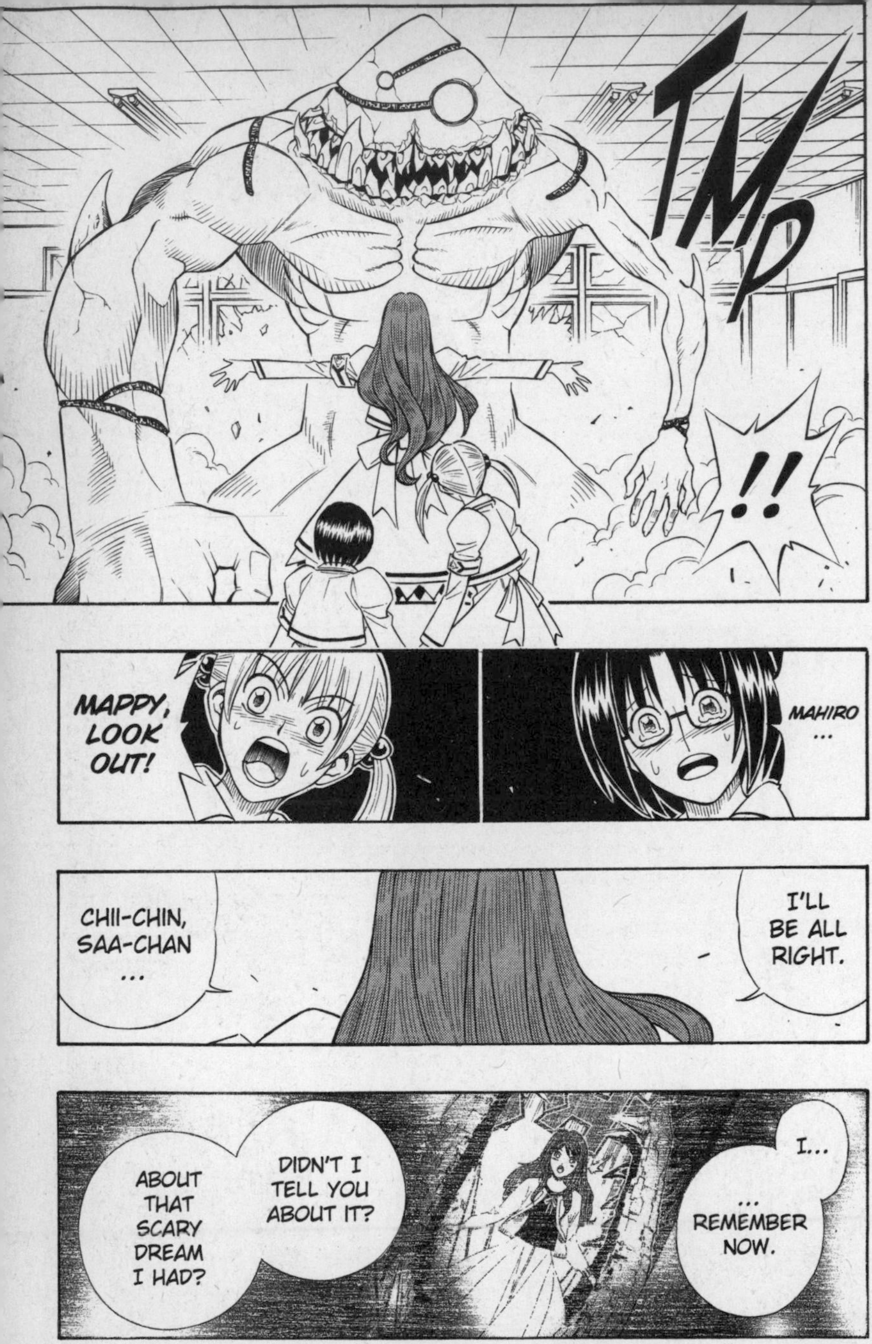
TMP
!!
MAHIRO ...
MAPPY, LOOK OUT!
I'LL BE ALL RIGHT.
CHII-CHIN, SAA-CHAN ...
I...
... REMEMBER NOW.
DIDN'T I TELL YOU ABOUT IT?
ABOUT THAT SCARY DREAM I HAD?

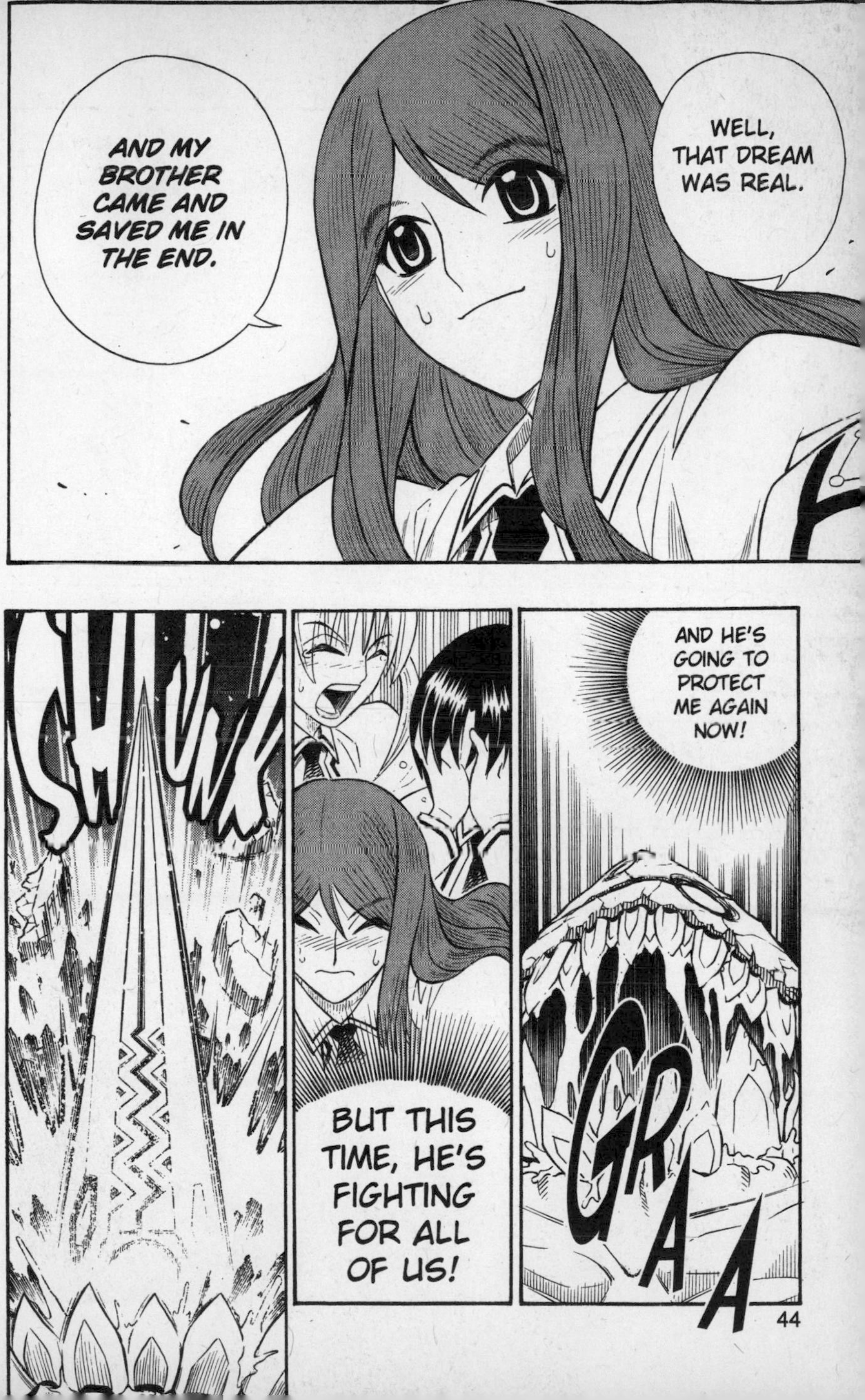
WELL, THAT DREAM WAS REAL.
AND MY BROTHER CAME AND SAVED ME IN THE END.
AND HE'S GOING TO PROTECT ME AGAIN NOW!
GRAAA
BUT THIS TIME, HE'S FIGHTING FOR ALL OF US!

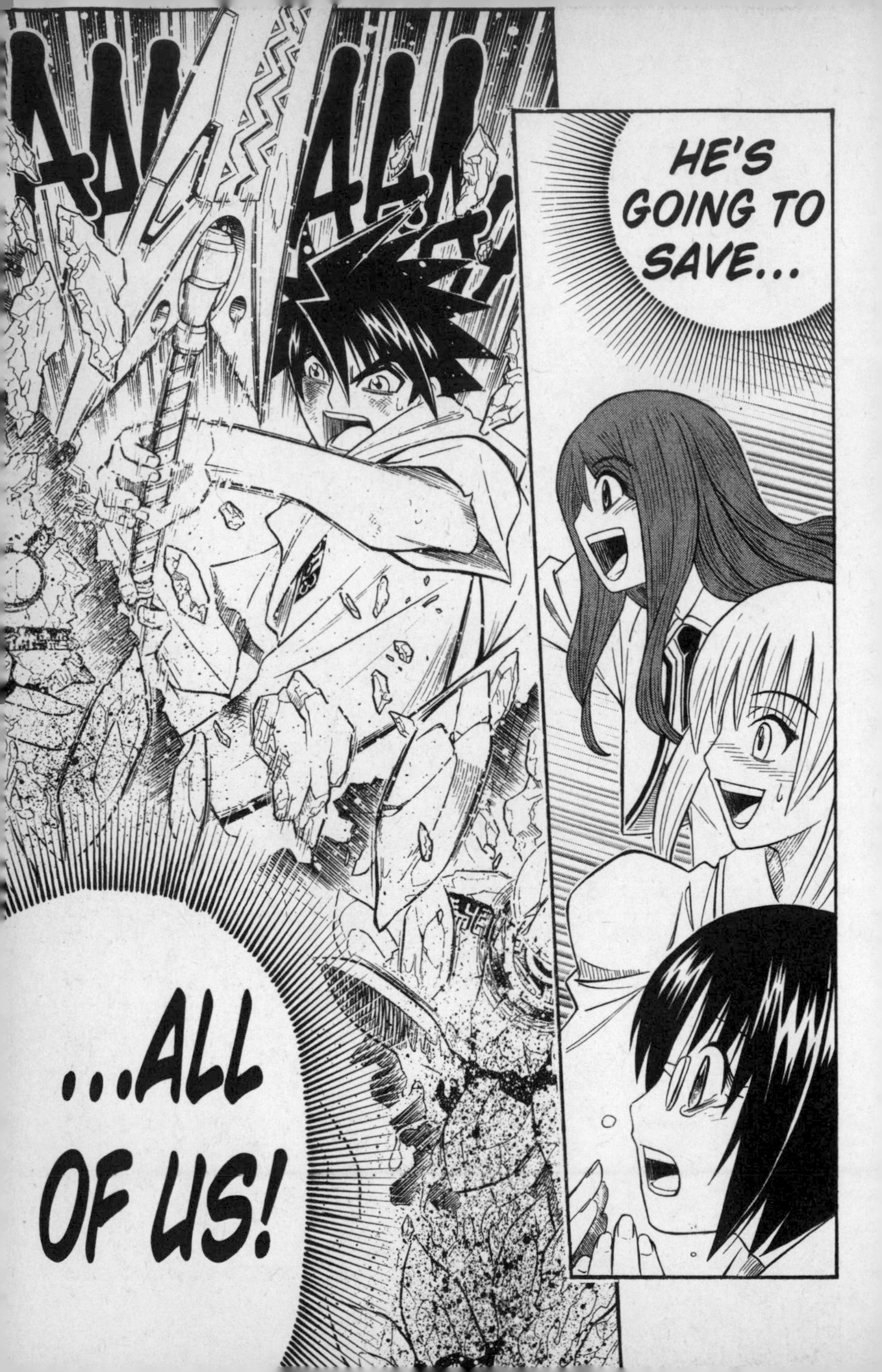
HE'S GOING TO SAVE...
...ALL OF US!

- Height: 152cm; Weight: 39kg
- Measurements: 75-54-79
- Born: January 13; Capricorn; Blood Type: B;
  Age: 15
- Likes: Mappy, Chii-Chin, Western confections
- Dislikes: Everything about studying
- Hobby: Searching for new sweets (especially
  Western ones)
- Special Ability: Sleeping for a long time (record is
  2 1/2 days)
- Affiliations: Ginsei Academy Year 1 Classroom A,
  Dorm resident

Character File No. 21

SAORI KAWAI

Author's Notes

- Like Chisato, she was created as a background character and was elevated to a supporting role.
- She's named after the younger of my two nieces. Since the design for Chisato was rather simple, I wanted to do the opposite with Saori so I gave her pigtails. The fact that her pigtails and bangs are different lengths every time I draw her is a secret that I'll only acknowledge here.
- Like most teenagers, she likes to play and follows the latest trends. Of Mahiro's group, she's the least psychologically rigid so she's better able to cope with crazy situations. You probably won't see it in the pages of this manga, but after school she drags Mahiro and Chisato out to go window-shopping and try out new restaurants. She's pretty normal, but in a different way than Chisato.

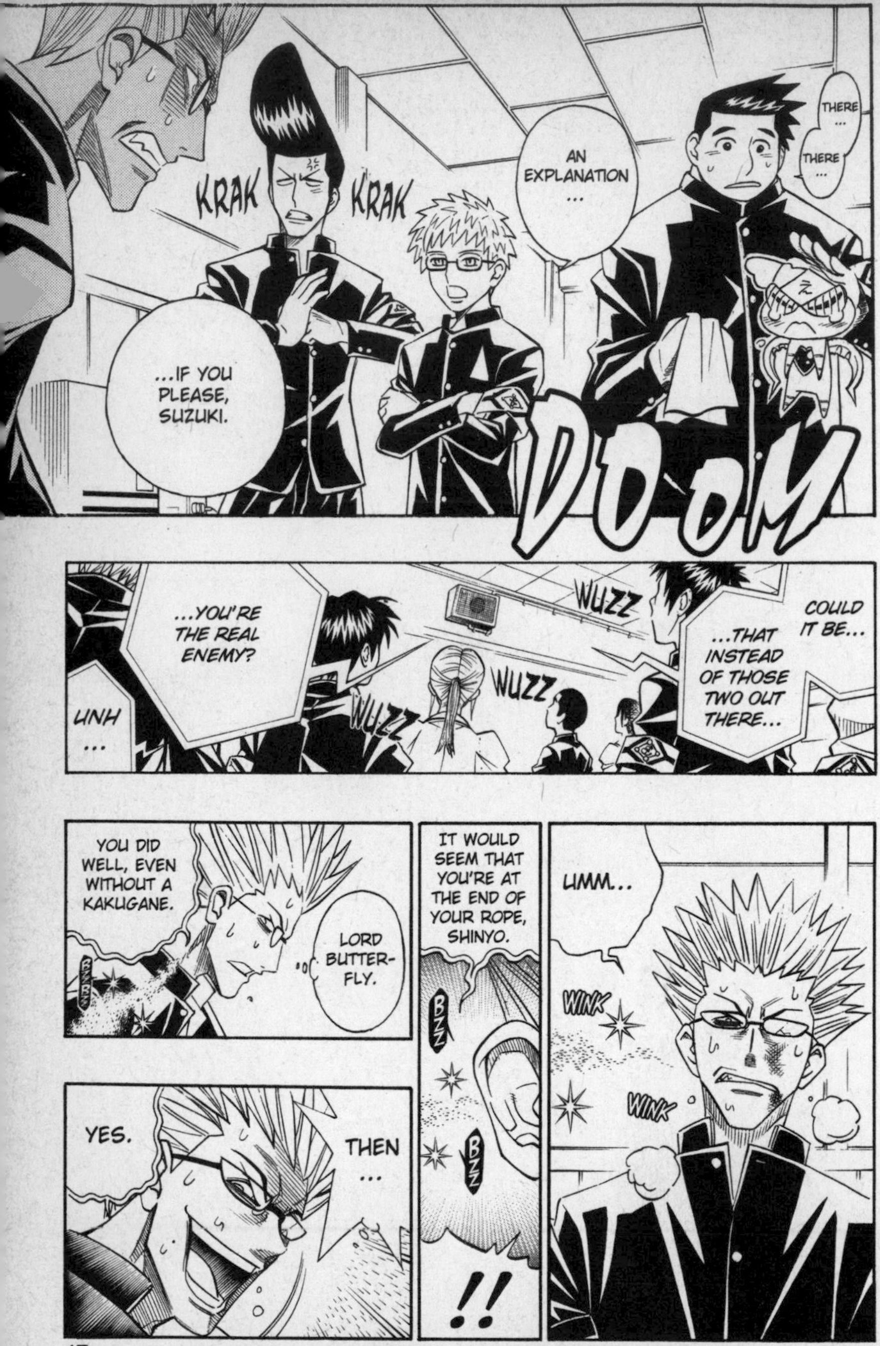
THERE ...
THERE ...
AN EXPLANATION ...
KRAK KRAK
...IF YOU PLEASE, SUZUKI.
DOOM
COULD IT BE...
...THAT INSTEAD OF THOSE TWO OUT THERE...
WUZZ
WUZZ
WUZZ
...YOU'RE THE REAL ENEMY?
UNH ...
UMM...
WINK
WINK
IT WOULD SEEM THAT YOU'RE AT THE END OF YOUR ROPE, SHINYO.
BZZ
BZZ
!!
LORD BUTTER-FLY.
YOU DID WELL, EVEN WITHOUT A KAKUGANE.
THEN ...
YES.

CHAPTER 39: OVERFLOWING POWER

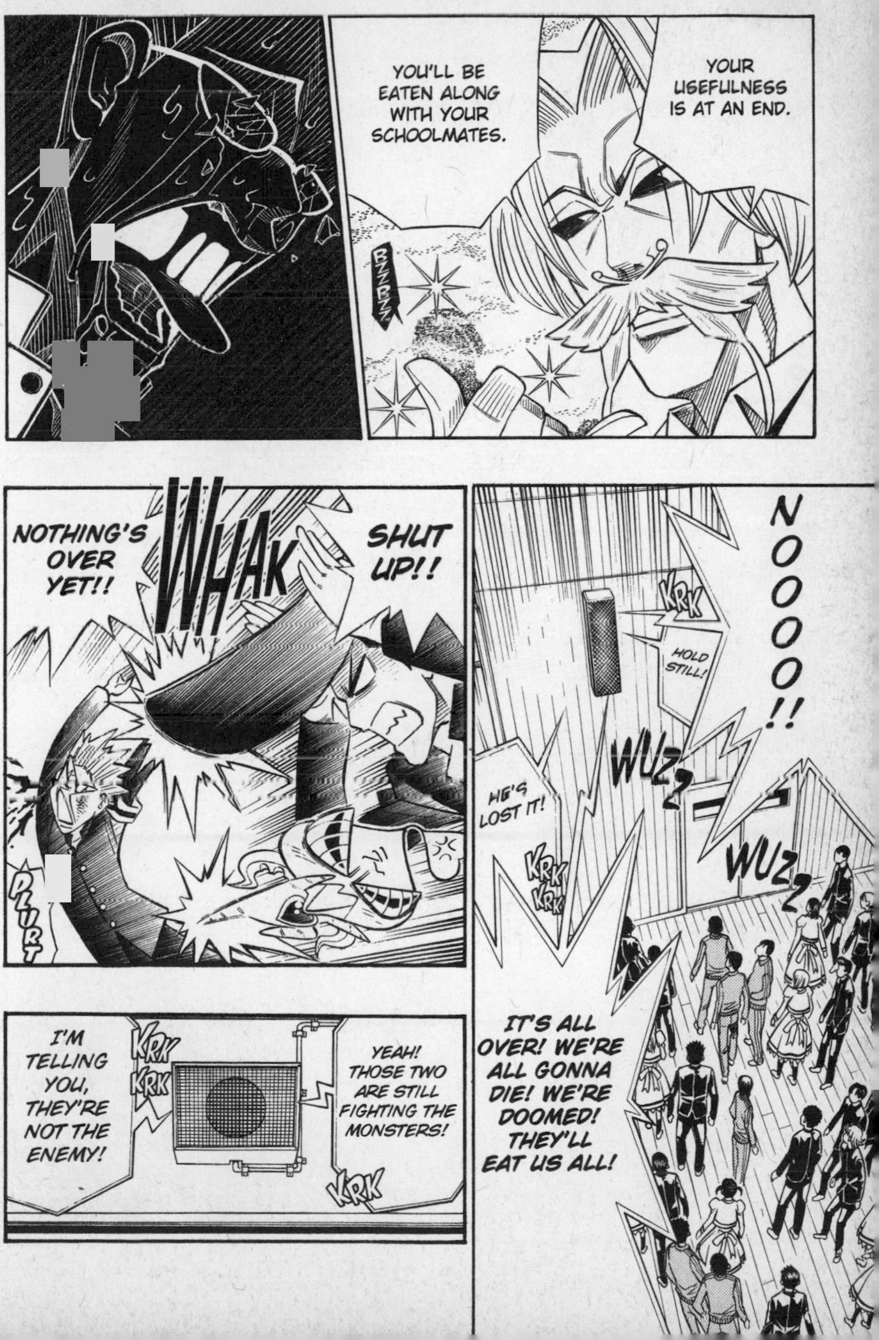

YOUR USEFULNESS IS AT AN END.
YOU'LL BE EATEN ALONG WITH YOUR SCHOOLMATES.
BZZBZZ
NOOOOO!!
KRK
HOLD STILL!
WUZZ
HE'S LOST IT!
WUZZ
KRK KRK
IT'S ALL OVER! WE'RE ALL GONNA DIE! WE'RE DOOMED! THEY'LL EAT US ALL!
SHUT UP!!
WHAK
NOTHING'S OVER YET!!
PLURT
YEAH! THOSE TWO ARE STILL FIGHTING THE MONSTERS!
KRK
KRK KRK
I'M TELLING YOU, THEY'RE NOT THE ENEMY!

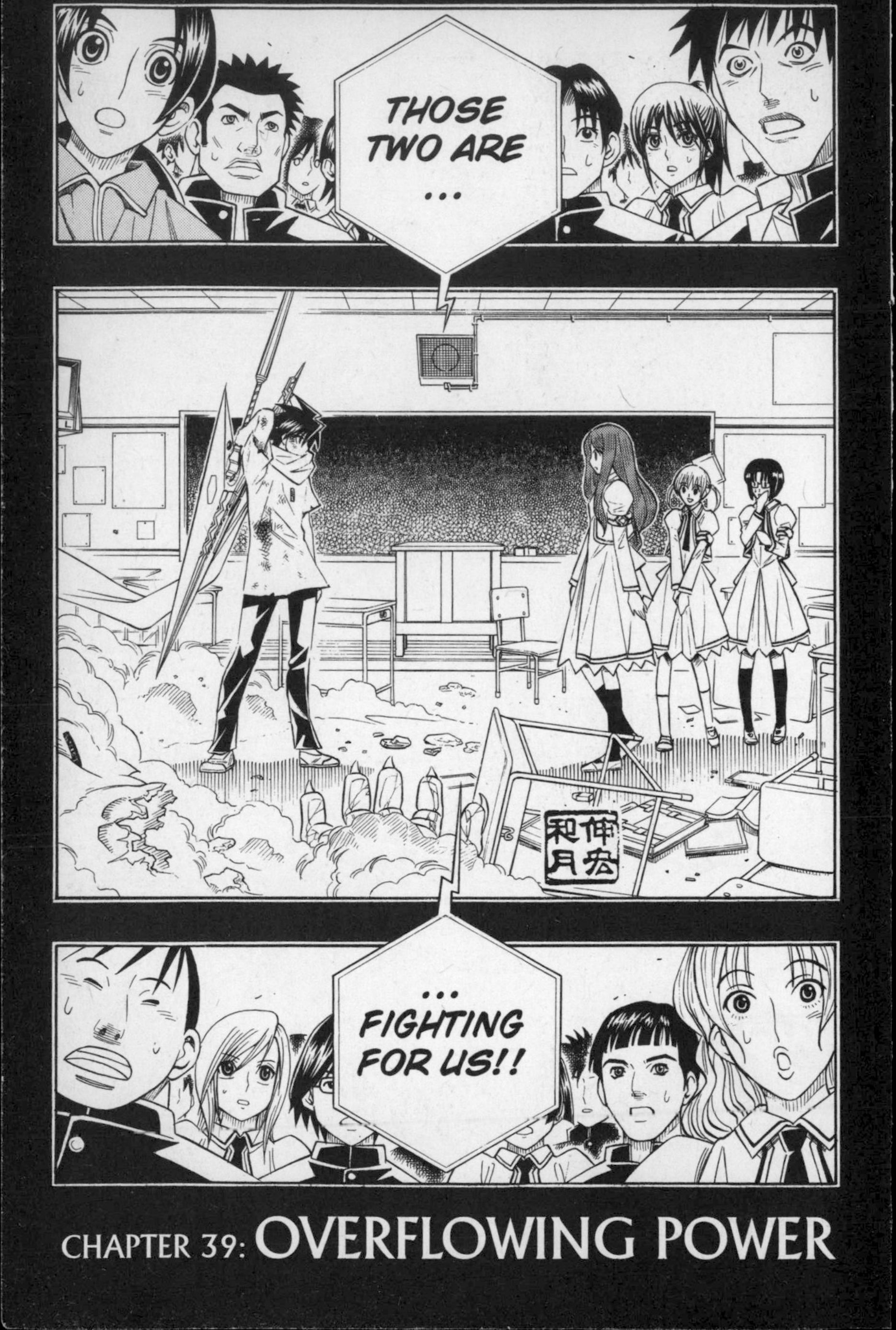
THOSE TWO ARE ...
伸宏和月
... FIGHTING FOR US!!

CHAPTER 39: OVERFLOWING POWER

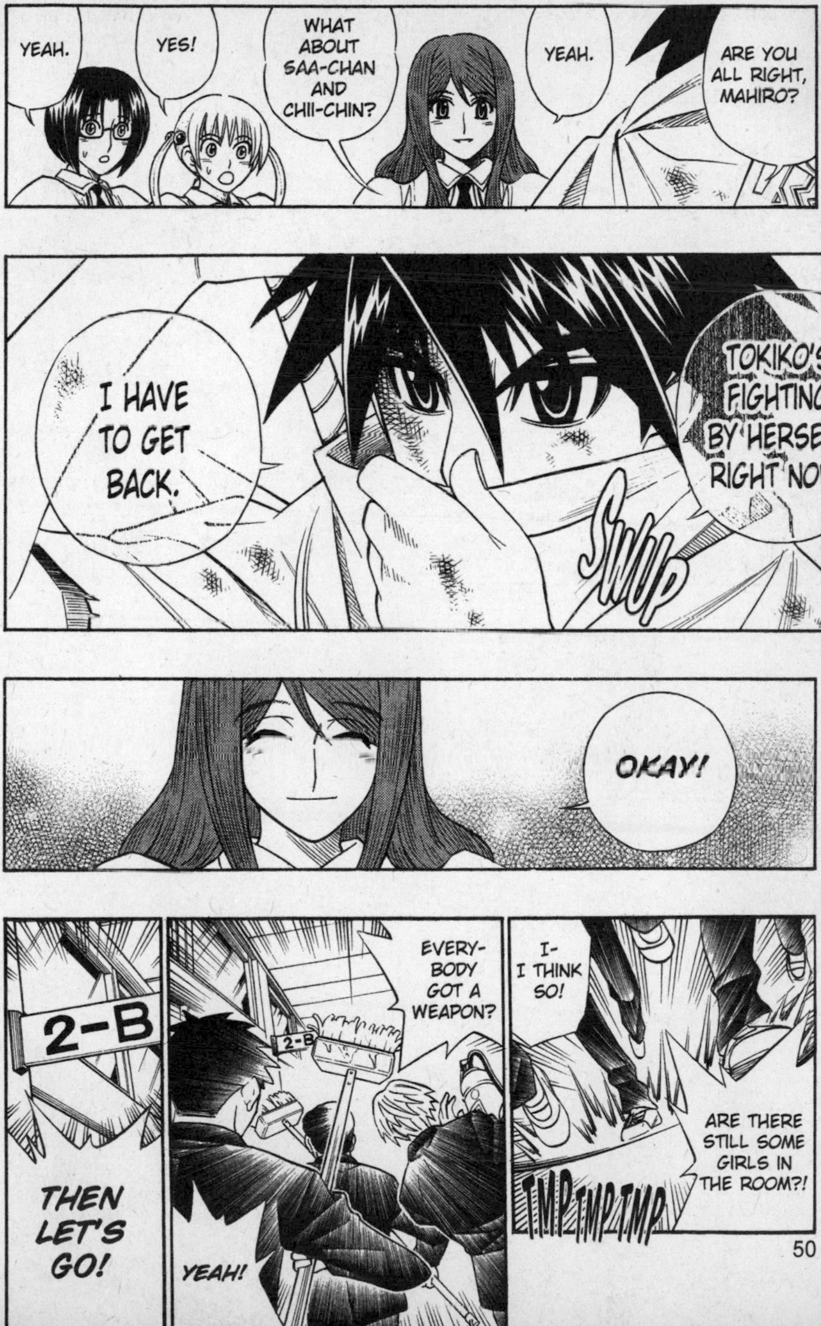
ARE YOU ALL RIGHT, MAHIRO?
YEAH.
WHAT ABOUT SAA-CHAN AND CHII-CHIN?
YES!
YEAH.
TOKIKO'S FIGHTING BY HERSELF RIGHT NOW.
SWUP
I HAVE TO GET BACK.
OKAY!
I- I THINK SO!
ARE THERE STILL SOME GIRLS IN THE ROOM?!
TMP TMP TMP
EVERY-BODY GOT A WEAPON?
2-B
YEAH!
2-B
THEN LET'S GO!

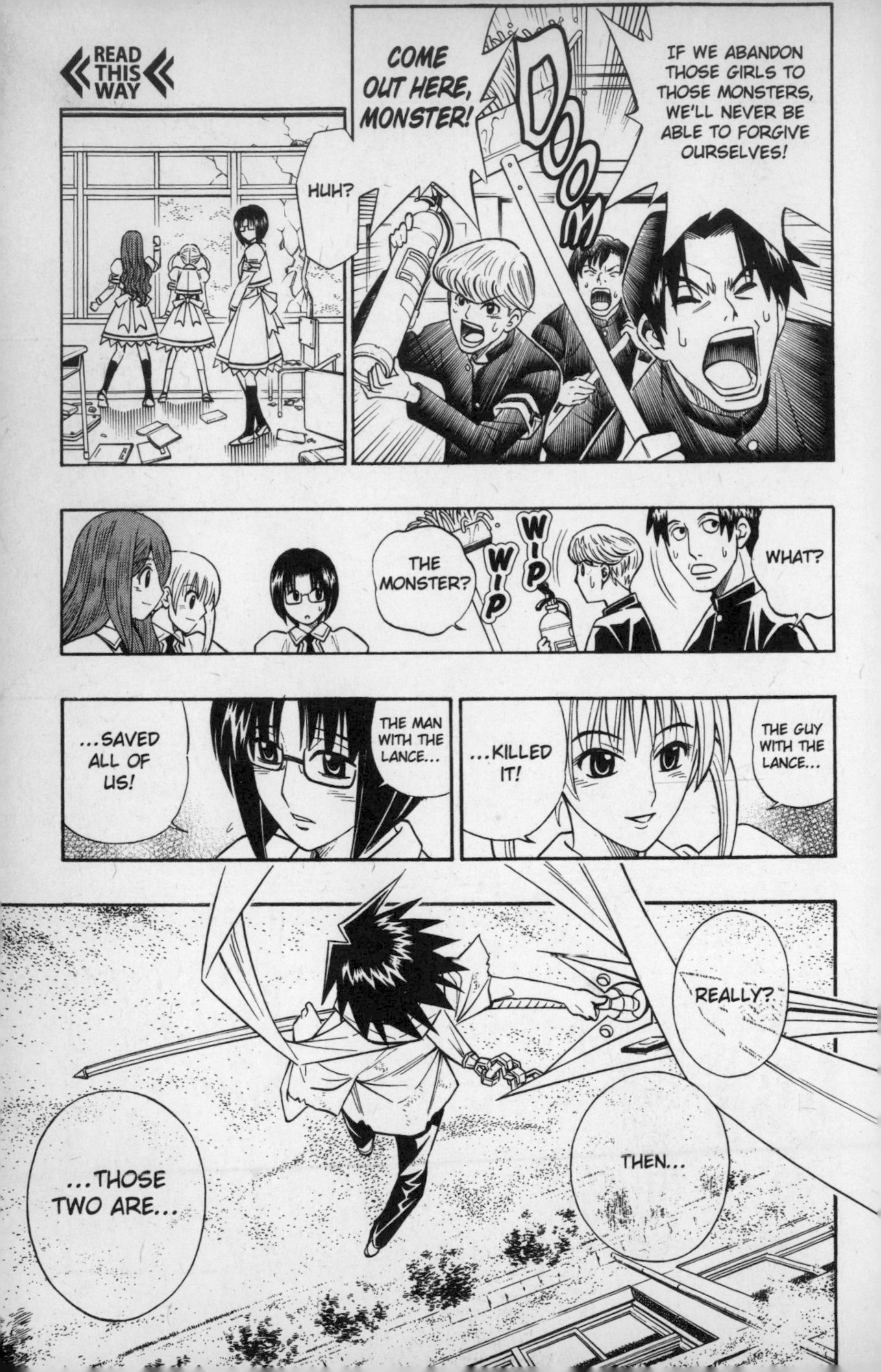
READ THIS WAY
IF WE ABANDON THOSE GIRLS TO THOSE MONSTERS, WE'LL NEVER BE ABLE TO FORGIVE OURSELVES!
COME OUT HERE, MONSTER!
DOOOM
HUH?
WHAT?
WIP
WIP
THE MONSTER?
THE GUY WITH THE LANCE...
...KILLED IT!
THE MAN WITH THE LANCE...
...SAVED ALL OF US!
REALLY?
THEN...
...THOSE TWO ARE...

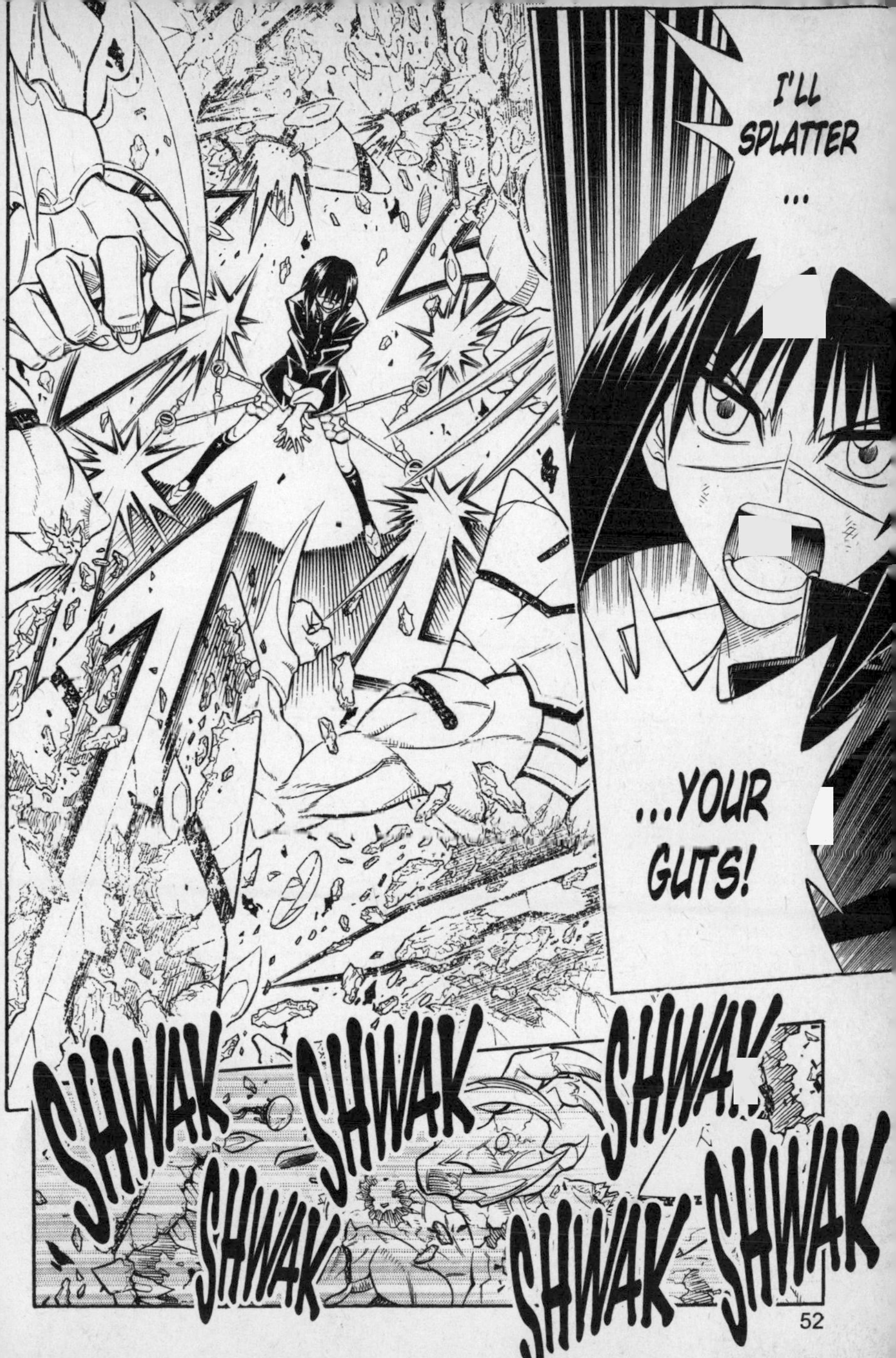
I'LL SPLATTER ...
...YOUR GUTS!
SHWAK SHWAK SHWAK
SHWAK SHWAK SHWAK SHWAK

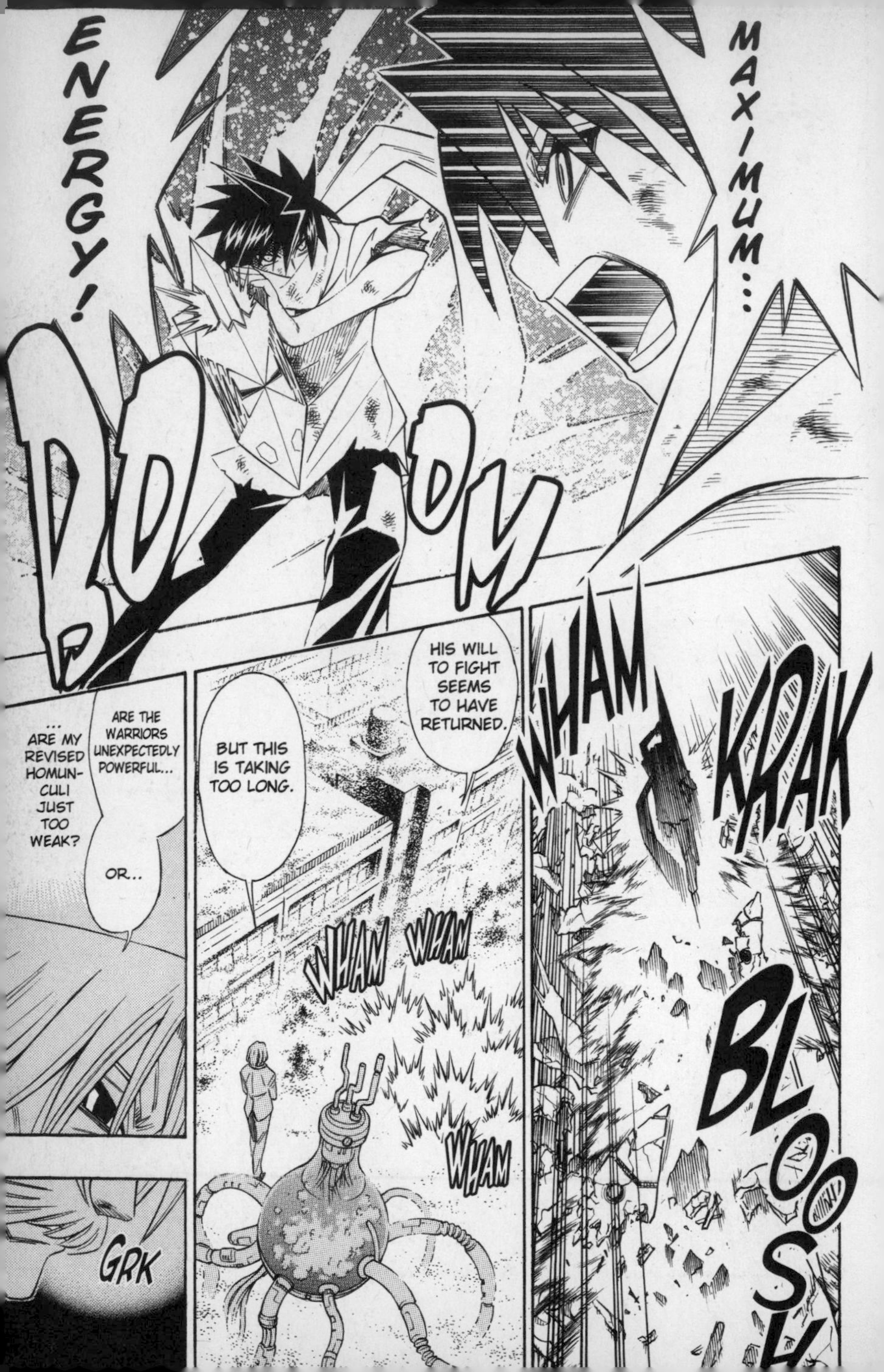
MAXIMUM...
ENERGY!
DOOM
WHAM
KRAK
BLOOSH
HIS WILL TO FIGHT SEEMS TO HAVE RETURNED.
BUT THIS IS TAKING TOO LONG.
WHAM
WHAM
WHAM
ARE THE WARRIORS UNEXPECTEDLY POWERFUL... OR...
...ARE MY REVISED HOMUN-CULI JUST TOO WEAK?
GRK

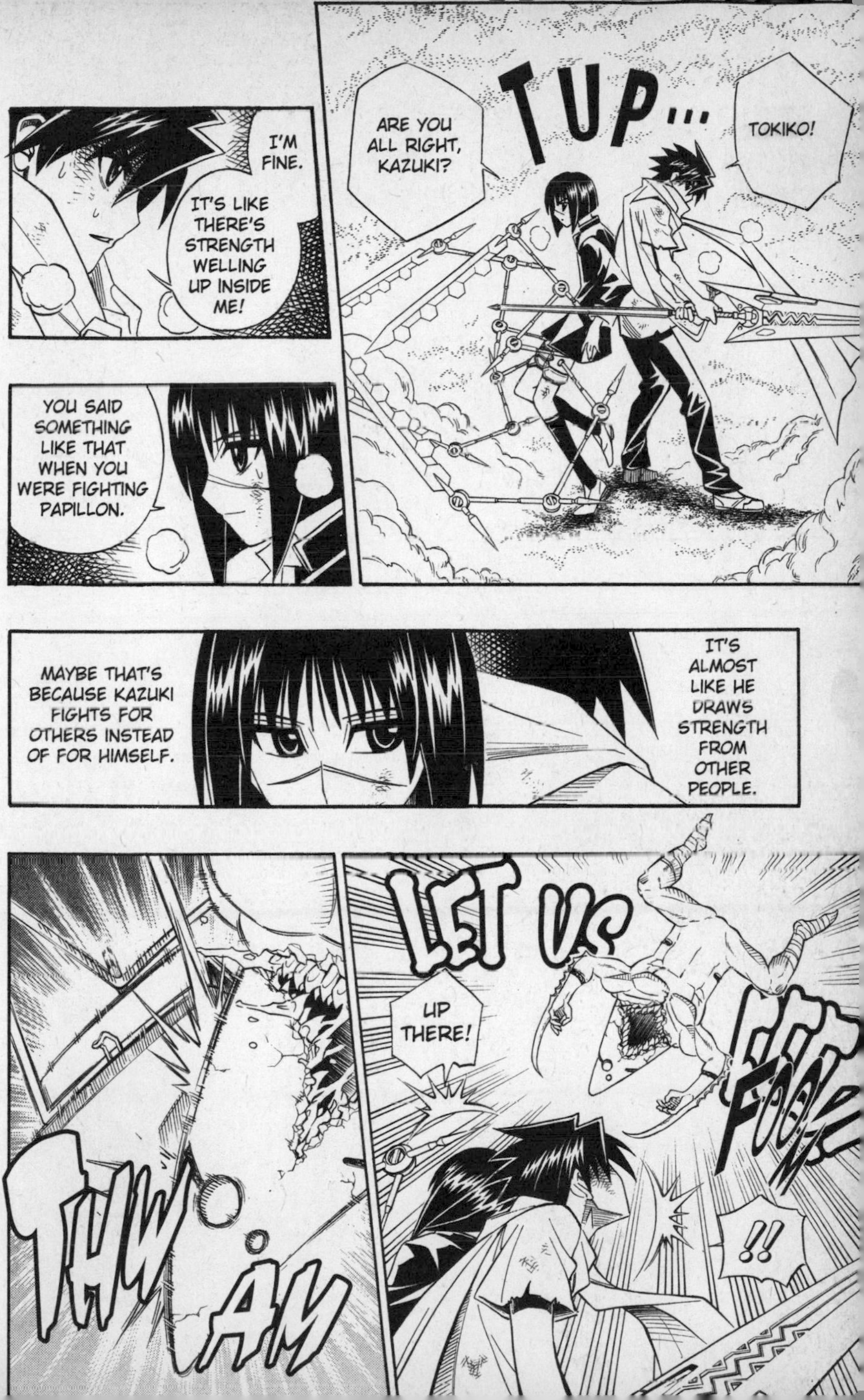
TOKIKO!
TUP...
ARE YOU ALL RIGHT, KAZUKI?
I'M FINE.
IT'S LIKE THERE'S STRENGTH WELLING UP INSIDE ME!
YOU SAID SOMETHING LIKE THAT WHEN YOU WERE FIGHTING PAPILLON.
IT'S ALMOST LIKE HE DRAWS STRENGTH FROM OTHER PEOPLE.
MAYBE THAT'S BECAUSE KAZUKI FIGHTS FOR OTHERS INSTEAD OF FOR HIMSELF.
LET US
UP THERE!
!!

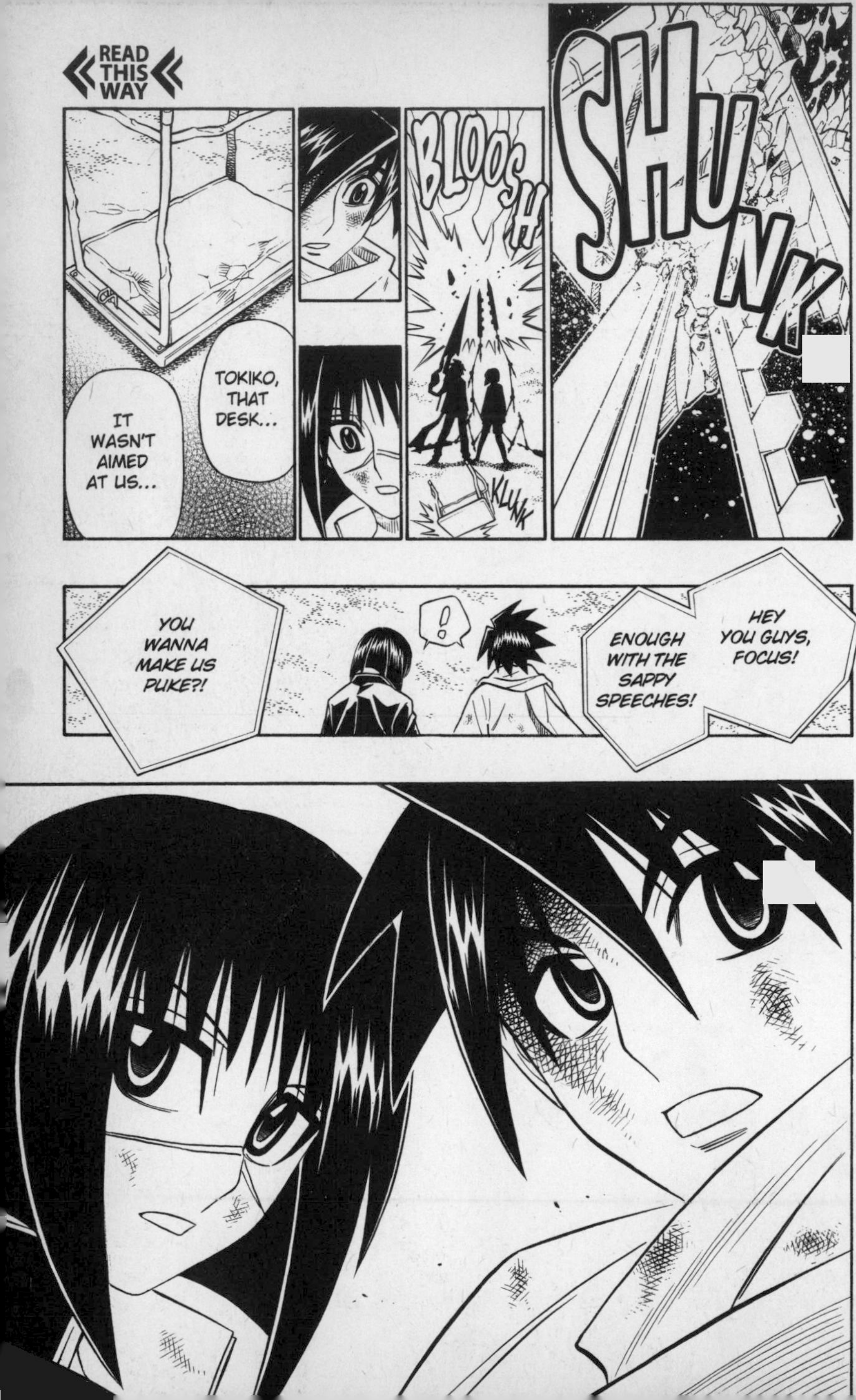
READ THIS WAY
SHUNK
BLOOSH
KLUNK
TOKIKO, THAT DESK...
IT WASN'T AIMED AT US...
HEY YOU GUYS, FOCUS!
ENOUGH WITH THE SAPPY SPEECHES!
!
YOU WANNA MAKE US PUKE?!

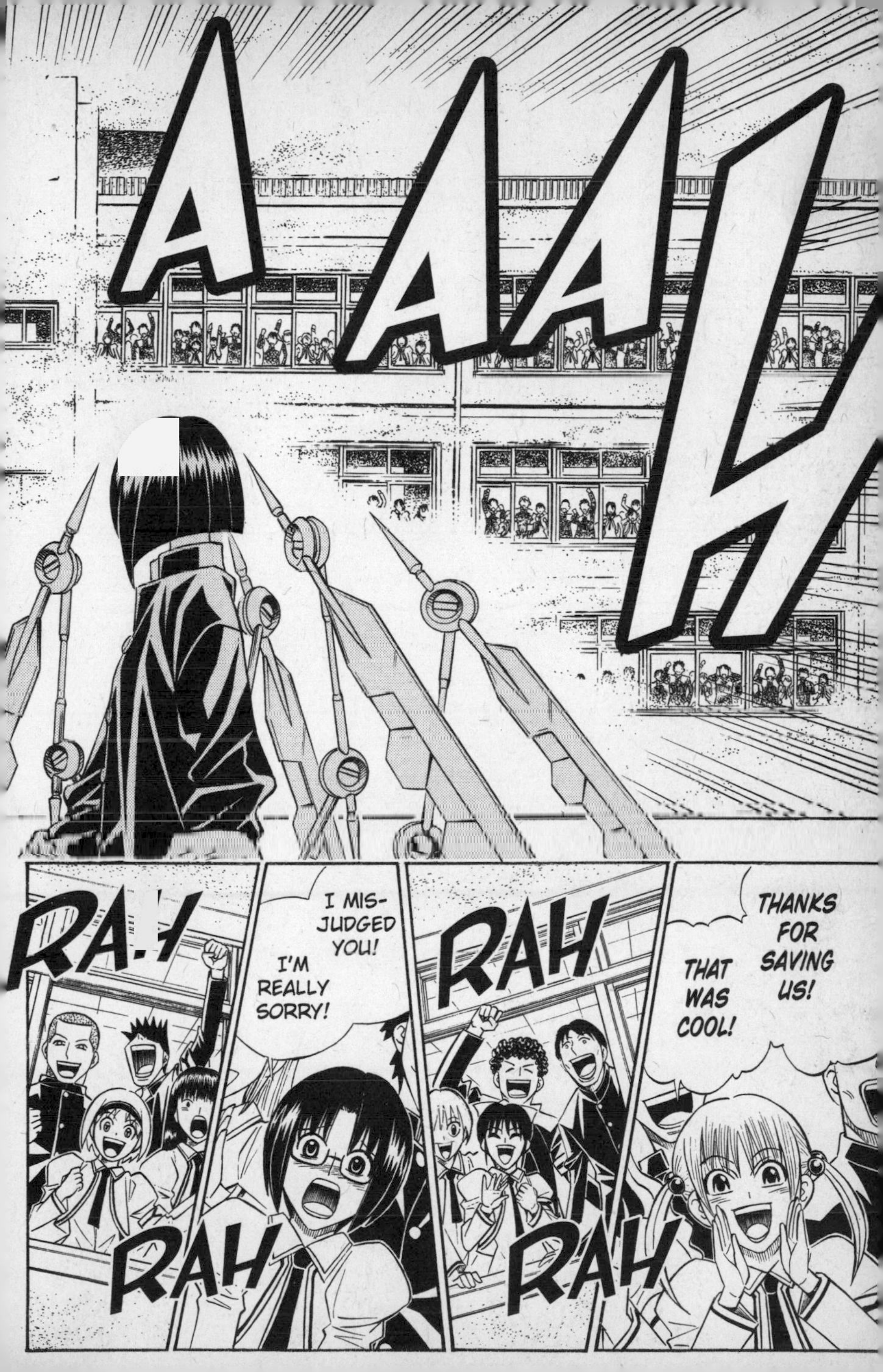
AAAH
THANKS FOR SAVING US!
THAT WAS COOL!
RAH
RAH
I MIS-JUDGED YOU!
I'M REALLY SORRY!
RAH

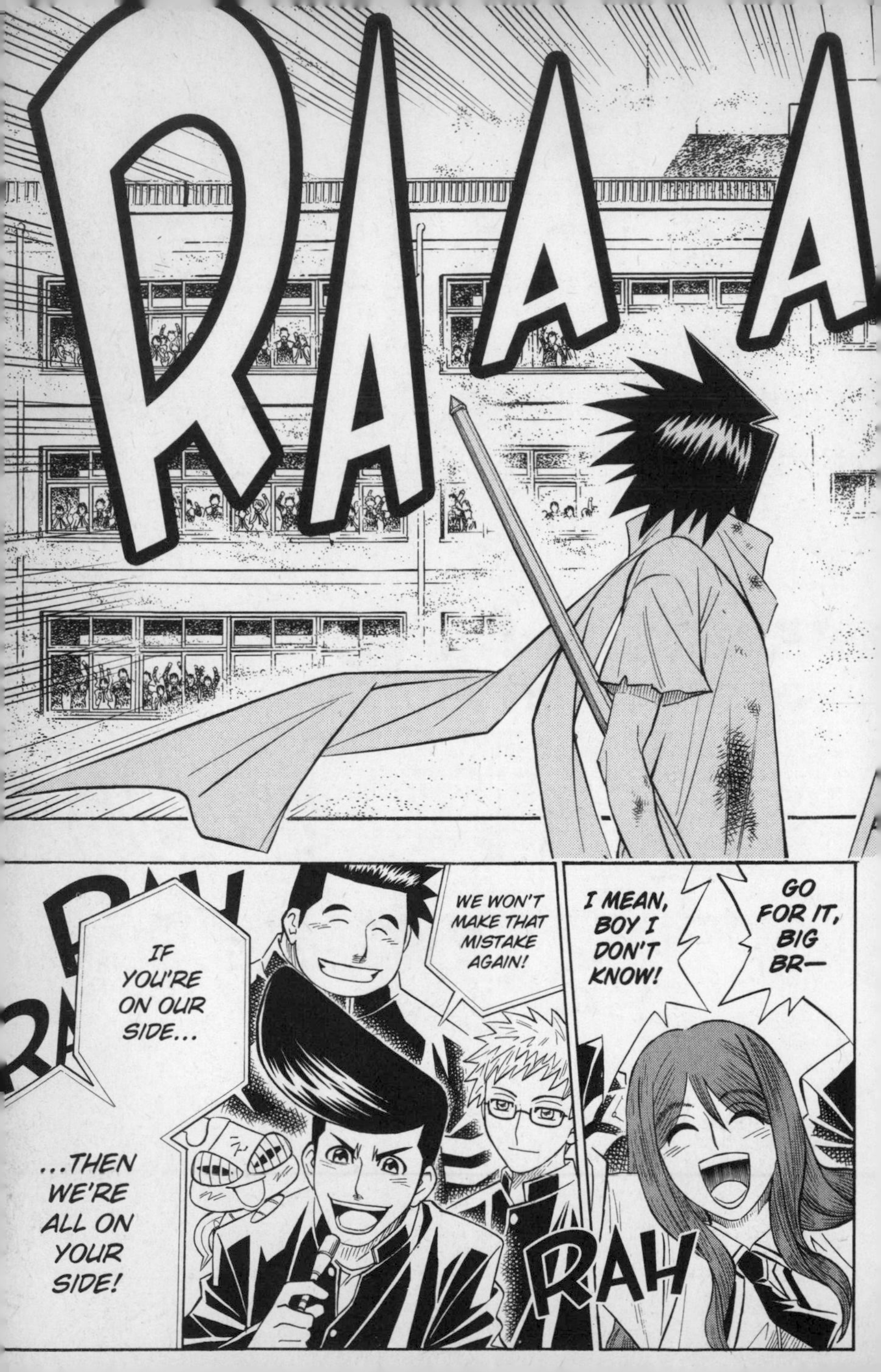
RAAAA
GO FOR IT, BIG BR—
I MEAN, BOY I DON'T KNOW!
RAH
WE WON'T MAKE THAT MISTAKE AGAIN!
IF YOU'RE ON OUR SIDE...
...THEN WE'RE ALL ON YOUR SIDE!

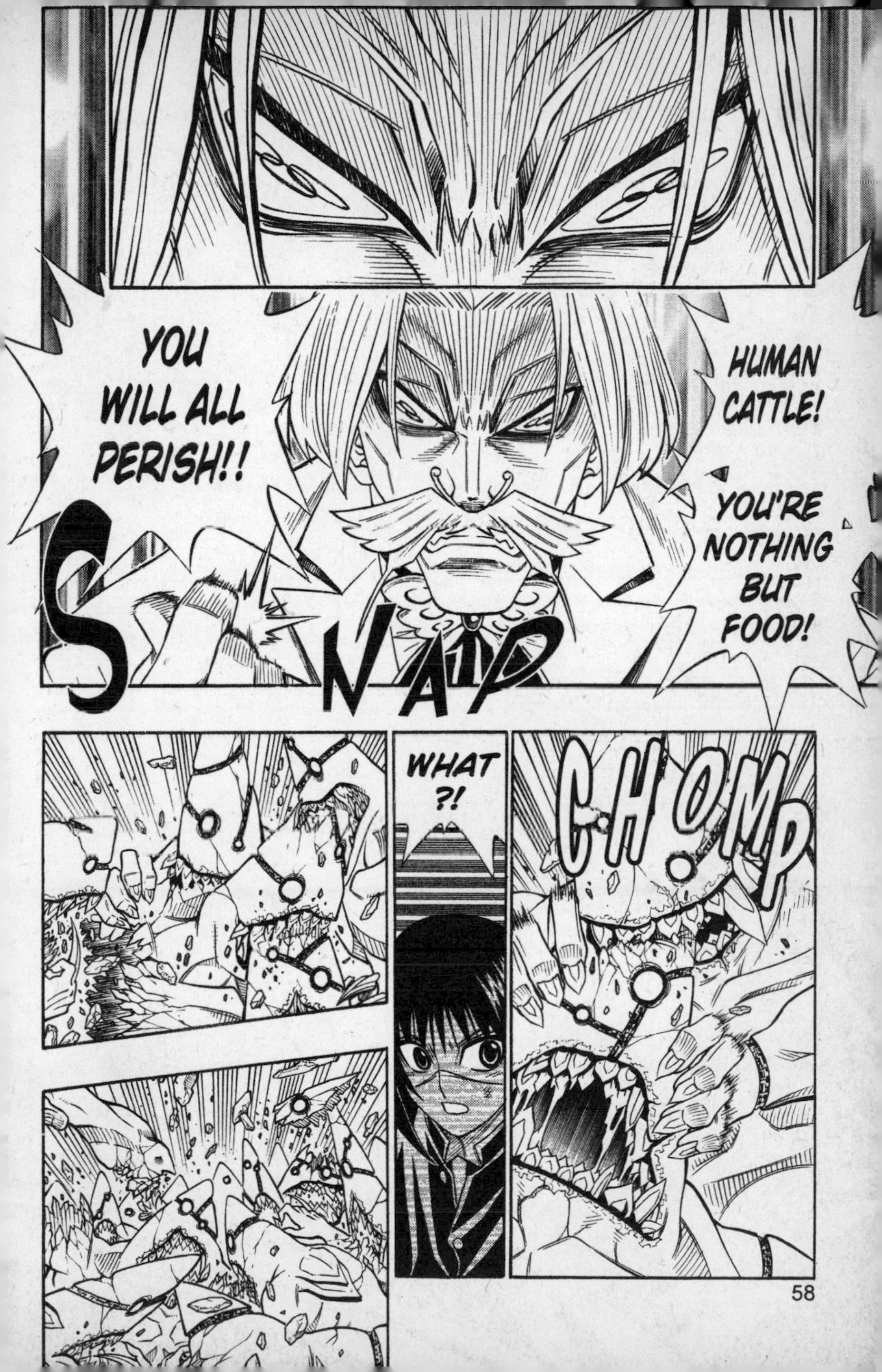
HUMAN CATTLE!
YOU'RE NOTHING BUT FOOD!
YOU WILL ALL PERISH!!
SNAP
CHOMP
WHAT ?!

READ THIS WAY

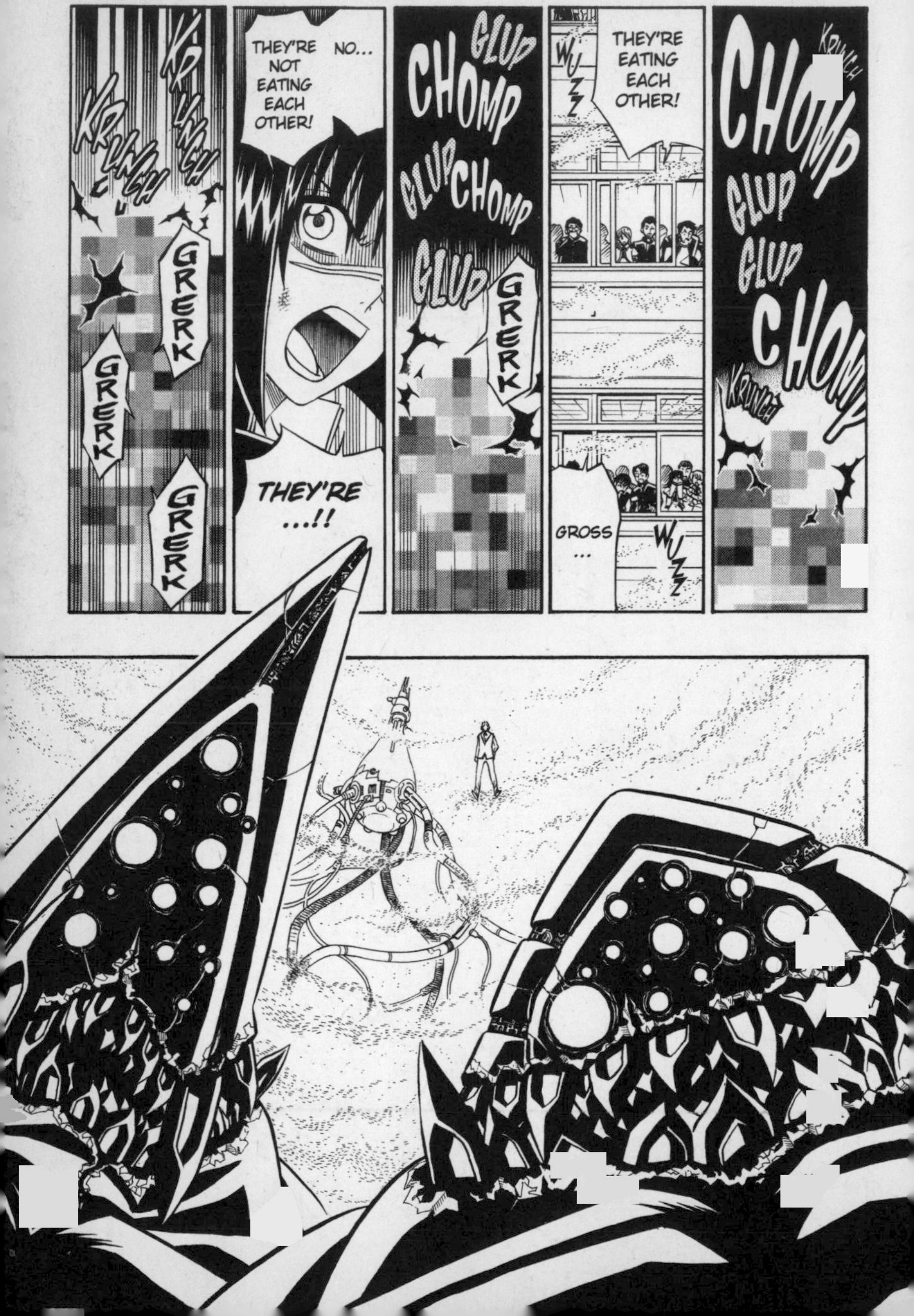

KRUNCH
CHOMP
GLUP
GLUP
CHOMP
KRUNCH
THEY'RE EATING EACH OTHER!
WUZZ
GROSS...
WUZZ
GLUP
CHOMP
GLUP
CHOMP
GLUP
GRERK
NO...
THEY'RE NOT EATING EACH OTHER!
THEY'RE...!!
KRUNCH
KRUNCH
GRERK
GRERK
GRERK

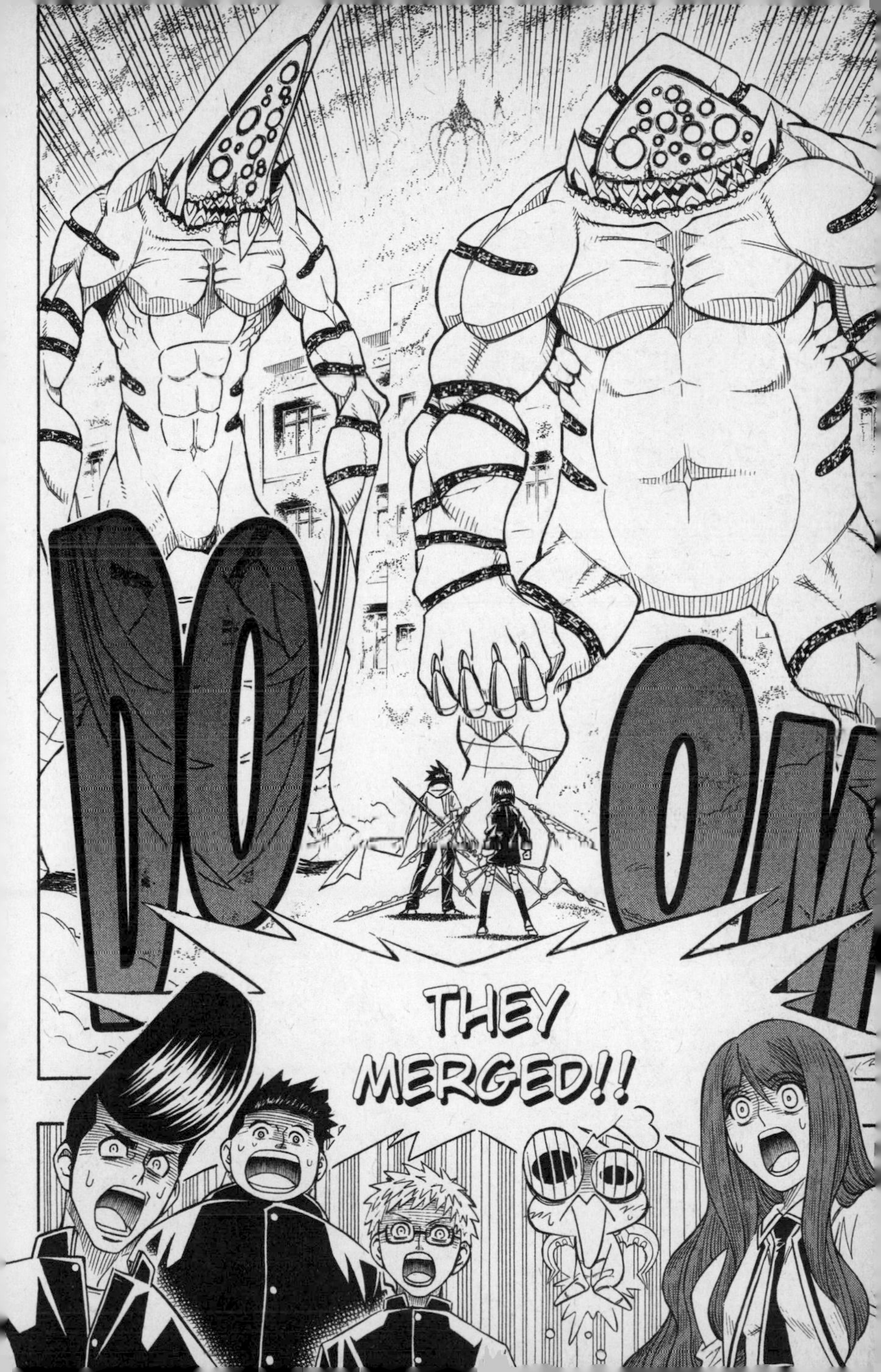
DOOM
THEY MERGED!!

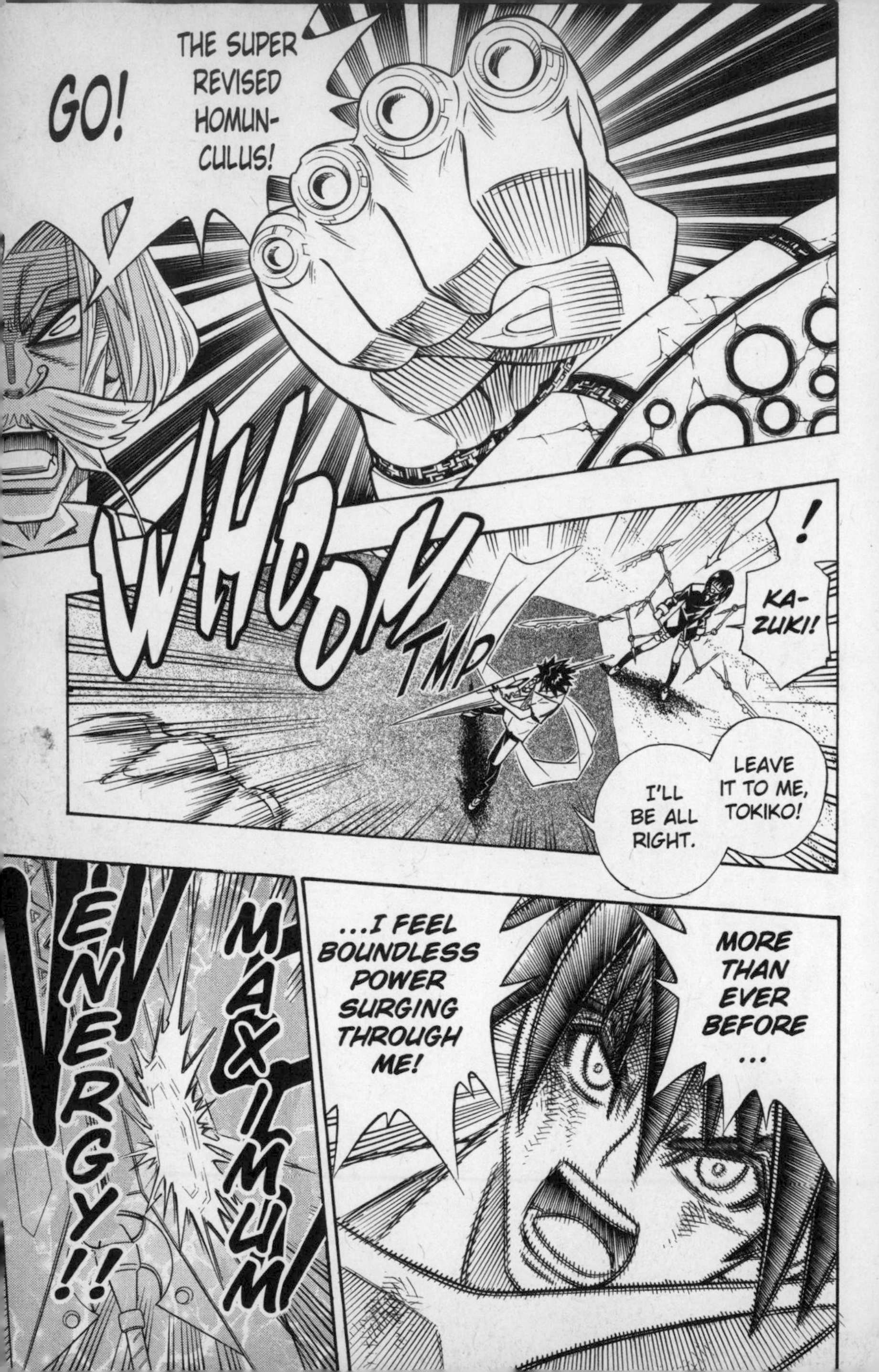
THE SUPER REVISED HOMUN-CULUS!
GO!
WHOOM
!
KA-ZUKI!
TMP
LEAVE IT TO ME, TOKIKO!
I'LL BE ALL RIGHT.
MORE THAN EVER BEFORE...
...I FEEL BOUNDLESS POWER SURGING THROUGH ME!
MAXIMUM
ENERGY!!

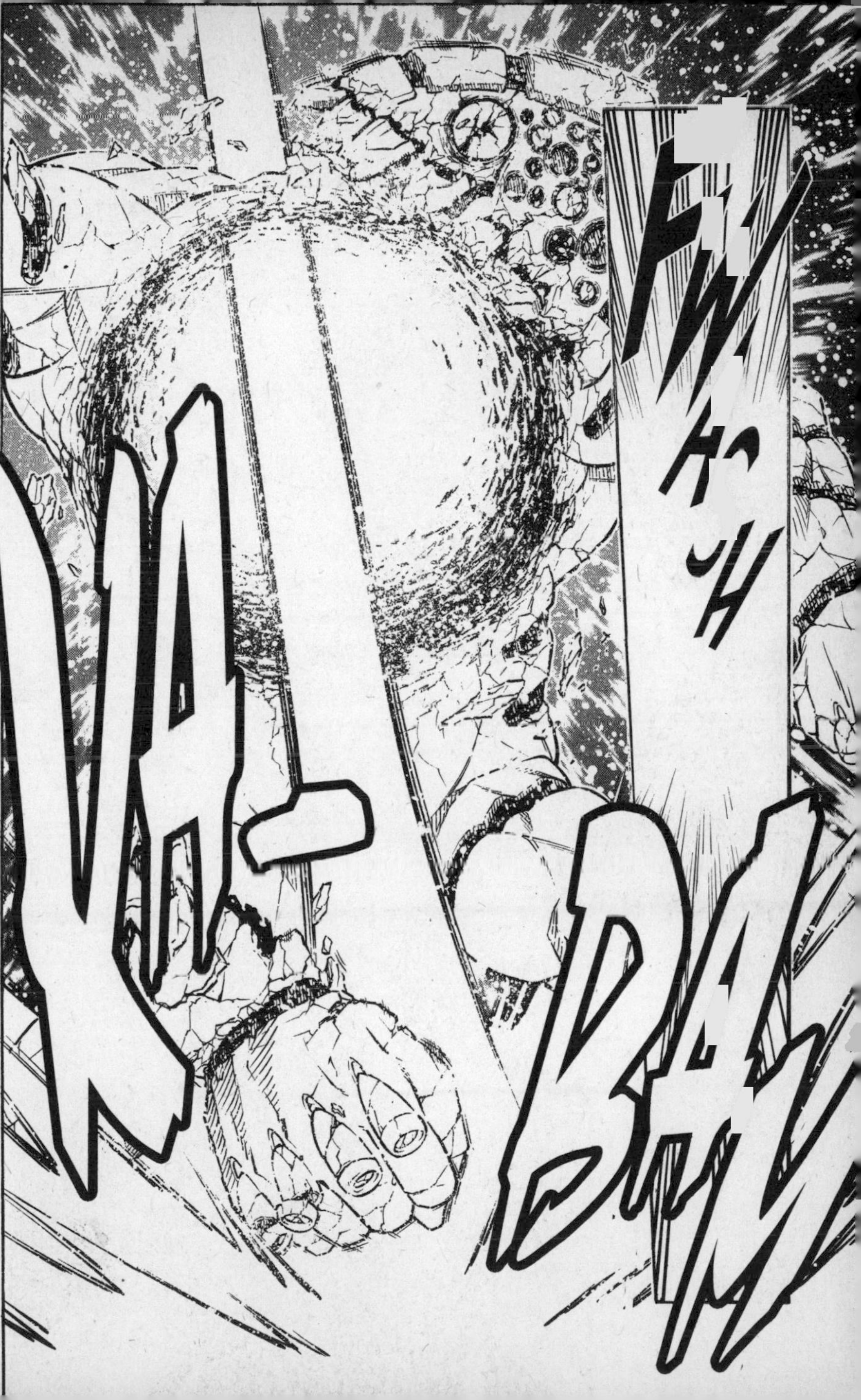

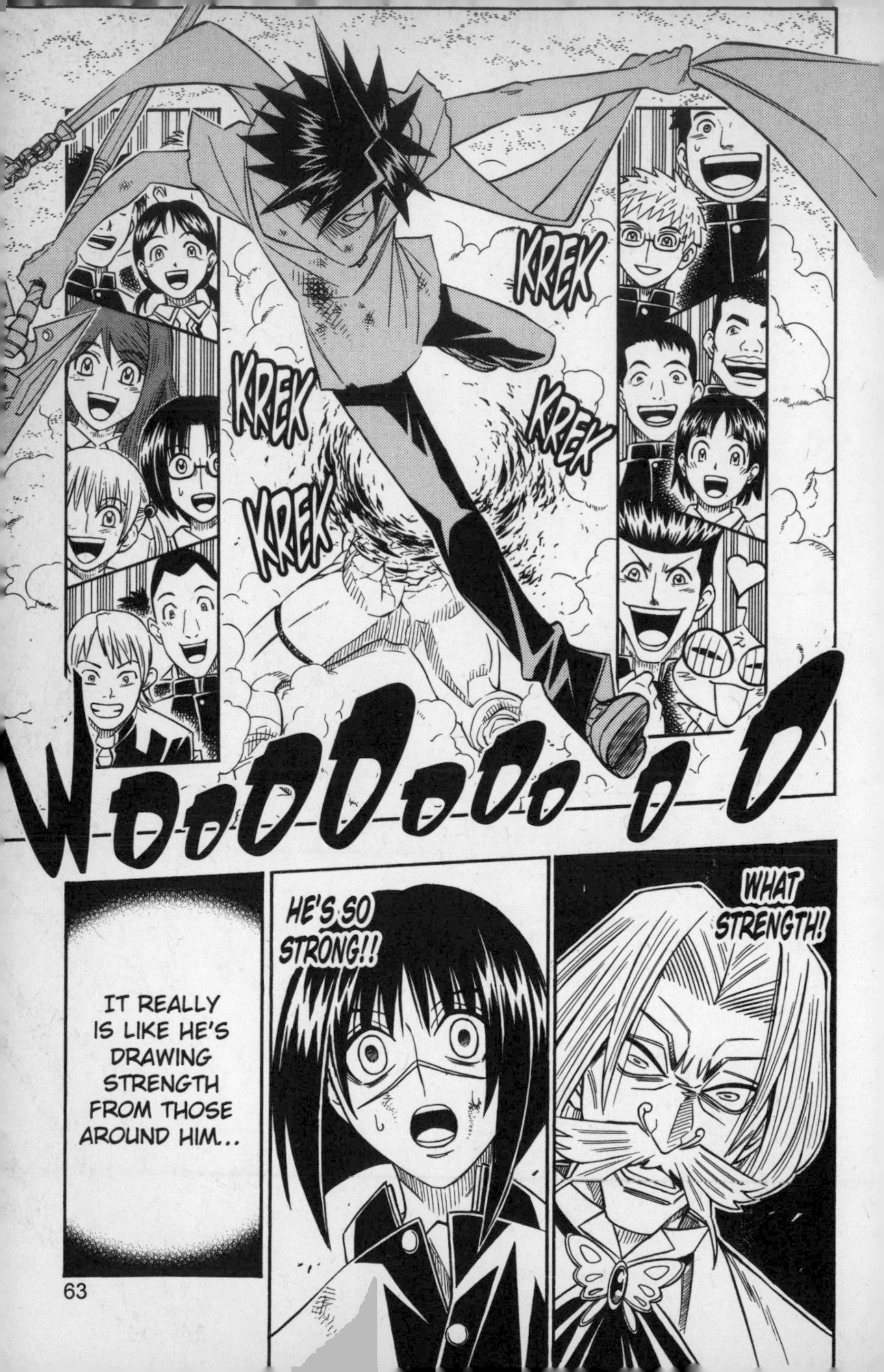
KREK
KREK
KREK
KREK
WOOOOOOOO O O
WHAT STRENGTH!
HE'S SO STRONG!!
IT REALLY IS LIKE HE'S DRAWING STRENGTH FROM THOSE AROUND HIM...

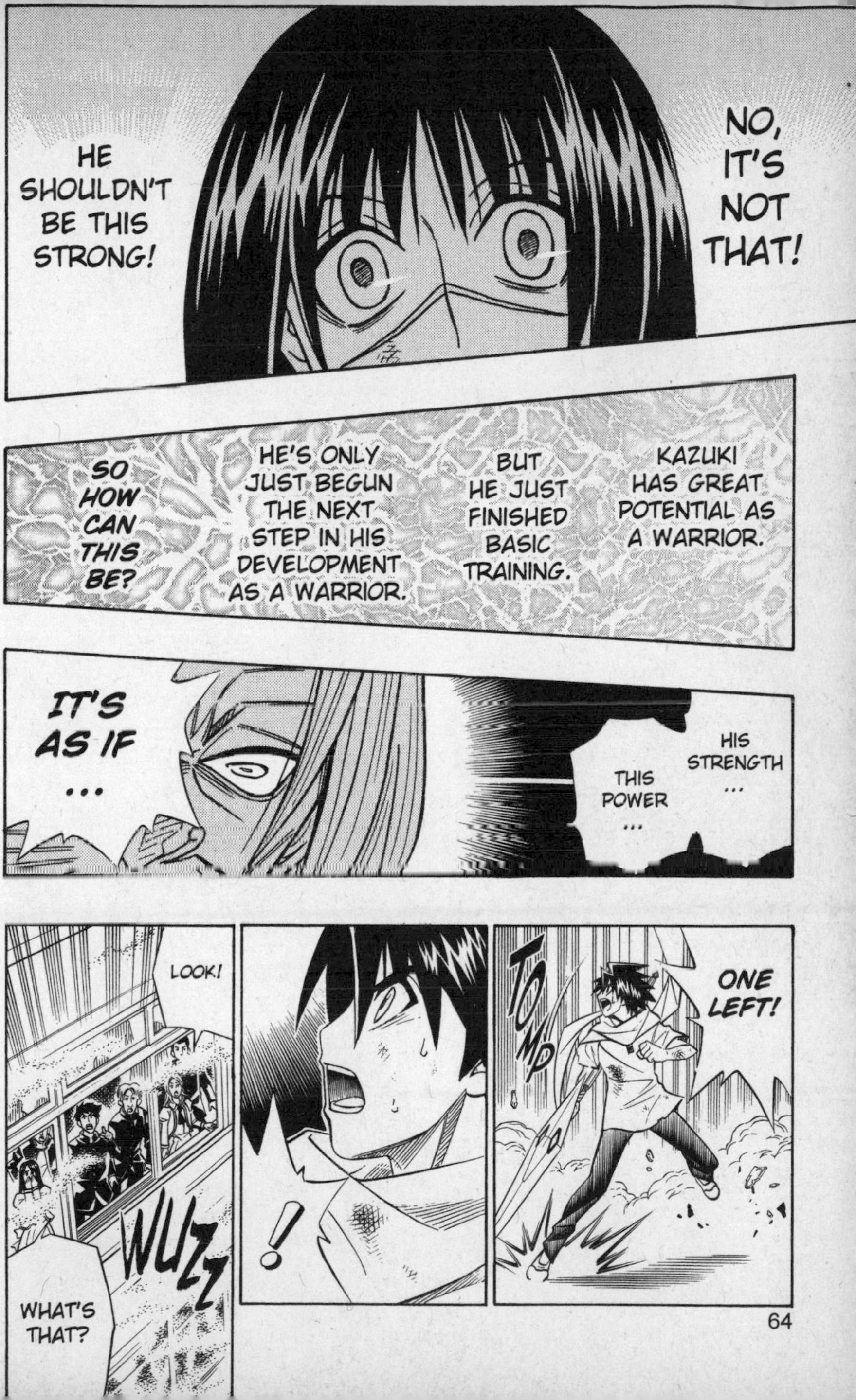
NO, IT'S NOT THAT!
HE SHOULDN'T BE THIS STRONG!
KAZUKI HAS GREAT POTENTIAL AS A WARRIOR.
BUT HE JUST FINISHED BASIC TRAINING.
HE'S ONLY JUST BEGUN THE NEXT STEP IN HIS DEVELOPMENT AS A WARRIOR.
SO HOW CAN THIS BE?
HIS STRENGTH...
THIS POWER...
IT'S AS IF...
TOMP
ONE LEFT!
!
LOOK!
WUZZ
WHAT'S THAT?

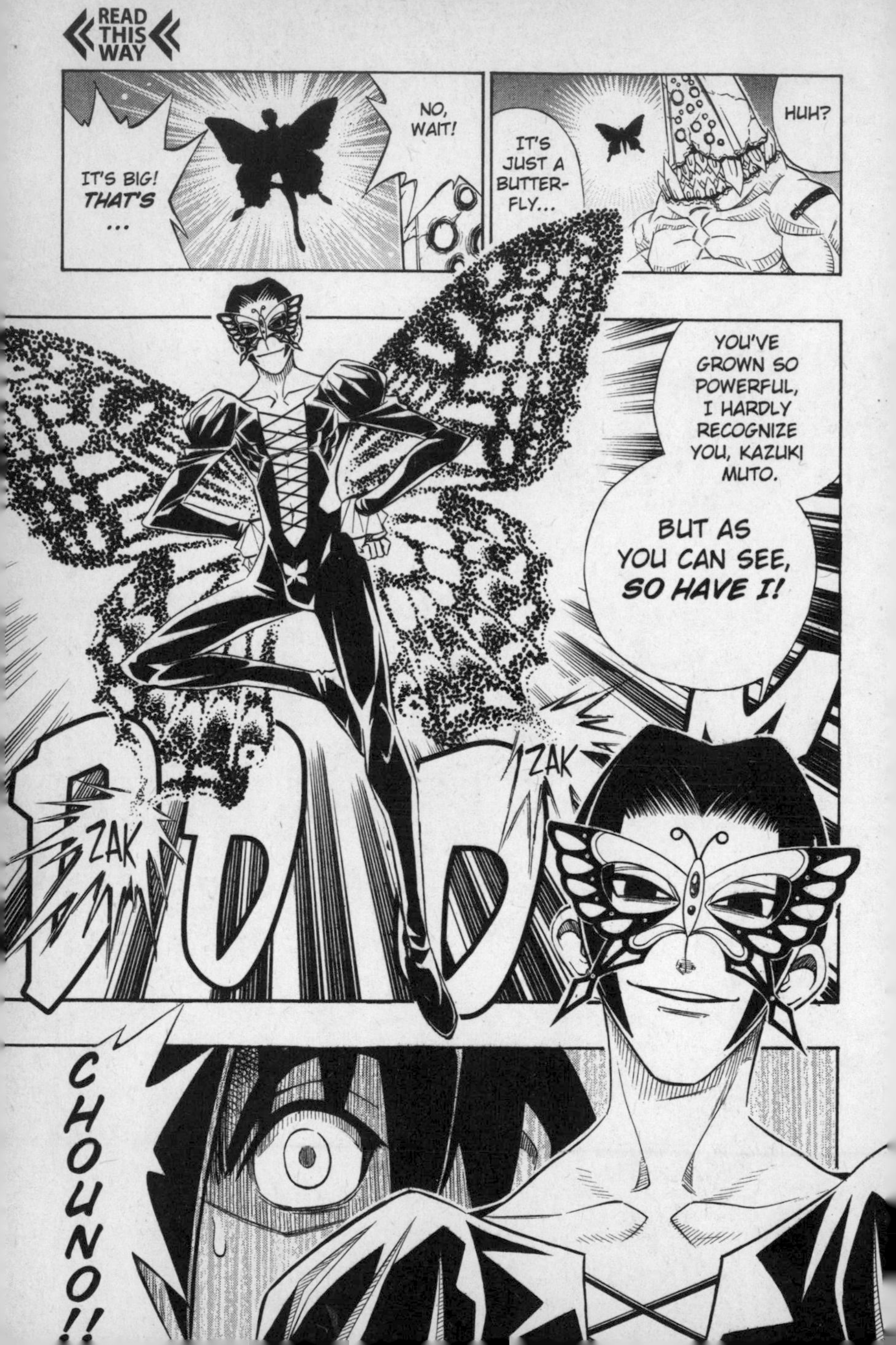

READ THIS WAY
HUH?
IT'S JUST A BUTTER-FLY...
NO, WAIT!
IT'S BIG! THAT'S ...
YOU'VE GROWN SO POWERFUL, I HARDLY RECOGNIZE YOU, KAZUKI MUTO.
BUT AS YOU CAN SEE, SO HAVE I!
ZAK
ZAK
CHOUNO!!

- Height: 174cm, Weight: 66kg
- Measurements: 83-57-85
- Born: November 9; Scorpio; Blood Type: AB; Age: 17
- Likes: Pencils
- Dislikes: Mechanical pencils
- Hobby: Reading (books about crime only)
- Special Ability: Debate
- Affiliations: Ginsei Academy Year 3 Classroom D L.X.E. (Familiar)

Author's Notes

- The name Shinyo comes from a WWII Japanese suicide weapon. Originally he was supposed to be a dangerous young murderer with a Buso Renkin, but story restraints wouldn't allow that.
- He ended up being a pretty pathetic character, but I think he served his function well. He will not appear again.

No. 22 SHINYO SUZUKI

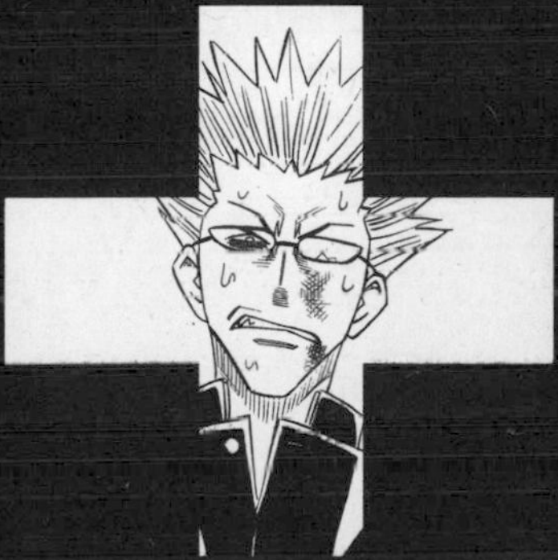

Character Files

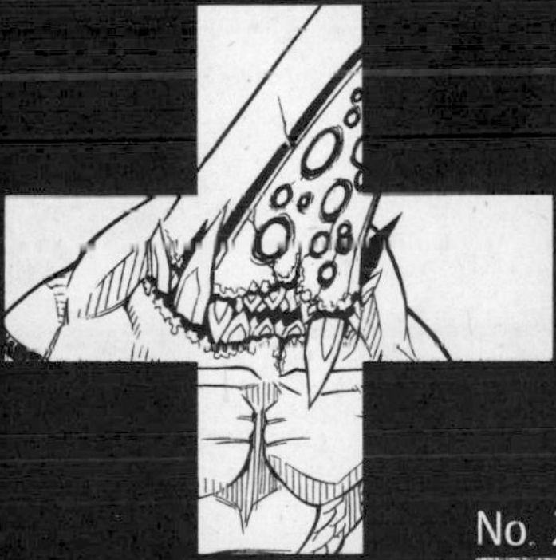

No. 23 REVISED HOMUNCULUS

- He's one of Dr. Butterfly's specially designed Homunculus, an amalgamation of animals and plants.
- Good fighters, but not very smart; puppets to Butterfly's will.
- Able to merge into a single, giant Homunculus by feeding on each other.

Author's Notes

- I needed an army of monsters for this story and this was what I came up with.
- The design concept combines the conical hats of the KKK with the physiques of bodybuilders.
- I found myself regretting making the giant Homunculus here.

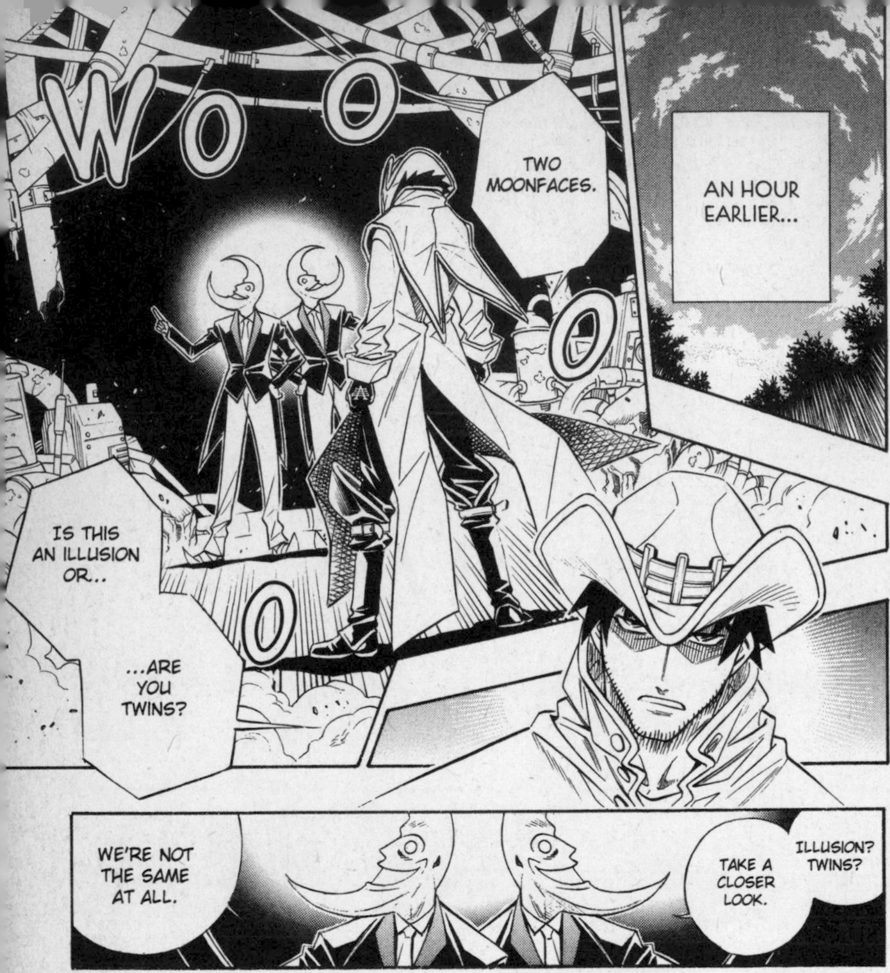
AN HOUR EARLIER...
WOO
TWO MOONFACES.
IS THIS AN ILLUSION OR..
...ARE YOU TWINS?
ILLUSION? TWINS?
TAKE A CLOSER LOOK.
WE'RE NOT THE SAME AT ALL.

CHAPTER 40: A SIGN OF DEATH

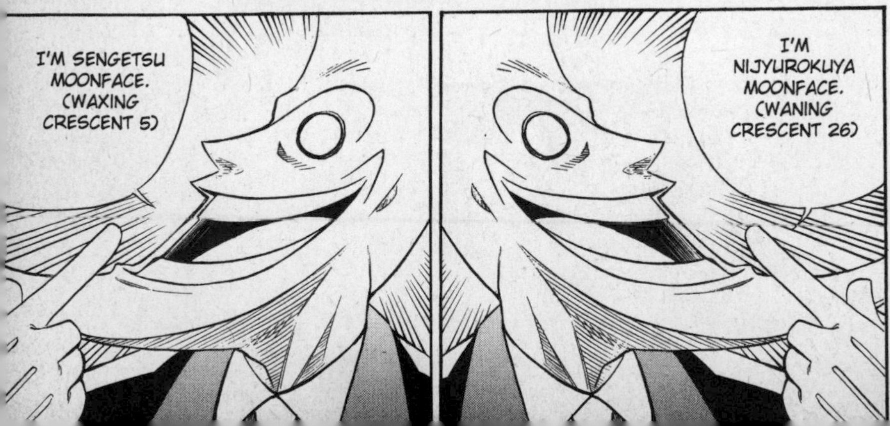
I'M NIJYUROKUYA MOONFACE. (WANING CRESCENT 26)
I'M SENGETSU MOONFACE. (WAXING CRESCENT 5)

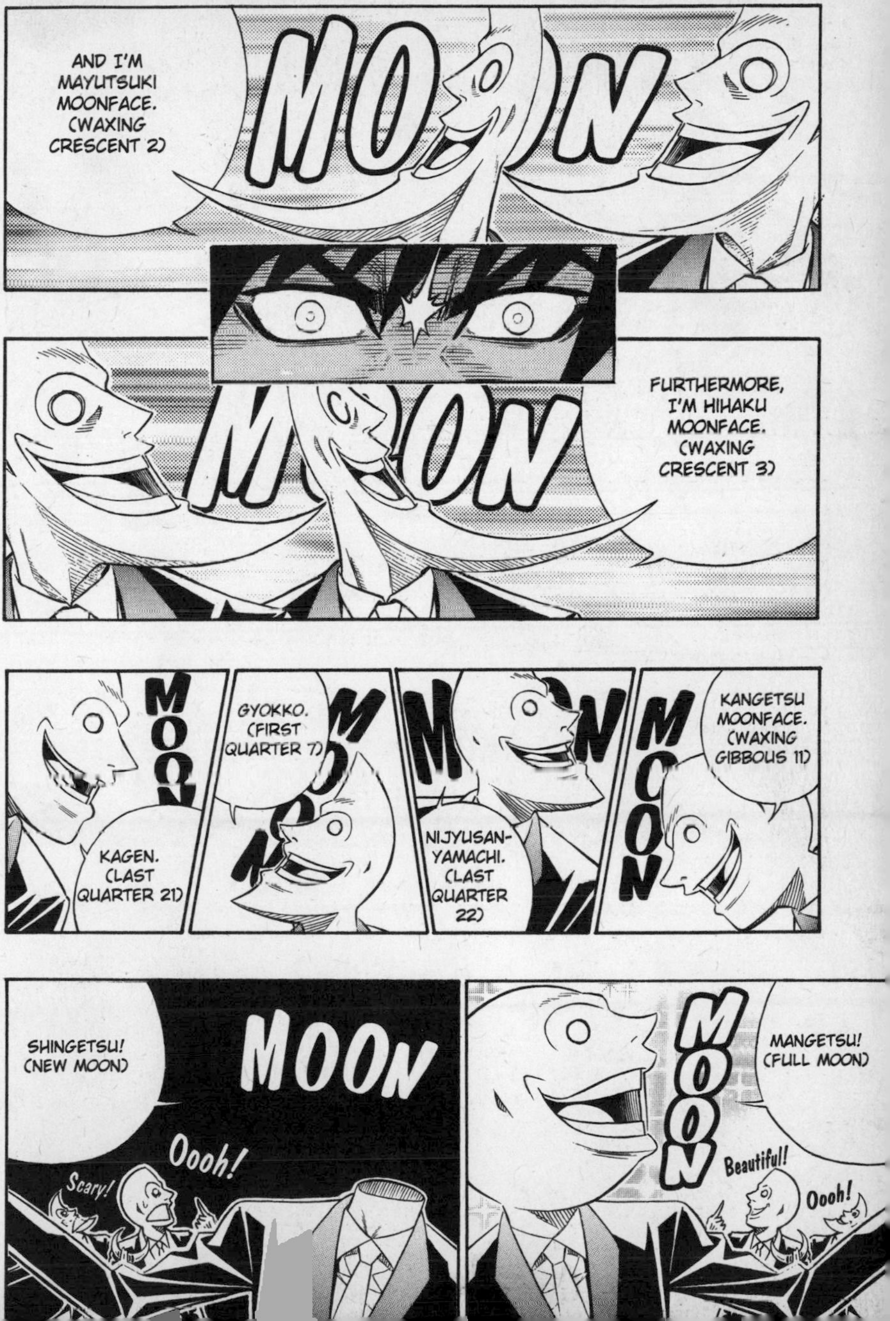
MOON
AND I'M MAYUTSUKI MOONFACE. (WAXING CRESCENT 2)
FURTHERMORE, I'M HIHAKU MOONFACE. (WAXING CRESCENT 3)
MOON
KANGETSU MOONFACE. (WAXING GIBBOUS 11)
MOON
NIJYUSAN-YAMACHI. (LAST QUARTER 22)
MOON
GYOKKO. (FIRST QUARTER 7)
MOON
MOON
KAGEN. (LAST QUARTER 21)
MANGETSU! (FULL MOON)
MOON
Beautiful!
Oooh!
SHINGETSU! (NEW MOON)
MOON
Oooh!
Scary!

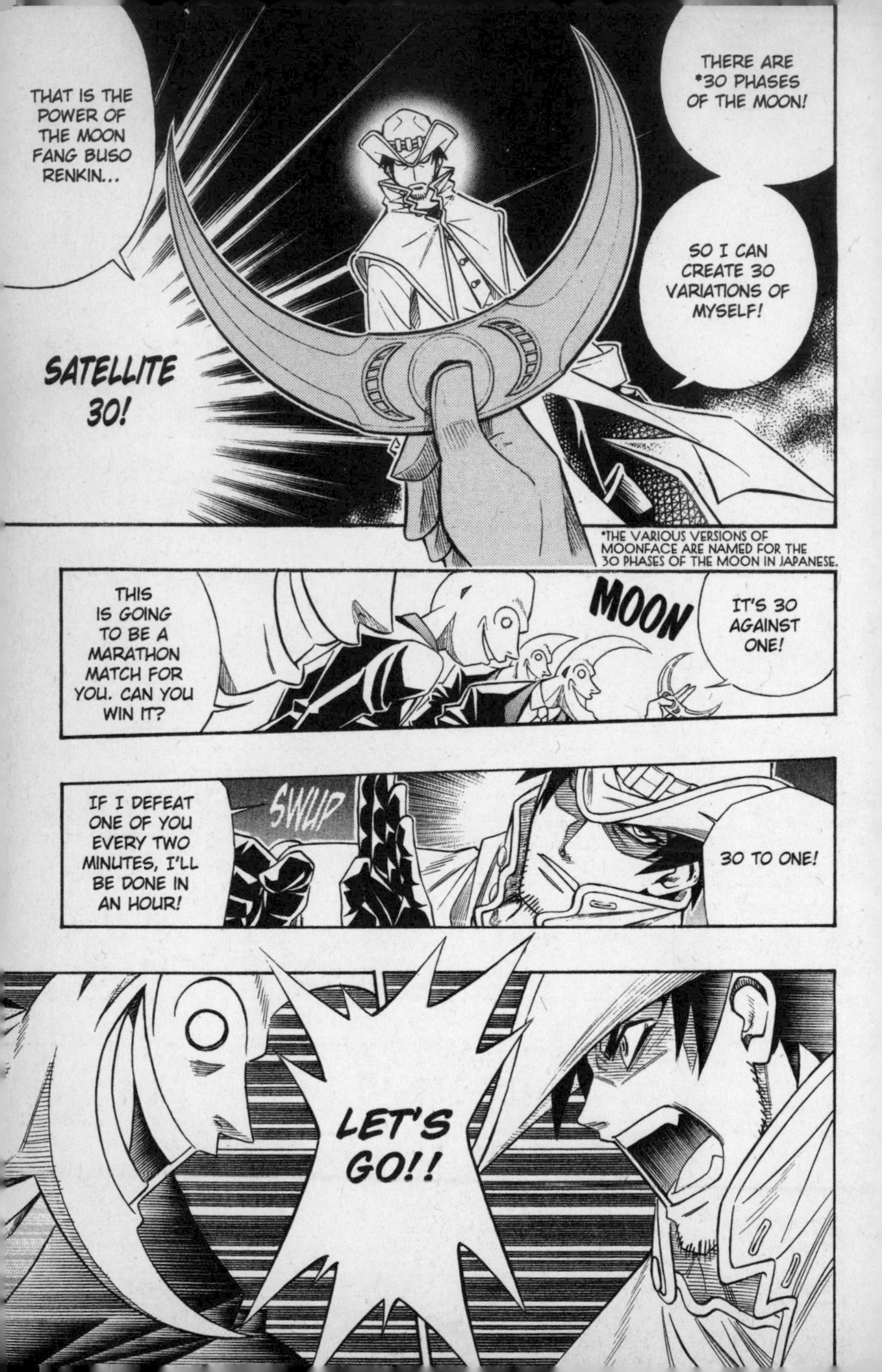
THERE ARE *30 PHASES OF THE MOON!
SO I CAN CREATE 30 VARIATIONS OF MYSELF!
THAT IS THE POWER OF THE MOON FANG BUSO RENKIN...
SATELLITE 30!
*THE VARIOUS VERSIONS OF MOONFACE ARE NAMED FOR THE 30 PHASES OF THE MOON IN JAPANESE.
IT'S 30 AGAINST ONE!
MOON
THIS IS GOING TO BE A MARATHON MATCH FOR YOU. CAN YOU WIN IT?
30 TO ONE!
SWUP
IF I DEFEAT ONE OF YOU EVERY TWO MINUTES, I'LL BE DONE IN AN HOUR!
LET'S GO!!

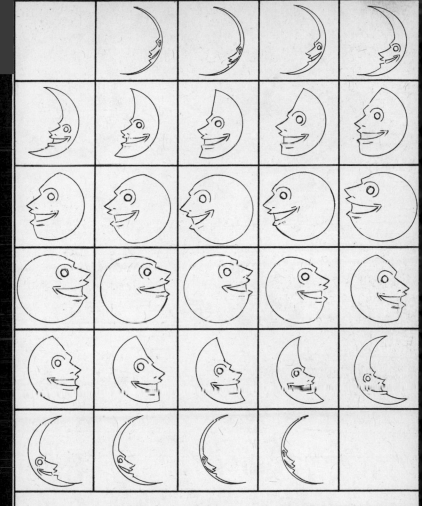

CHAPTER 40:
A SIGN OF DEATH

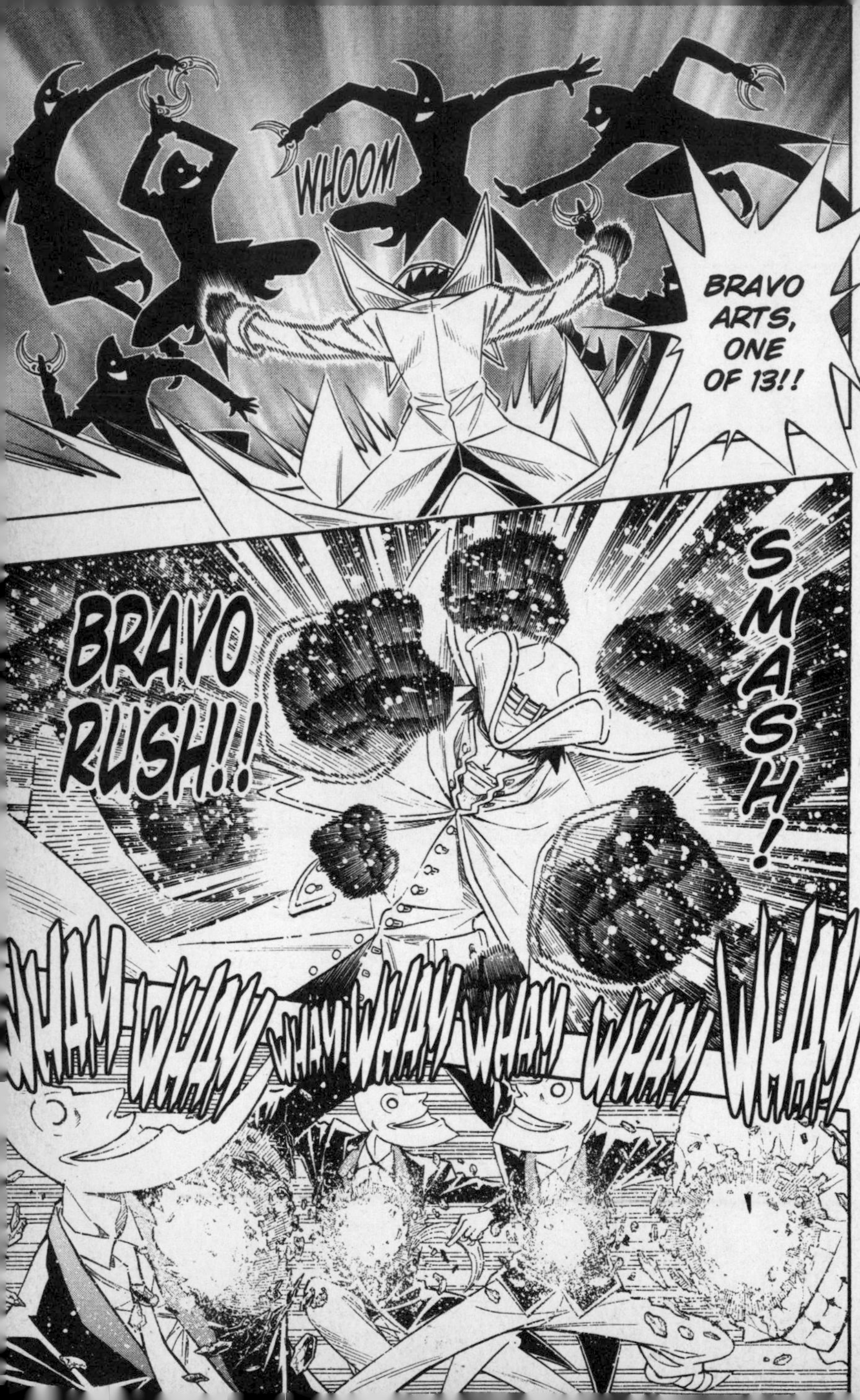
BRAVO ARTS, ONE OF 13!!
WHOOM
SMASH!
BRAVO RUSH!!
WHAM WHAM WHAM WHAM WHAM WHAM WHAM

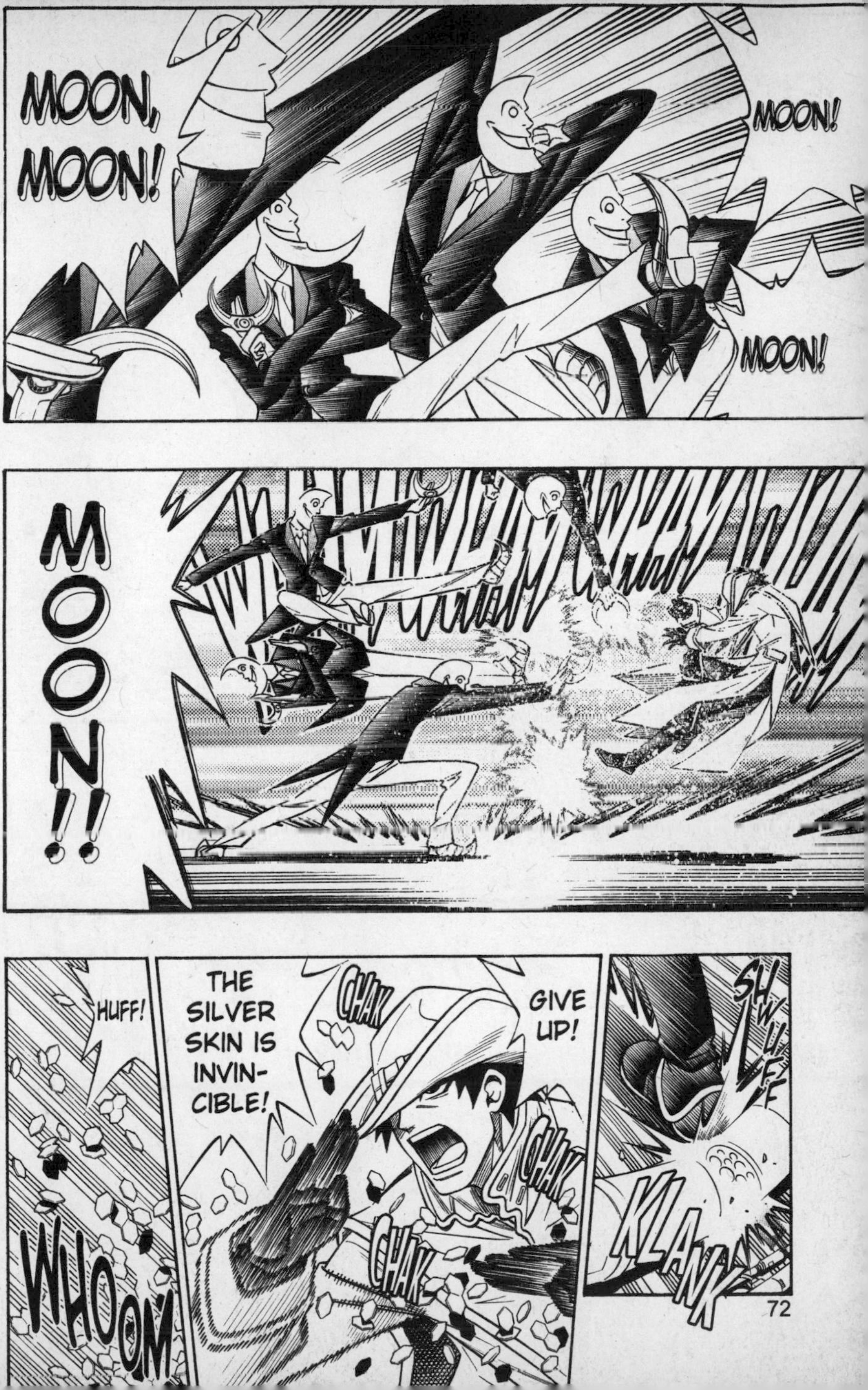
MOON!
MOON, MOON!
MOON!
MOON!!
SHWUFF
KLANK
GIVE UP!
CHAK
THE SILVER SKIN IS INVINCIBLE!
CHAK
CHAK
HUFF!
WHOOM

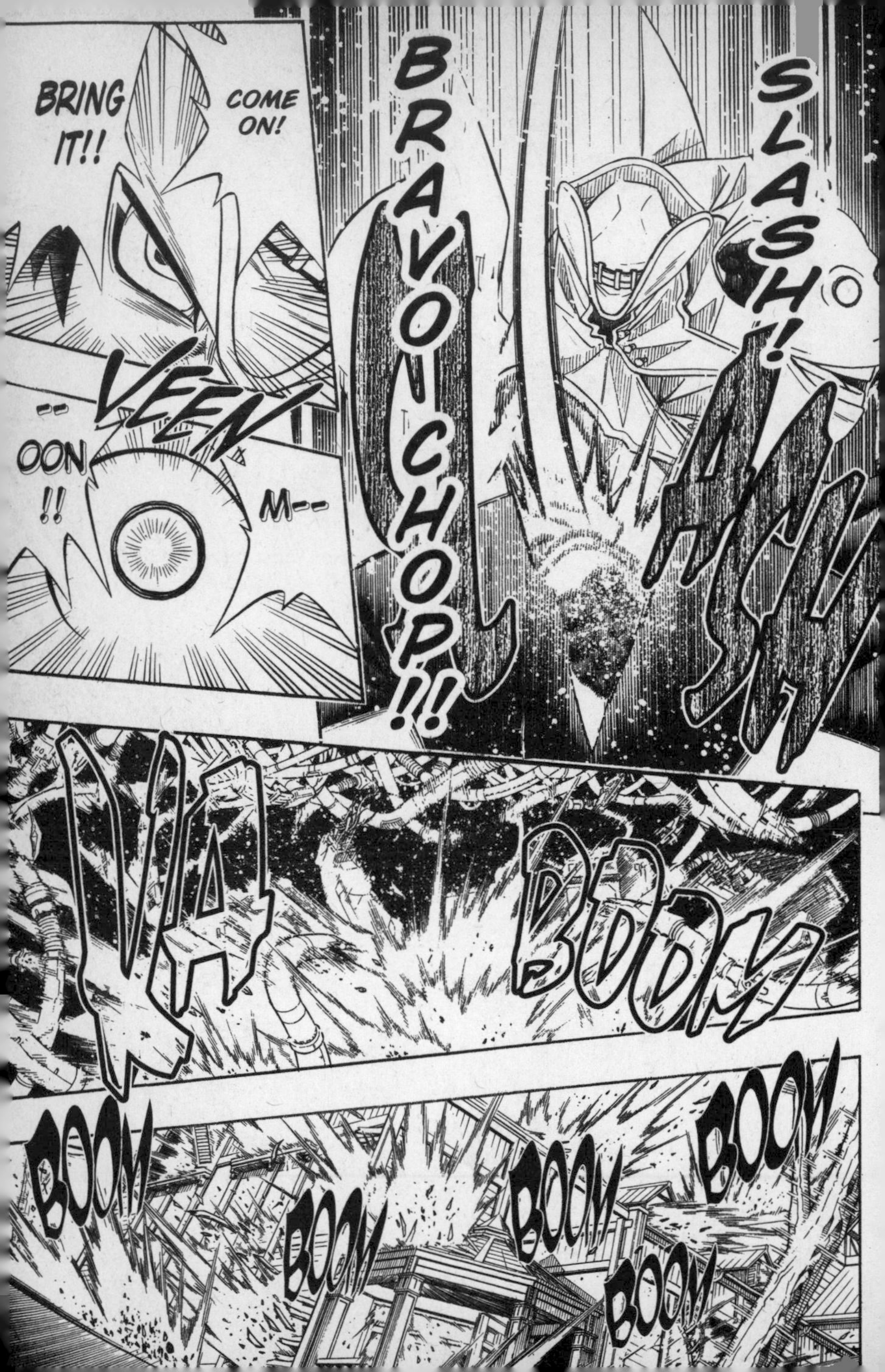
SLASH!
BRAVO CHOP!!
COME ON!
BRING IT!!
VEEN
M--
--OON!!
BOOM
VA
BOOM
BOOM
BOOM
BOOM
BOOM

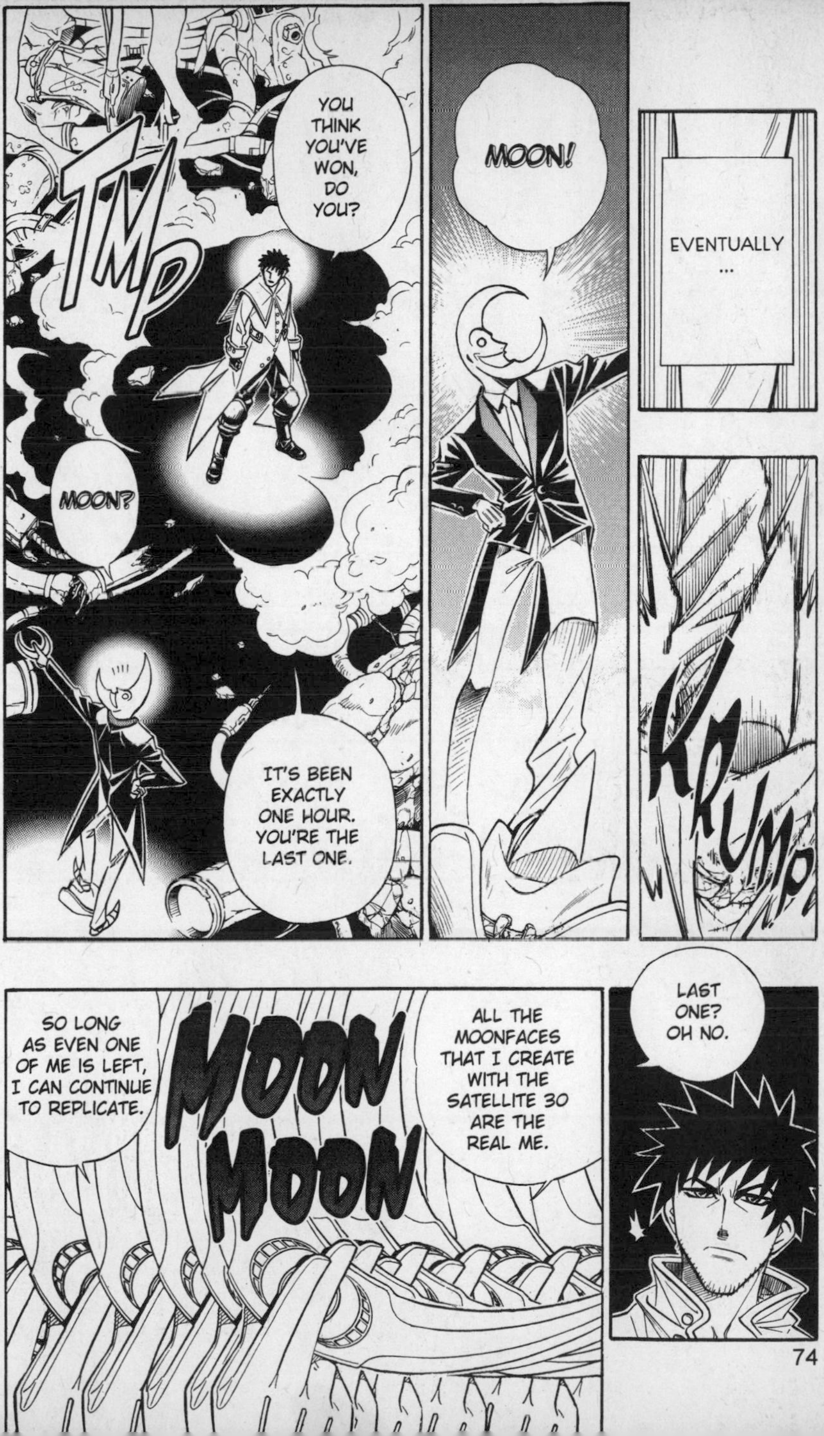

EVENTUALLY ...
KRUMP
MOON!
YOU THINK YOU'VE WON, DO YOU?
TMP
MOON?
IT'S BEEN EXACTLY ONE HOUR. YOU'RE THE LAST ONE.
LAST ONE? OH NO.
ALL THE MOONFACES THAT I CREATE WITH THE SATELLITE 30 ARE THE REAL ME.
MOON MOON
SO LONG AS EVEN ONE OF ME IS LEFT, I CAN CONTINUE TO REPLICATE.

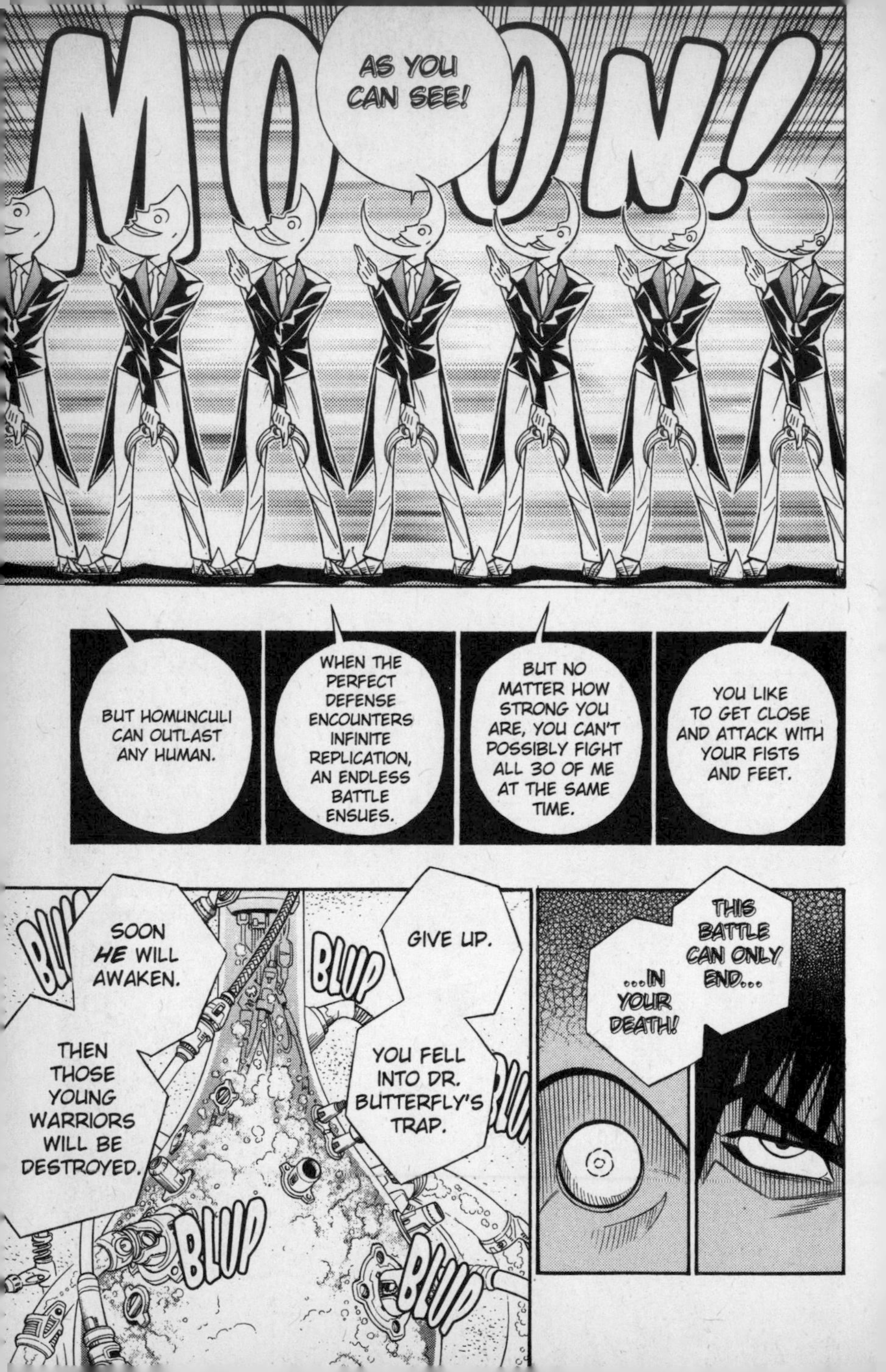
MOOON!
AS YOU CAN SEE!
YOU LIKE TO GET CLOSE AND ATTACK WITH YOUR FISTS AND FEET.
BUT NO MATTER HOW STRONG YOU ARE, YOU CAN'T POSSIBLY FIGHT ALL 30 OF ME AT THE SAME TIME.
WHEN THE PERFECT DEFENSE ENCOUNTERS INFINITE REPLICATION, AN ENDLESS BATTLE ENSUES.
BUT HOMUNCULI CAN OUTLAST ANY HUMAN.
THIS BATTLE CAN ONLY END...
...IN YOUR DEATH!
BLUP
GIVE UP.
YOU FELL INTO DR. BUTTERFLY'S TRAP.
SOON *HE* WILL AWAKEN.
THEN THOSE YOUNG WARRIORS WILL BE DESTROYED.
BLUP
BLUP

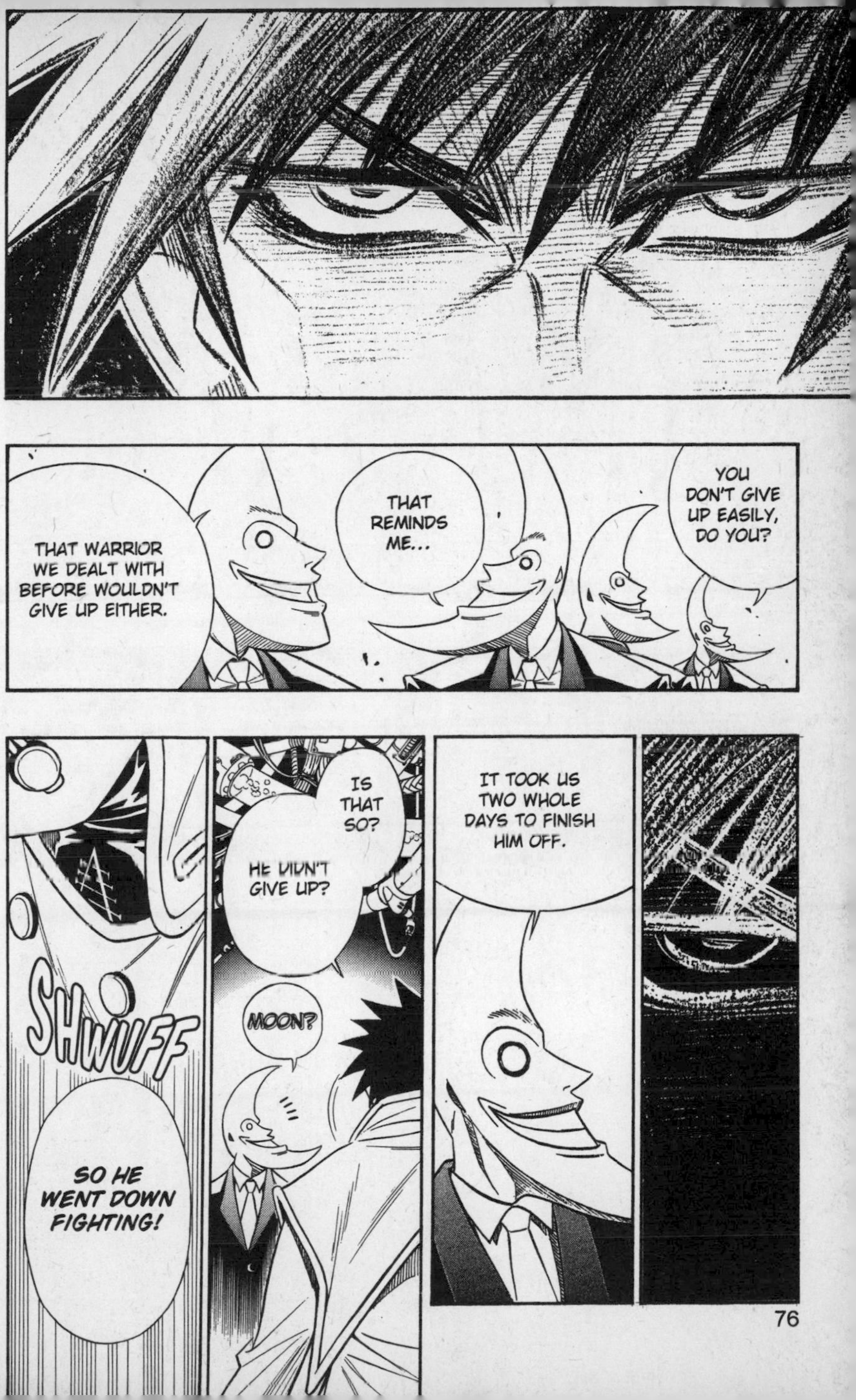
YOU DON'T GIVE UP EASILY, DO YOU?
THAT REMINDS ME...
THAT WARRIOR WE DEALT WITH BEFORE WOULDN'T GIVE UP EITHER.
IT TOOK US TWO WHOLE DAYS TO FINISH HIM OFF.
IS THAT SO?
HE DIDN'T GIVE UP?
MOON?
SHWUFF
SO HE WENT DOWN FIGHTING!

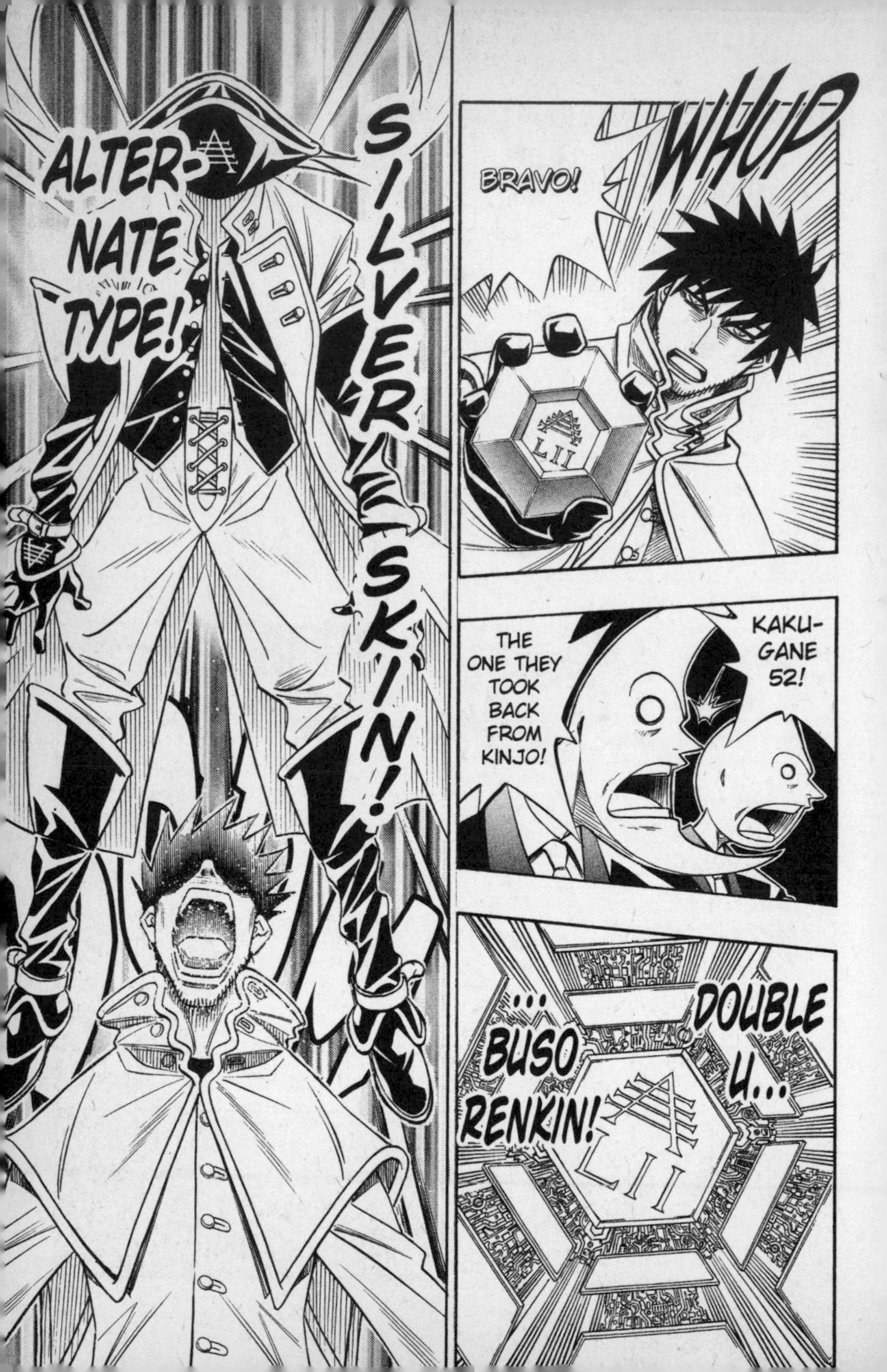
WHUP
BRAVO!
KAKU-GANE 52!
THE ONE THEY TOOK BACK FROM KINJO!
DOUBLE U...
...BUSO RENKIN!
SILVER SKIN!
ALTER-NATE TYPE!

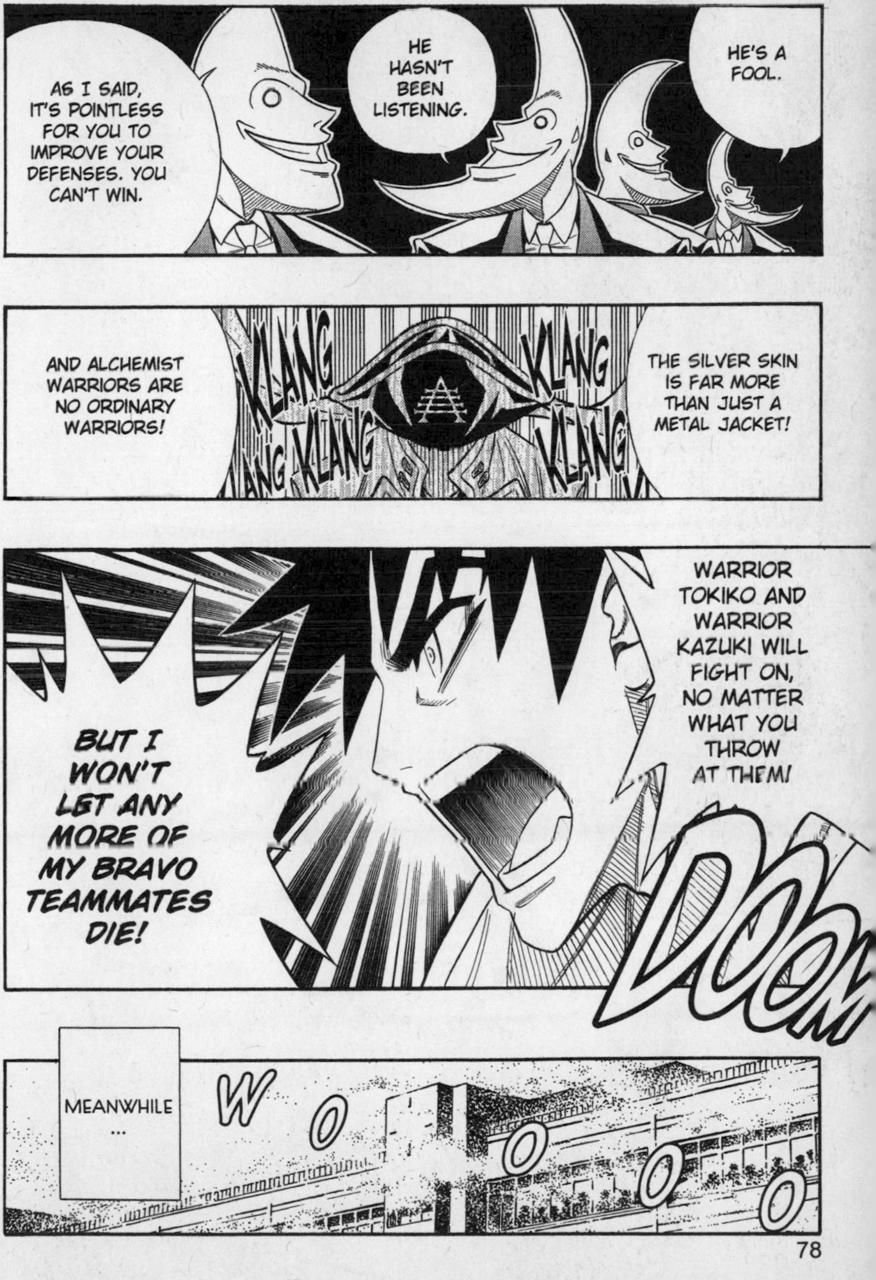
HE'S A FOOL.
HE HASN'T BEEN LISTENING.
AS I SAID, IT'S POINTLESS FOR YOU TO IMPROVE YOUR DEFENSES. YOU CAN'T WIN.
THE SILVER SKIN IS FAR MORE THAN JUST A METAL JACKET!
KLANG KLANG KLANG KLANG KLANG KLANG
AND ALCHEMIST WARRIORS ARE NO ORDINARY WARRIORS!
WARRIOR TOKIKO AND WARRIOR KAZUKI WILL FIGHT ON, NO MATTER WHAT YOU THROW AT THEM!
BUT I WON'T LET ANY MORE OF MY BRAVO TEAMMATES DIE!
DOOM
MEANWHILE ...
WOOOOO

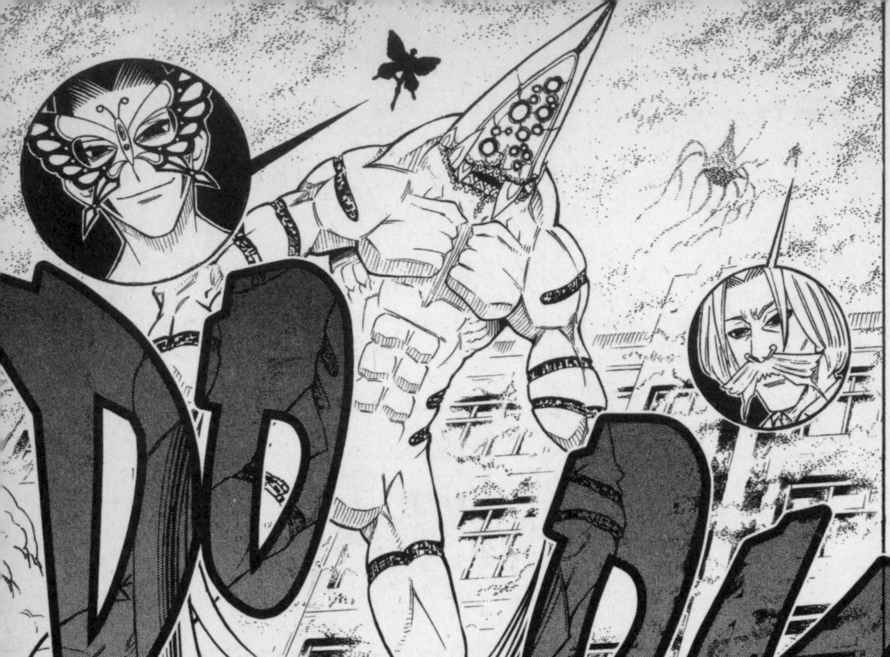
DODON
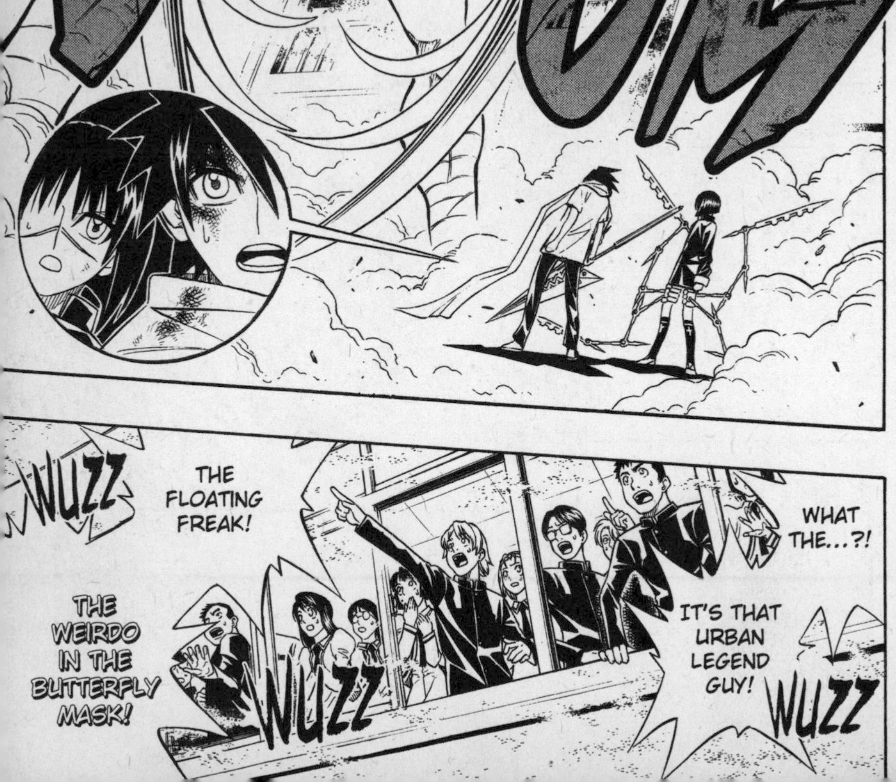
WHAT THE...?!
IT'S THAT URBAN LEGEND GUY!
WUZZ
THE FLOATING FREAK!
WUZZ
THE WEIRDO IN THE BUTTERFLY MASK!
WUZZ

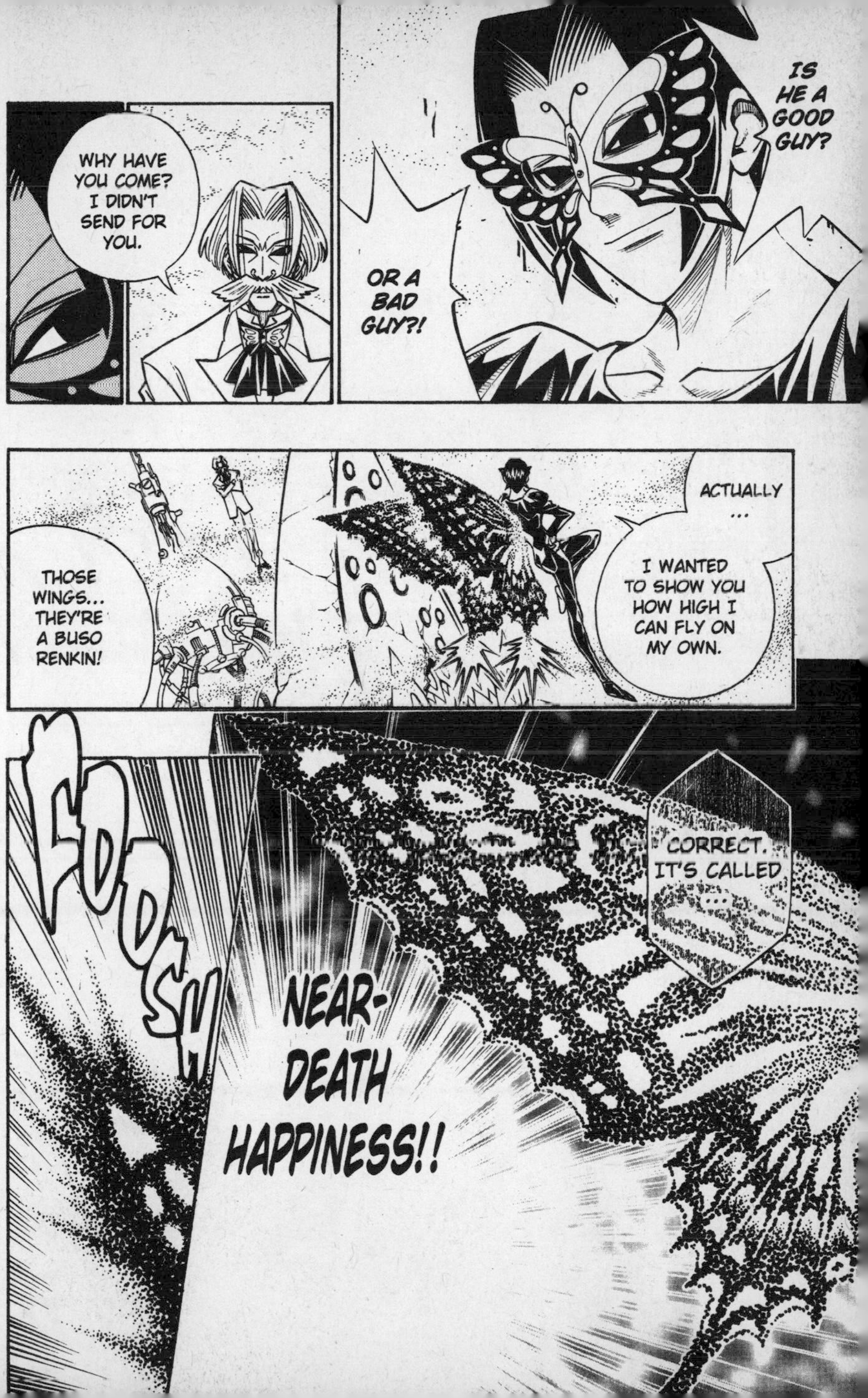
IS HE A GOOD GUY?
OR A BAD GUY?!
WHY HAVE YOU COME? I DIDN'T SEND FOR YOU.
ACTUALLY ...
I WANTED TO SHOW YOU HOW HIGH I CAN FLY ON MY OWN.
THOSE WINGS... THEY'RE A BUSO RENKIN!
CORRECT. IT'S CALLED ...
NEAR-DEATH HAPPINESS!!
FOOSH

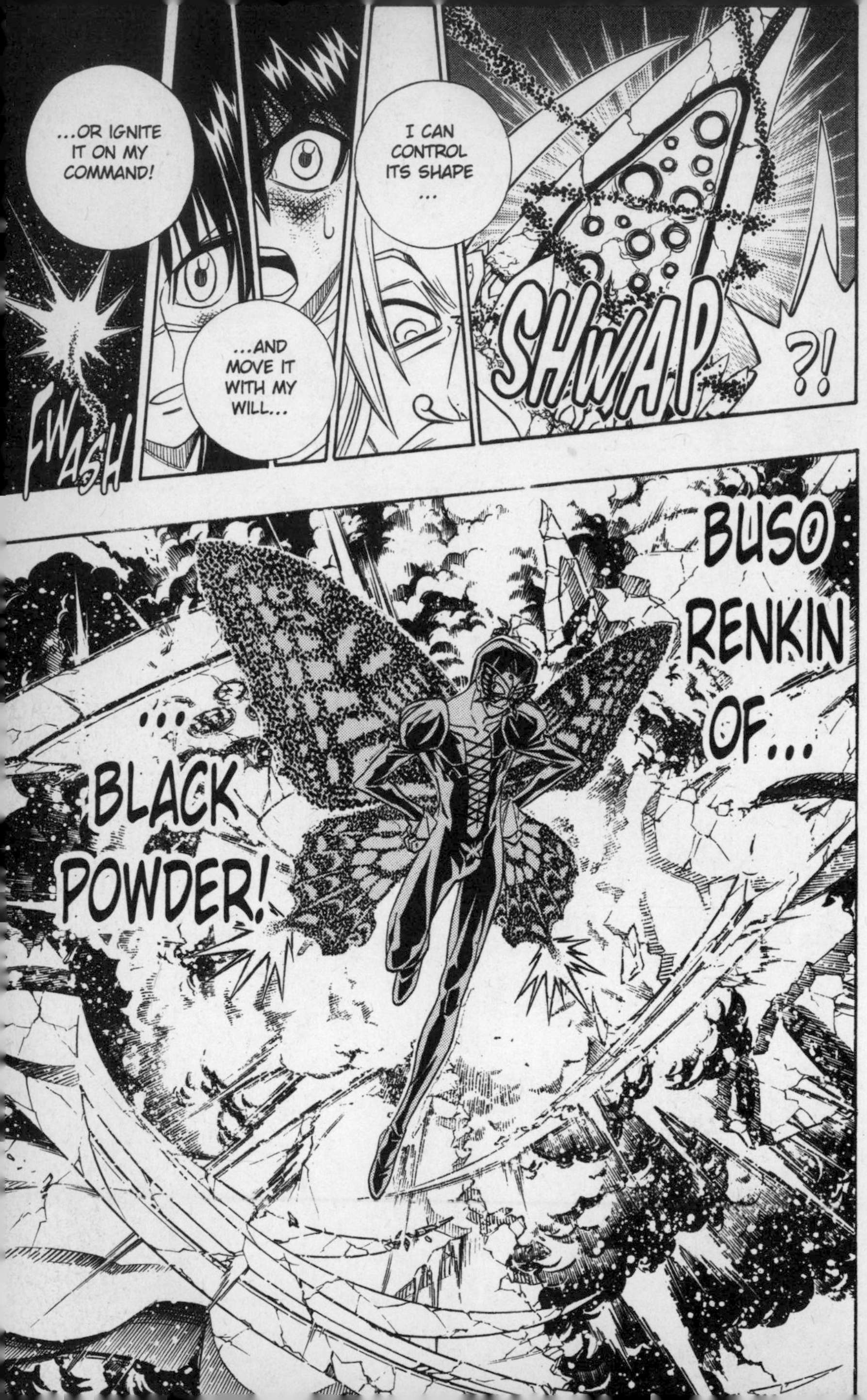
SHWAP
?!
I CAN CONTROL ITS SHAPE ...
...AND MOVE IT WITH MY WILL...
...OR IGNITE IT ON MY COMMAND!
FWASH
BUSO RENKIN OF...
...BLACK POWDER!

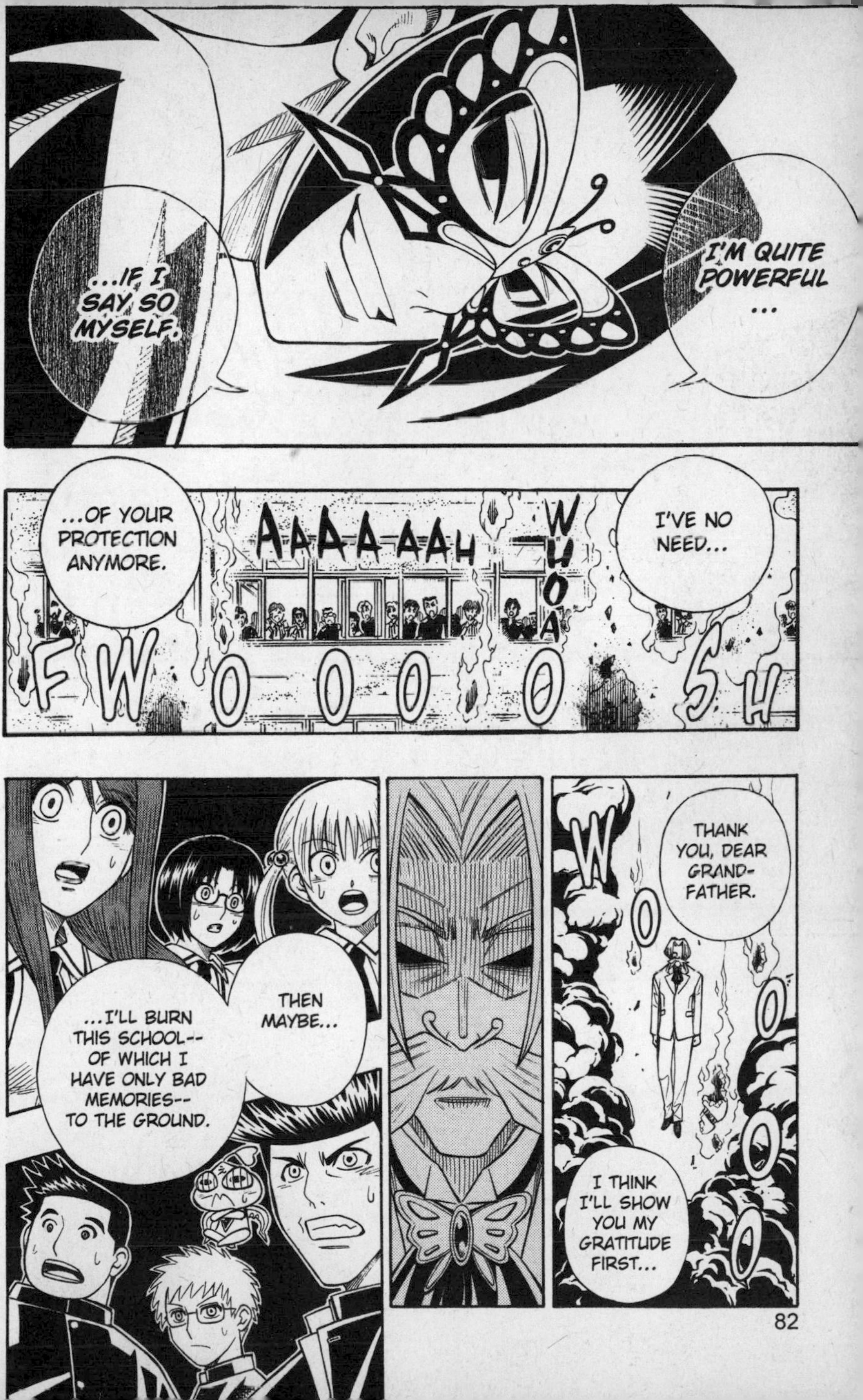
I'M QUITE POWERFUL...
...IF I SAY SO MYSELF.
I'VE NO NEED...
WHOA
AAAAAAH
...OF YOUR PROTECTION ANYMORE.
FWOOOOSH
THANK YOU, DEAR GRAND-FATHER.
WOOOOOO
I THINK I'LL SHOW YOU MY GRATITUDE FIRST...
THEN MAYBE...
...I'LL BURN THIS SCHOOL-- OF WHICH I HAVE ONLY BAD MEMORIES-- TO THE GROUND.

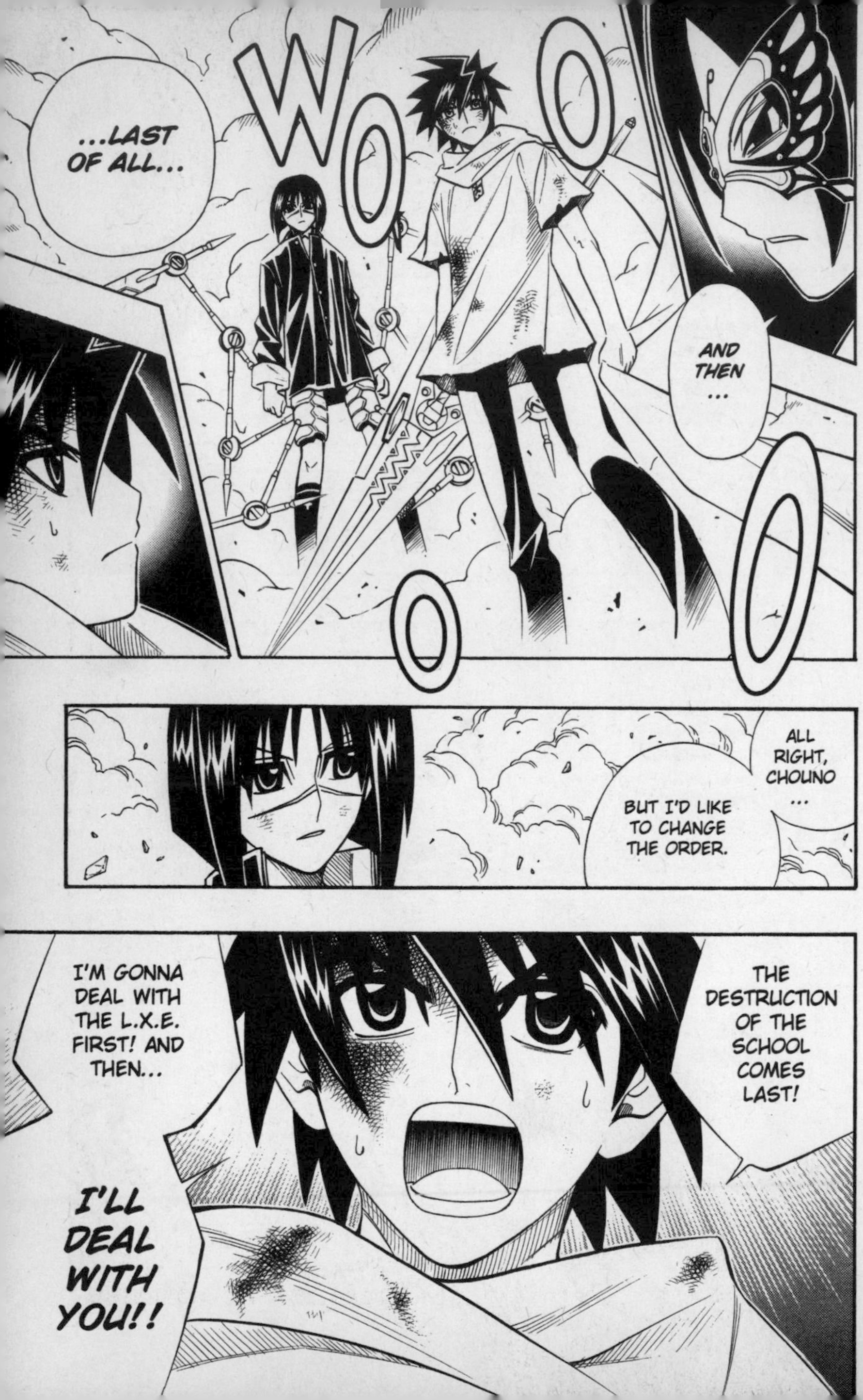
AND THEN ...
...LAST OF ALL...
WOOOOO
ALL RIGHT, CHOUNO ...
BUT I'D LIKE TO CHANGE THE ORDER.
THE DESTRUCTION OF THE SCHOOL COMES LAST!
I'M GONNA DEAL WITH THE L.X.E. FIRST! AND THEN...
I'LL DEAL WITH YOU!!

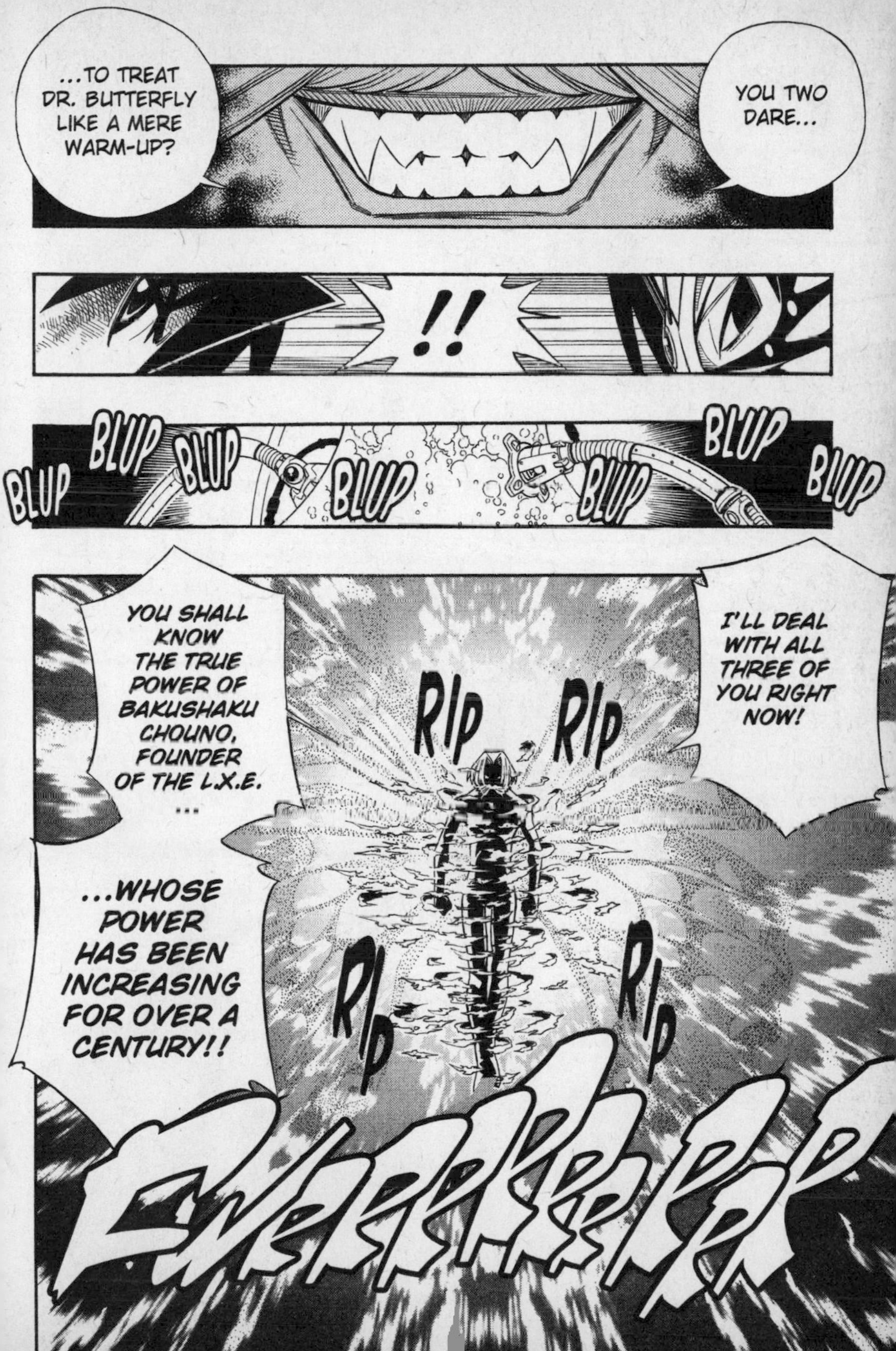
YOU TWO DARE...
...TO TREAT DR. BUTTERFLY LIKE A MERE WARM-UP?
!!
BLUP
BLUP
BLUP
BLUP
BLUP
BLUP
BLUP
I'LL DEAL WITH ALL THREE OF YOU RIGHT NOW!
YOU SHALL KNOW THE TRUE POWER OF BAKUSHAKU CHOUNO, FOUNDER OF THE L.X.E. ...
...WHOSE POWER HAS BEEN INCREASING FOR OVER A CENTURY!!
RIP
RIP
RIP
RIP

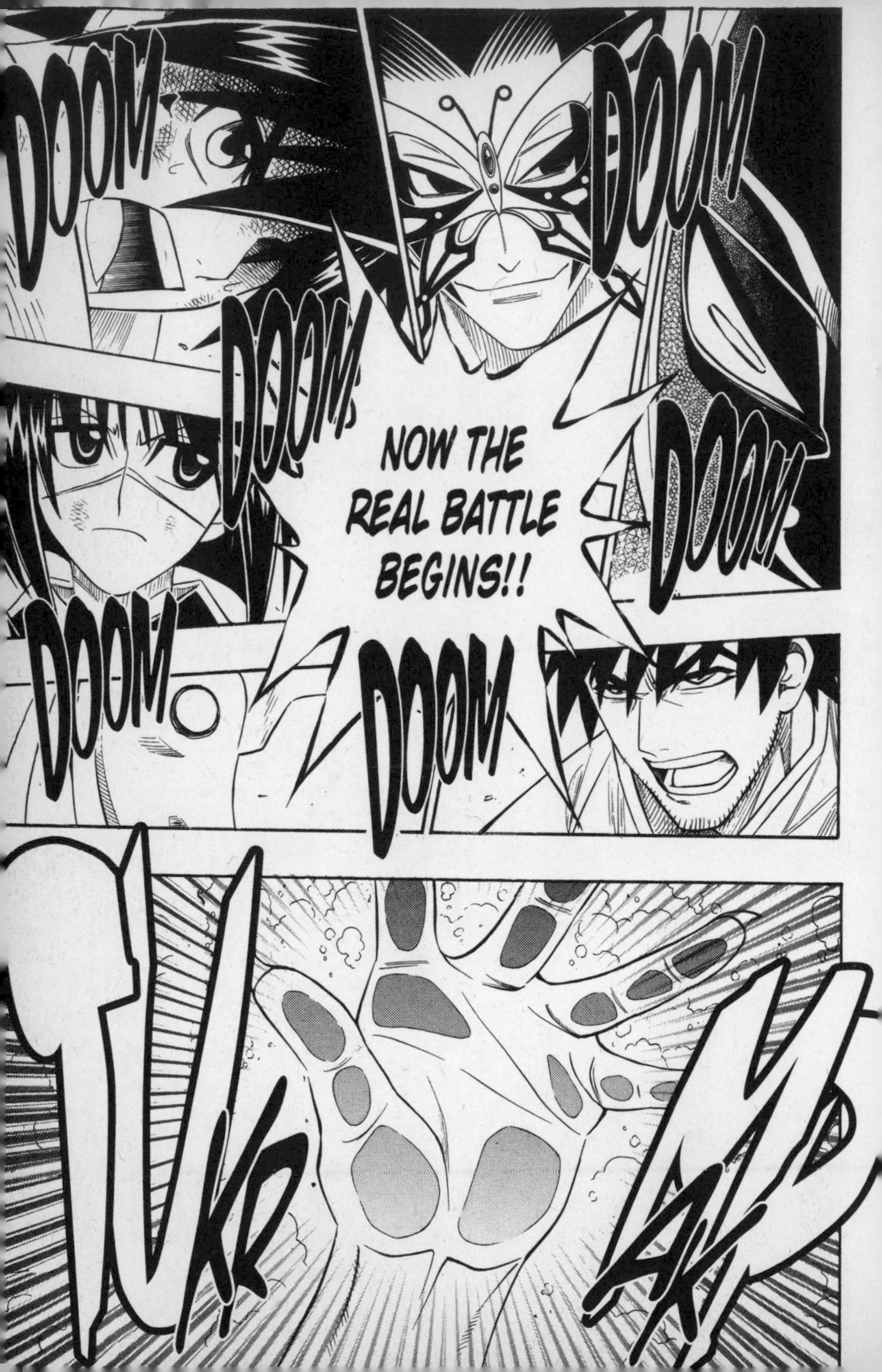
DOOM
DOOM
DOOM
DOOM
NOW THE REAL BATTLE BEGINS!!
DOOM
DOOM

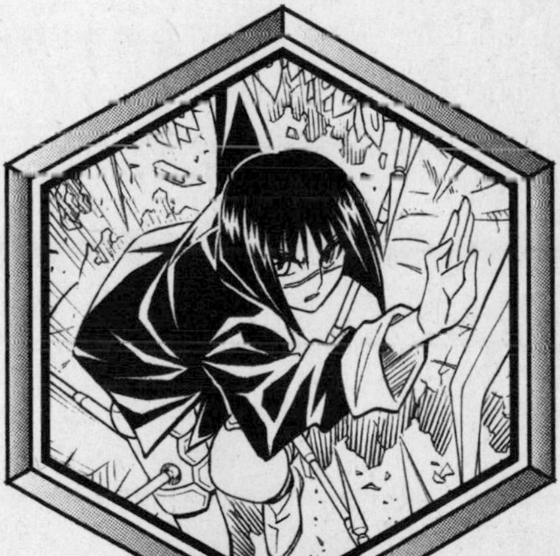

Buso Renkin

ブソウレンキン

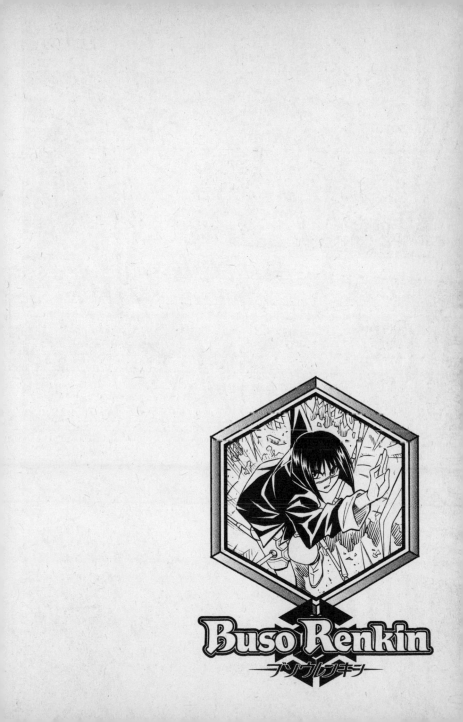

CHAPTER 41: PAPILLON VS. BUTTERFLY, Part I

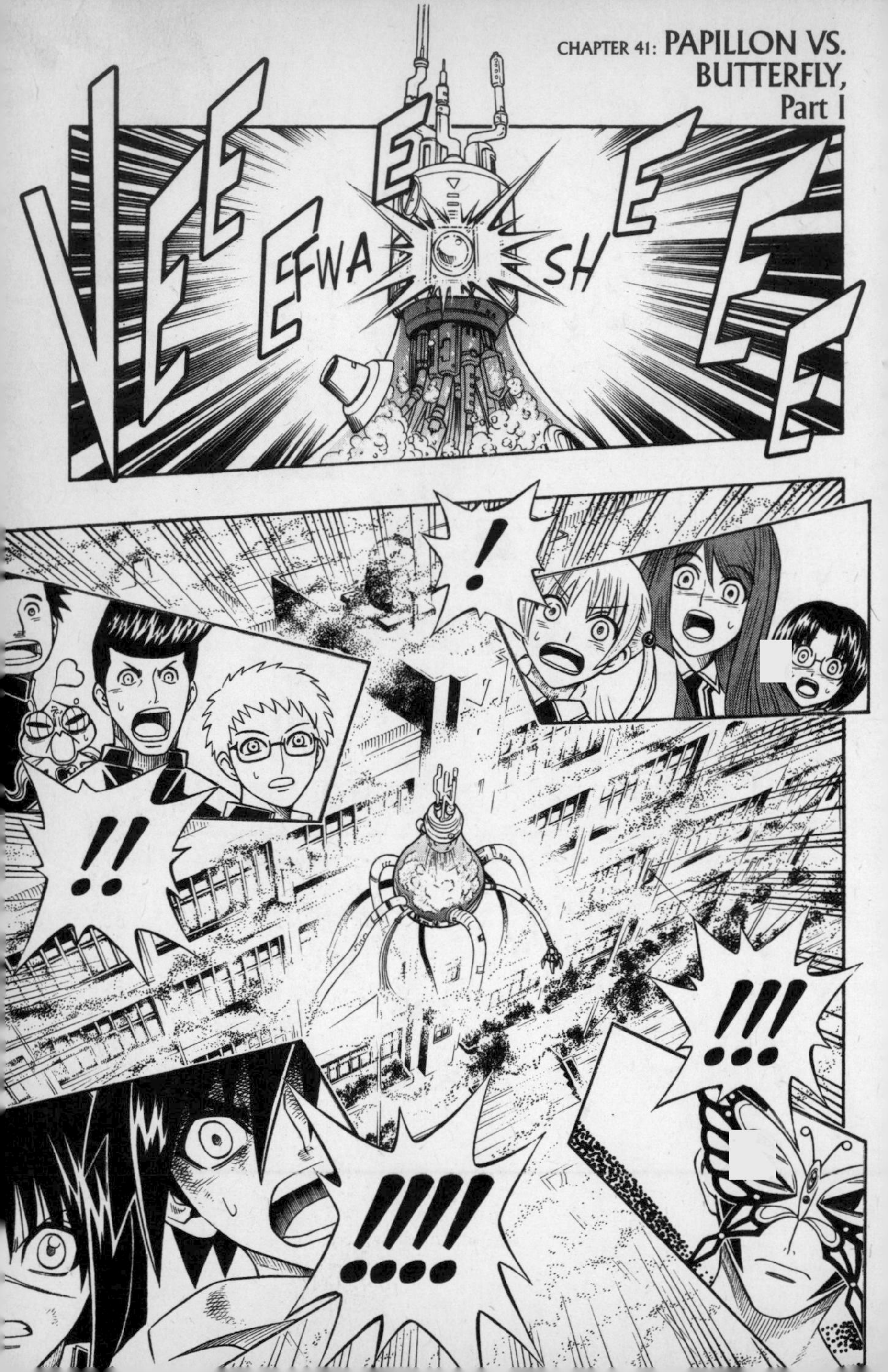
VEEEEFWASHEEEEE
!
!!
!!!
!!!!

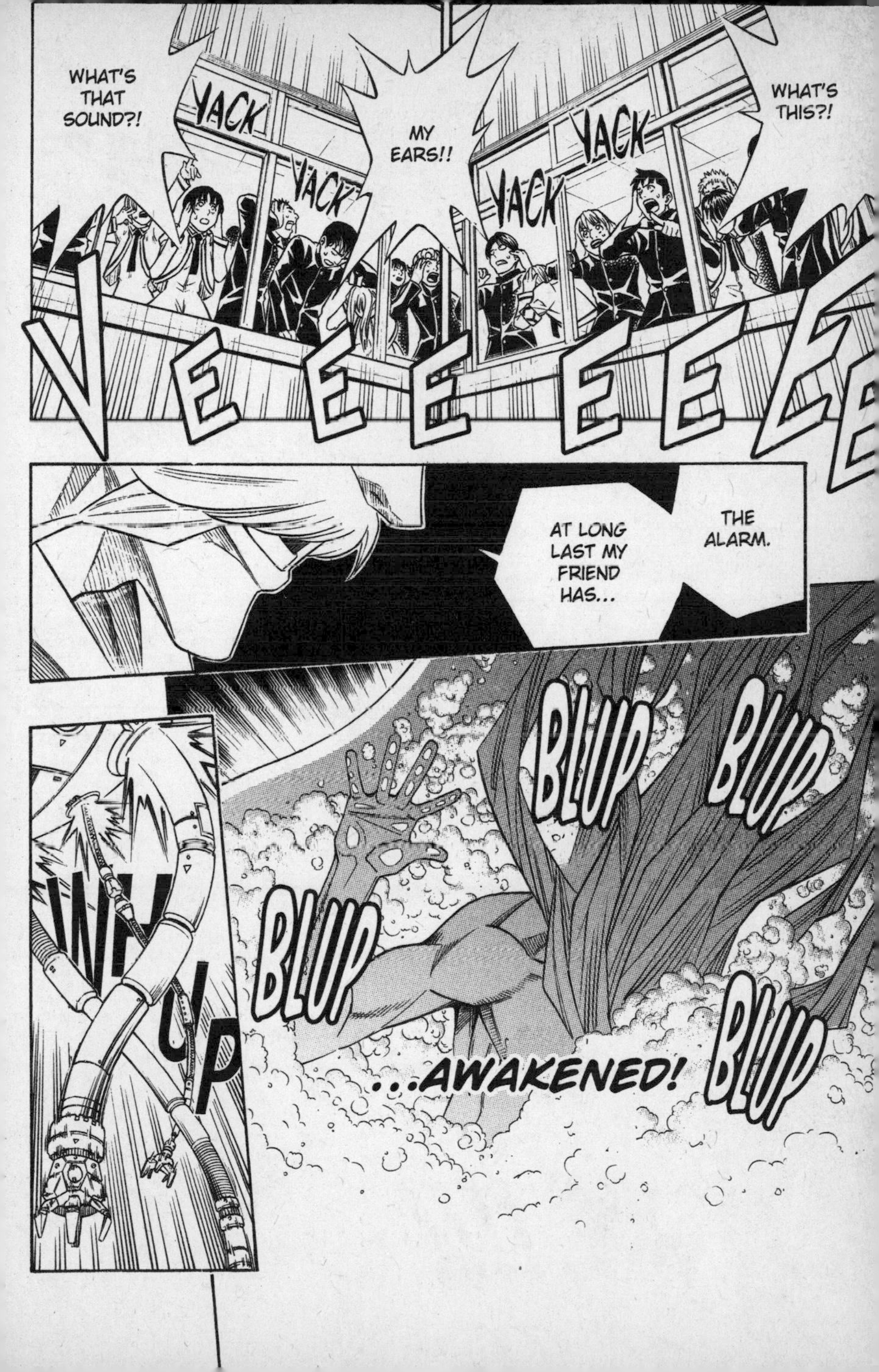
WHAT'S THIS?!
YACK
YACK
MY EARS!!
YACK
YACK
WHAT'S THAT SOUND?!
VEEEEEE
THE ALARM.
AT LONG LAST MY FRIEND HAS...
BLUP
BLUP
BLUP
BLUP
...AWAKENED!

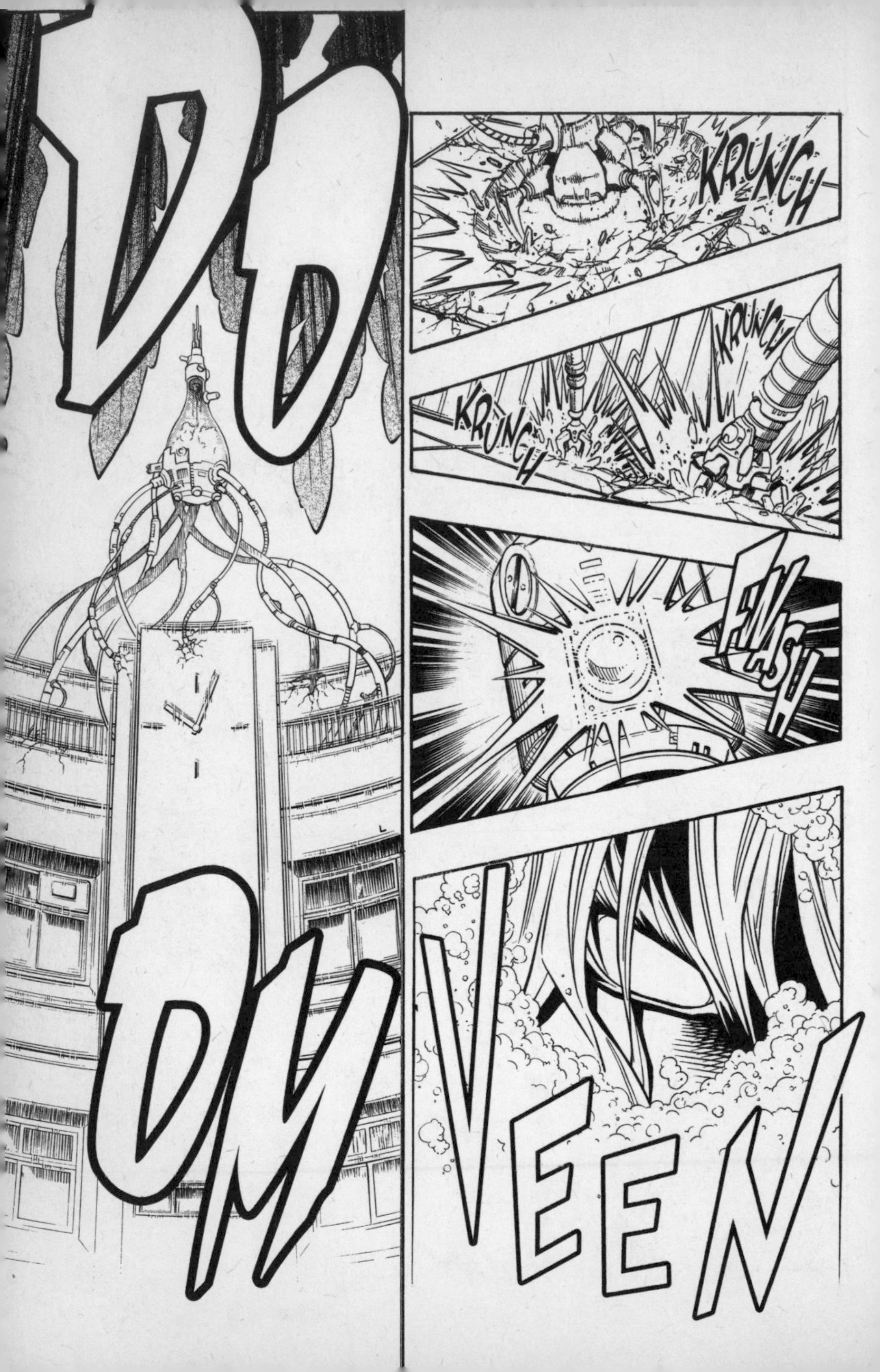
KRUNCH
KRUNCH
KRUNCH
FLASH
VEEN
DO
DOY

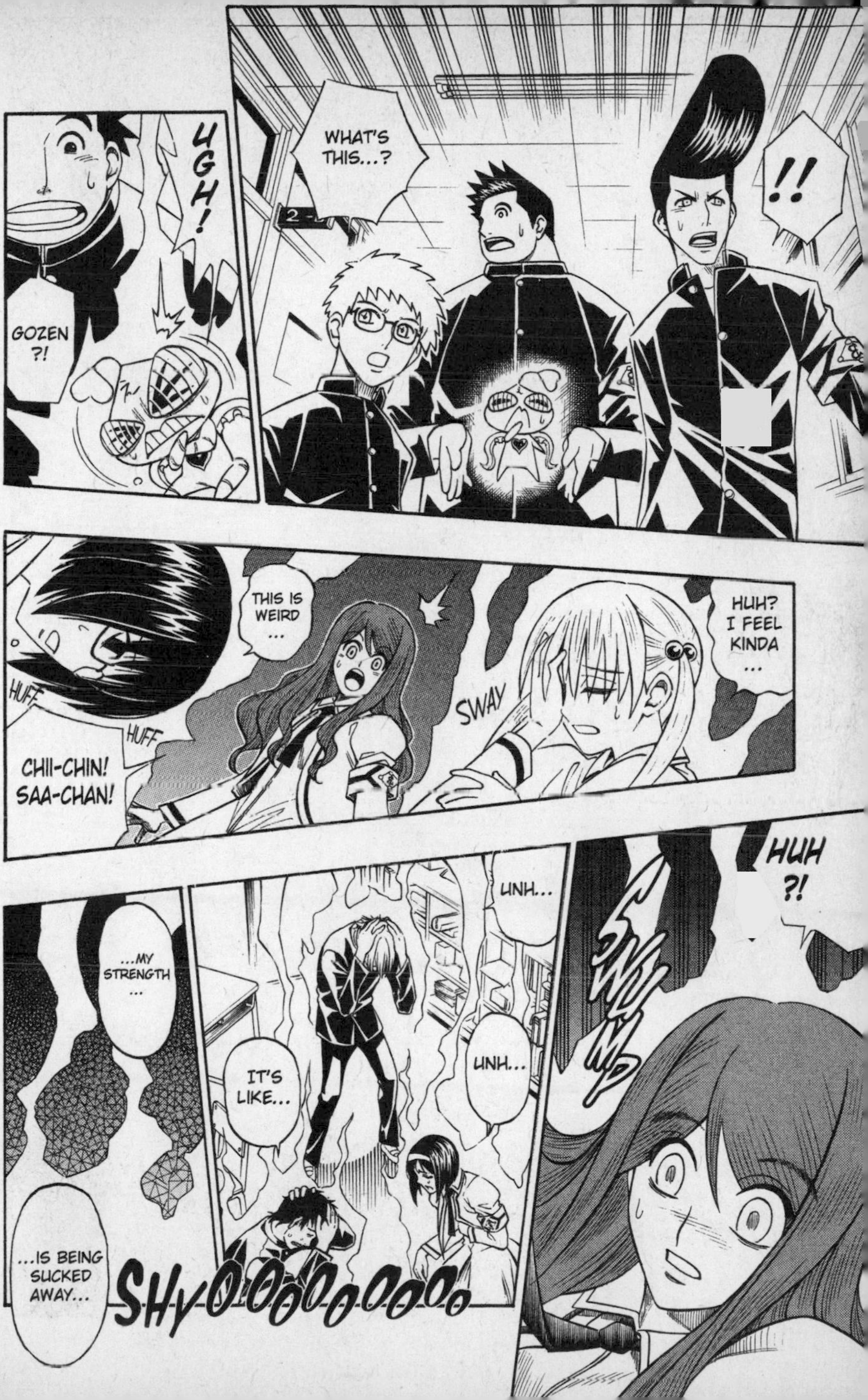
!!
WHAT'S THIS...?
UGH!
GOZEN ?!
HUH? I FEEL KINDA ...
SWAY
THIS IS WEIRD ...
HUFF
HUFF
CHII-CHIN! SAA-CHAN!
HUH ?!
UNH...
UNH...
IT'S LIKE...
...MY STRENGTH ...
...IS BEING SUCKED AWAY...
SHYOOOOOOOOOo

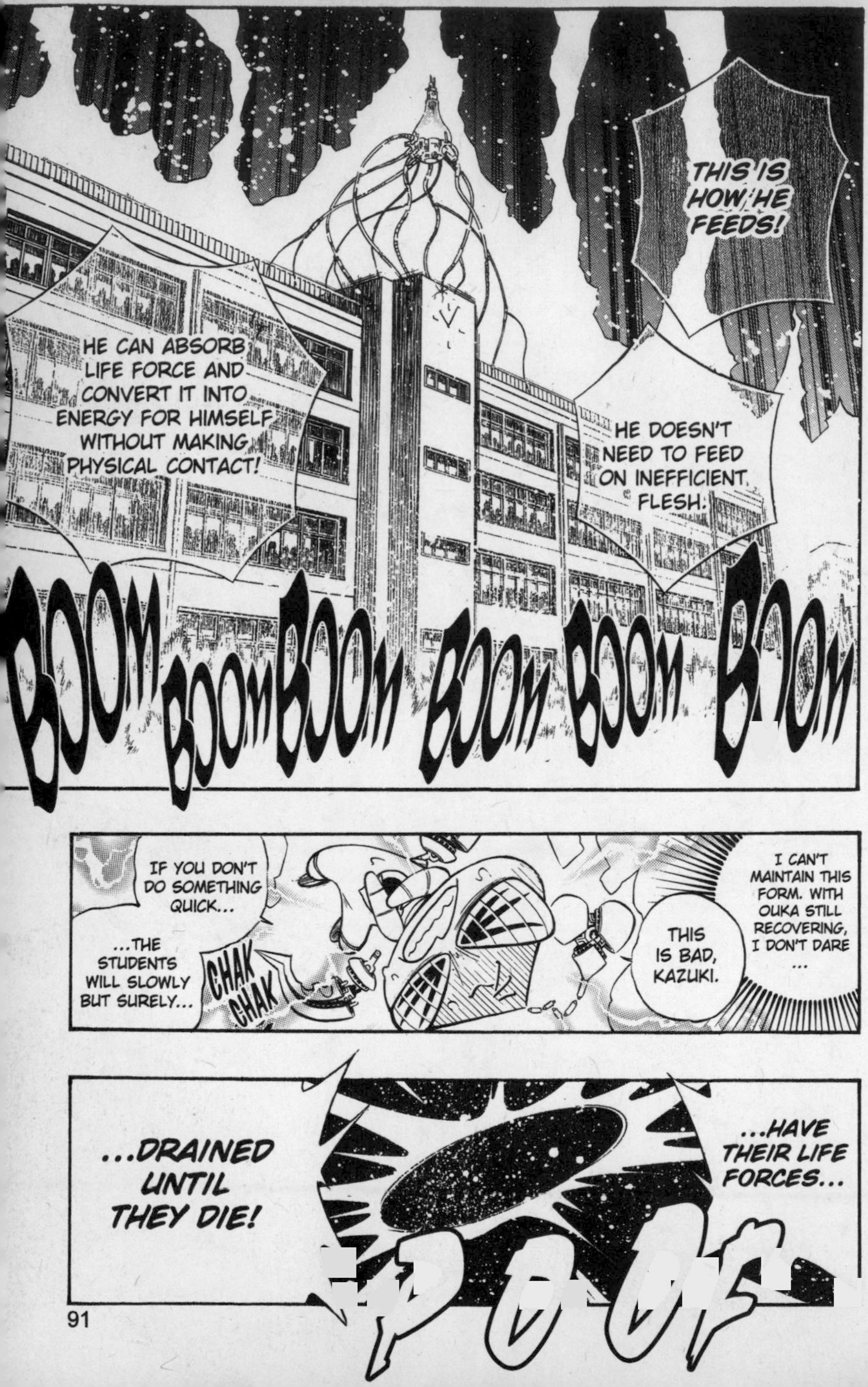
THIS IS HOW HE FEEDS!
HE DOESN'T NEED TO FEED ON INEFFICIENT FLESH.
HE CAN ABSORB LIFE FORCE AND CONVERT IT INTO ENERGY FOR HIMSELF WITHOUT MAKING PHYSICAL CONTACT!
BOOM BOOM BOOM BOOM BOOM BOOM
I CAN'T MAINTAIN THIS FORM. WITH OUKA STILL RECOVERING, I DON'T DARE ...
THIS IS BAD, KAZUKI.
IF YOU DON'T DO SOMETHING QUICK...
...THE STUDENTS WILL SLOWLY BUT SURELY...
CHAK CHAK
...HAVE THEIR LIFE FORCES...
...DRAINED UNTIL THEY DIE!

CHAPTER 41: PAPILLON VS. BUTTERFLY, Part I

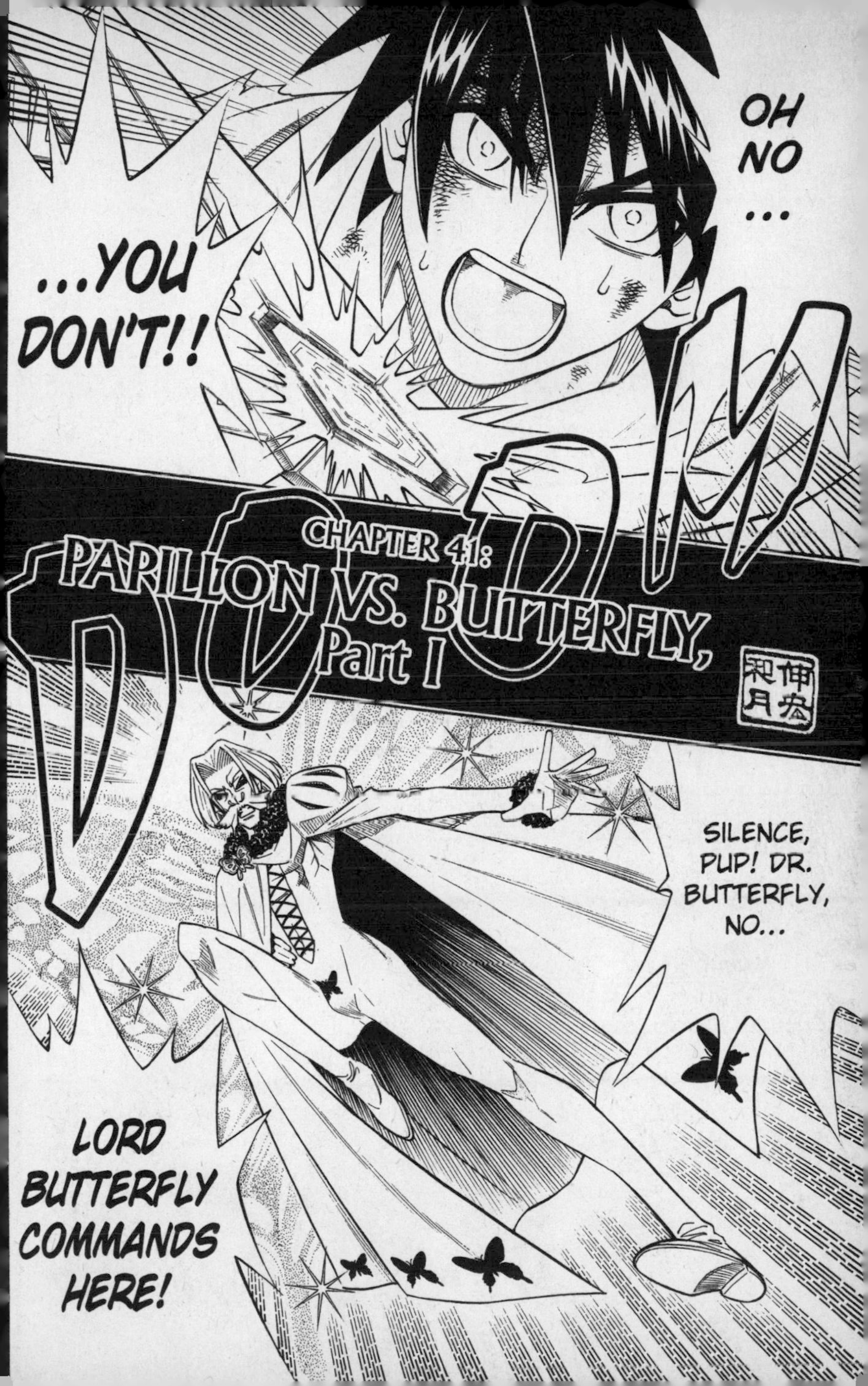
OH NO ...
...YOU DON'T!!
SILENCE, PUP! DR. BUTTERFLY, NO...
LORD BUTTERFLY COMMANDS HERE!

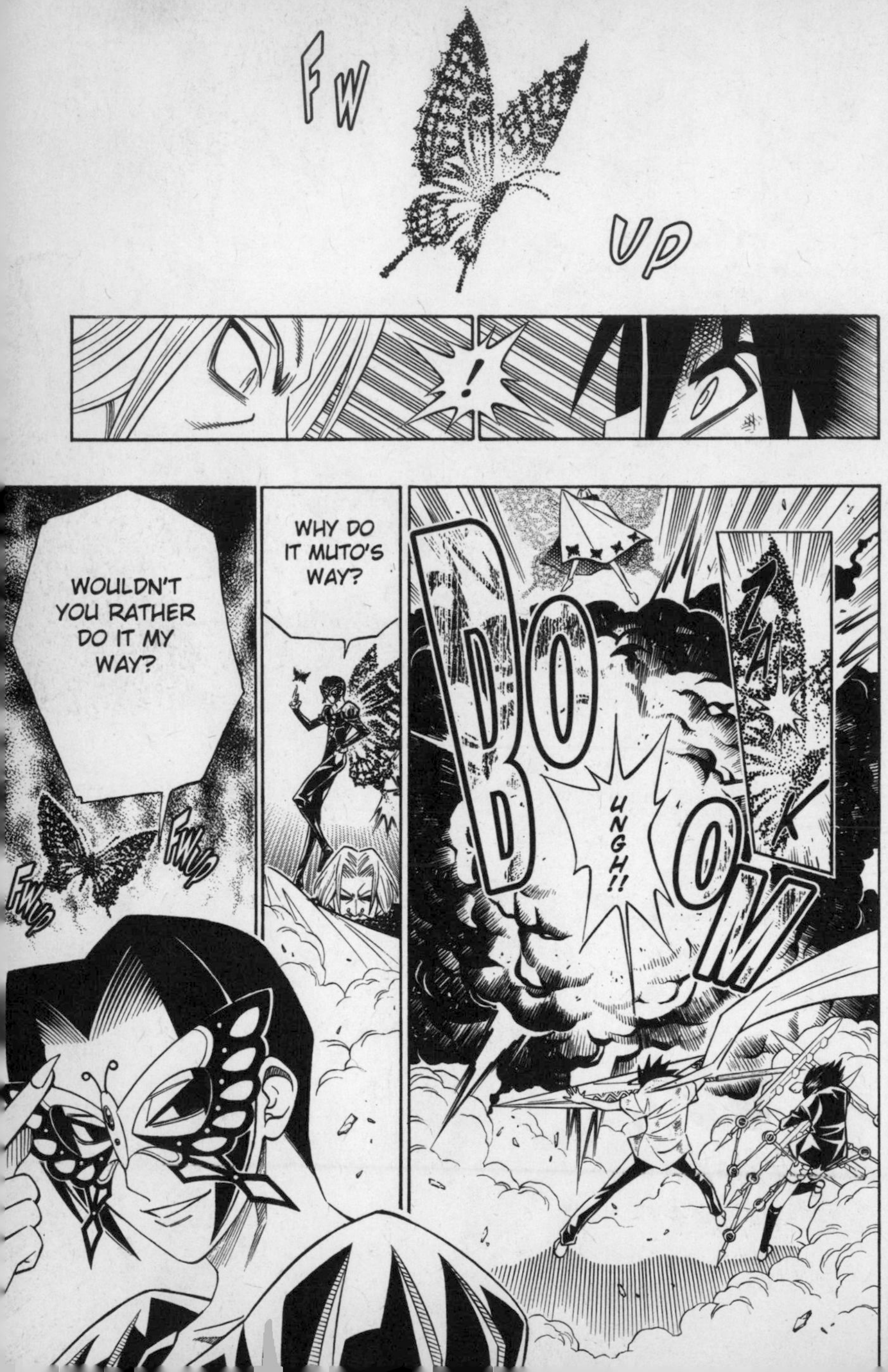
FW
UP
!
BOOM
ZAK
UNGH!!
WHY DO IT MUTO'S WAY?
WOULDN'T YOU RATHER DO IT MY WAY?
FWP
FWP

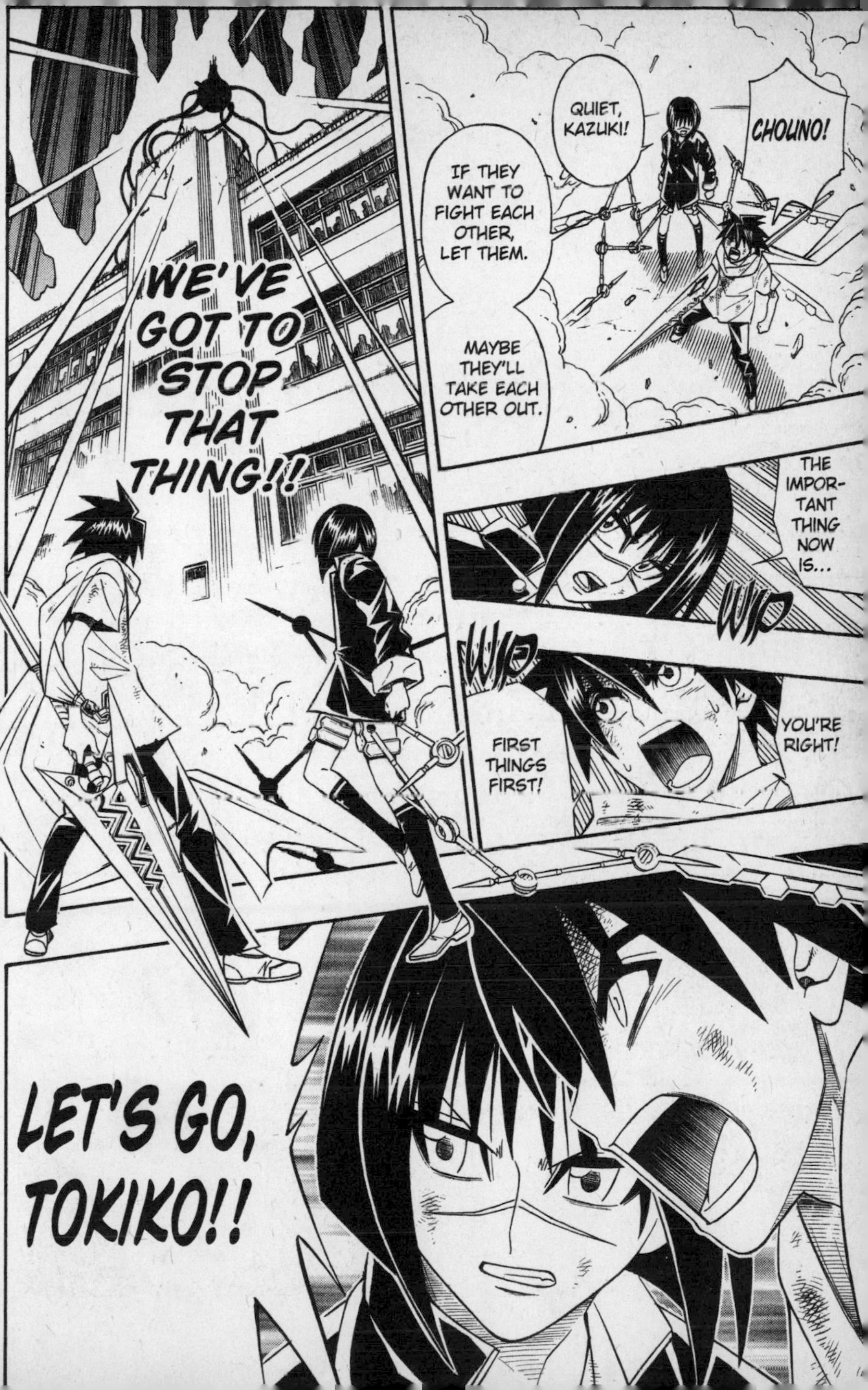
CHOUNO!
QUIET, KAZUKI!
IF THEY WANT TO FIGHT EACH OTHER, LET THEM.
MAYBE THEY'LL TAKE EACH OTHER OUT.
THE IMPORTANT THING NOW IS...
WUP
WUP
YOU'RE RIGHT!
FIRST THINGS FIRST!
WE'VE GOT TO STOP THAT THING!!
LET'S GO, TOKIKO!!

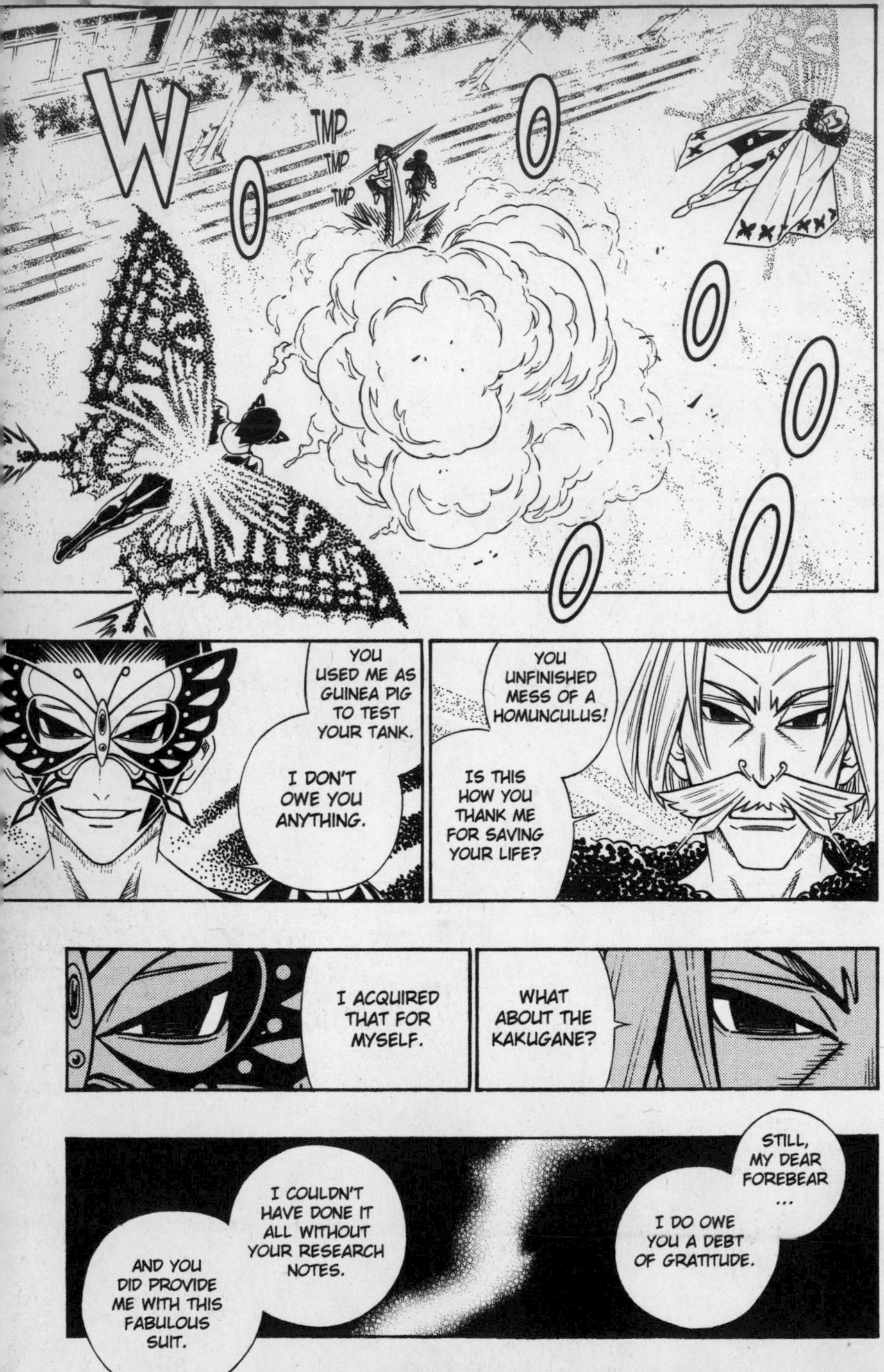
WOOOOOO
TMP TMP TMP
YOU UNFINISHED MESS OF A HOMUNCULUS!
IS THIS HOW YOU THANK ME FOR SAVING YOUR LIFE?
YOU USED ME AS GUINEA PIG TO TEST YOUR TANK.
I DON'T OWE YOU ANYTHING.
WHAT ABOUT THE KAKUGANE?
I ACQUIRED THAT FOR MYSELF.
STILL, MY DEAR FOREBEAR ...
I DO OWE YOU A DEBT OF GRATITUDE.
I COULDN'T HAVE DONE IT ALL WITHOUT YOUR RESEARCH NOTES.
AND YOU DID PROVIDE ME WITH THIS FABULOUS SUIT.

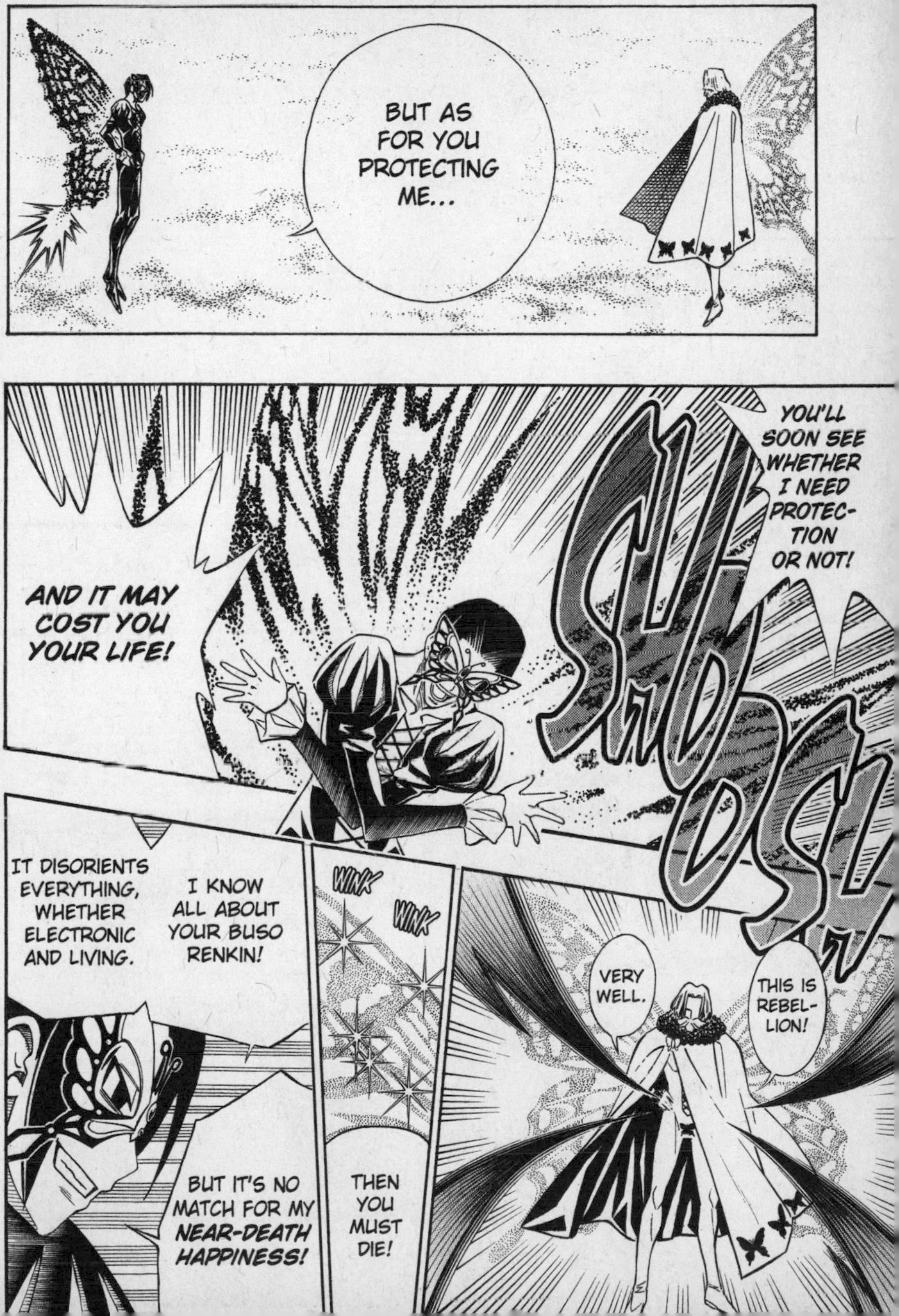
BUT AS FOR YOU PROTECTING ME...
YOU'LL SOON SEE WHETHER I NEED PROTECTION OR NOT!
AND IT MAY COST YOU YOUR LIFE!
THIS IS REBELLION!
VERY WELL.
WINK
WINK
THEN YOU MUST DIE!
I KNOW ALL ABOUT YOUR BUSO RENKIN!
IT DISORIENTS EVERYTHING, WHETHER ELECTRONIC AND LIVING.
BUT IT'S NO MATCH FOR MY *NEAR-DEATH HAPPINESS!*

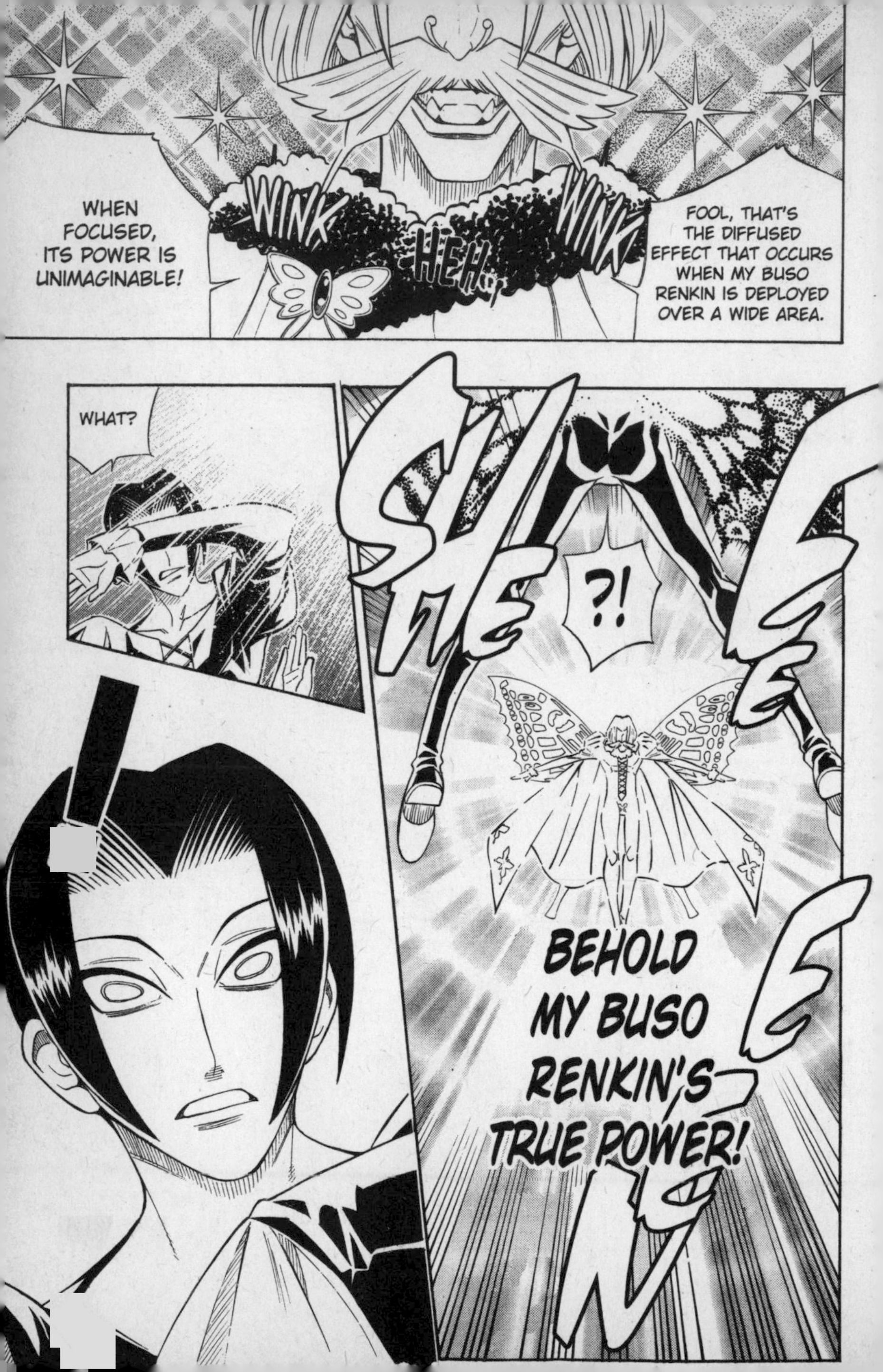
FOOL, THAT'S THE DIFFUSED EFFECT THAT OCCURS WHEN MY BUSO RENKIN IS DEPLOYED OVER A WIDE AREA.
WINK
HEH...
WINK
WHEN FOCUSED, ITS POWER IS UNIMAGINABLE!
?!
BEHOLD MY BUSO RENKIN'S TRUE POWER!
WHAT?

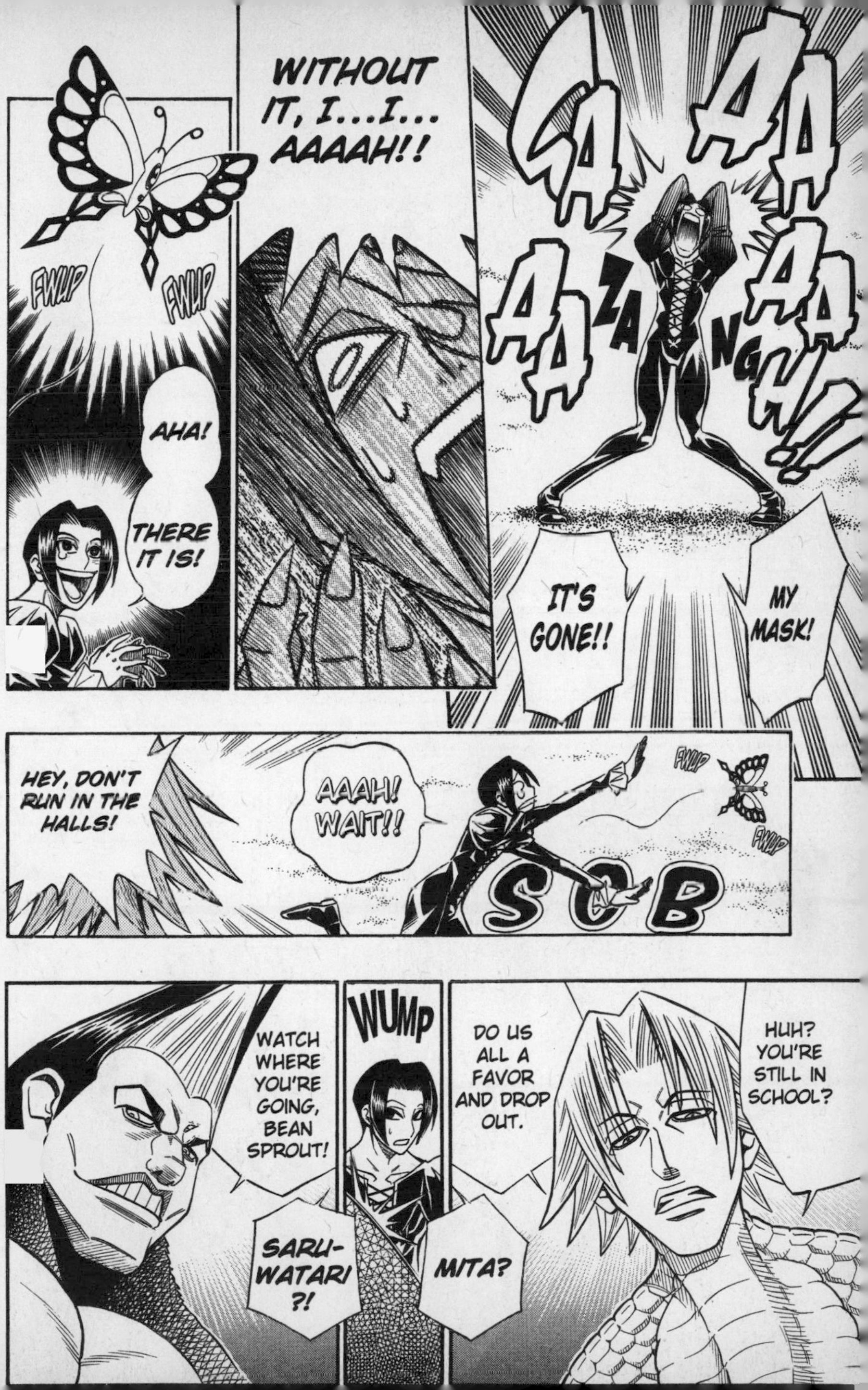
MY MASK!
IT'S GONE!!
WITHOUT IT, I...I... AAAAH!!
FWUP
FWUP
AHA!
THERE IT IS!
FWUP
FWUP
SOB
AAAH! WAIT!!
HEY, DON'T RUN IN THE HALLS!
HUH? YOU'RE STILL IN SCHOOL?
DO US ALL A FAVOR AND DROP OUT.
MITA?
WUMP
WATCH WHERE YOU'RE GOING, BEAN SPROUT!
SARU-WATARI?!

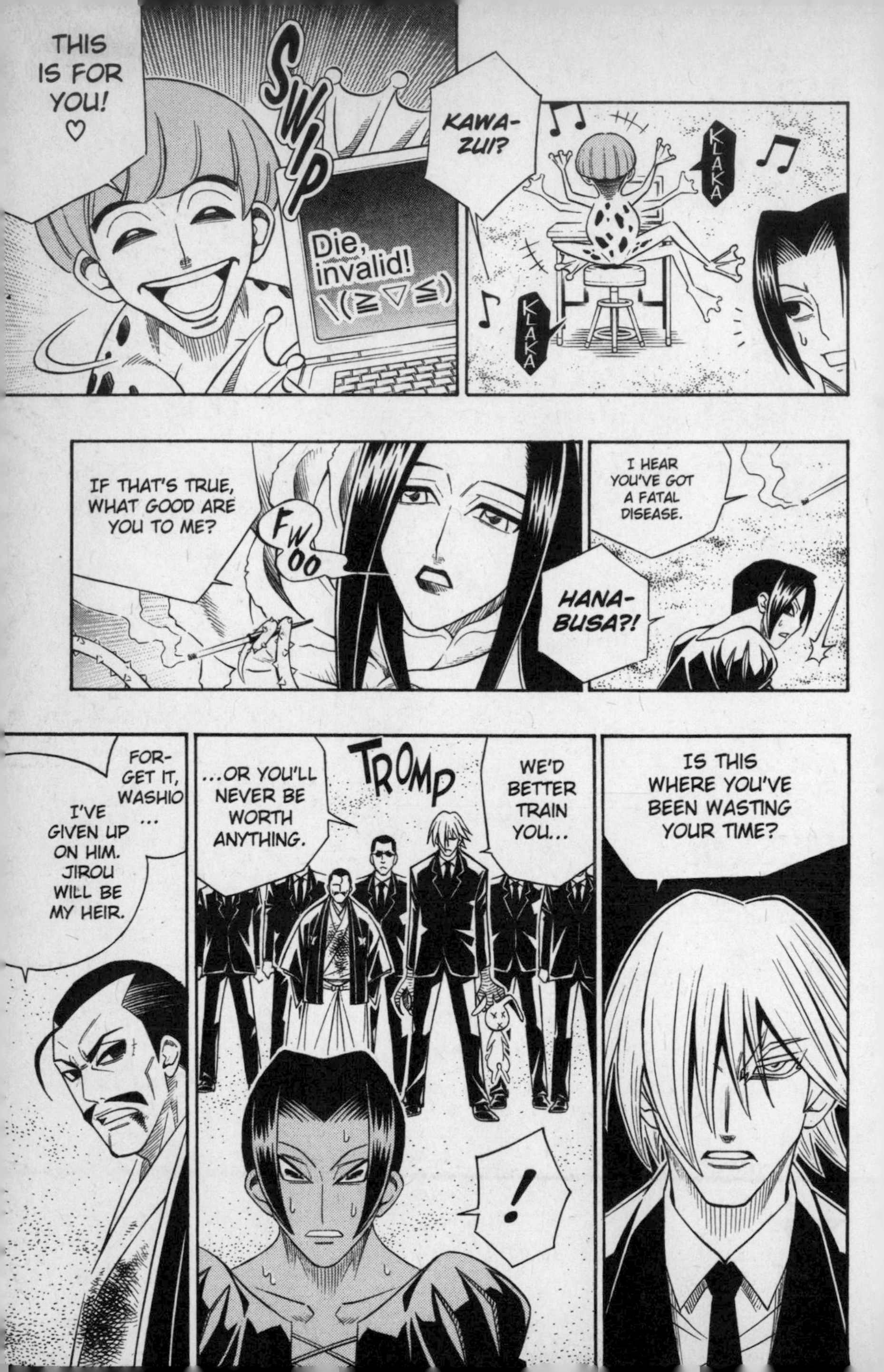
KAWA-ZUI?
KLAKA
KLAKA
THIS IS FOR YOU! ♡
SWIP
Die, invalid! \(≧▽≦)
I HEAR YOU'VE GOT A FATAL DISEASE.
HANA-BUSA?!
IF THAT'S TRUE, WHAT GOOD ARE YOU TO ME?
FWOO
IS THIS WHERE YOU'VE BEEN WASTING YOUR TIME?
WE'D BETTER TRAIN YOU...
TROMP
...OR YOU'LL NEVER BE WORTH ANYTHING.
!
FOR-GET IT, WASHIO...
I'VE GIVEN UP ON HIM. JIROU WILL BE MY HEIR.

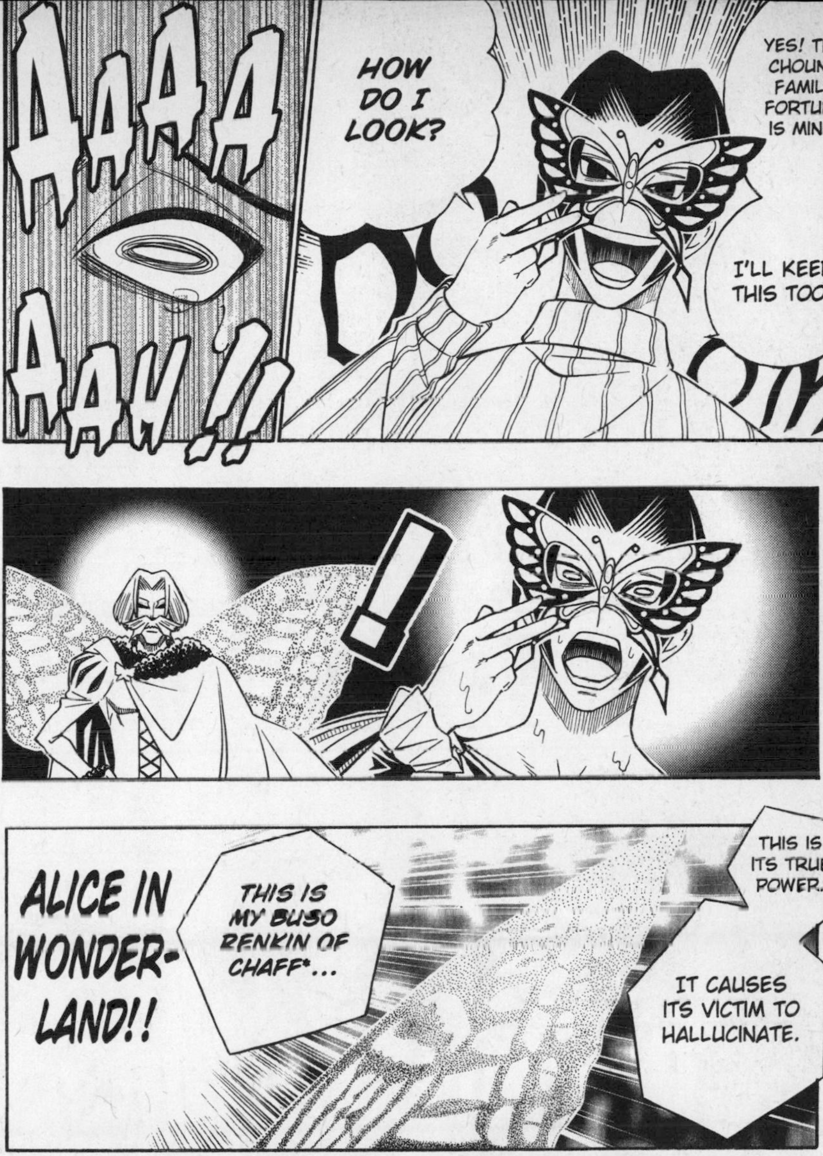
YES! THE CHOUNO FAMILY FORTUNE IS MINE!
I'LL KEEP THIS TOO!
HOW DO I LOOK?
AAAA AAH!!
!
THIS IS ITS TRUE POWER.
IT CAUSES ITS VICTIM TO HALLUCINATE.
THIS IS MY BUSO RENKIN OF CHAFF*...
ALICE IN WONDER-LAND!!

※CHAFF--BITS OF METAL OR PLASTIC SCATTERED TO CONFUSE ENEMY RADAR.

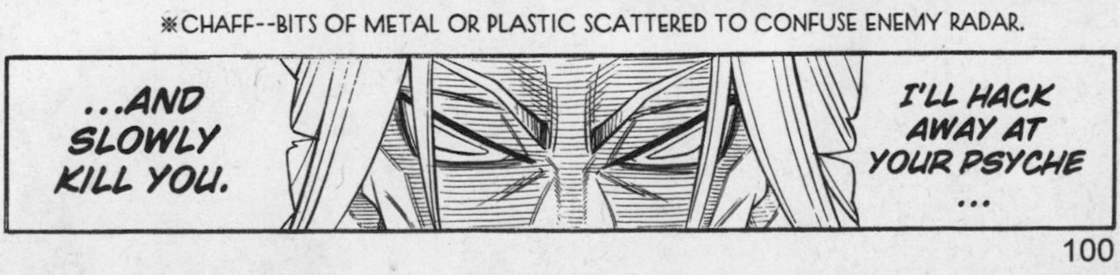
I'LL HACK AWAY AT YOUR PSYCHE ...
...AND SLOWLY KILL YOU.

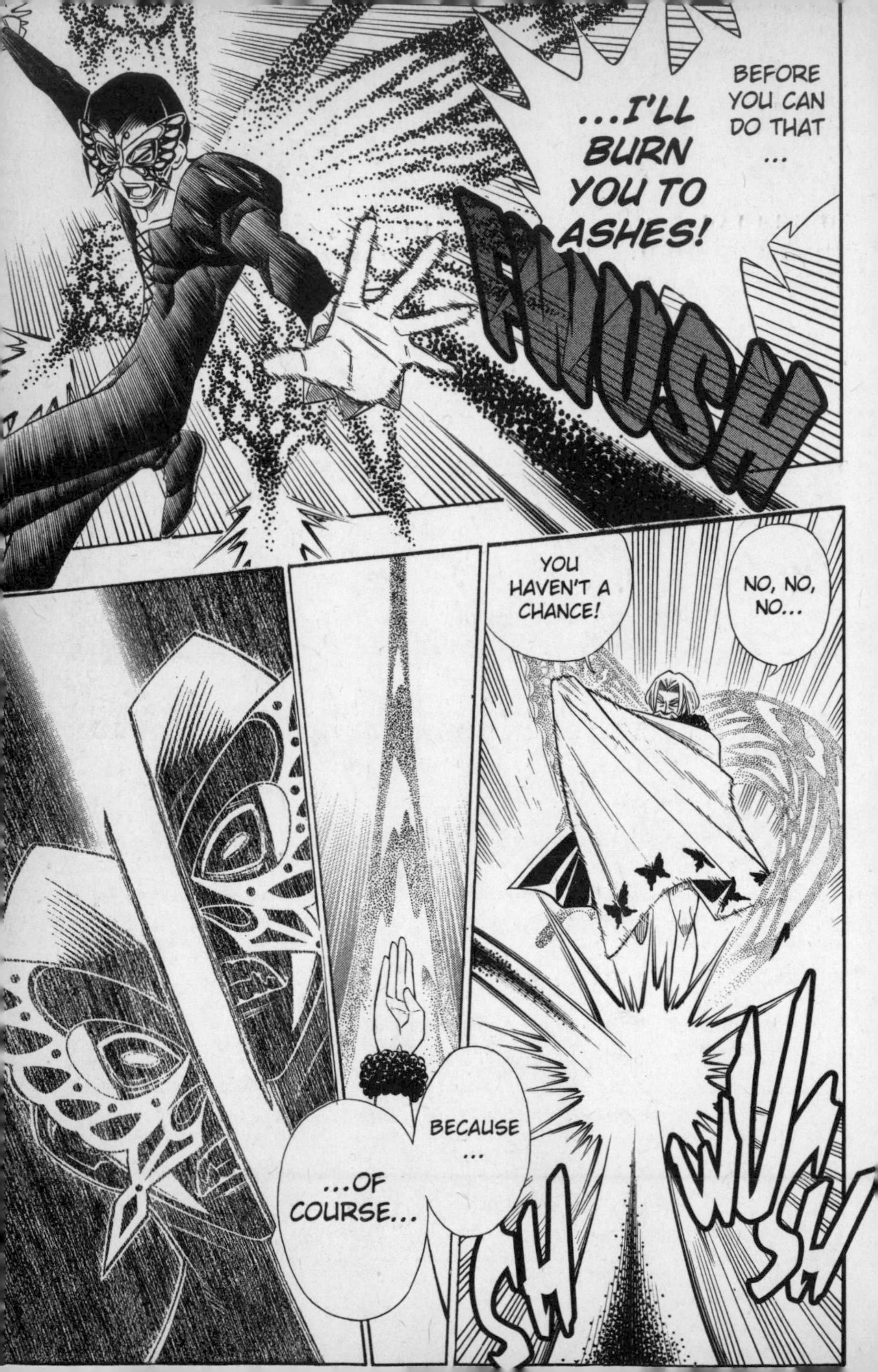
BEFORE YOU CAN DO THAT ...
...I'LL BURN YOU TO ASHES!
FWUSH
NO, NO, NO...
YOU HAVEN'T A CHANCE!
WUSH
SH
BECAUSE ...
...OF COURSE...

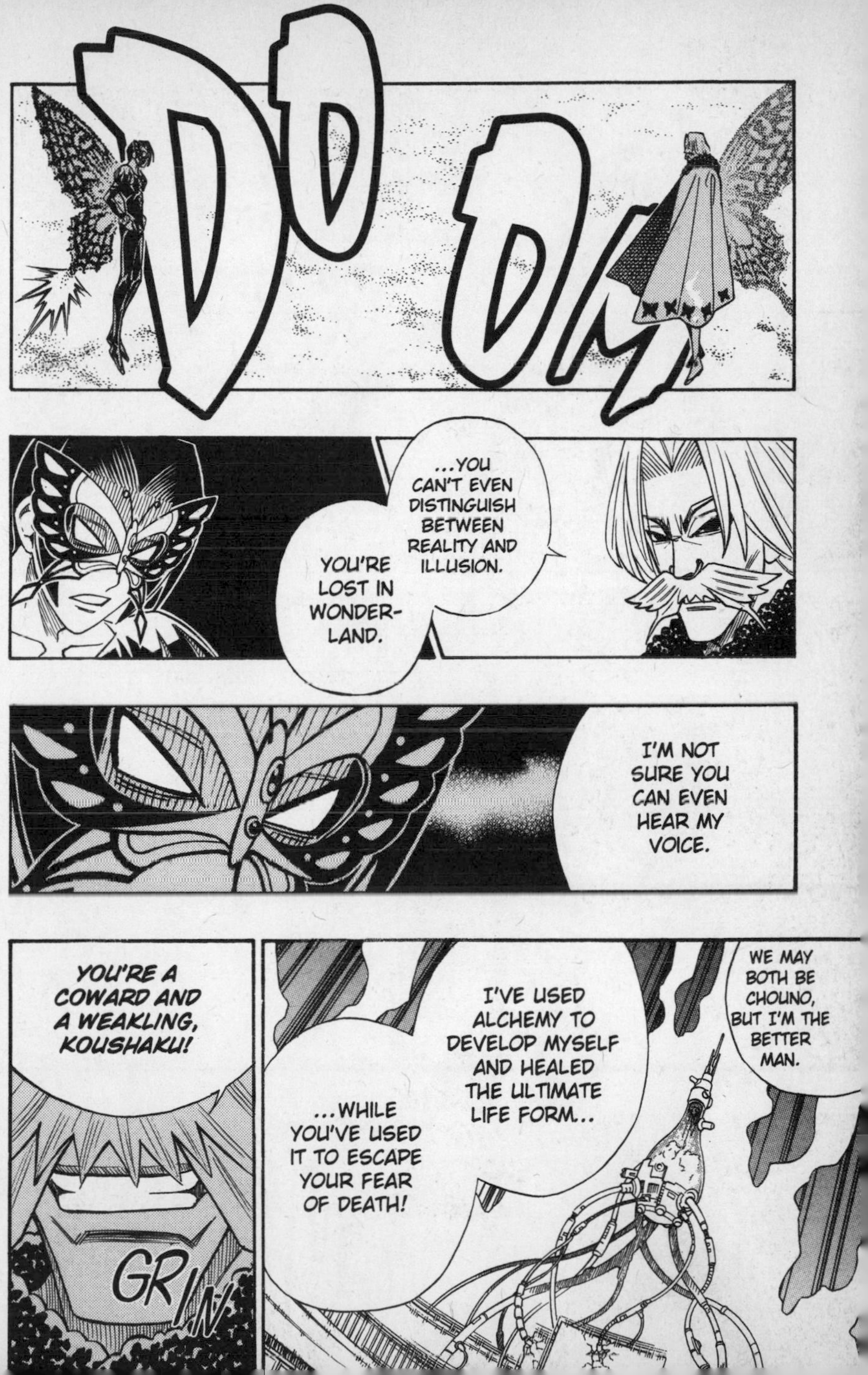
DODOM
...YOU CAN'T EVEN DISTINGUISH BETWEEN REALITY AND ILLUSION.
YOU'RE LOST IN WONDER-LAND.
I'M NOT SURE YOU CAN EVEN HEAR MY VOICE.
WE MAY BOTH BE CHOUNO, BUT I'M THE BETTER MAN.
I'VE USED ALCHEMY TO DEVELOP MYSELF AND HEALED THE ULTIMATE LIFE FORM...
...WHILE YOU'VE USED IT TO ESCAPE YOUR FEAR OF DEATH!
YOU'RE A COWARD AND A WEAKLING, KOUSHAKU!
GRIN

READ THIS WAY

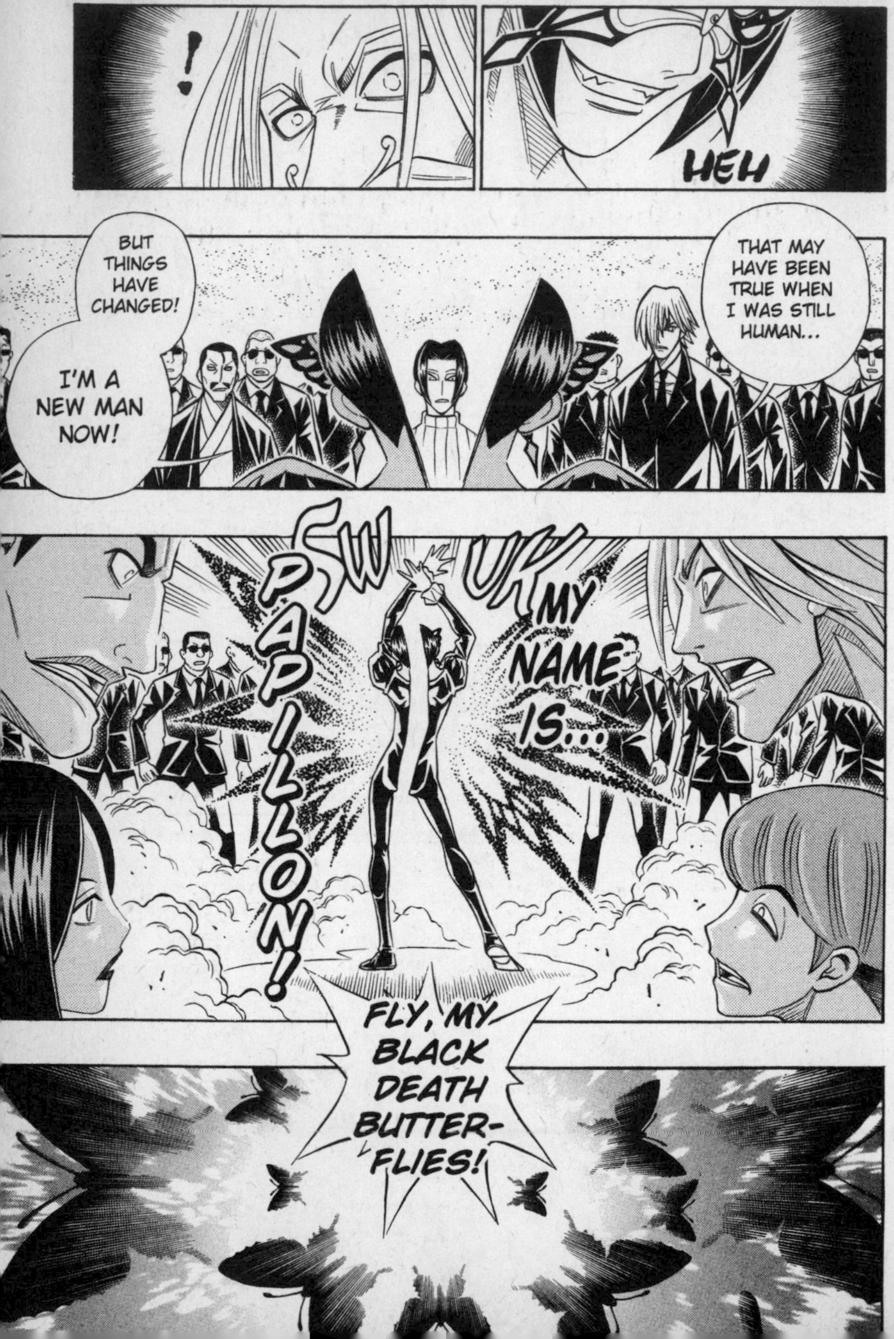
HEH
!
THAT MAY HAVE BEEN TRUE WHEN I WAS STILL HUMAN...
BUT THINGS HAVE CHANGED!
I'M A NEW MAN NOW!
SWUK
MY NAME IS...
PAPILLON!
FLY, MY BLACK DEATH BUTTER-FLIES!

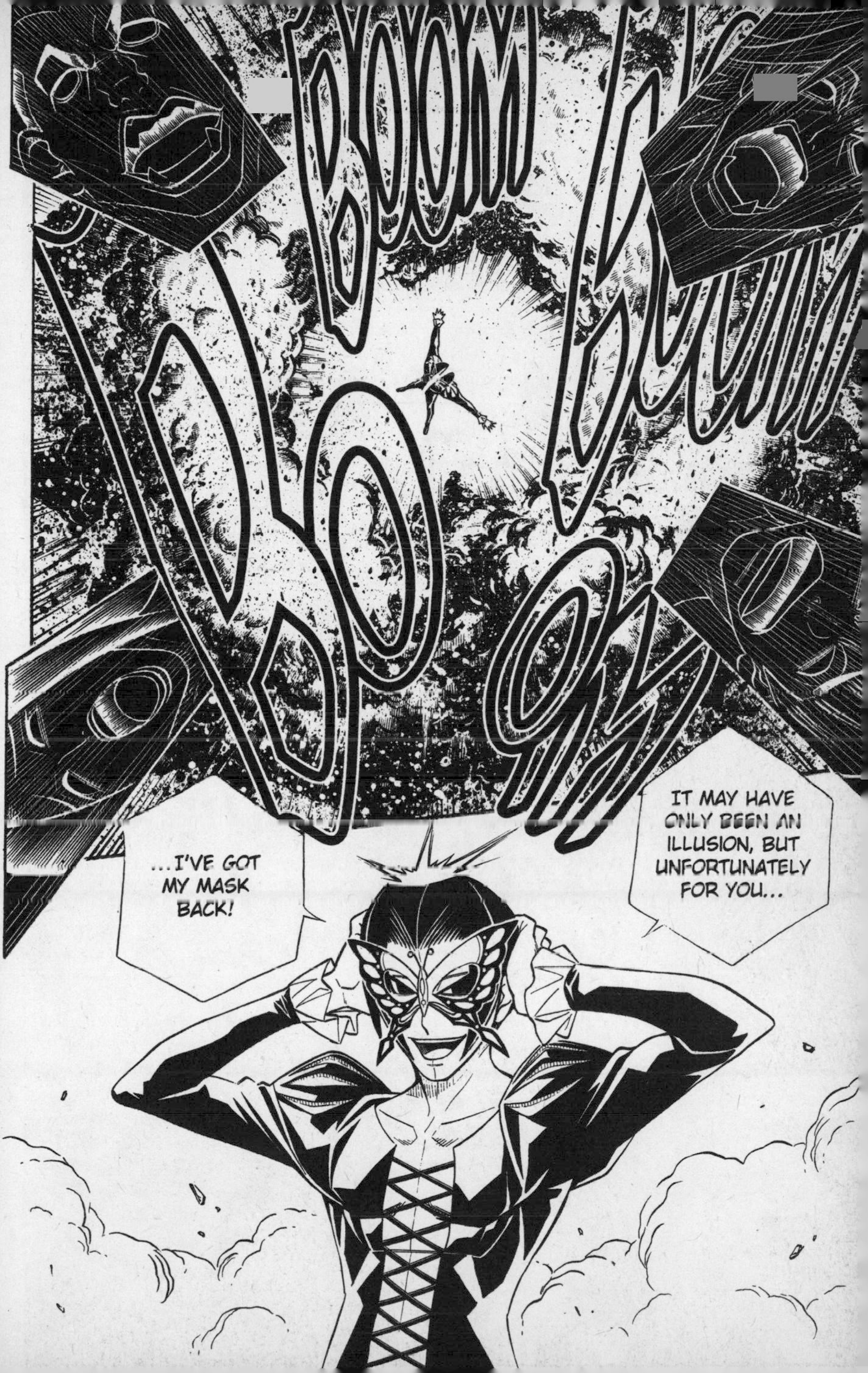
IT MAY HAVE ONLY BEEN AN ILLUSION, BUT UNFORTUNATELY FOR YOU...
...I'VE GOT MY MASK BACK!

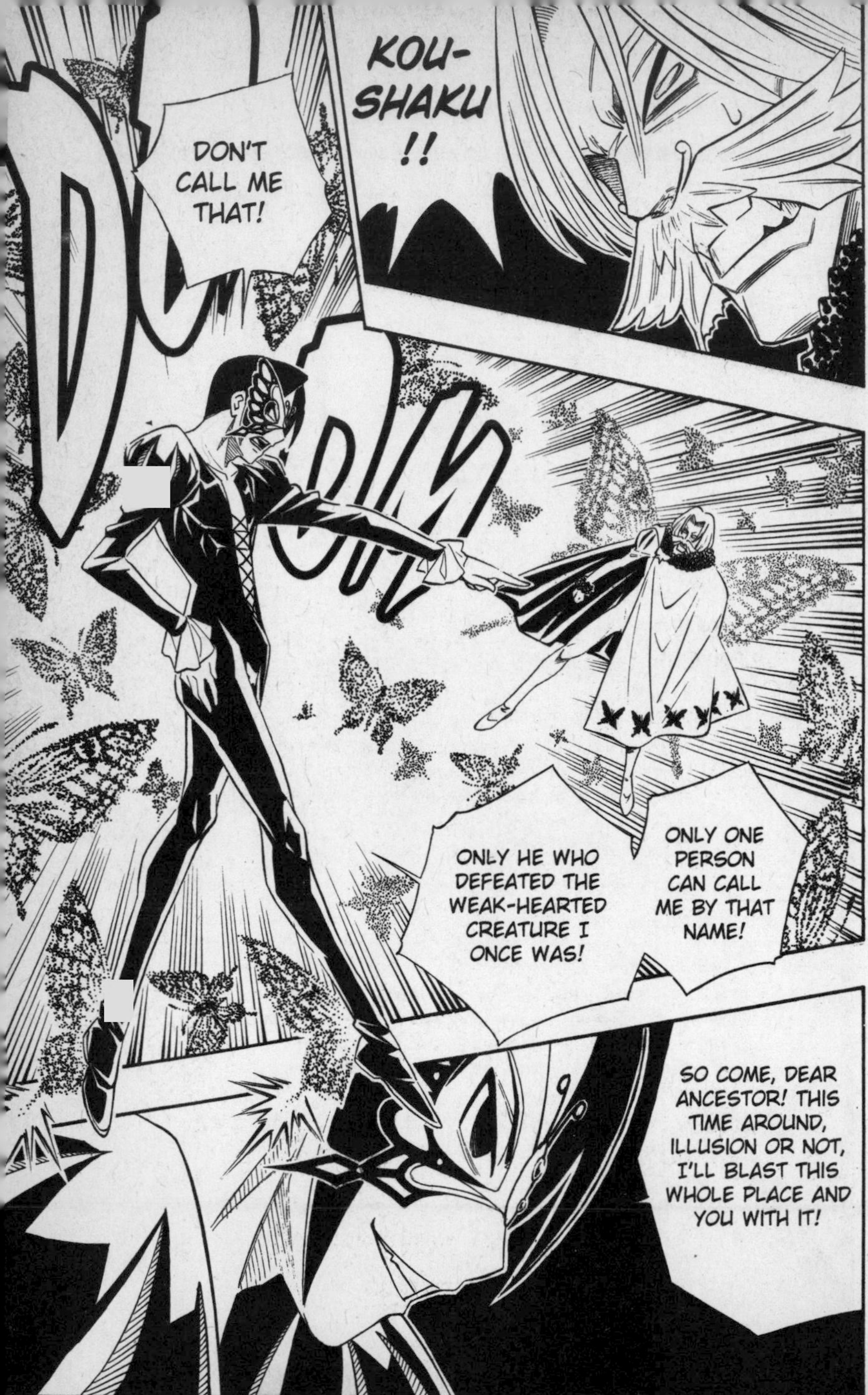
KOU-SHAKU!!
DON'T CALL ME THAT!
DOOM
ONLY ONE PERSON CAN CALL ME BY THAT NAME!
ONLY HE WHO DEFEATED THE WEAK-HEARTED CREATURE I ONCE WAS!
SO COME, DEAR ANCESTOR! THIS TIME AROUND, ILLUSION OR NOT, I'LL BLAST THIS WHOLE PLACE AND YOU WITH IT!

Hyahooo!

Buso Renkin File No. 4

ピーキー
ガリバー
PEAKY GULLIVER

- ○ Kakugane Serial Number: LII (52)
- ○ Creator: Homunculus Kinjo
- ○ Form: Right Gauntlet
- ○ Main Color: Moss Green
- ○ Special Abilities: · Able to grow to gigantic size
- ○ Special Traits: · Able to instantly suck elements out of the air to increase
  the Buso Renkin's size and mass.
  · It is a simple impact weapon, but if it connects, the effects
  can be devastating.
  · Overall, it's kind of a plain weapon…

- ○ Author's Notes:
  · The truth is, until just before the pages were finalized, this weapon's
  special ability was the Rocket Punch. Its little wings are left over from that.
  But in the end that seemed too ordinary.
  · In terms of design, I used a *Gundam* model kit as a reference and based
  it on a Gatling gun.
  · Whenever I got stuck with this character, I could always just have him yell,
  "Hyahoo!"

CHAPTER 42: PAPILLON VS. BUTTERFLY, Part II

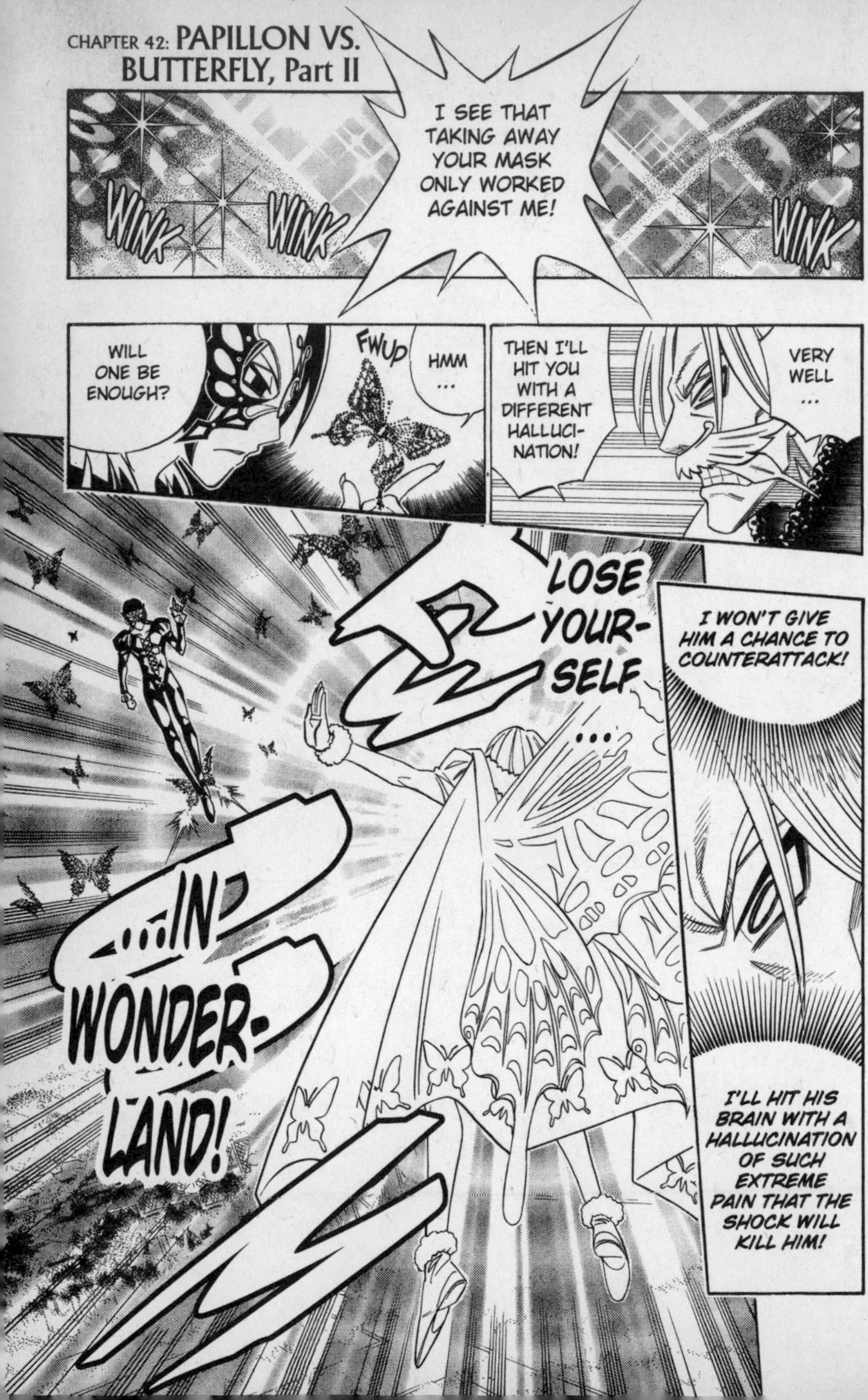
WINK
I SEE THAT TAKING AWAY YOUR MASK ONLY WORKED AGAINST ME!
WINK
WINK
VERY WELL ...
THEN I'LL HIT YOU WITH A DIFFERENT HALLUCI-NATION!
HMM ...
FWUP
WILL ONE BE ENOUGH?
I WON'T GIVE HIM A CHANCE TO COUNTERATTACK!
I'LL HIT HIS BRAIN WITH A HALLUCINATION OF SUCH EXTREME PAIN THAT THE SHOCK WILL KILL HIM!
LOSE YOUR-SELF ...
...IN WONDER-LAND!

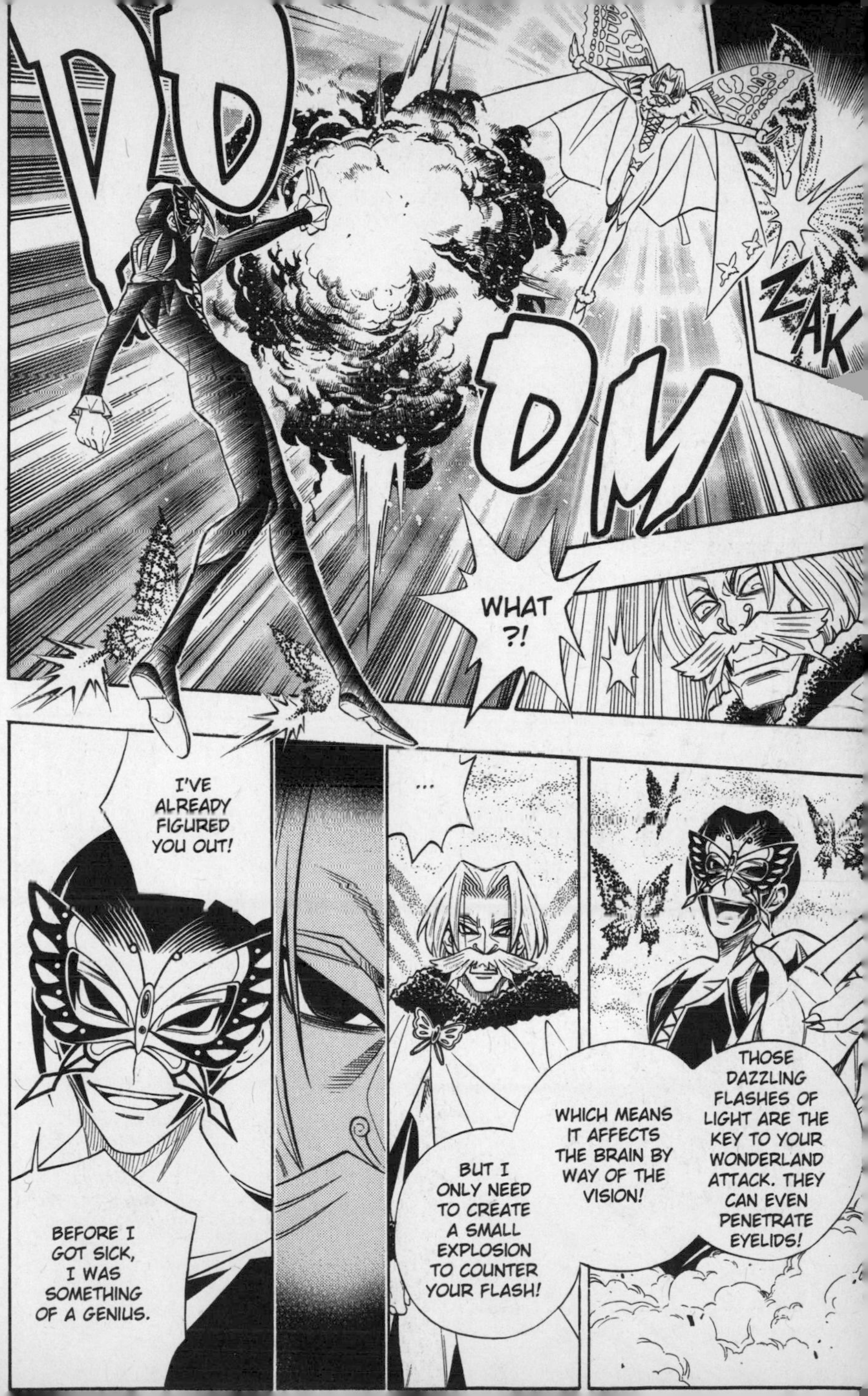
ZAK
WHAT ?!
THOSE DAZZLING FLASHES OF LIGHT ARE THE KEY TO YOUR WONDERLAND ATTACK. THEY CAN EVEN PENETRATE EYELIDS!
WHICH MEANS IT AFFECTS THE BRAIN BY WAY OF THE VISION!
...
BUT I ONLY NEED TO CREATE A SMALL EXPLOSION TO COUNTER YOUR FLASH!
I'VE ALREADY FIGURED YOU OUT!
BEFORE I GOT SICK, I WAS SOMETHING OF A GENIUS.

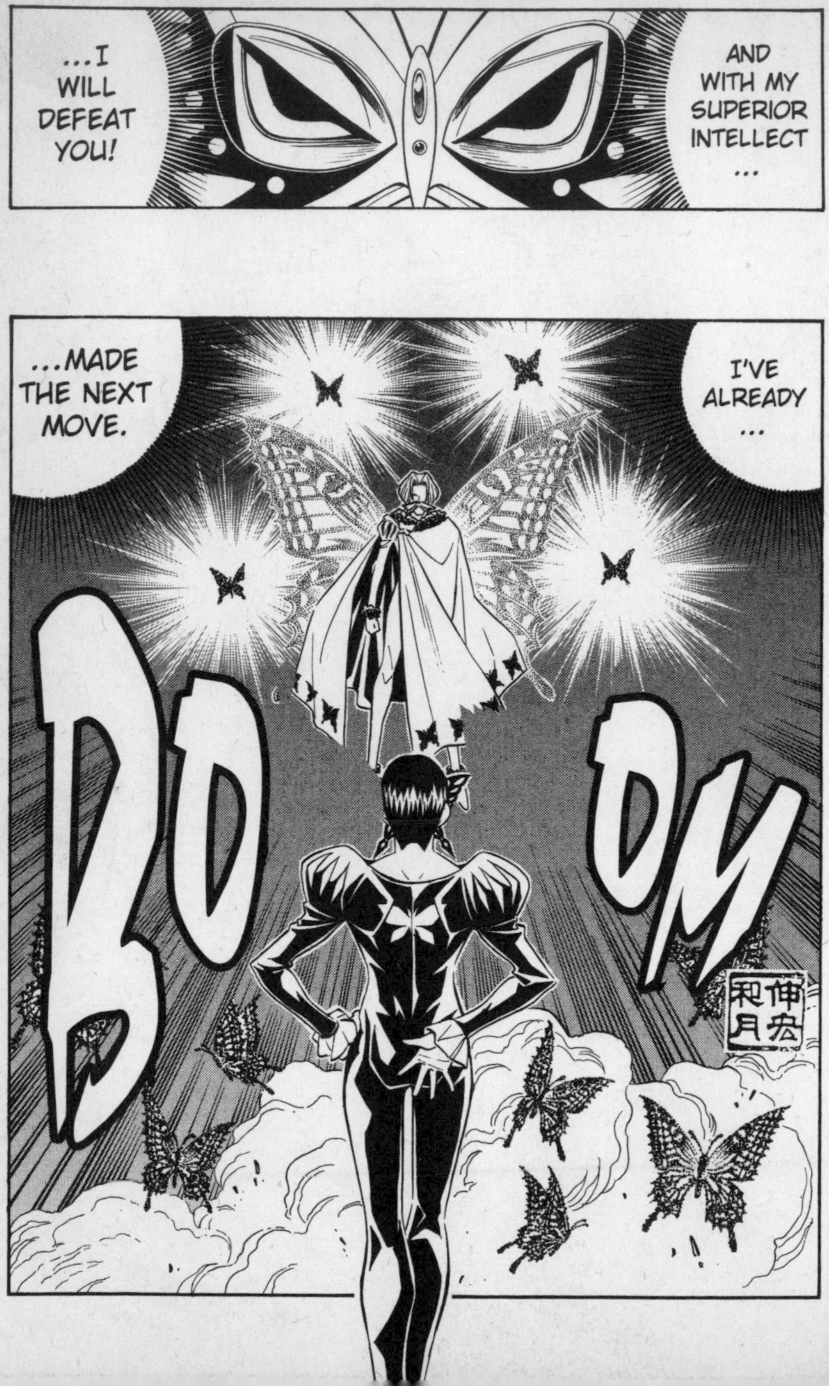
AND WITH MY SUPERIOR INTELLECT ...
...I WILL DEFEAT YOU!
I'VE ALREADY ...
...MADE THE NEXT MOVE.
BOOM

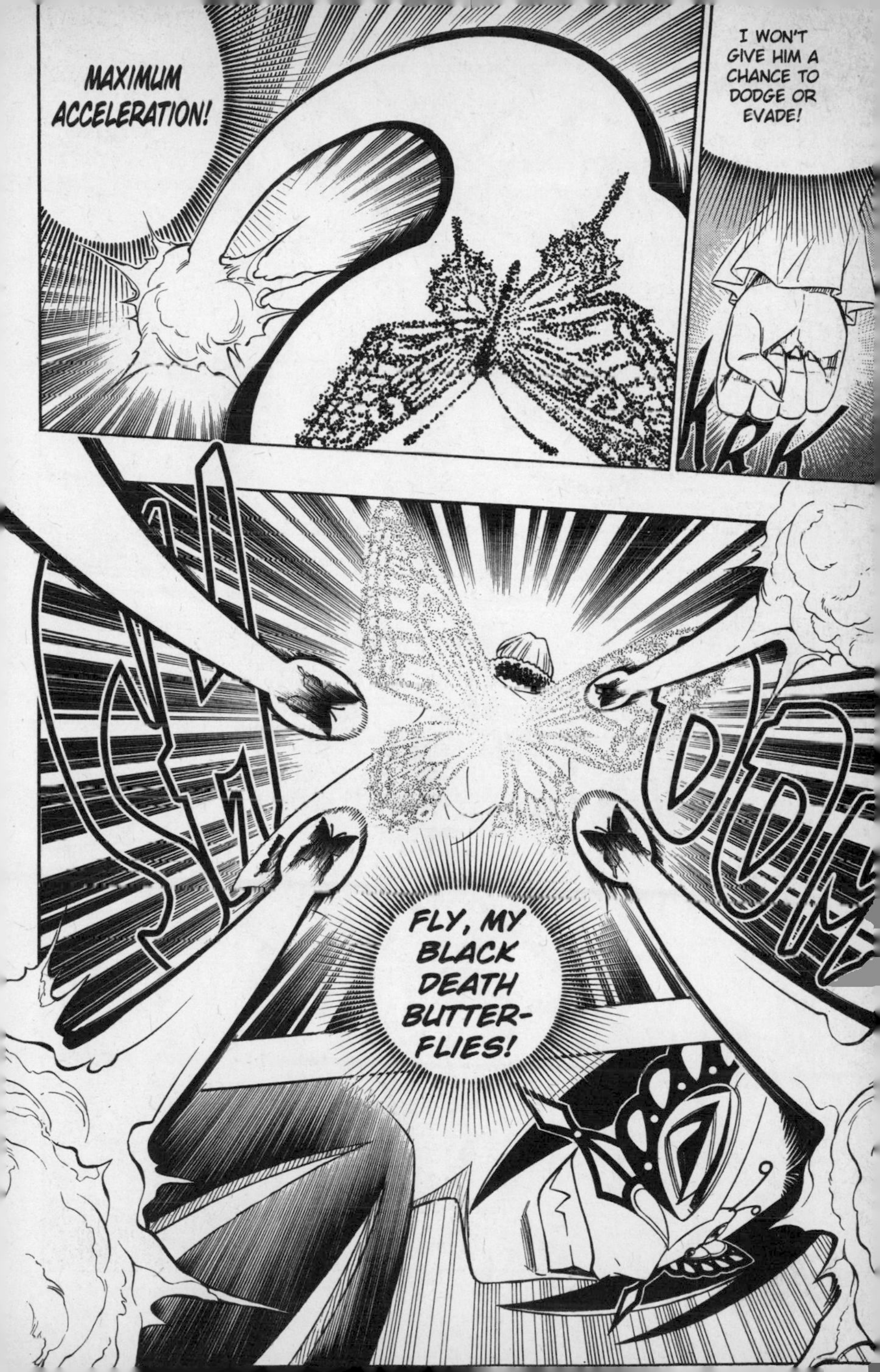
I WON'T GIVE HIM A CHANCE TO DODGE OR EVADE!
MAXIMUM ACCELERATION!
FLY, MY BLACK DEATH BUTTER-FLIES!

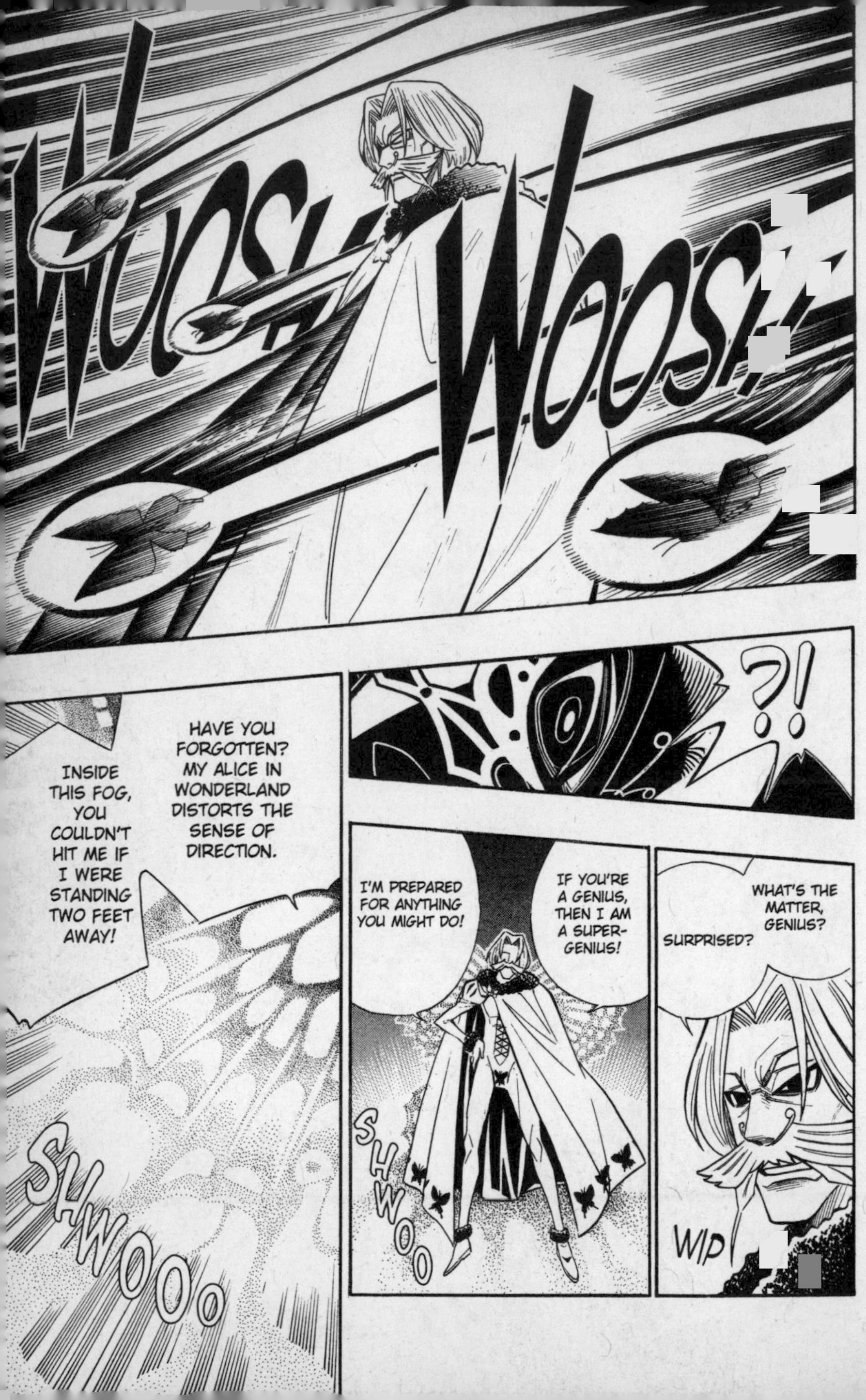
WOOSH
WOOSH
?!
WHAT'S THE MATTER, GENIUS?
SURPRISED?
WIP
IF YOU'RE A GENIUS, THEN I AM A SUPER-GENIUS!
I'M PREPARED FOR ANYTHING YOU MIGHT DO!
SHWOO
HAVE YOU FORGOTTEN? MY ALICE IN WONDERLAND DISTORTS THE SENSE OF DIRECTION.
INSIDE THIS FOG, YOU COULDN'T HIT ME IF I WERE STANDING TWO FEET AWAY!
SHWOOO

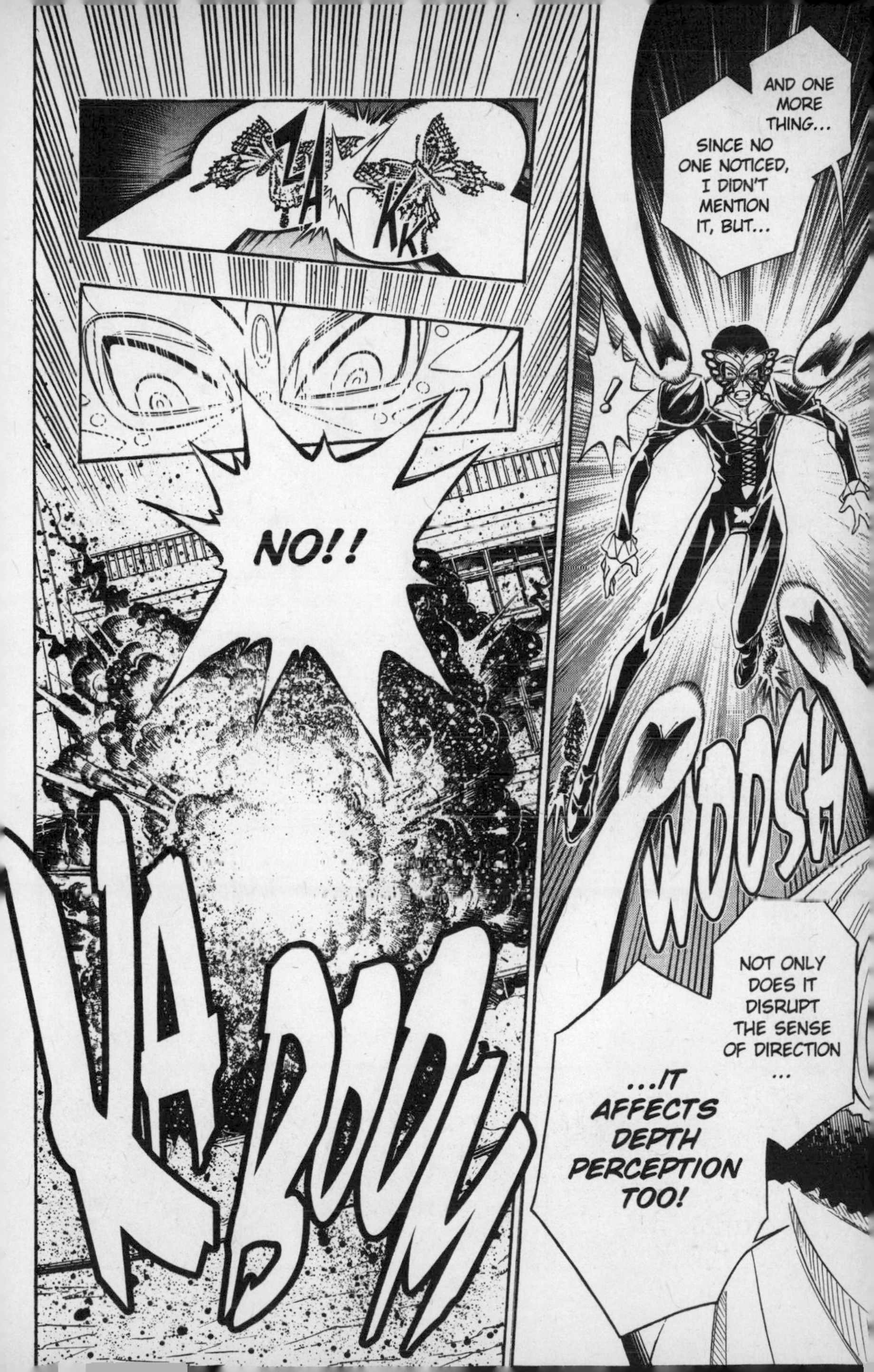
AND ONE MORE THING...
SINCE NO ONE NOTICED, I DIDN'T MENTION IT, BUT...
!
WOOSH
NOT ONLY DOES IT DISRUPT THE SENSE OF DIRECTION ...
...IT AFFECTS DEPTH PERCEPTION TOO!
ZAKK
NO!!
KABOOM

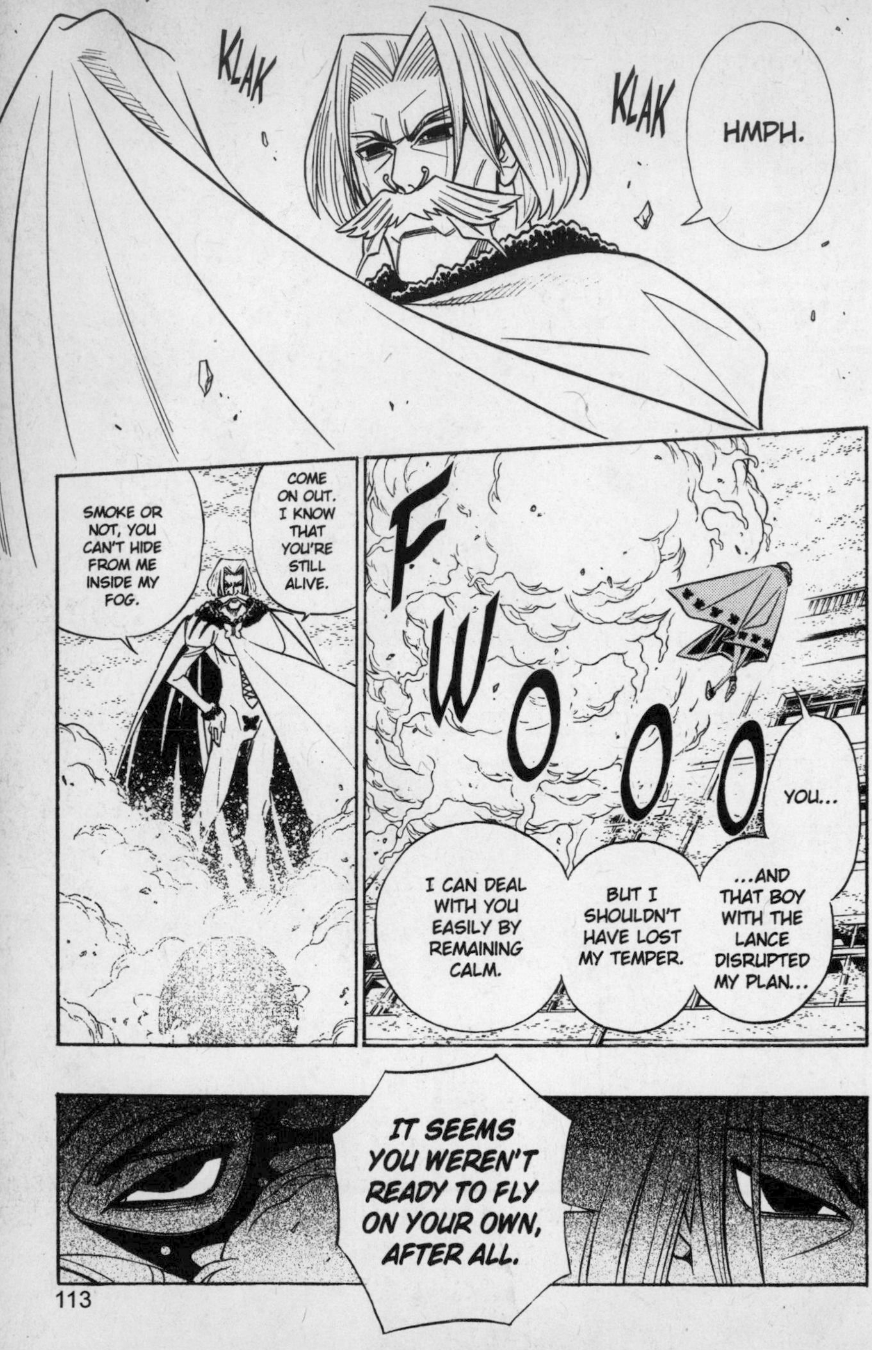
HMPH.
KLAK
KLAK
FWOOO
YOU...
...AND THAT BOY WITH THE LANCE DISRUPTED MY PLAN...
BUT I SHOULDN'T HAVE LOST MY TEMPER.
I CAN DEAL WITH YOU EASILY BY REMAINING CALM.
COME ON OUT. I KNOW THAT YOU'RE STILL ALIVE.
SMOKE OR NOT, YOU CAN'T HIDE FROM ME INSIDE MY FOG.
IT SEEMS YOU WEREN'T READY TO FLY ON YOUR OWN, AFTER ALL.

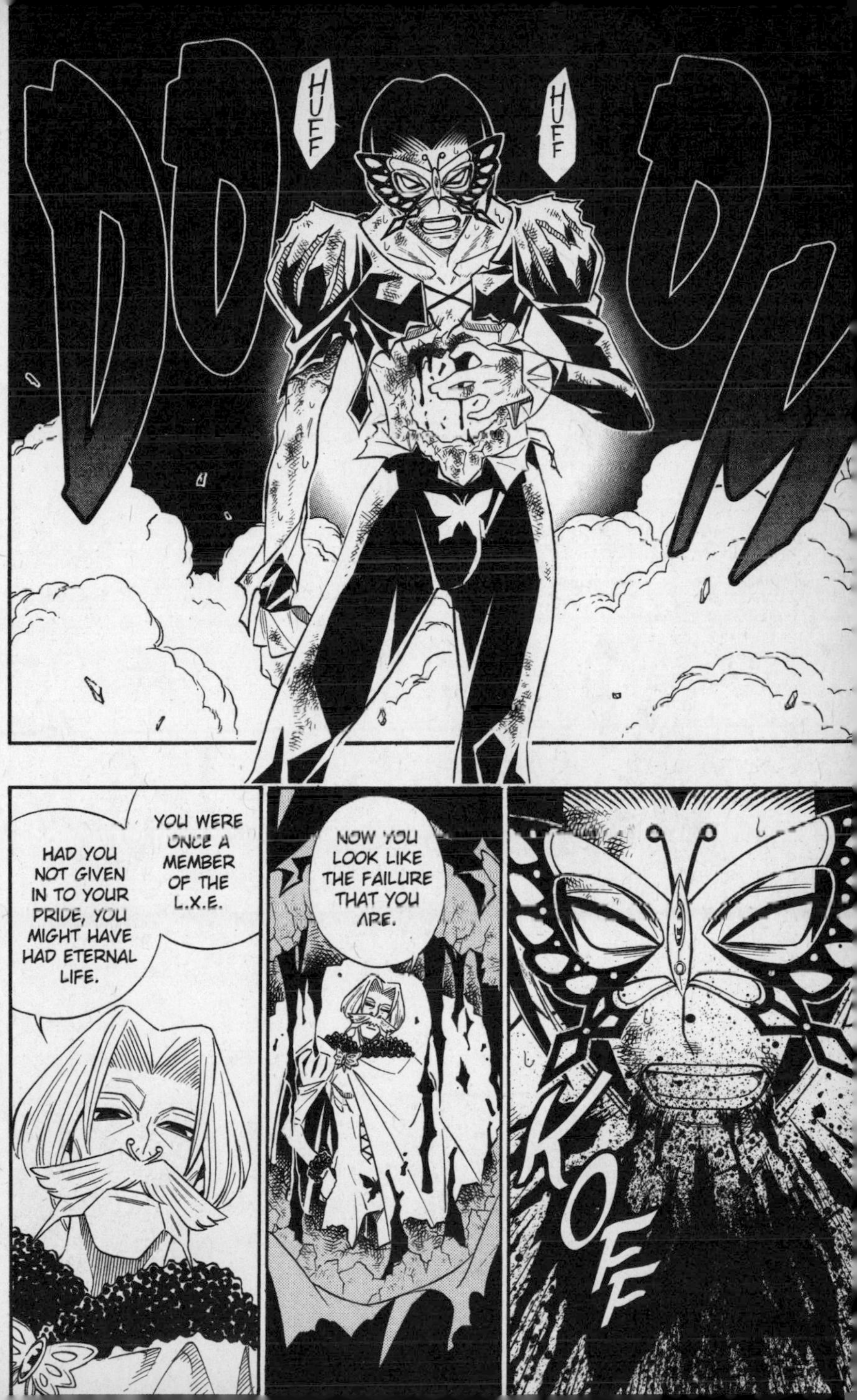
HUFF
HUFF
DOOM
KOFF
NOW YOU LOOK LIKE THE FAILURE THAT YOU ARE.
YOU WERE ONCE A MEMBER OF THE L.X.E.
HAD YOU NOT GIVEN IN TO YOUR PRIDE, YOU MIGHT HAVE HAD ETERNAL LIFE.

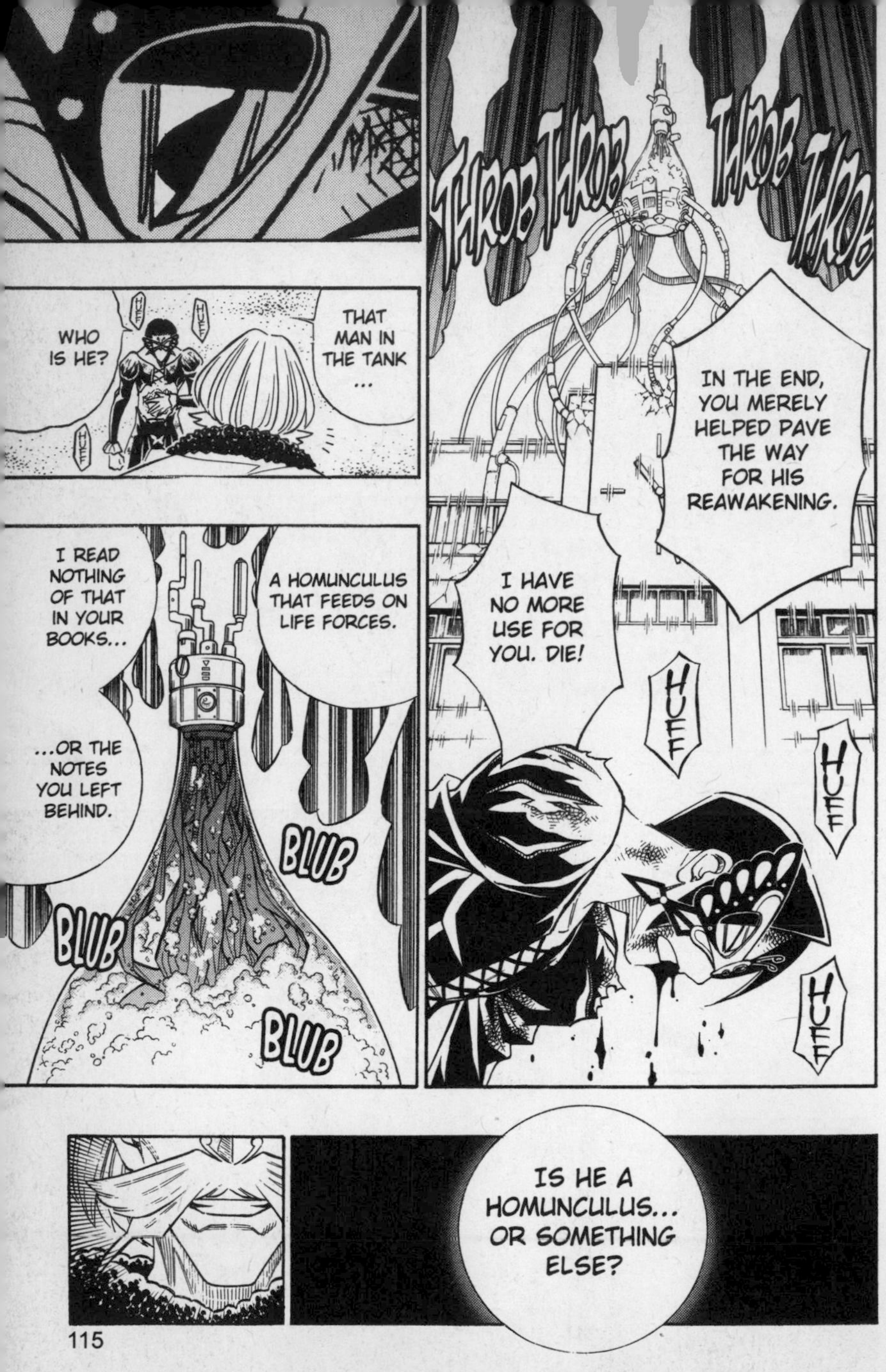
THROB THROB THROB THROB
IN THE END, YOU MERELY HELPED PAVE THE WAY FOR HIS REAWAKENING.
I HAVE NO MORE USE FOR YOU. DIE!
HUFF
HUFF
HUFF
HUFF
HUFF
THAT MAN IN THE TANK ...
WHO IS HE?
HUFF
A HOMUNCULUS THAT FEEDS ON LIFE FORCES.
I READ NOTHING OF THAT IN YOUR BOOKS...
...OR THE NOTES YOU LEFT BEHIND.
BLUB
BLUB
BLUB
IS HE A HOMUNCULUS... OR SOMETHING ELSE?

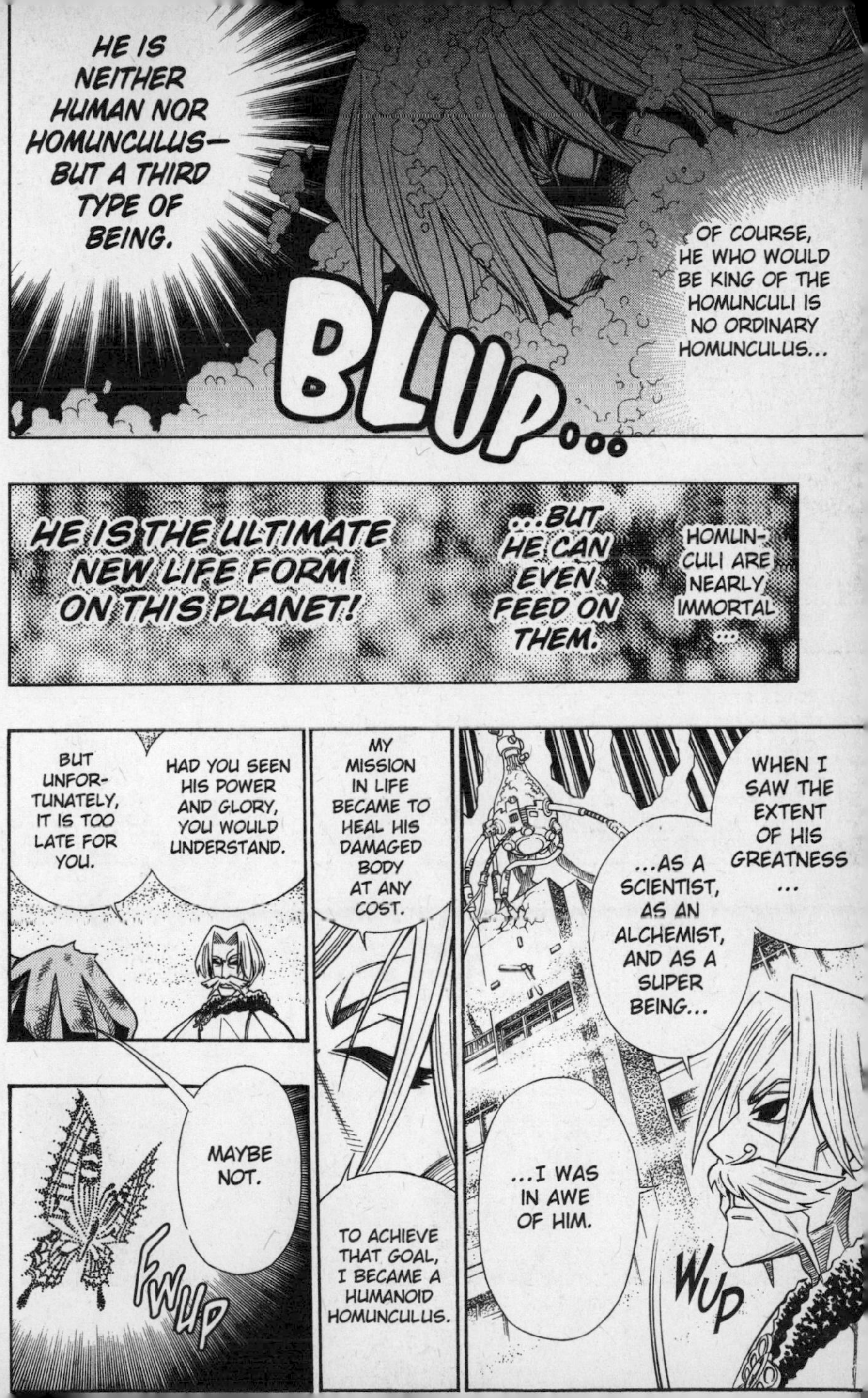
OF COURSE, HE WHO WOULD BE KING OF THE HOMUNCULI IS NO ORDINARY HOMUNCULUS...
HE IS NEITHER HUMAN NOR HOMUNCULUS— BUT A THIRD TYPE OF BEING.
BLUP...
HOMUN-CULI ARE NEARLY IMMORTAL...
...BUT HE CAN EVEN FEED ON THEM.
HE IS THE ULTIMATE NEW LIFE FORM ON THIS PLANET!
WHEN I SAW THE EXTENT OF HIS GREATNESS...
...AS A SCIENTIST, AS AN ALCHEMIST, AND AS A SUPER BEING...
...I WAS IN AWE OF HIM.
WUP
MY MISSION IN LIFE BECAME TO HEAL HIS DAMAGED BODY AT ANY COST.
TO ACHIEVE THAT GOAL, I BECAME A HUMANOID HOMUNCULUS.
HAD YOU SEEN HIS POWER AND GLORY, YOU WOULD UNDERSTAND.
BUT UNFOR-TUNATELY, IT IS TOO LATE FOR YOU.
MAYBE NOT.
FWUP

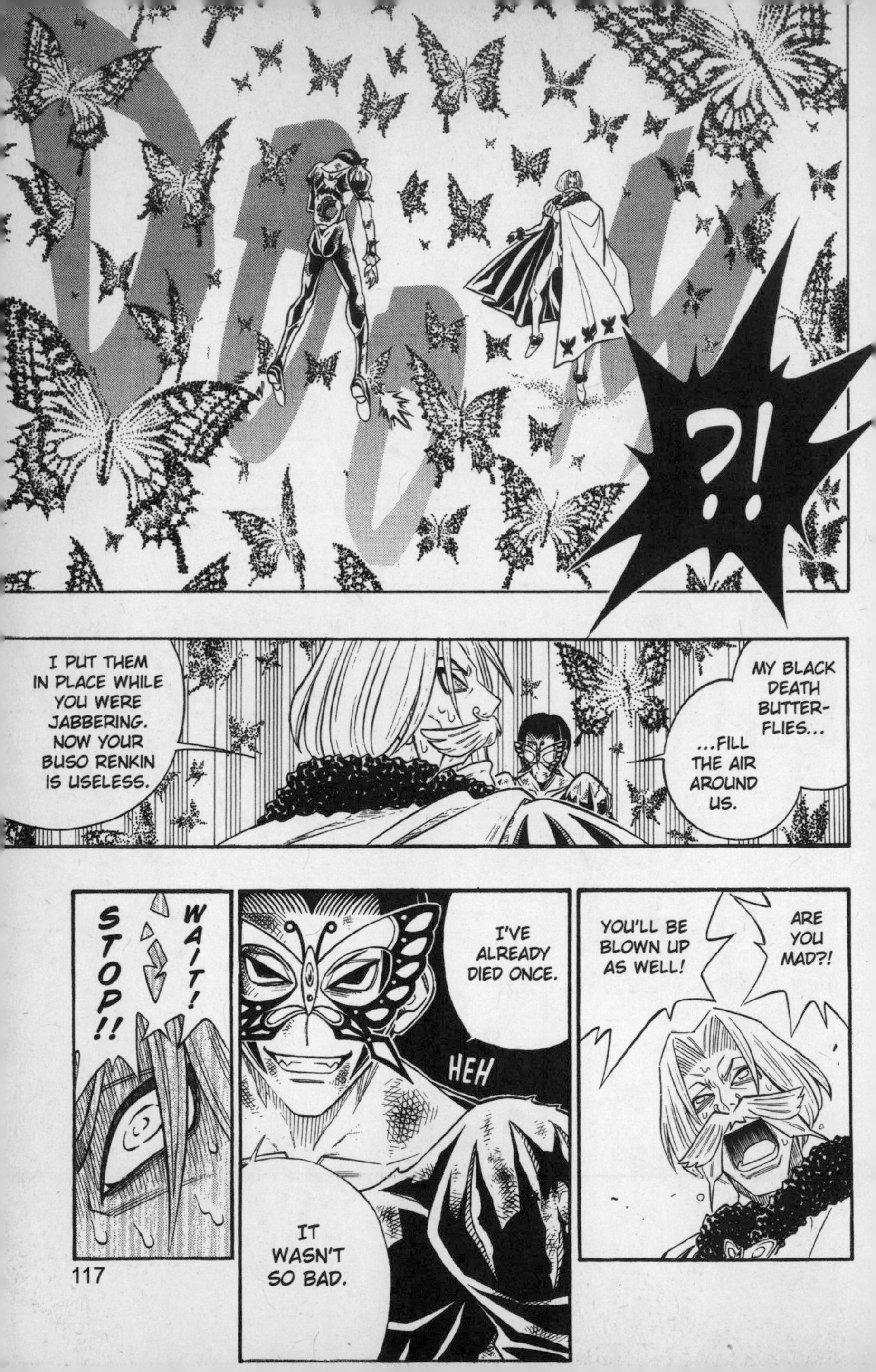
?!
MY BLACK DEATH BUTTER-FLIES...
...FILL THE AIR AROUND US.
I PUT THEM IN PLACE WHILE YOU WERE JABBERING. NOW YOUR BUSO RENKIN IS USELESS.
ARE YOU MAD?!
YOU'LL BE BLOWN UP AS WELL!
I'VE ALREADY DIED ONCE.
HEH
IT WASN'T SO BAD.
WAIT!
STOP!!

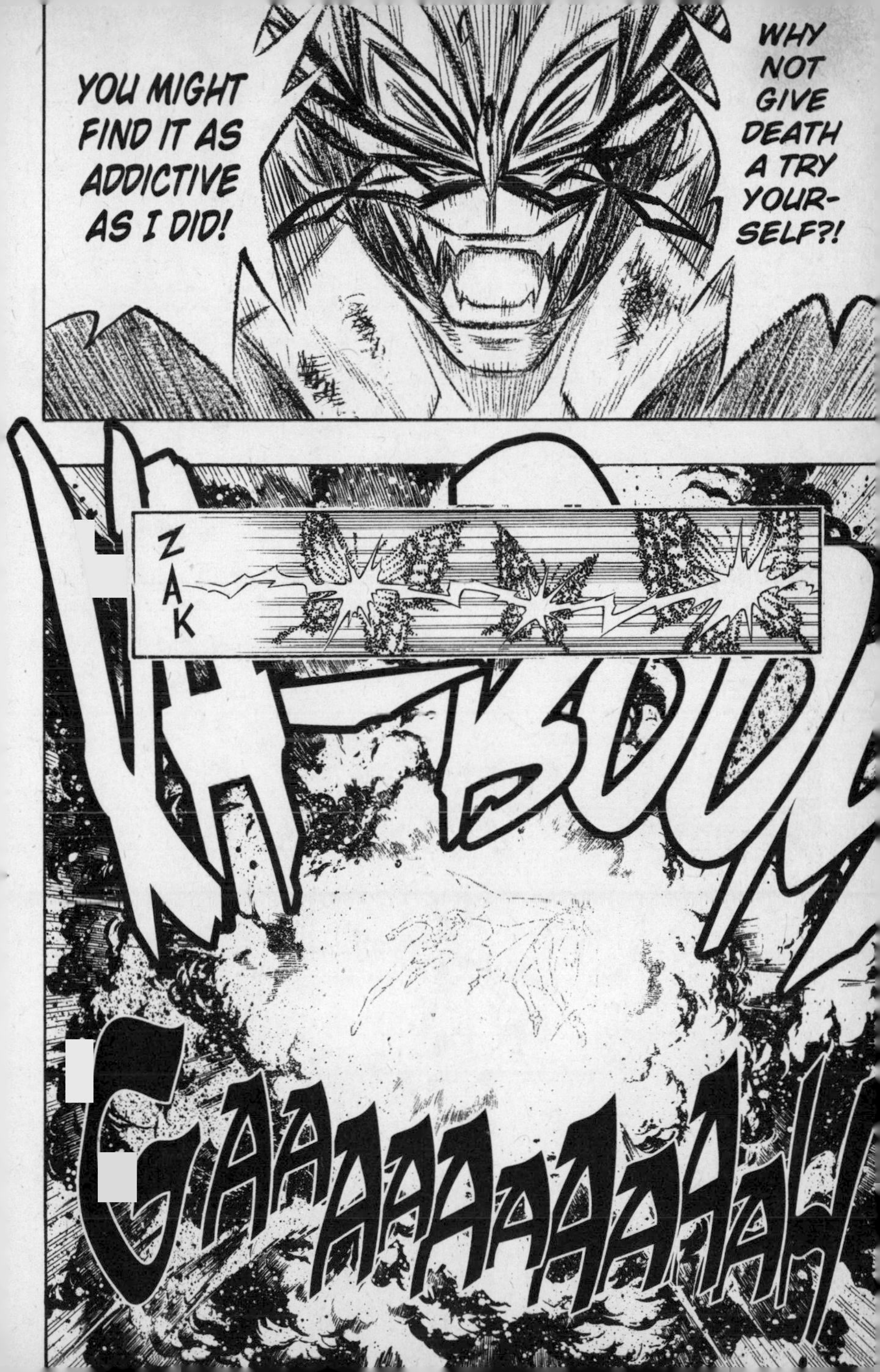
WHY NOT GIVE DEATH A TRY YOUR-SELF?!
YOU MIGHT FIND IT AS ADDICTIVE AS I DID!
ZAK
GAAAAAAAAAAH!

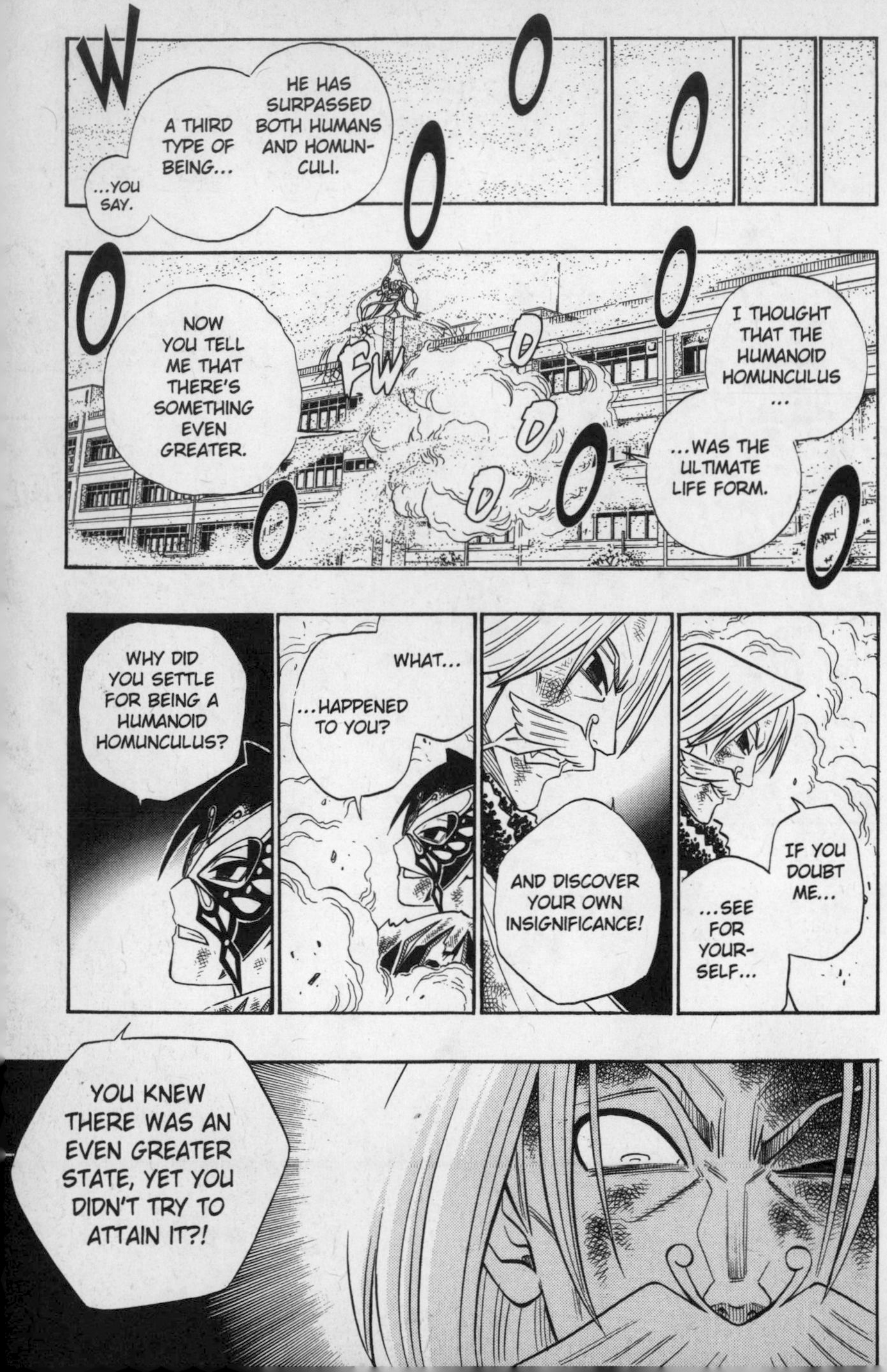
WOOOOOOOO
HE HAS SURPASSED BOTH HUMANS AND HOMUN-CULI.
A THIRD TYPE OF BEING...
...YOU SAY.
I THOUGHT THAT THE HUMANOID HOMUNCULUS...
...WAS THE ULTIMATE LIFE FORM.
FWDDD
NOW YOU TELL ME THAT THERE'S SOMETHING EVEN GREATER.
IF YOU DOUBT ME...
...SEE FOR YOUR-SELF...
AND DISCOVER YOUR OWN INSIGNIFICANCE!
WHAT...
...HAPPENED TO YOU?
WHY DID YOU SETTLE FOR BEING A HUMANOID HOMUNCULUS?
YOU KNEW THERE WAS AN EVEN GREATER STATE, YET YOU DIDN'T TRY TO ATTAIN IT?!

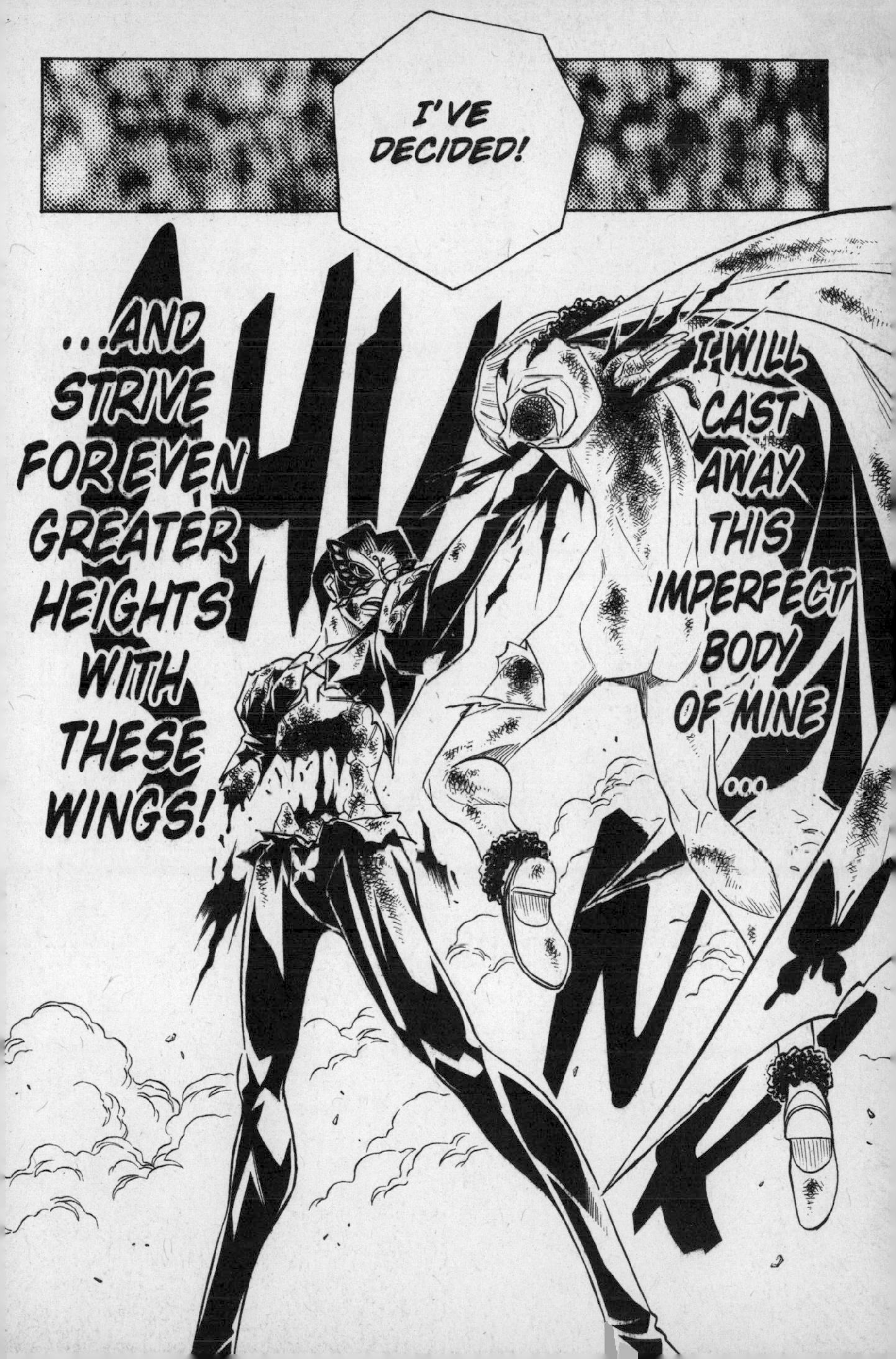
I'VE DECIDED!
I WILL CAST AWAY THIS IMPERFECT BODY OF MINE...
...AND STRIVE FOR EVEN GREATER HEIGHTS WITH THESE WINGS!

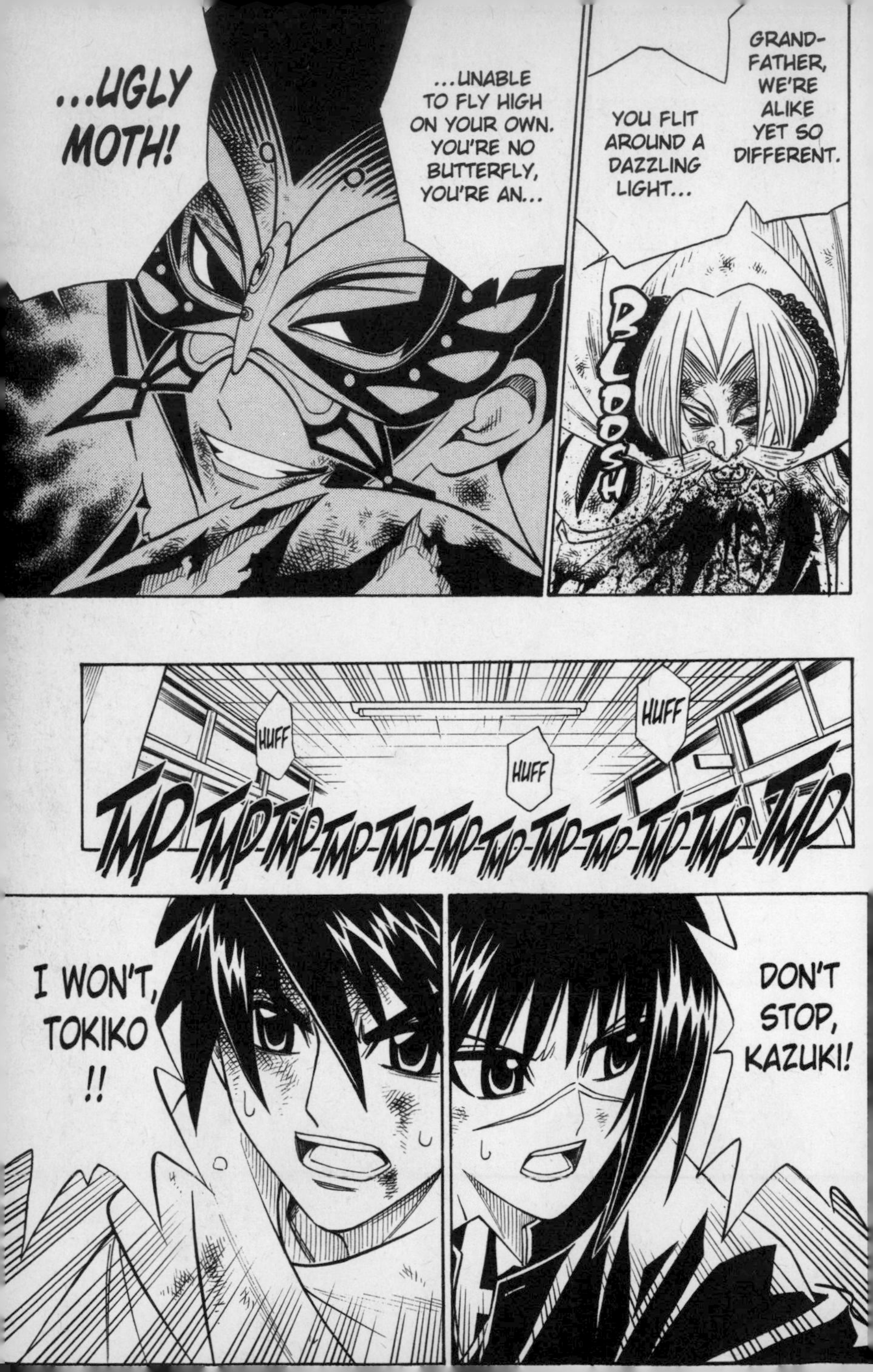
GRAND-FATHER, WE'RE ALIKE YET SO DIFFERENT.
YOU FLIT AROUND A DAZZLING LIGHT...
BLOOSH
...UNABLE TO FLY HIGH ON YOUR OWN. YOU'RE NO BUTTERFLY, YOU'RE AN...
...UGLY MOTH!
HUFF
HUFF
HUFF
TMP TMP-TMP-TMP-TMP-TMP-TMP-TMP-TMP-TMP-TMP TMP
DON'T STOP, KAZUKI!
I WON'T, TOKIKO !!

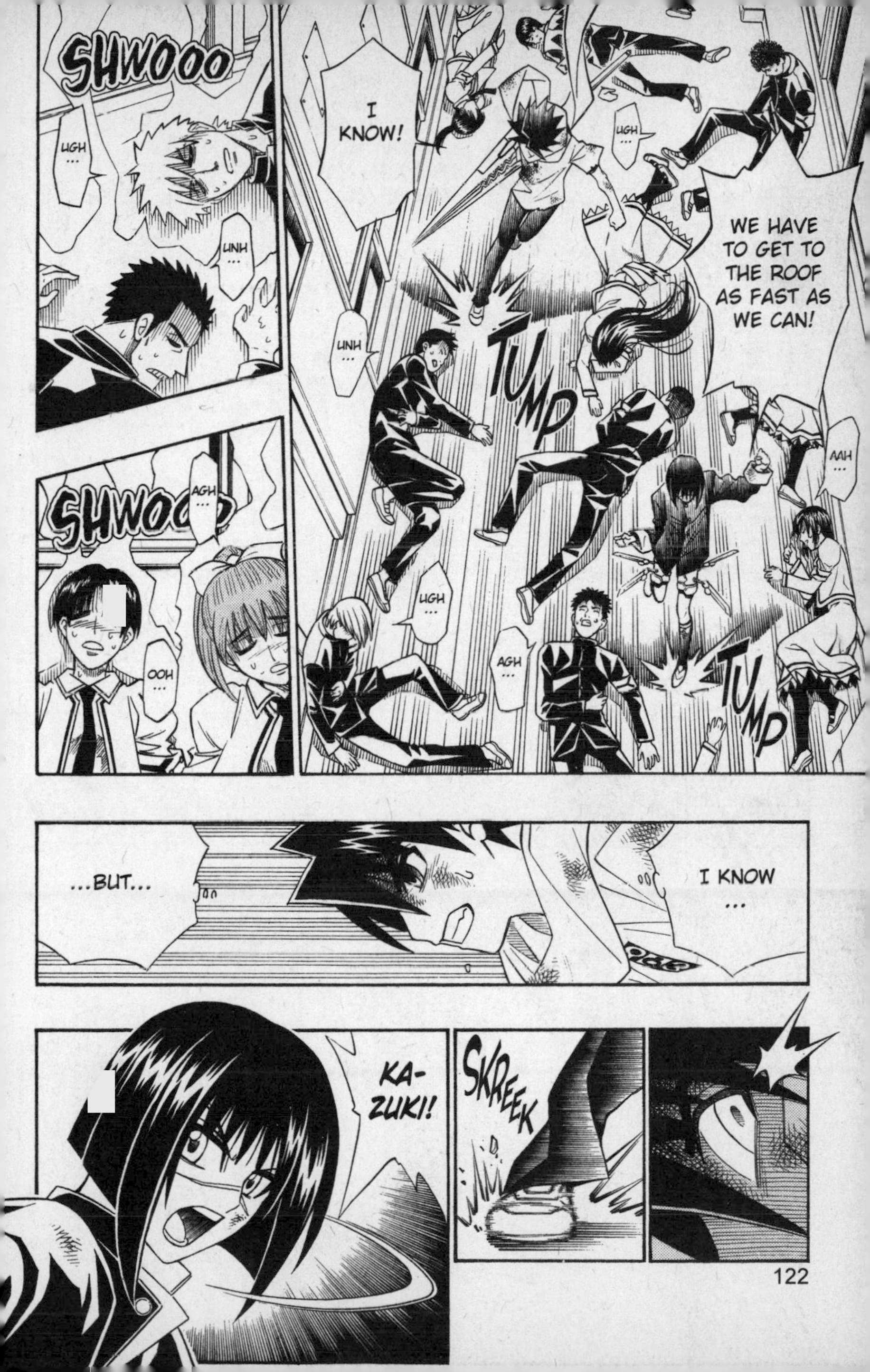
WE HAVE TO GET TO THE ROOF AS FAST AS WE CAN!
UGH ...
I KNOW!
AAH ...
TUMP
TUMP
UNH ...
AGH ...
UGH ...
SHWOOO
UGH ...
UNH ...
SHWOOO
AGH
OOH ...
I KNOW ...
...BUT...
SKREEK
KA-ZUKI!

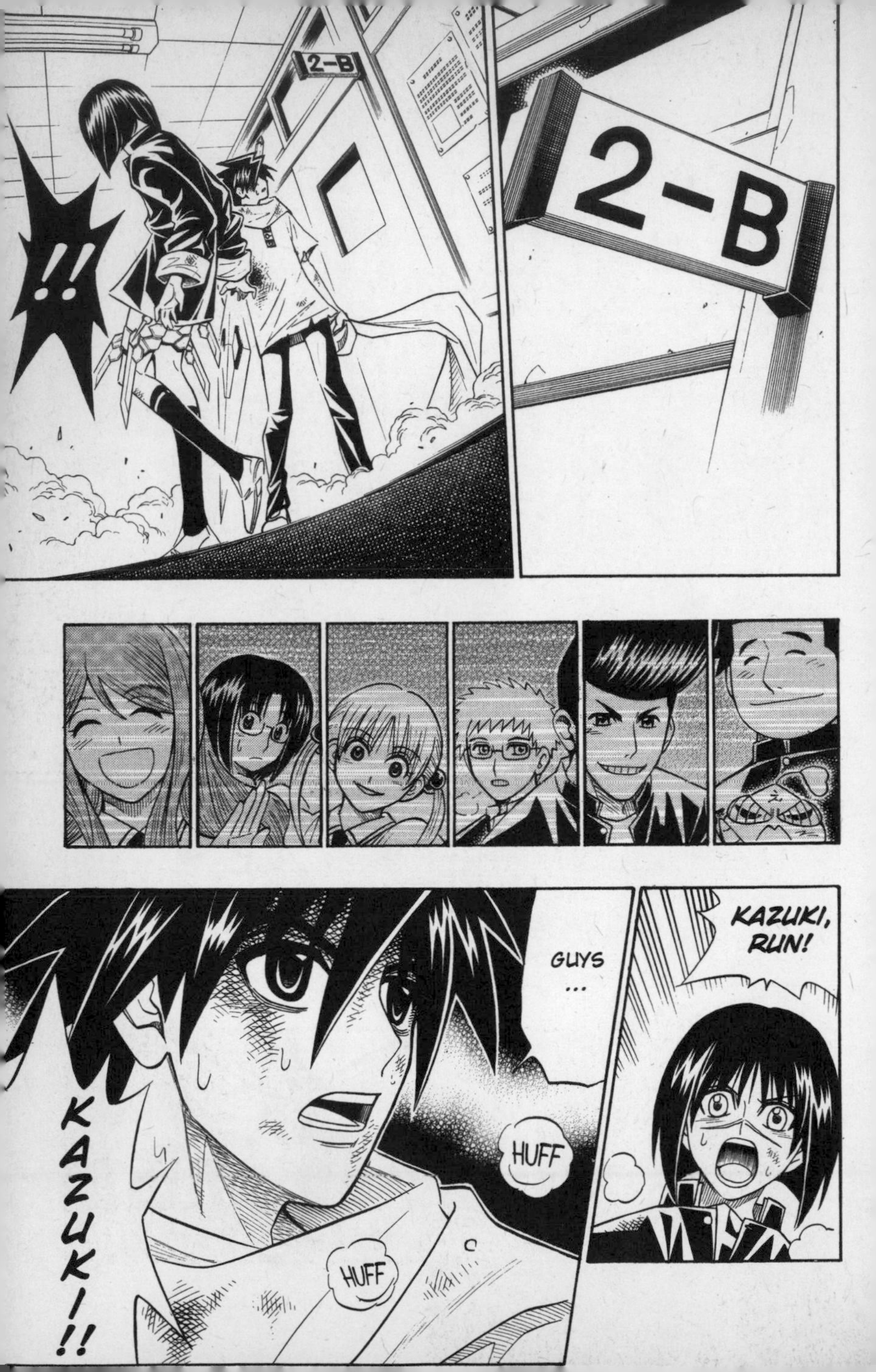
2-B
2-B
!!
KAZUKI, RUN!
GUYS ...
HUFF
HUFF
KAZUKI!!

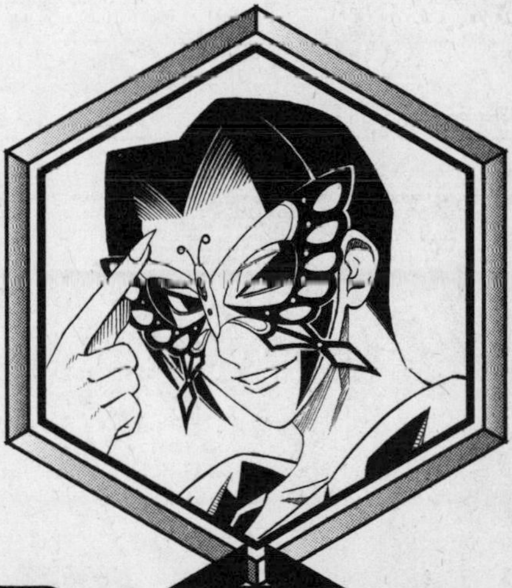

Buso Renkin

ブソウレンキン

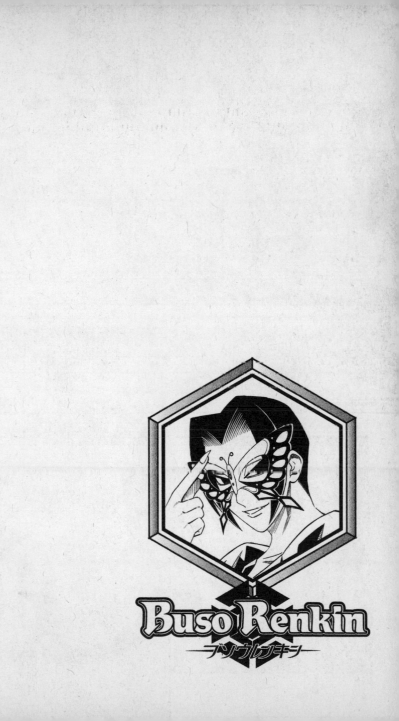

CHAPTER 43:
WHO ARE YOU?

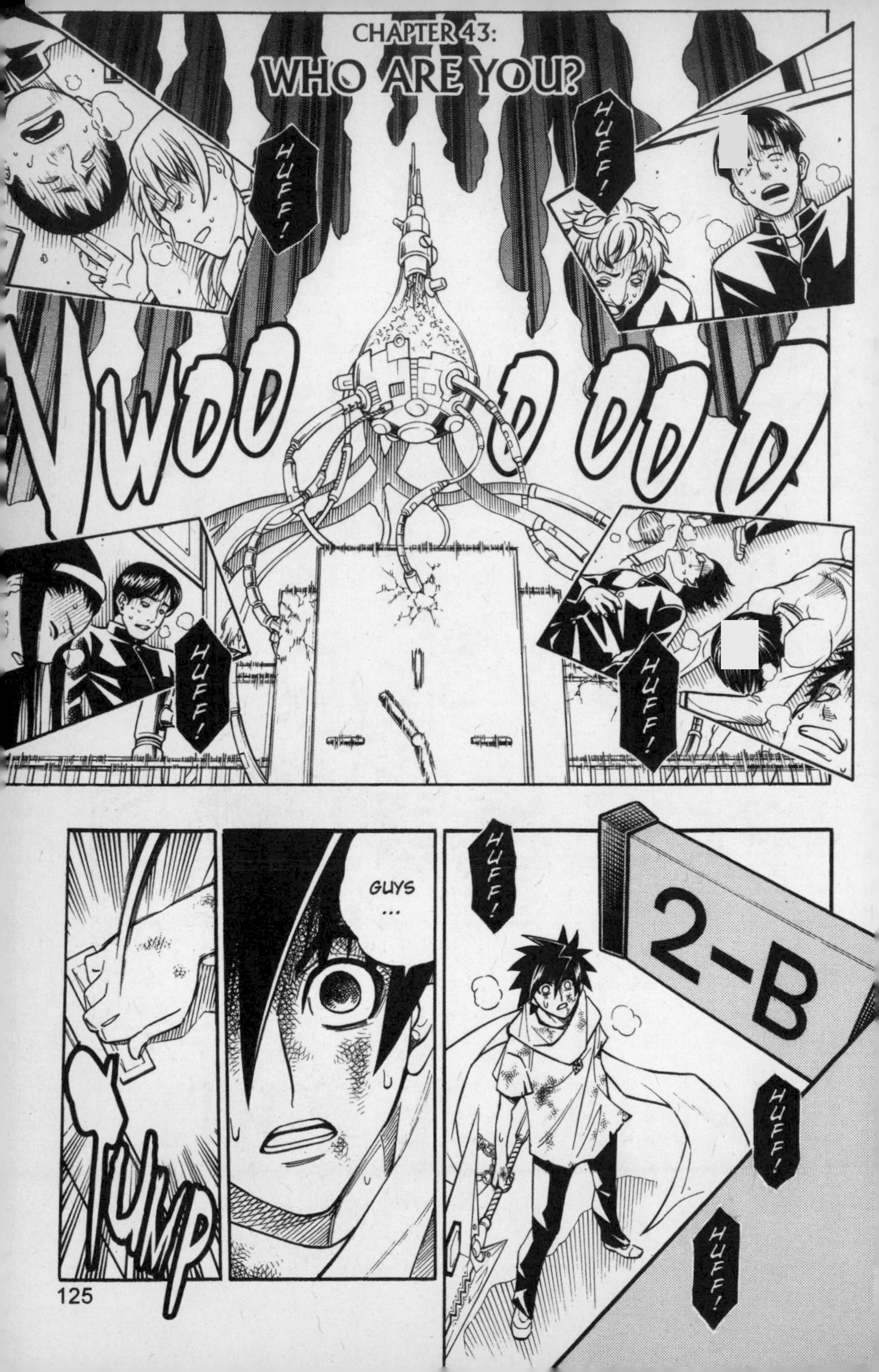
HUFF!
HUFF!
VWOOOOOOOOO
HUFF!
HUFF!
HUFF!
HUFF!
HUFF!
GUYS...
TUMP

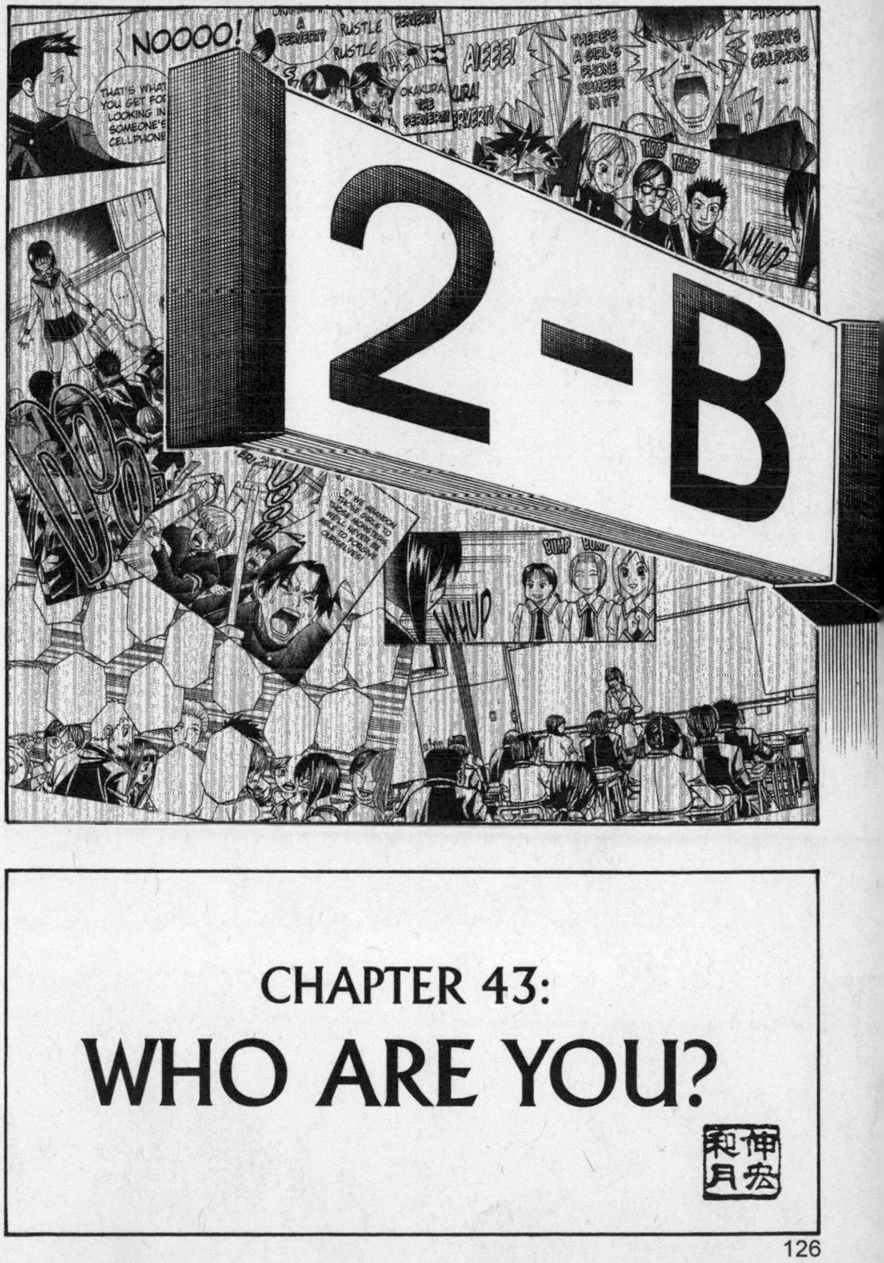
KAZUKI'S CELLPHONE ...
THERE'S A GIRL'S PHONE NUMBER IN IT?
AIEEE!
THROB THROB
WHUP
OKAKURA THE PERVERT!!
RUSTLE RUSTLE
A PERVERT?
NOOOO!
THAT'S WHAT YOU GET FOR LOOKING IN SOMEONE'S CELLPHONE
2-B
BUMP BUMP
WHUP
IF WE ABANDON THOSE GIRLS TO THOSE MONSTERS, WE'LL NEVER BE ABLE TO FORGIVE OURSELVES!

CHAPTER 43:
WHO ARE YOU?

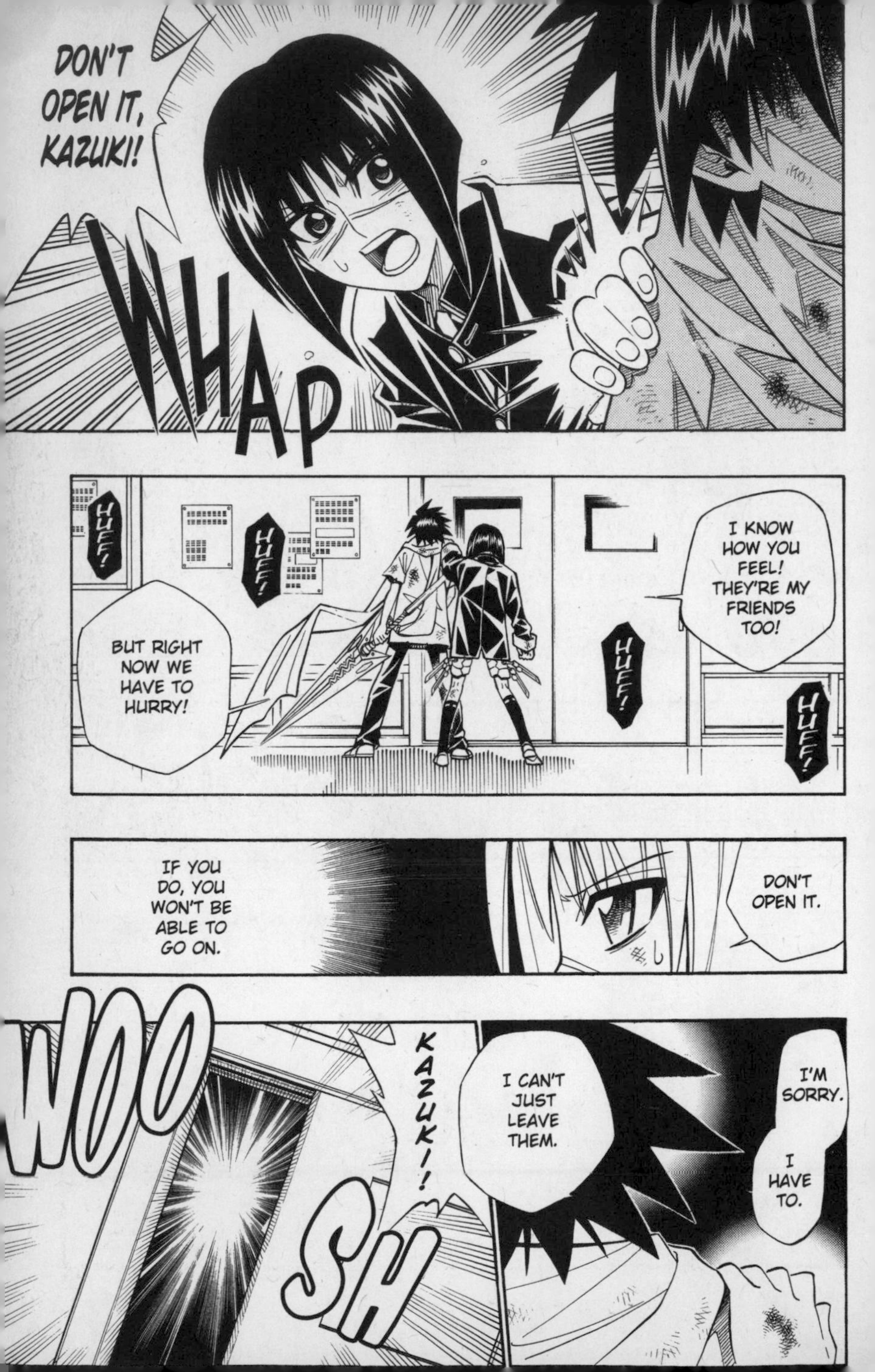
DON'T OPEN IT, KAZUKI!
WHAP
I KNOW HOW YOU FEEL! THEY'RE MY FRIENDS TOO!
HUFF!
HUFF!
HUFF!
HUFF!
BUT RIGHT NOW WE HAVE TO HURRY!
DON'T OPEN IT.
IF YOU DO, YOU WON'T BE ABLE TO GO ON.
I'M SORRY.
I HAVE TO.
I CAN'T JUST LEAVE THEM.
KAZUKI!!
WOO
SH

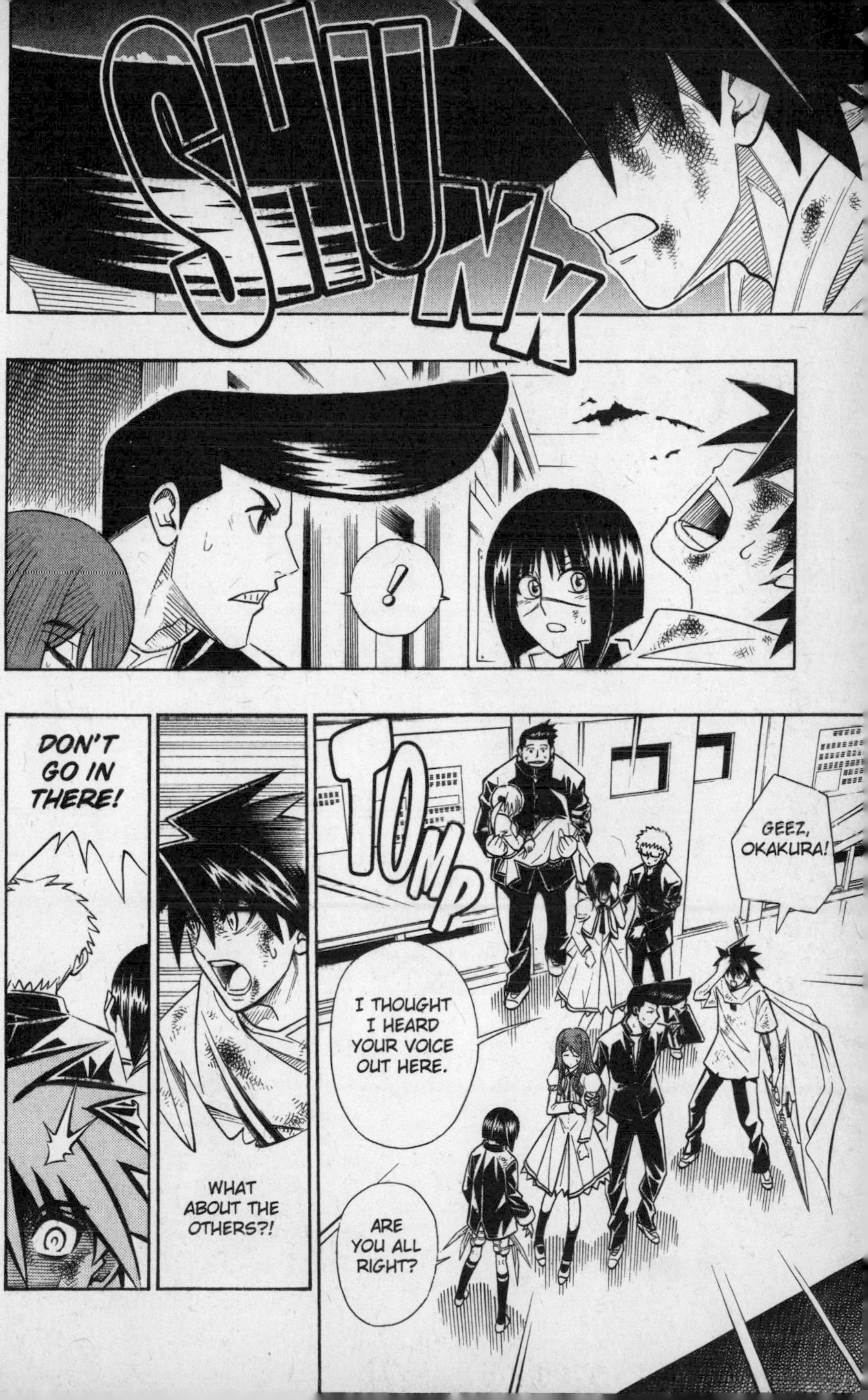
SHUNK
!
GEEZ, OKAKURA!
TOMP
I THOUGHT I HEARD YOUR VOICE OUT HERE.
ARE YOU ALL RIGHT?
WHAT ABOUT THE OTHERS?!
DON'T GO IN THERE!

READ THIS WAY

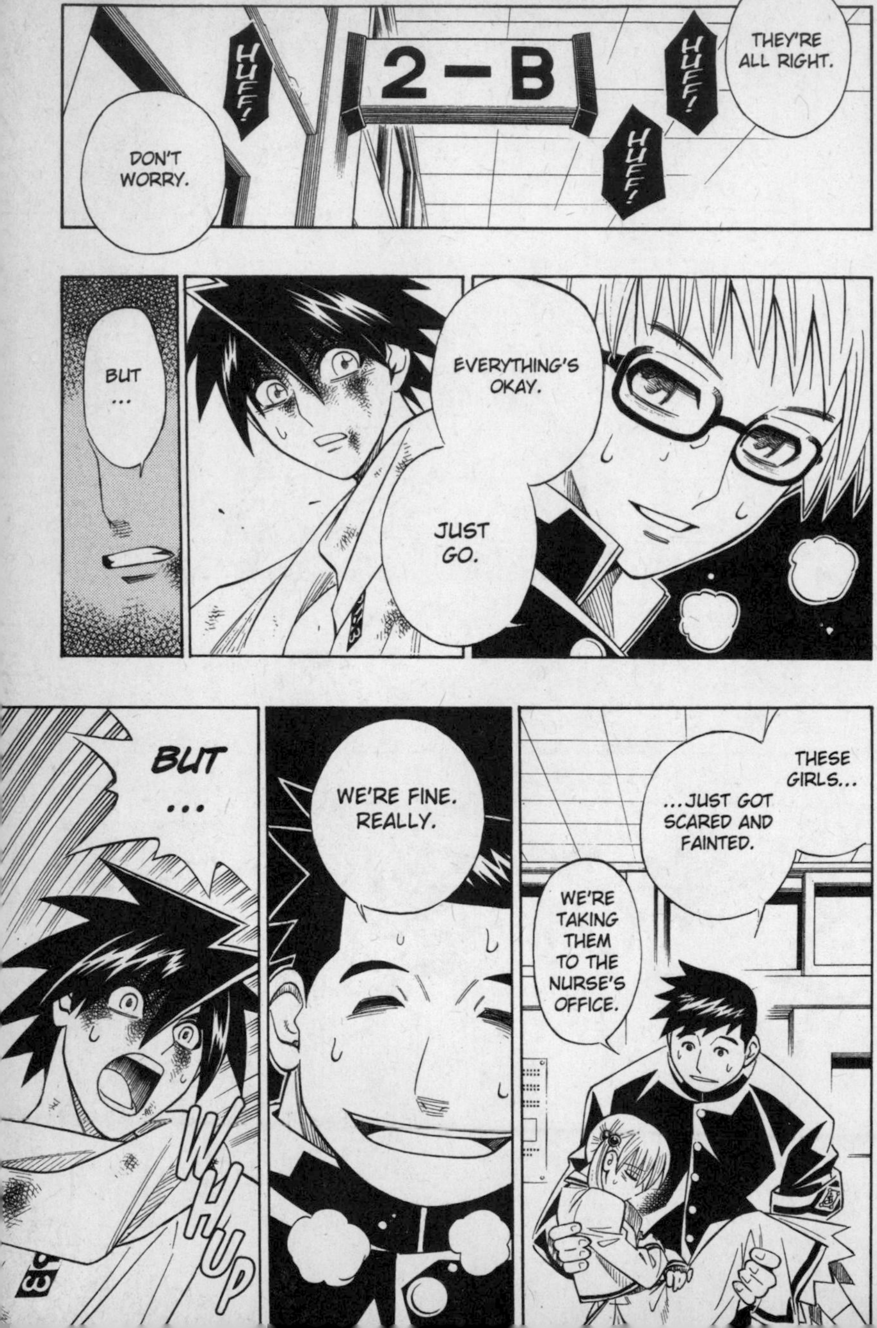

THEY'RE ALL RIGHT.
HUFF!
HUFF!
2-B
HUFF!
DON'T WORRY.
EVERYTHING'S OKAY.
JUST GO.
BUT ...
THESE GIRLS...
...JUST GOT SCARED AND FAINTED.
WE'RE TAKING THEM TO THE NURSE'S OFFICE.
WE'RE FINE. REALLY.
BUT ...
WHUP

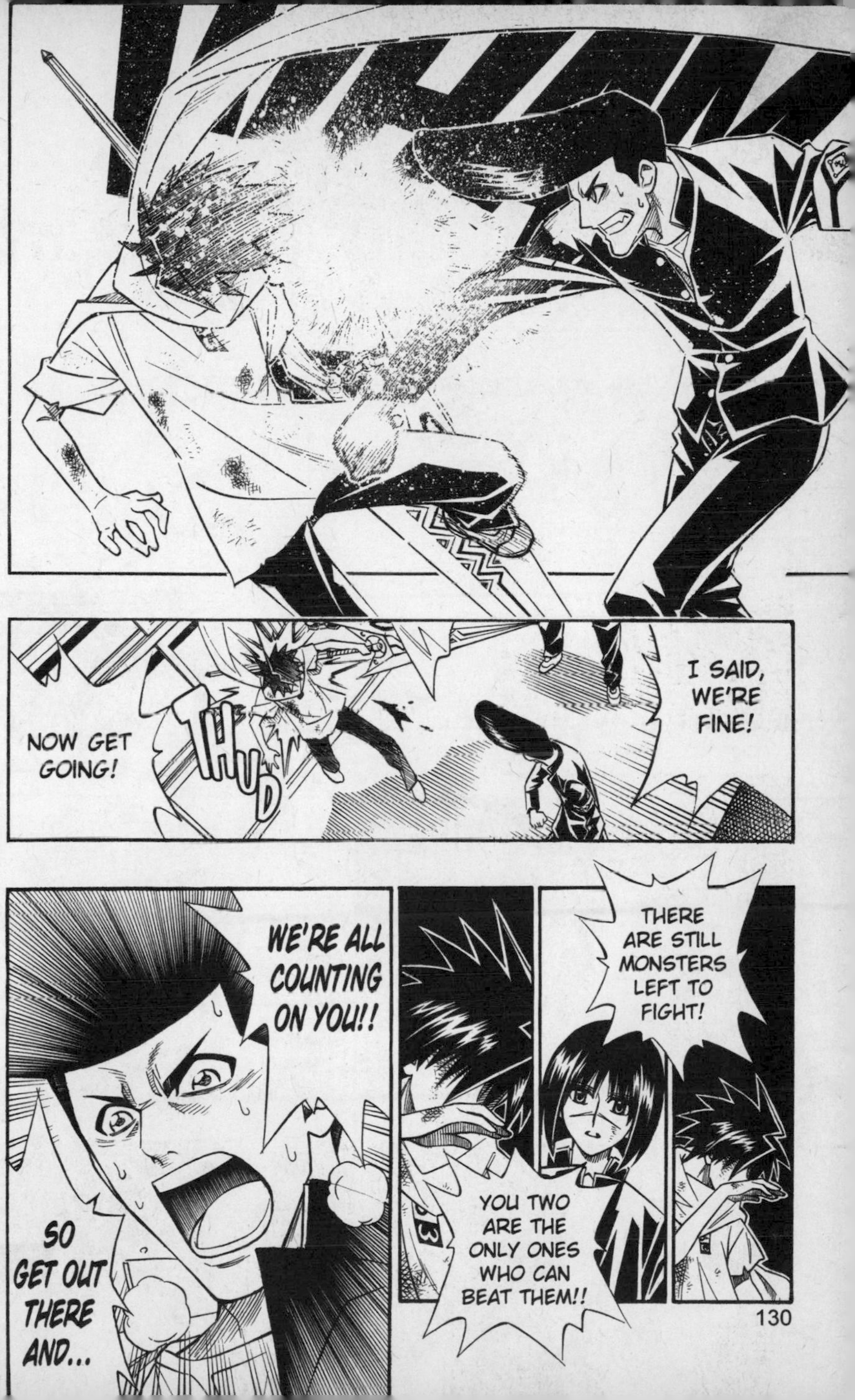
I SAID, WE'RE FINE!
THUD
NOW GET GOING!
THERE ARE STILL MONSTERS LEFT TO FIGHT!
YOU TWO ARE THE ONLY ONES WHO CAN BEAT THEM!!
WE'RE ALL COUNTING ON YOU!!
SO GET OUT THERE AND...

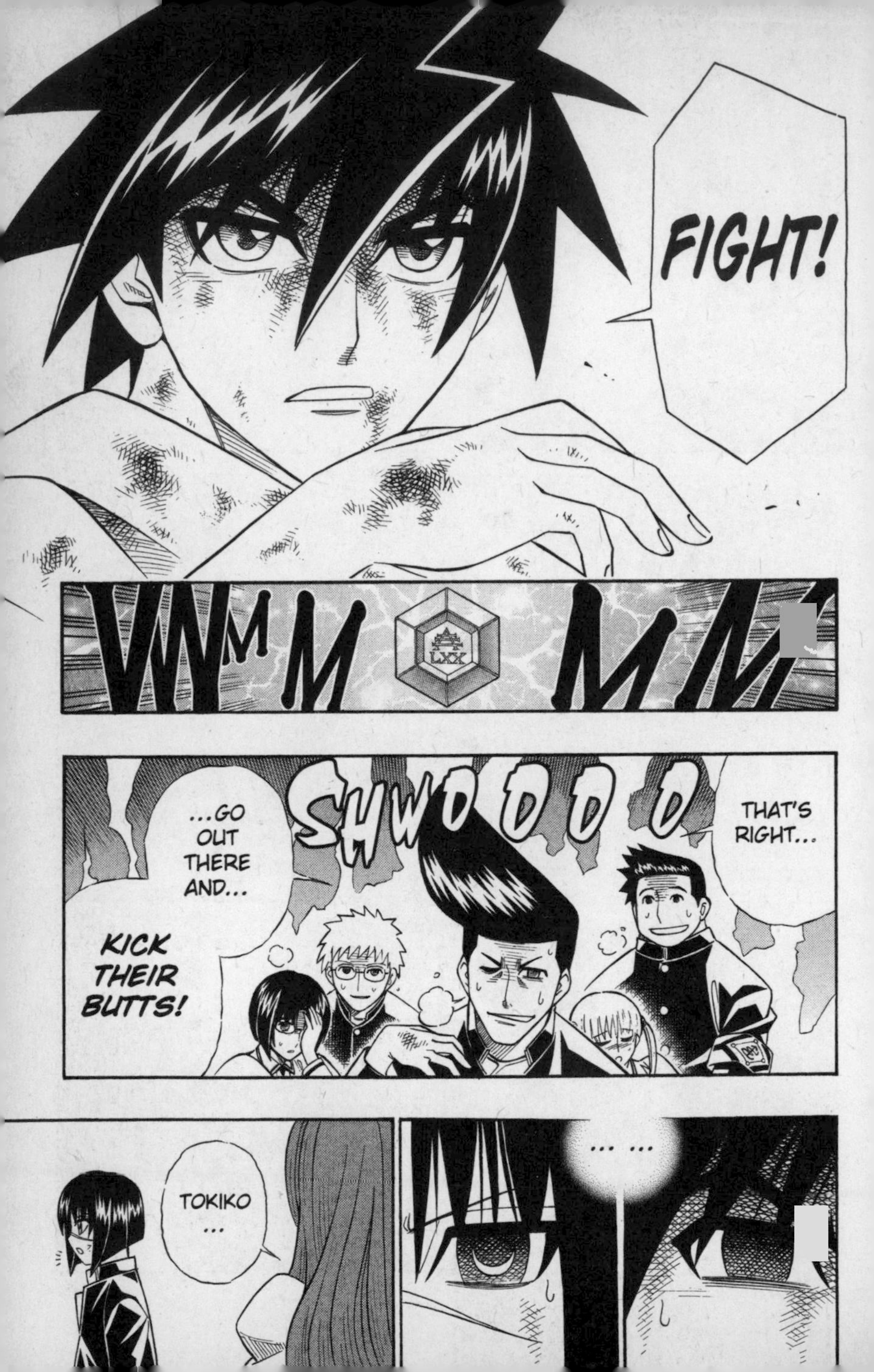
FIGHT!
VMMMMMM
THAT'S RIGHT...
SHWOOOO
...GO OUT THERE AND...
KICK THEIR BUTTS!
... ...
TOKIKO ...

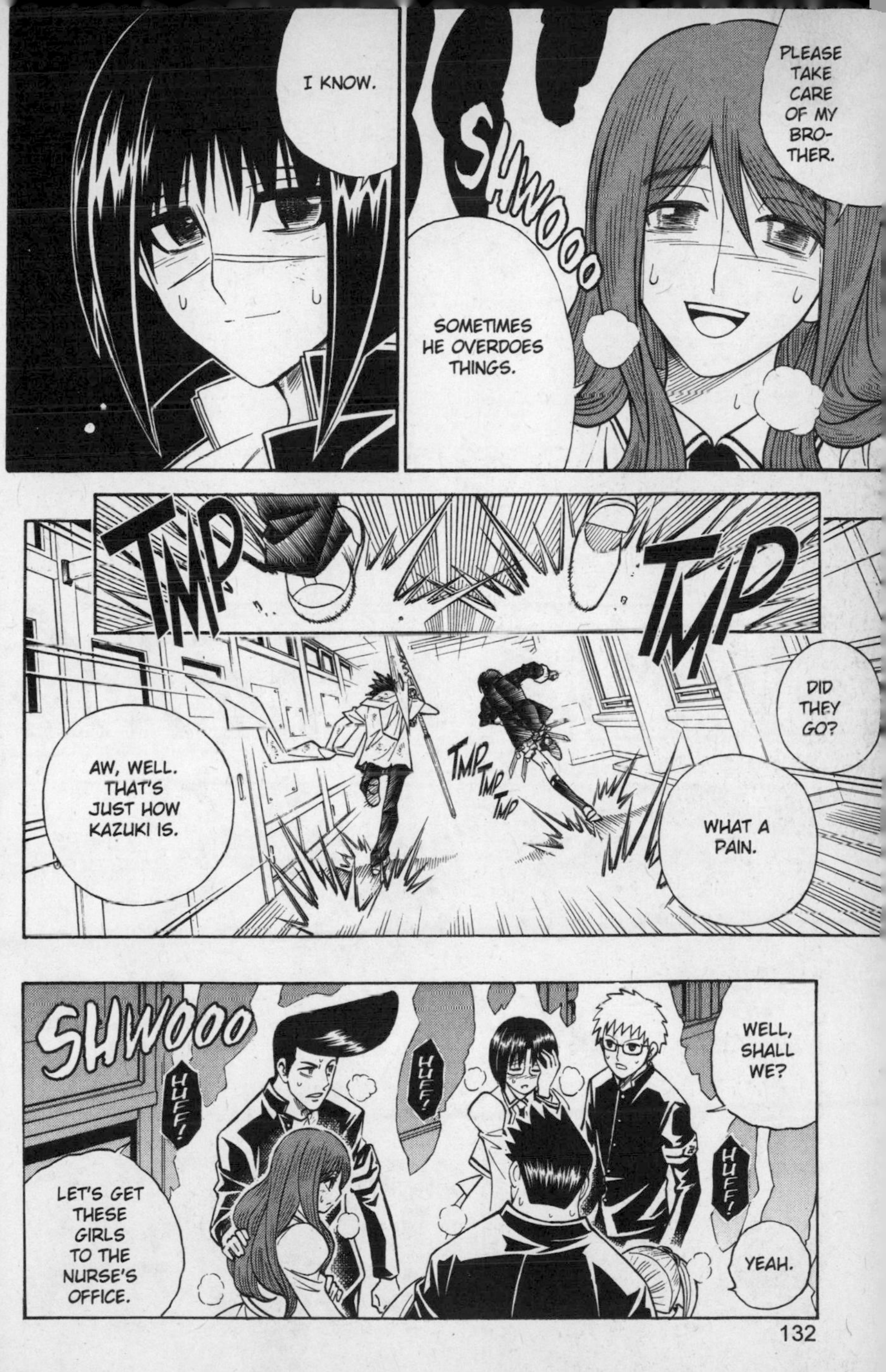
PLEASE TAKE CARE OF MY BRO-THER.
SHWOOOO
SOMETIMES HE OVERDOES THINGS.
I KNOW.
TMP
TMP
DID THEY GO?
WHAT A PAIN.
TMP TMP TMP
AW, WELL. THAT'S JUST HOW KAZUKI IS.
WELL, SHALL WE?
HUFF!
YEAH.
HUFF!
HUFF!
LET'S GET THESE GIRLS TO THE NURSE'S OFFICE.
SHWOOO

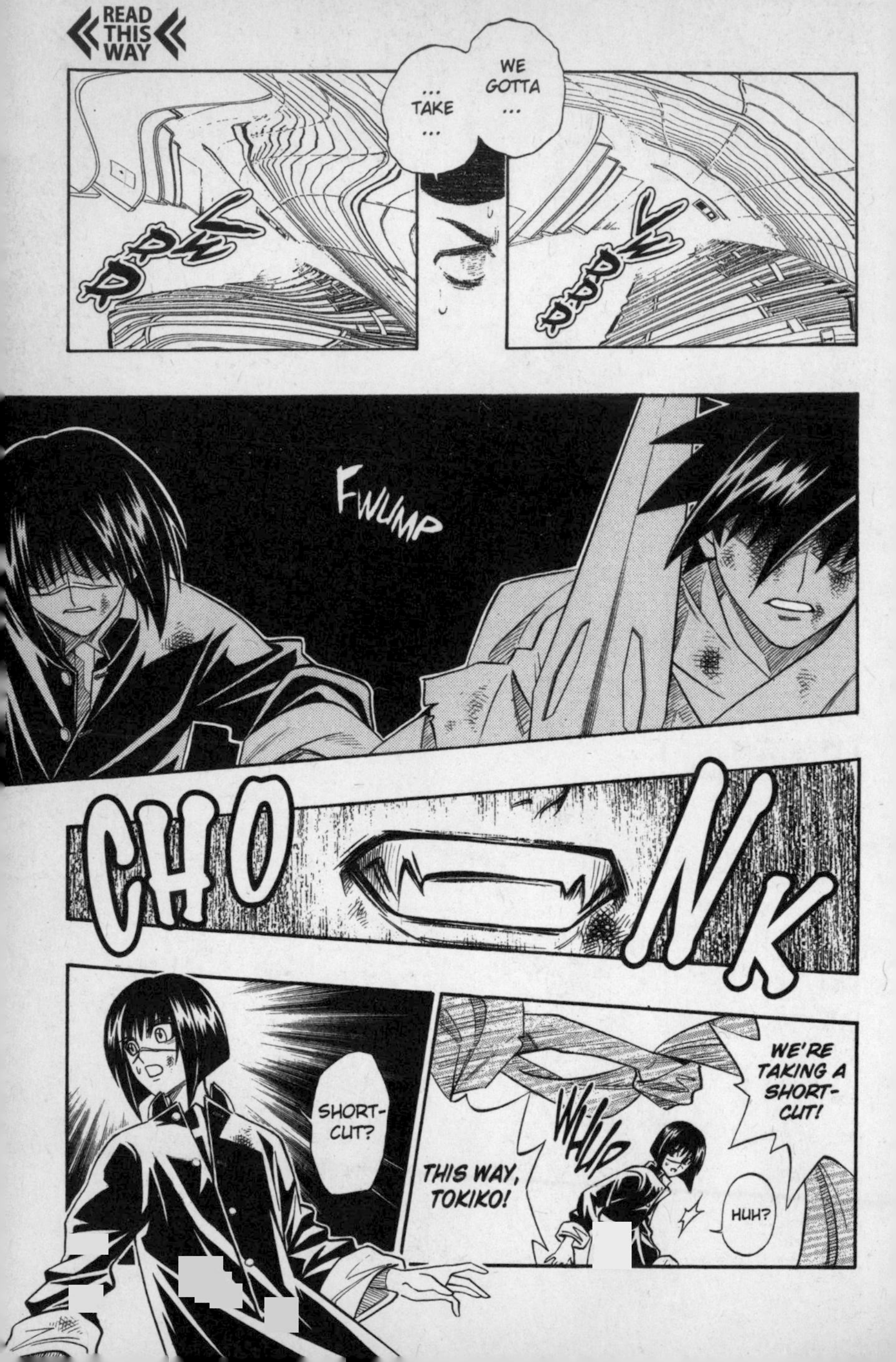
READ THIS WAY
WE GOTTA ...
... TAKE ...
FWUMP
CHONK
WE'RE TAKING A SHORT-CUT!
WHUP
THIS WAY, TOKIKO!
HUH?
SHORT-CUT?

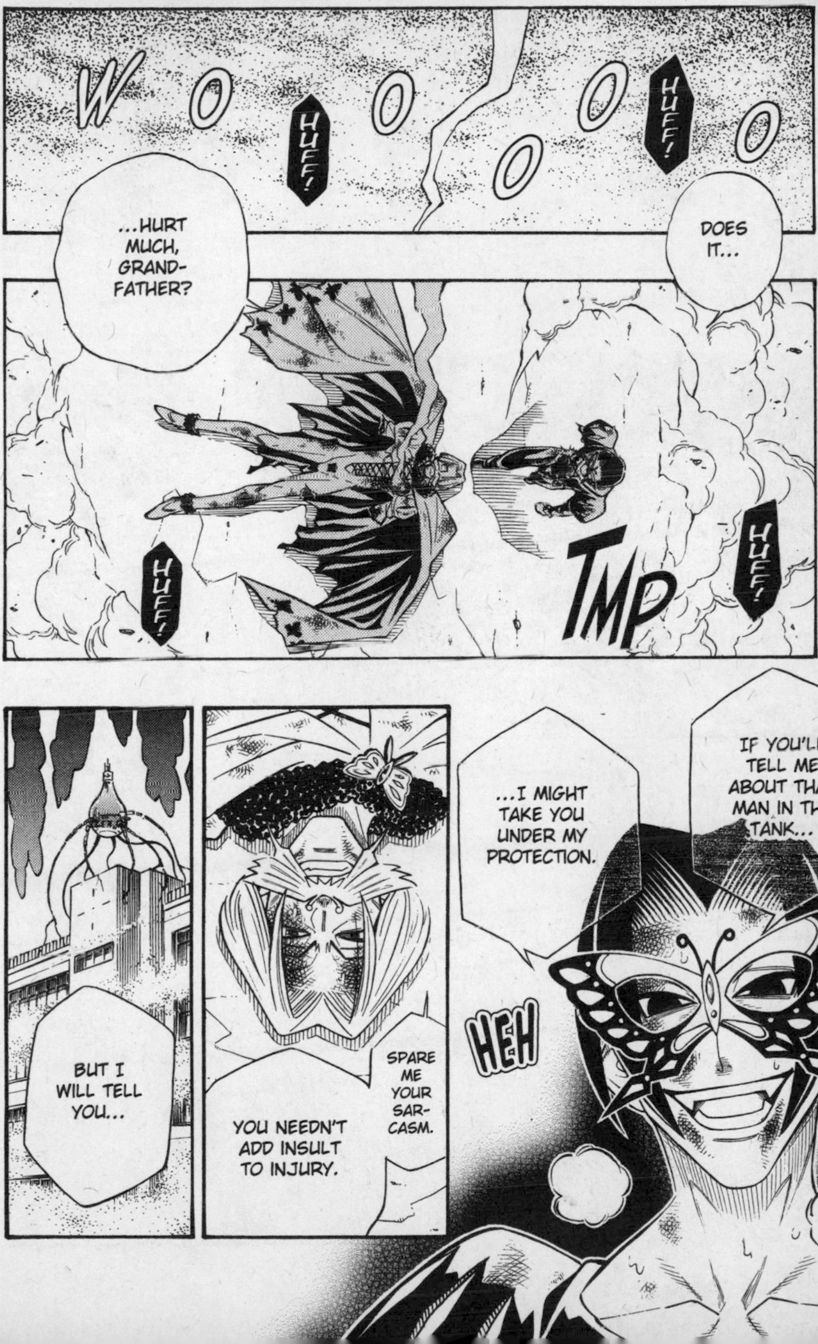
WOOOOOO
HUFF!
HUFF!
DOES IT...
...HURT MUCH, GRANDFATHER?
HUFF!
TMP
HUFF!
IF YOU'LL TELL ME ABOUT THAT MAN IN THE TANK...
...I MIGHT TAKE YOU UNDER MY PROTECTION.
HEH
SPARE ME YOUR SARCASM.
YOU NEEDN'T ADD INSULT TO INJURY.
BUT I WILL TELL YOU...

READ THIS WAY

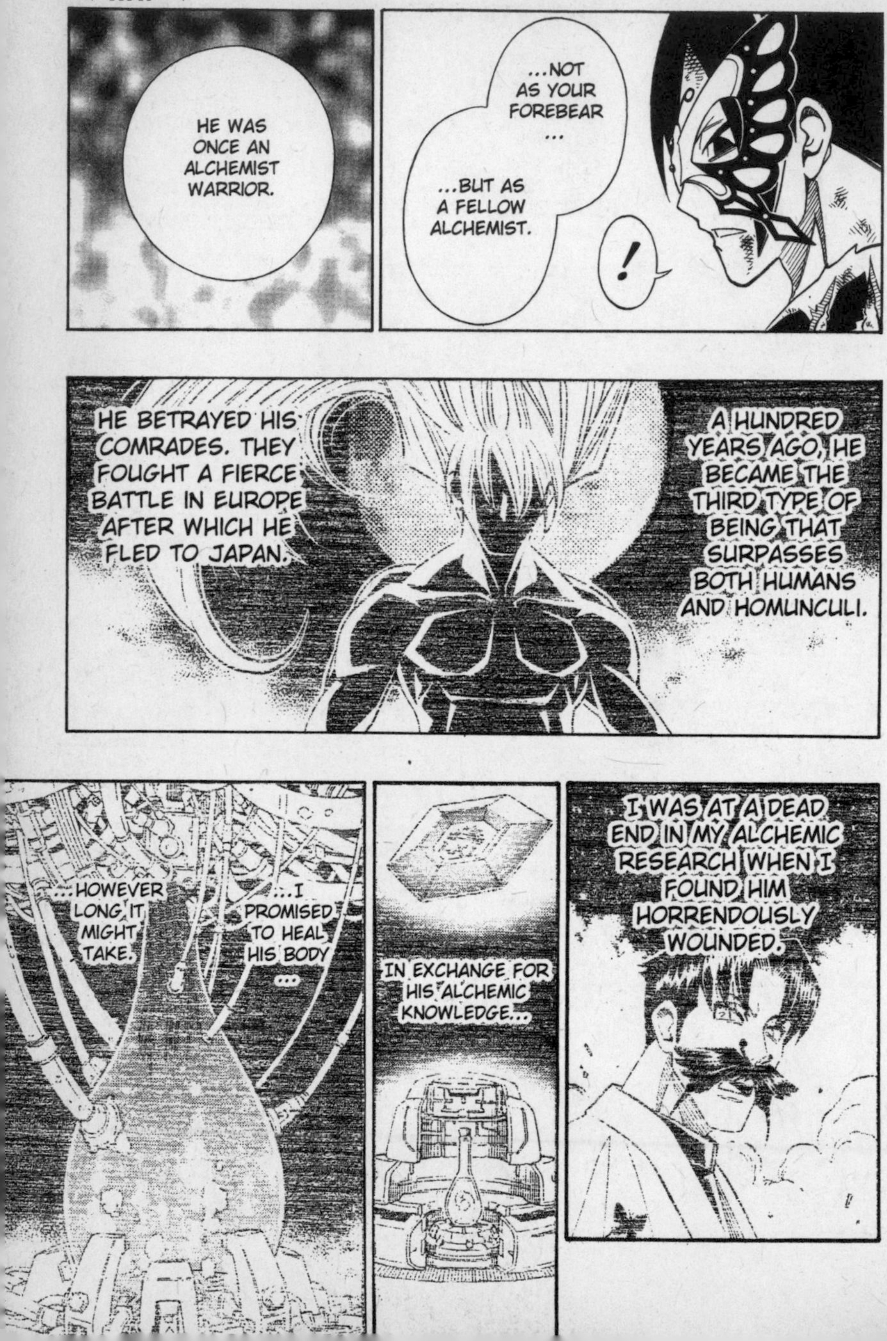
...NOT AS YOUR FOREBEAR ...
...BUT AS A FELLOW ALCHEMIST.
!
HE WAS ONCE AN ALCHEMIST WARRIOR.
A HUNDRED YEARS AGO, HE BECAME THE THIRD TYPE OF BEING THAT SURPASSES BOTH HUMANS AND HOMUNCULI.
HE BETRAYED HIS COMRADES. THEY FOUGHT A FIERCE BATTLE IN EUROPE AFTER WHICH HE FLED TO JAPAN.
I WAS AT A DEAD END IN MY ALCHEMIC RESEARCH WHEN I FOUND HIM HORRENDOUSLY WOUNDED.
IN EXCHANGE FOR HIS ALCHEMIC KNOWLEDGE...
...I PROMISED TO HEAL HIS BODY ...
...HOWEVER LONG IT MIGHT TAKE.

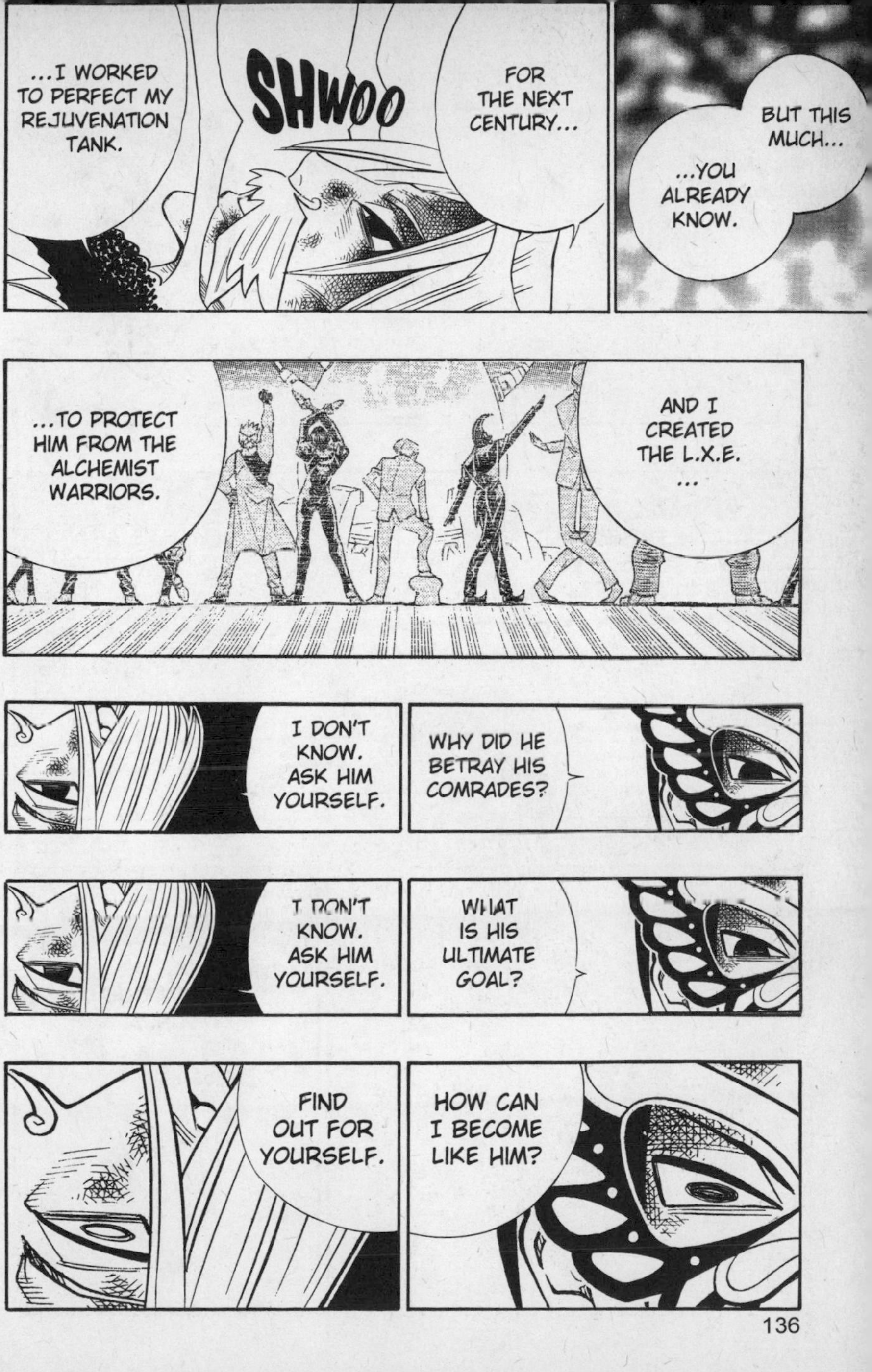
BUT THIS MUCH...
...YOU ALREADY KNOW.
FOR THE NEXT CENTURY...
SHWOO
...I WORKED TO PERFECT MY REJUVENATION TANK.
AND I CREATED THE L.X.E. ...
...TO PROTECT HIM FROM THE ALCHEMIST WARRIORS.
WHY DID HE BETRAY HIS COMRADES?
I DON'T KNOW. ASK HIM YOURSELF.
WHAT IS HIS ULTIMATE GOAL?
I DON'T KNOW. ASK HIM YOURSELF.
HOW CAN I BECOME LIKE HIM?
FIND OUT FOR YOURSELF.

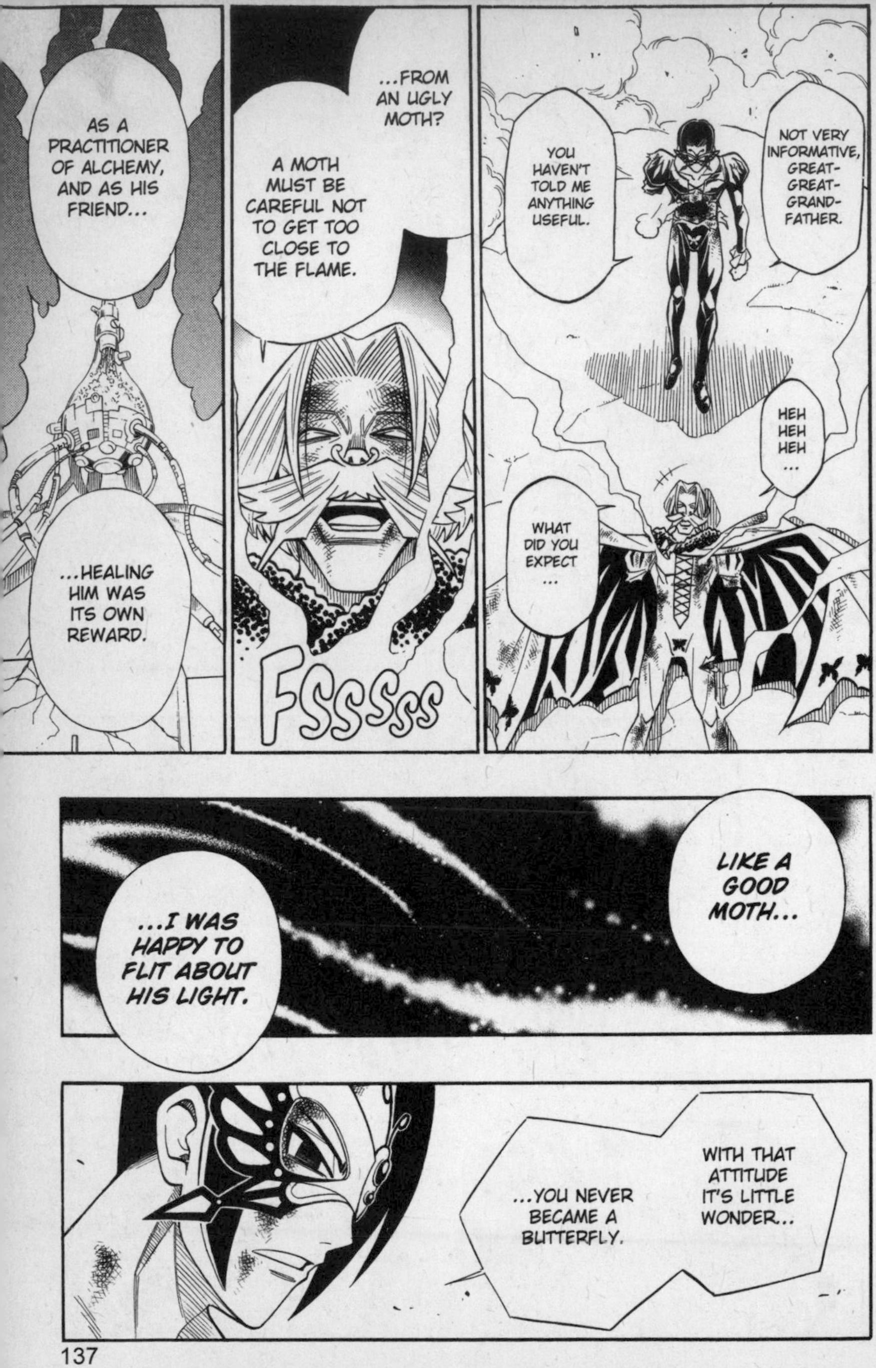
NOT VERY INFORMATIVE, GREAT-GREAT-GRANDFATHER.
YOU HAVEN'T TOLD ME ANYTHING USEFUL.
HEH HEH HEH ...
WHAT DID YOU EXPECT ...
...FROM AN UGLY MOTH?
A MOTH MUST BE CAREFUL NOT TO GET TOO CLOSE TO THE FLAME.
FSSSSS
AS A PRACTITIONER OF ALCHEMY, AND AS HIS FRIEND...
...HEALING HIM WAS ITS OWN REWARD.
LIKE A GOOD MOTH...
...I WAS HAPPY TO FLIT ABOUT HIS LIGHT.
WITH THAT ATTITUDE IT'S LITTLE WONDER...
...YOU NEVER BECAME A BUTTERFLY.

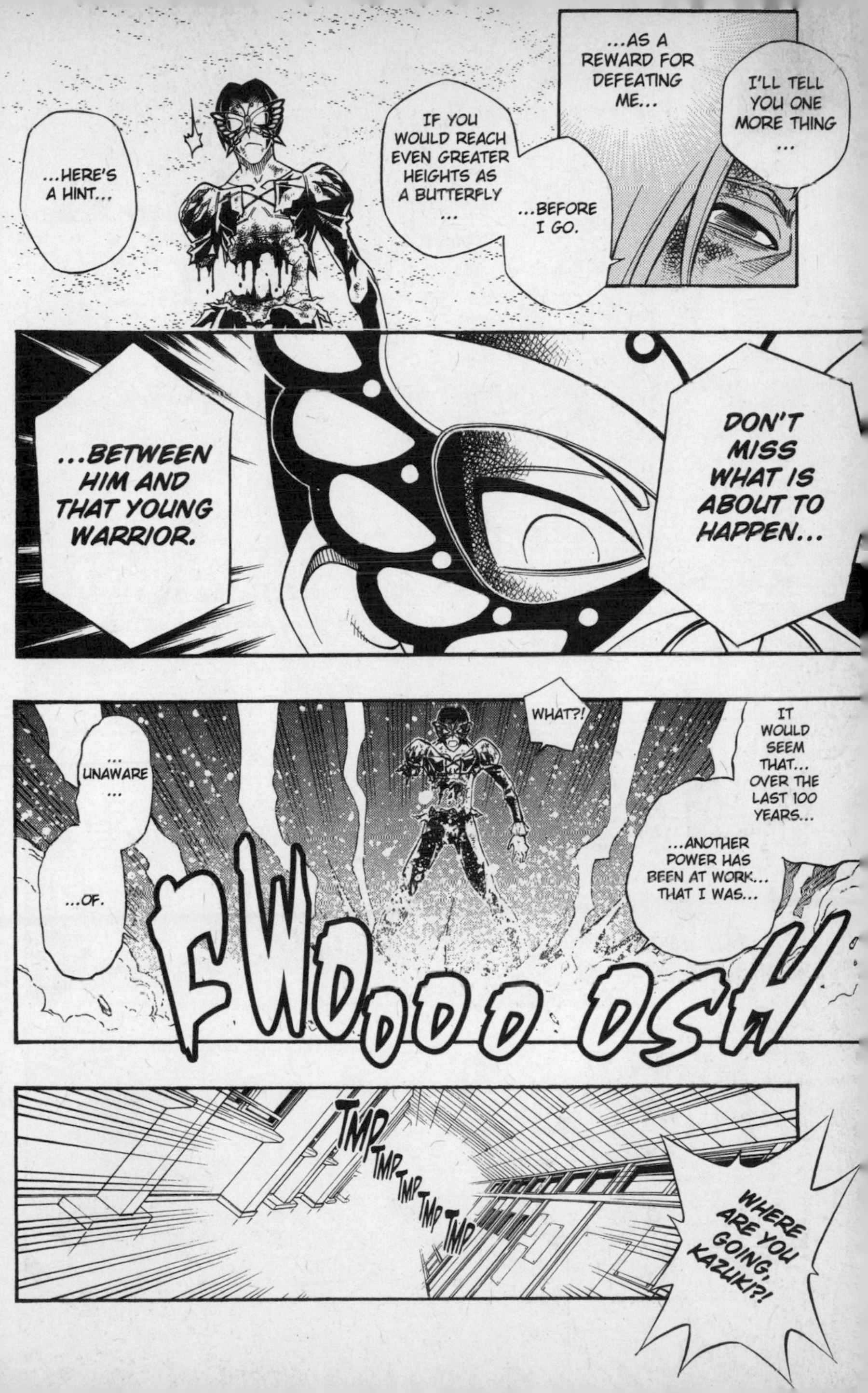

...AS A REWARD FOR DEFEATING ME...
I'LL TELL YOU ONE MORE THING...
...BEFORE I GO.
IF YOU WOULD REACH EVEN GREATER HEIGHTS AS A BUTTERFLY...
...HERE'S A HINT...
DON'T MISS WHAT IS ABOUT TO HAPPEN...
...BETWEEN HIM AND THAT YOUNG WARRIOR.
IT WOULD SEEM THAT... OVER THE LAST 100 YEARS...
...ANOTHER POWER HAS BEEN AT WORK... THAT I WAS...
WHAT?!
...UNAWARE...
...OF.
FWOOOOOSH
WHERE ARE YOU GOING, KAZUKI?!
TMP TMP TMP TMP TMP TMP

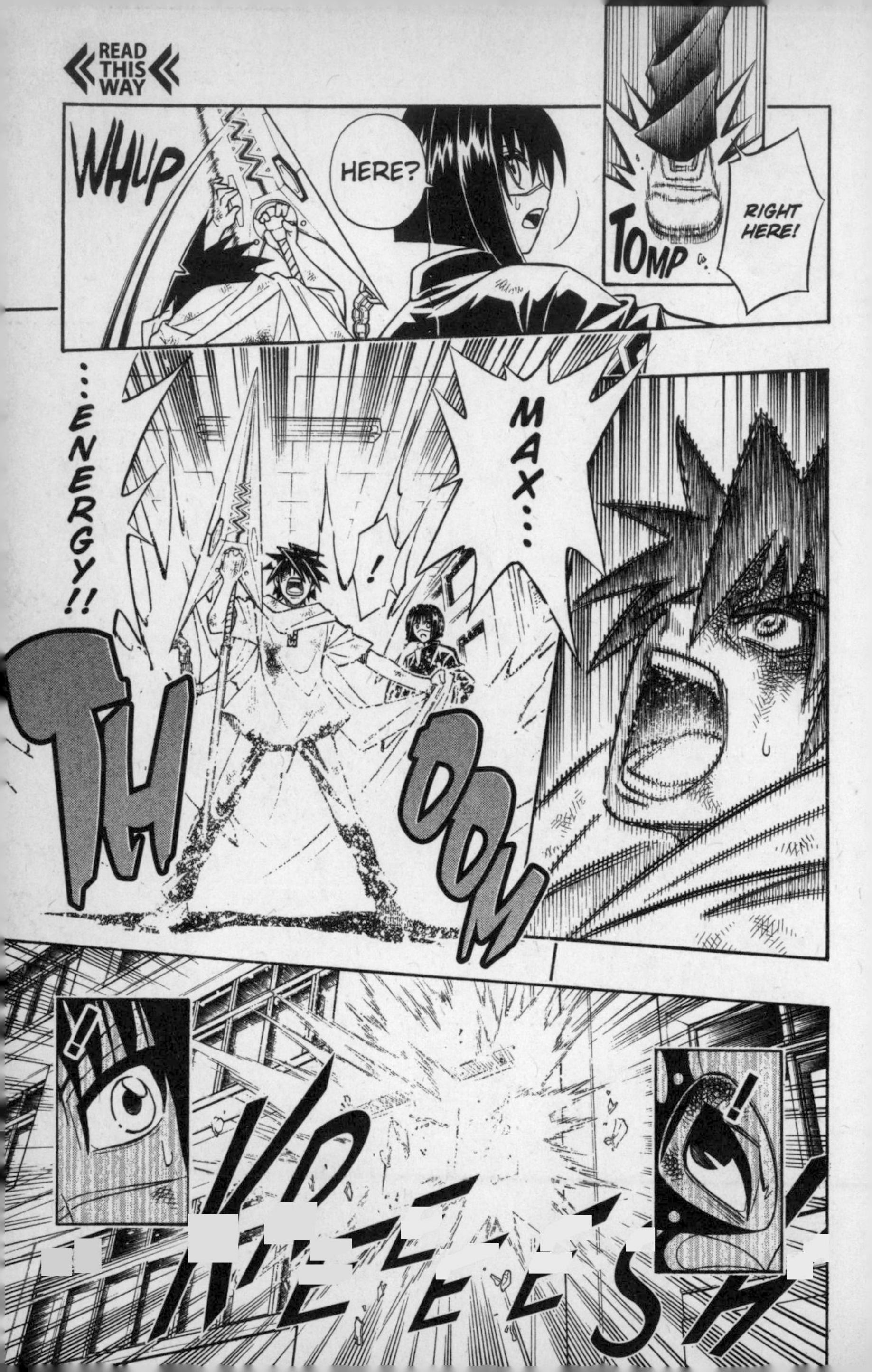
READ THIS WAY
RIGHT HERE!
TOMP
HERE?
WHUP
MAX...
...ENERGY!!
!
THOOM
!
!

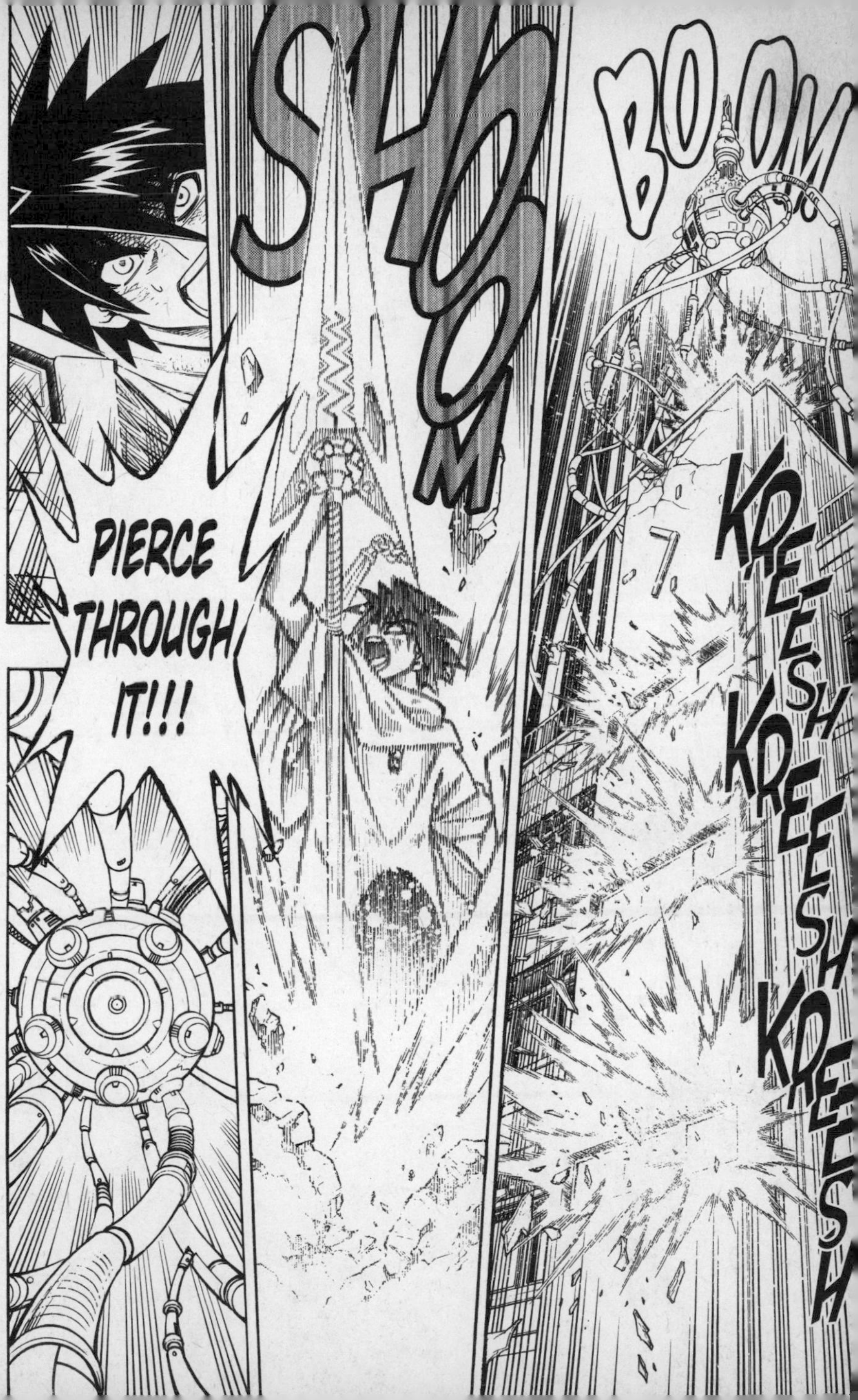
BOOM
KREESH
KREESH
KREESH
SHOOM
PIERCE THROUGH IT!!!

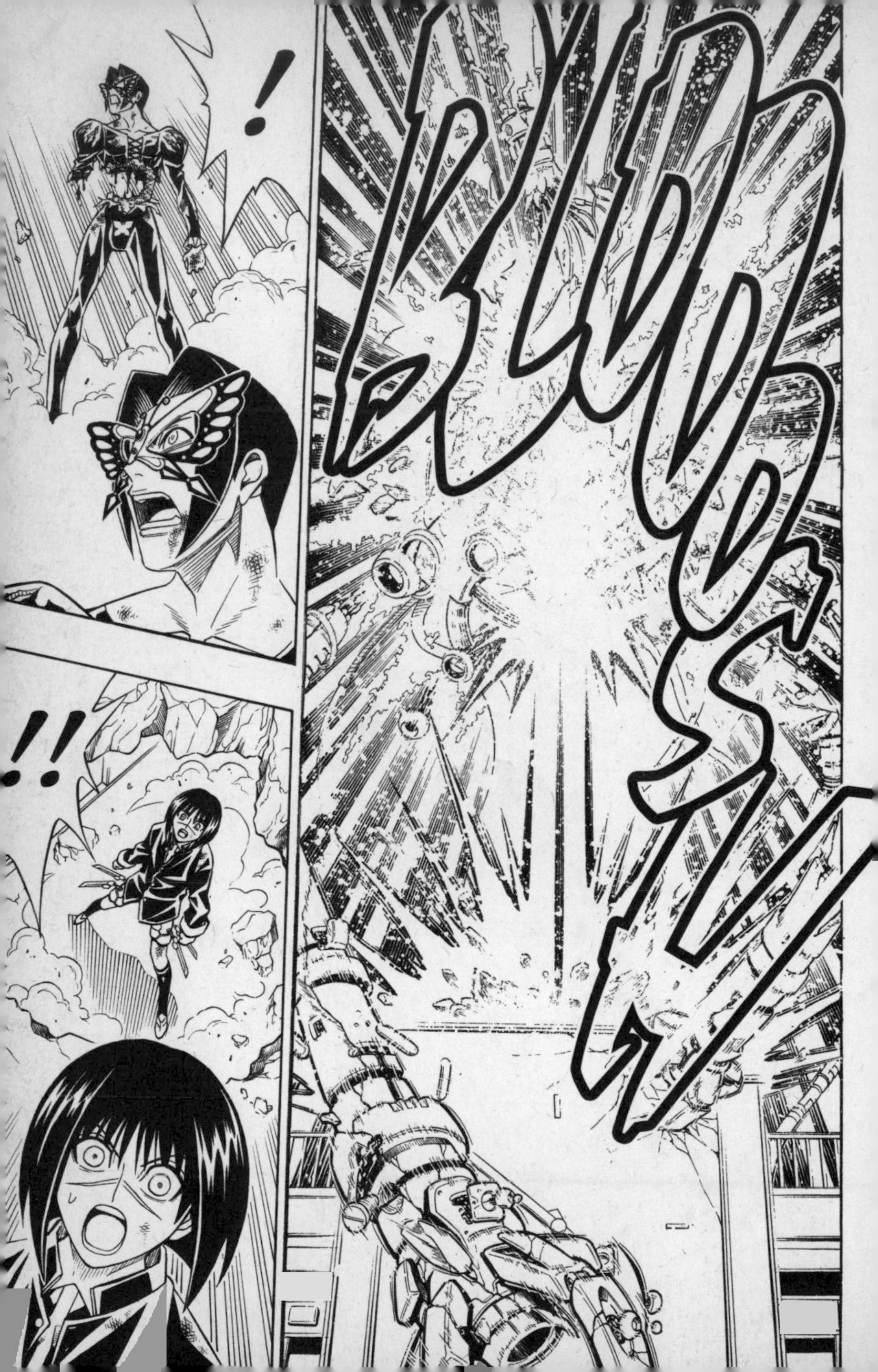
!
!!

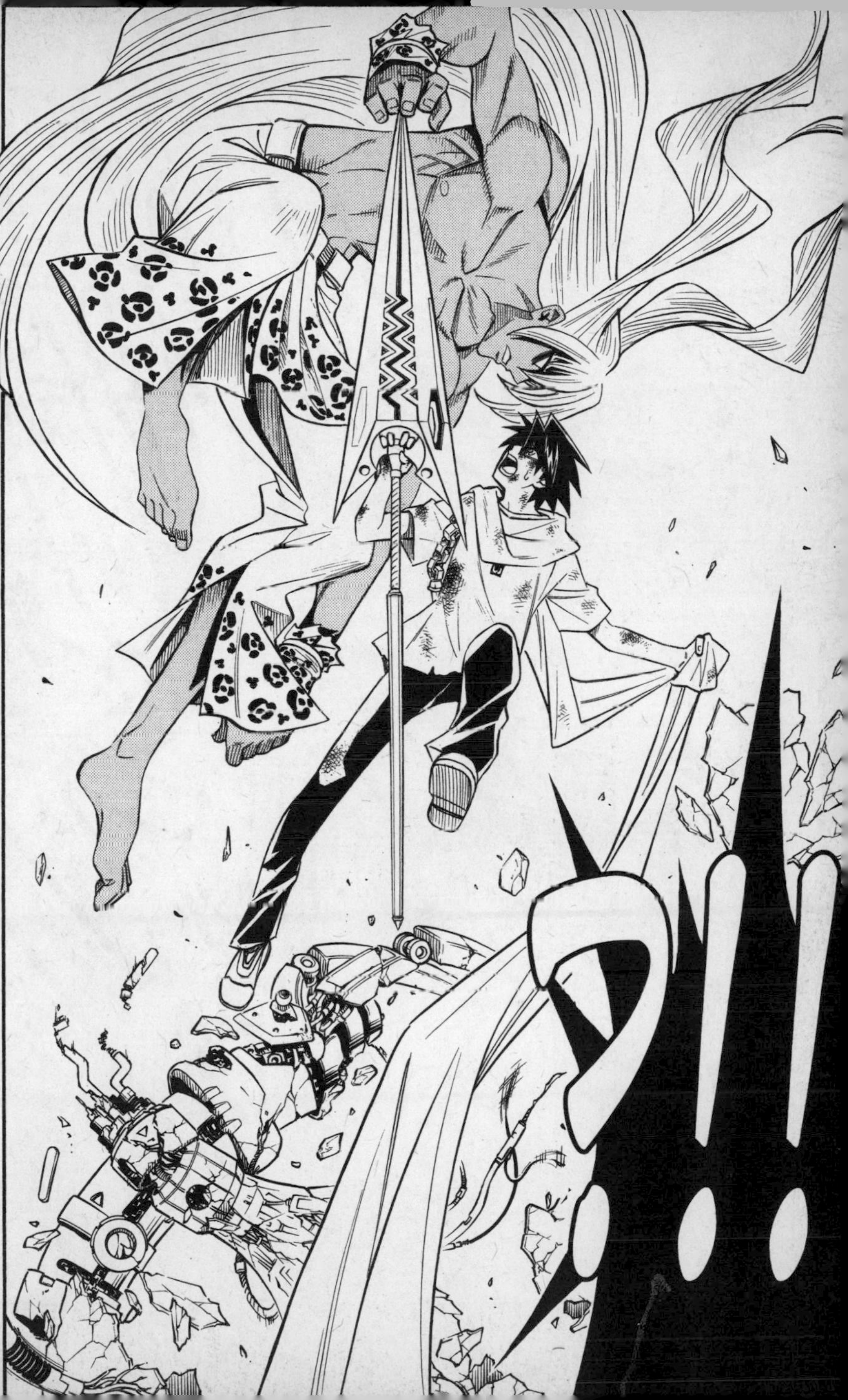
?!!

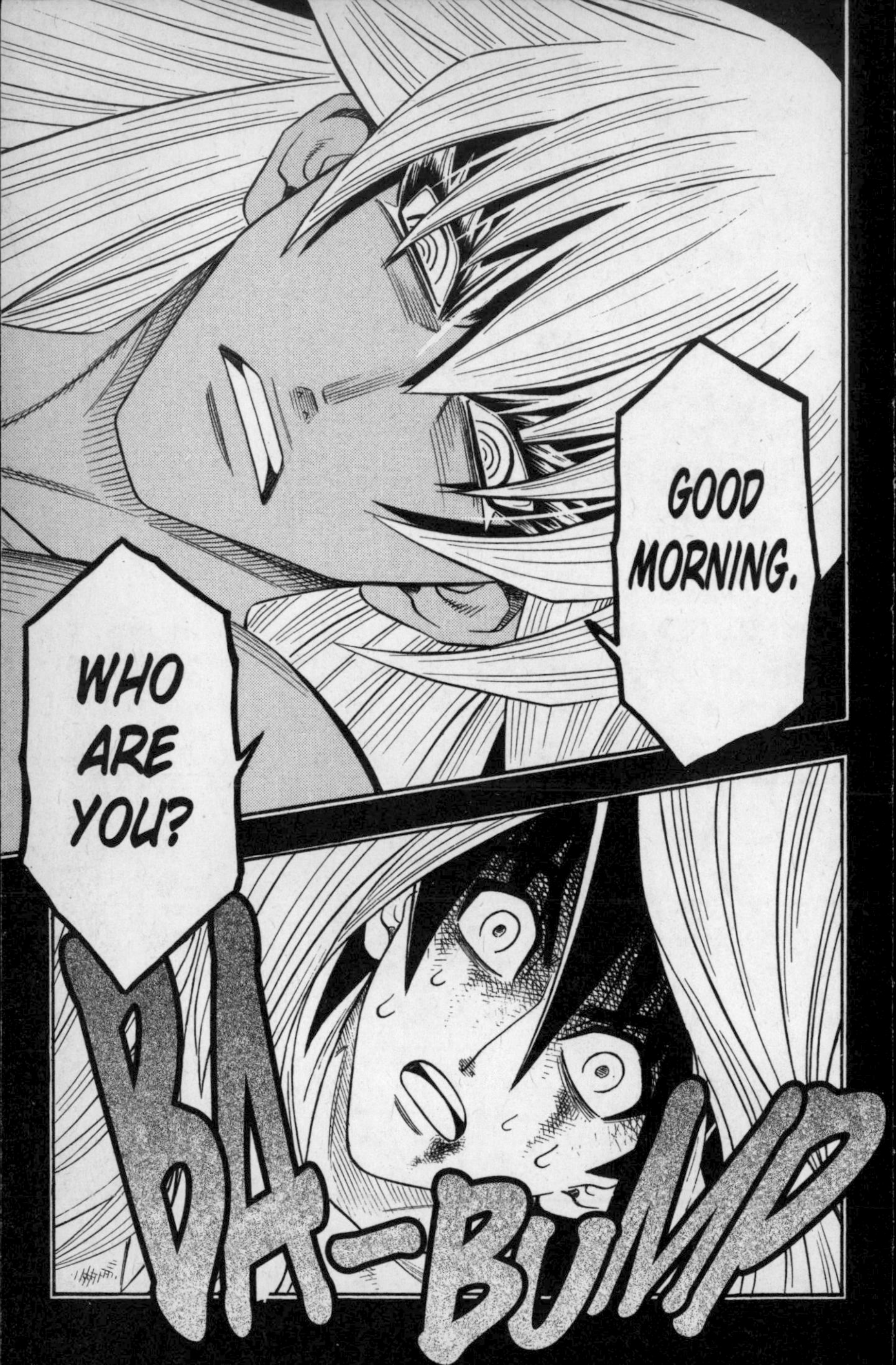
GOOD MORNING.
WHO ARE YOU?
BA-BUMP

· Height: 180cm; Weight: 64kg
· Born: June 28; Cancer; Blood Type: AB; Age: 55
· Likes: Himself, butterflies, beings greater than himself
· Dislikes: Beings who are inferior to himself
· Hobby: Maintaining his mustache, alchemic research
· Special Ability: Comical stomach tricks
· Affiliations: L.X.E. (Founder)

Character File No. 24

BAKUSHAKU CHOUNO (DOKTOR BUTTERFLY)

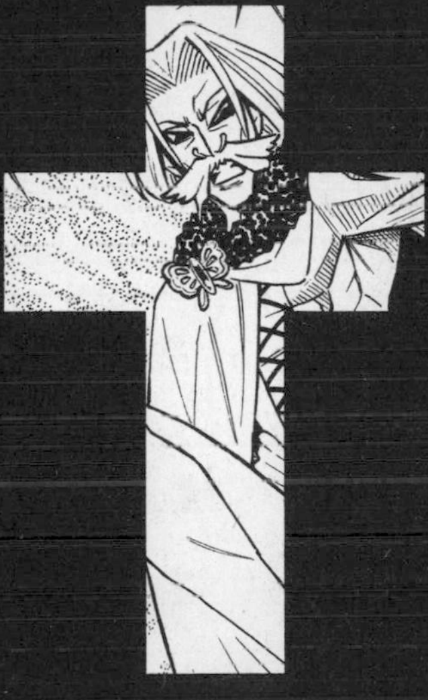

Author's Notes

· No matter how brilliant Koushaku might be, I knew he couldn't become a homunculus on his own, so I came up with this character. The idea for the L.X.E. came to me as I developed the story.
· I wanted him to be one of Papillon's ancestors, but I didn't want them to be after the same thing. They're similar, but each of them is unique.
· In the middle of this character's run, I thought he didn't have enough presence, but I'm pleased with how he turned out in the end.
· The main design motif is his trademark butterfly mustache. As with Papillon and his mask, Dr. Butterfly wouldn't be Dr. Butterfly without it.
· I know that "Doktor" is German and "Butterfly" is English, but don't pay any attention to it. Ignore the man behind the curtain...please.

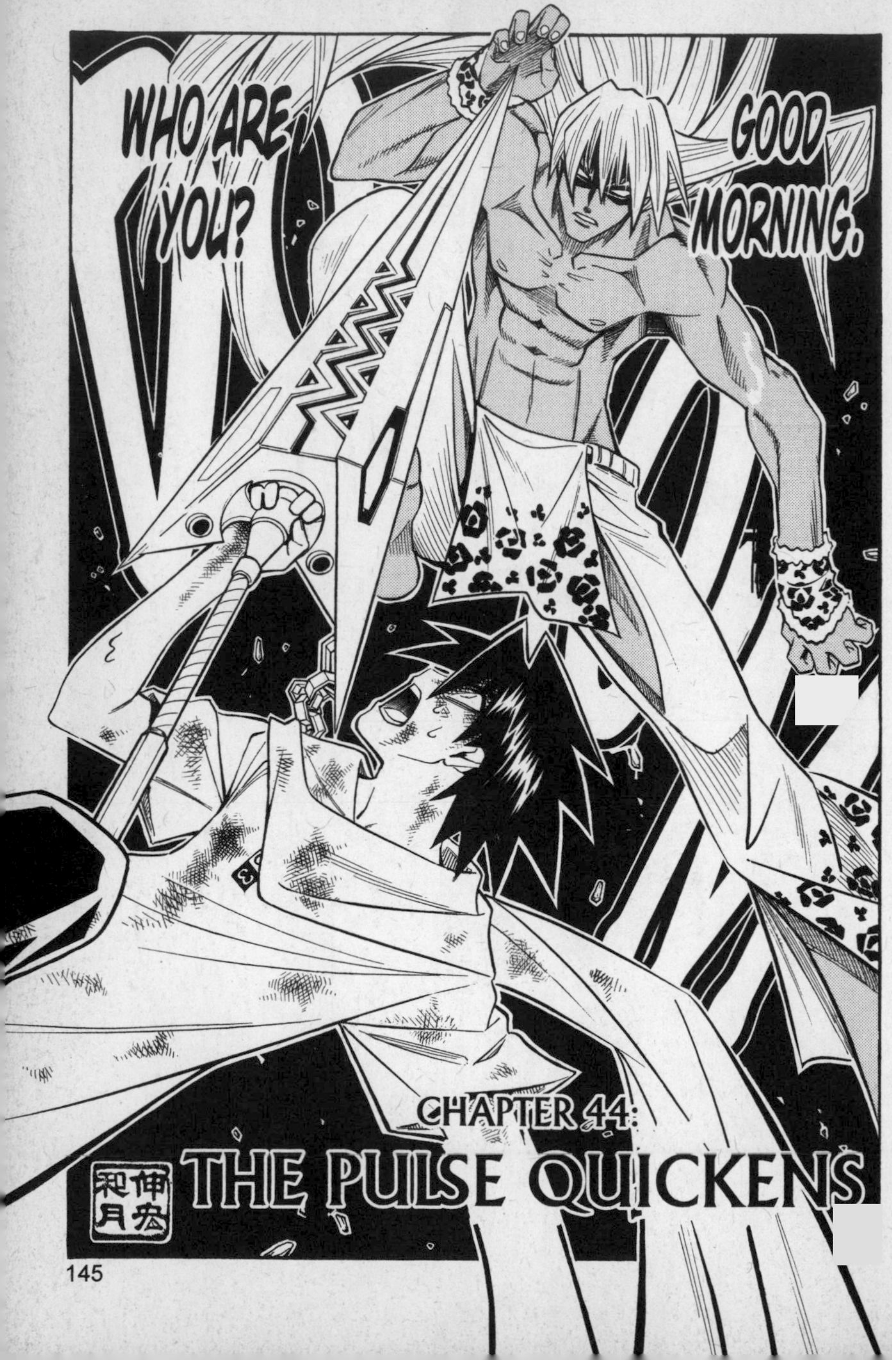
GOOD MORNING.
WHO ARE YOU?
CHAPTER 44:
THE PULSE QUICKENS

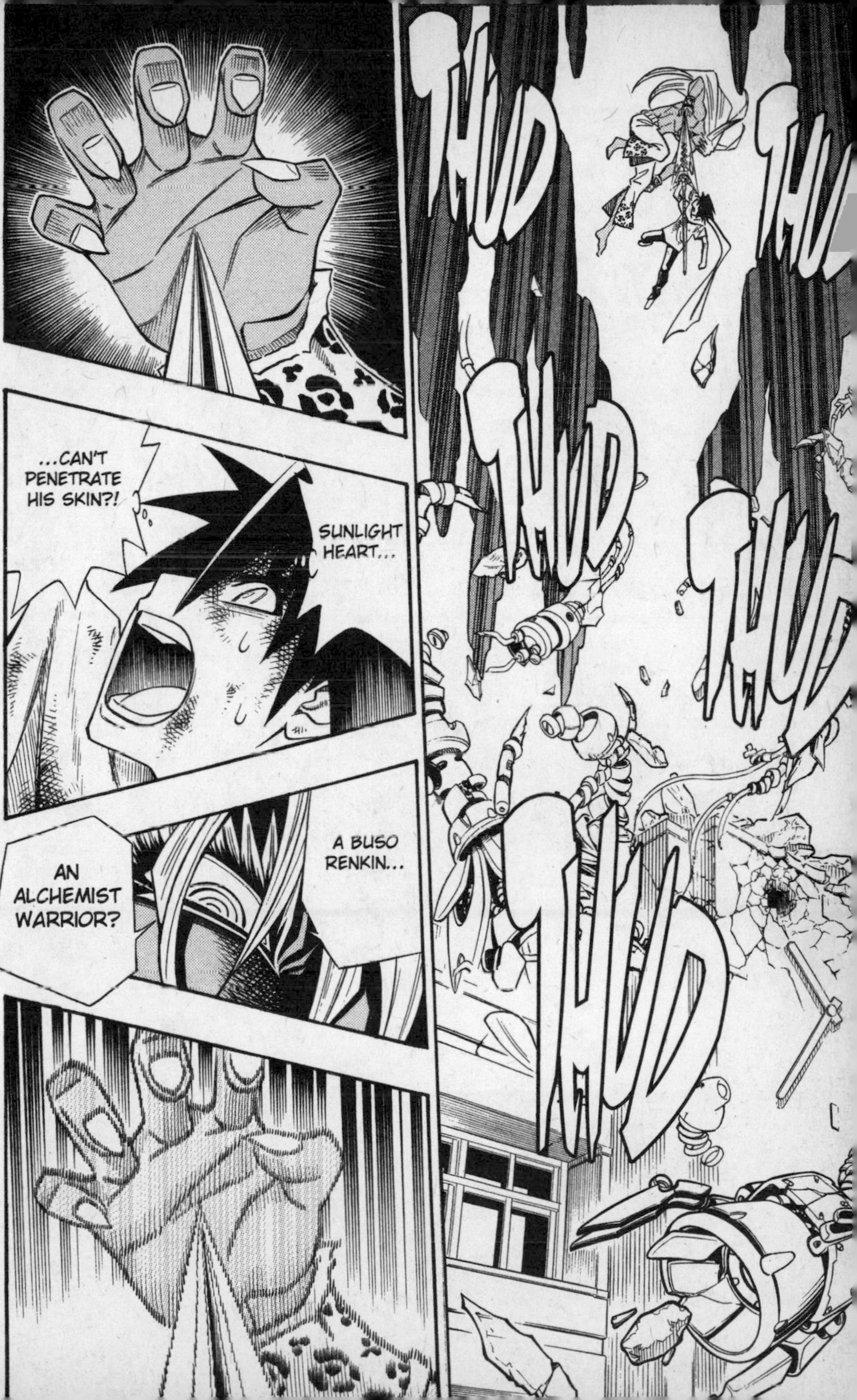
THU
THUD
THU
THUD
THUD
SUNLIGHT HEART...
...CAN'T PENETRATE HIS SKIN?!
A BUSO RENKIN...
AN ALCHEMIST WARRIOR?

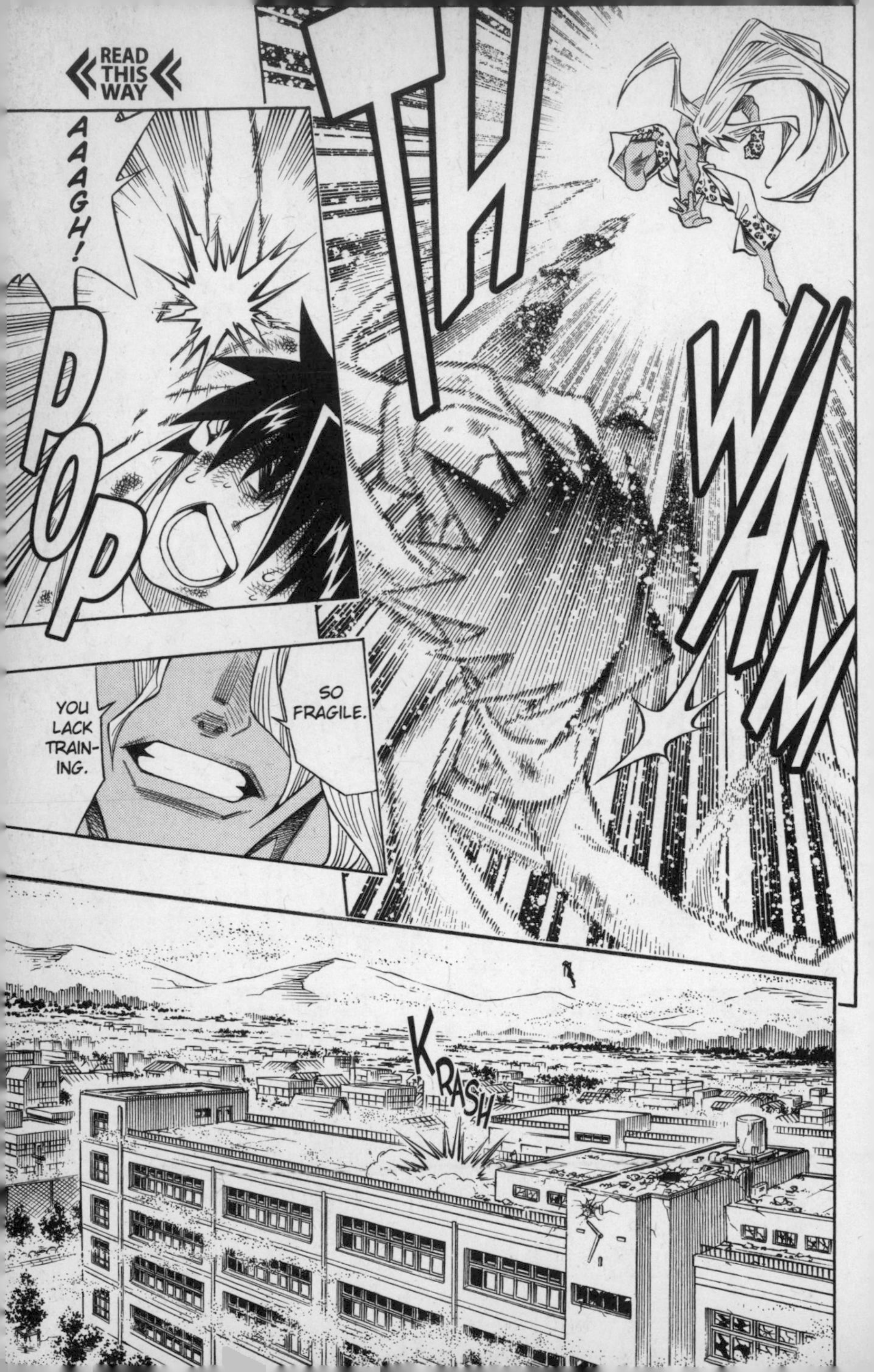
READ THIS WAY
THWAM
AAAAGH!
POP
SO FRAGILE.
YOU LACK TRAIN-ING.
KRASH

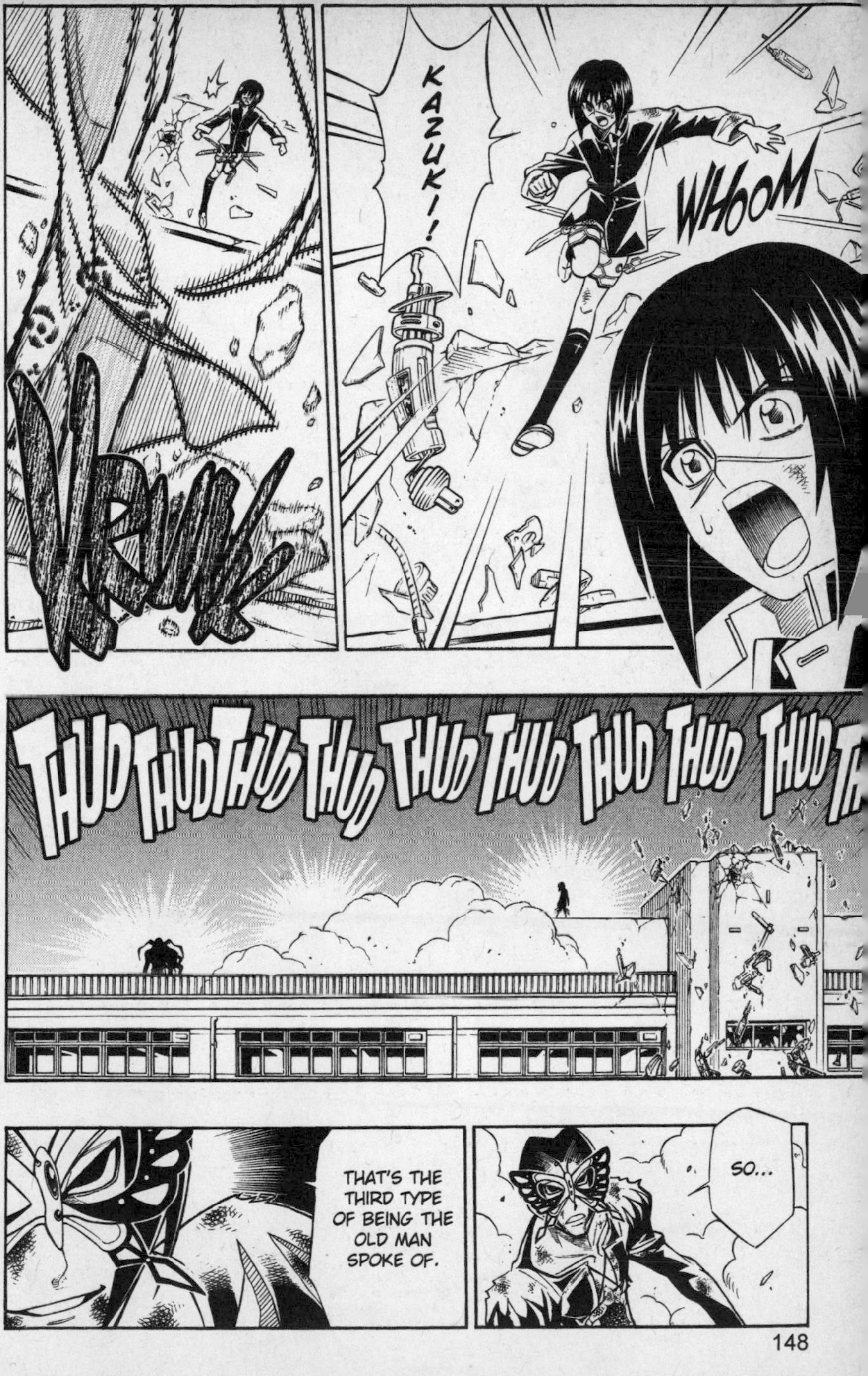
KAZUKI!
WHOOM
THUD THUD THUD THUD THUD THUD THUD THUD THUD TH
SO...
THAT'S THE THIRD TYPE OF BEING THE OLD MAN SPOKE OF.

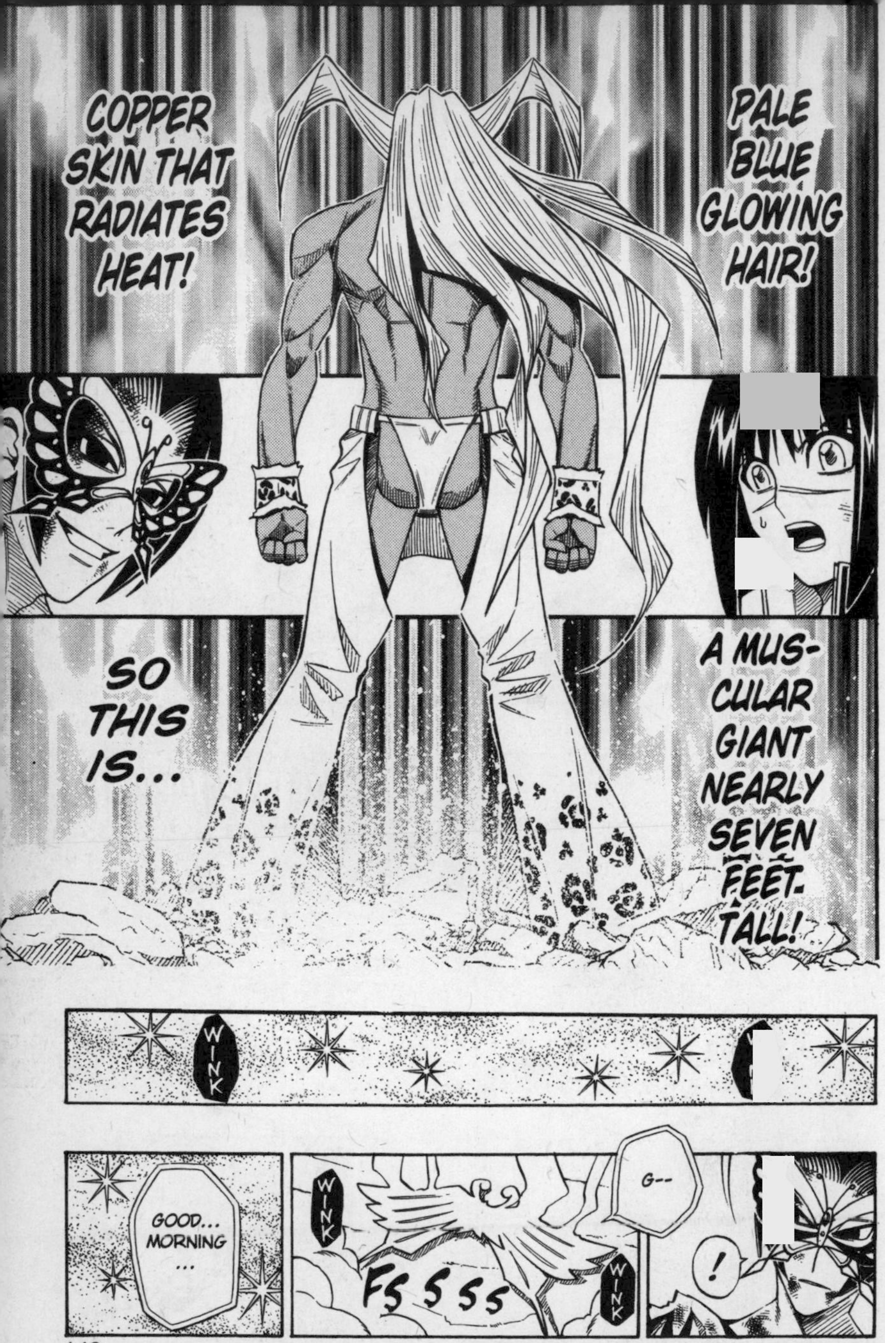
PALE BLUE GLOWING HAIR!
COPPER SKIN THAT RADIATES HEAT!
A MUS-CULAR GIANT NEARLY SEVEN FEET TALL!
SO THIS IS...
WINK
!
G--
WINK
FSSSS
WINK
GOOD... MORNING ...

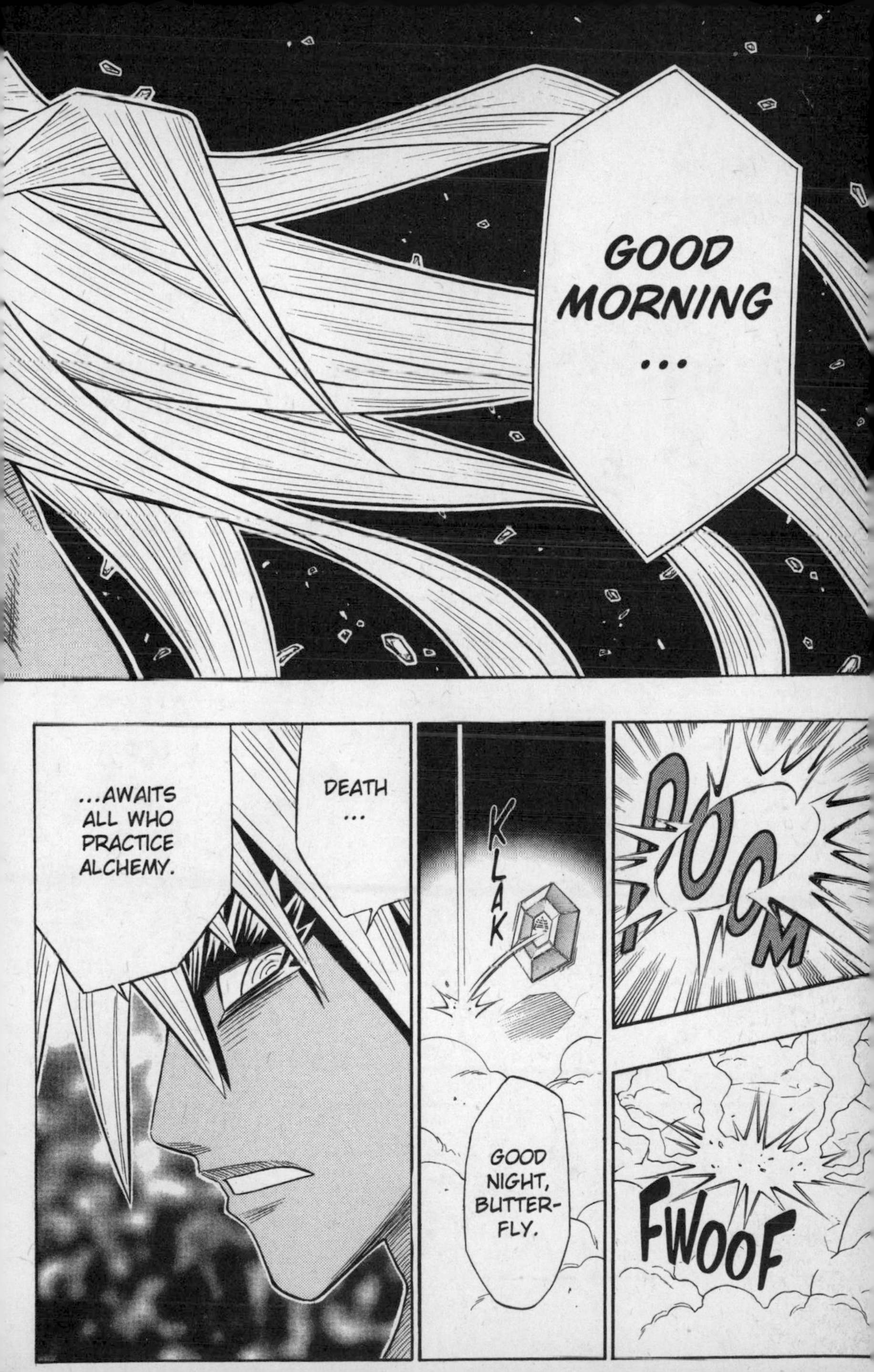
GOOD MORNING ...
BOOM
FWOOF
KLAK
GOOD NIGHT, BUTTER-FLY.
DEATH ...
...AWAITS ALL WHO PRACTICE ALCHEMY.

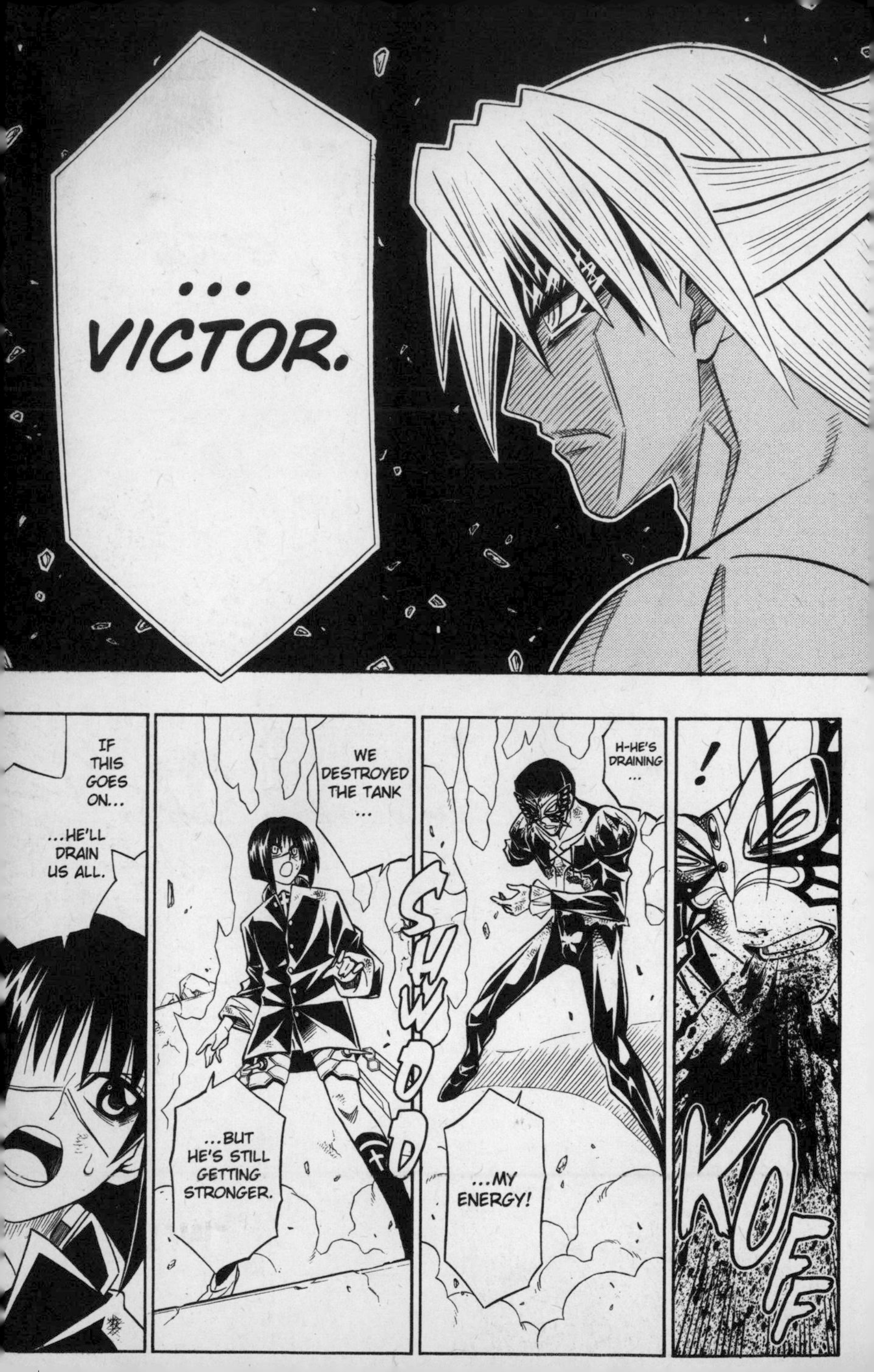
...VICTOR.
!
KOFF
H-HE'S DRAINING ...
...MY ENERGY!
SHWOOD
WE DESTROYED THE TANK ...
...BUT HE'S STILL GETTING STRONGER.
IF THIS GOES ON...
...HE'LL DRAIN US ALL.

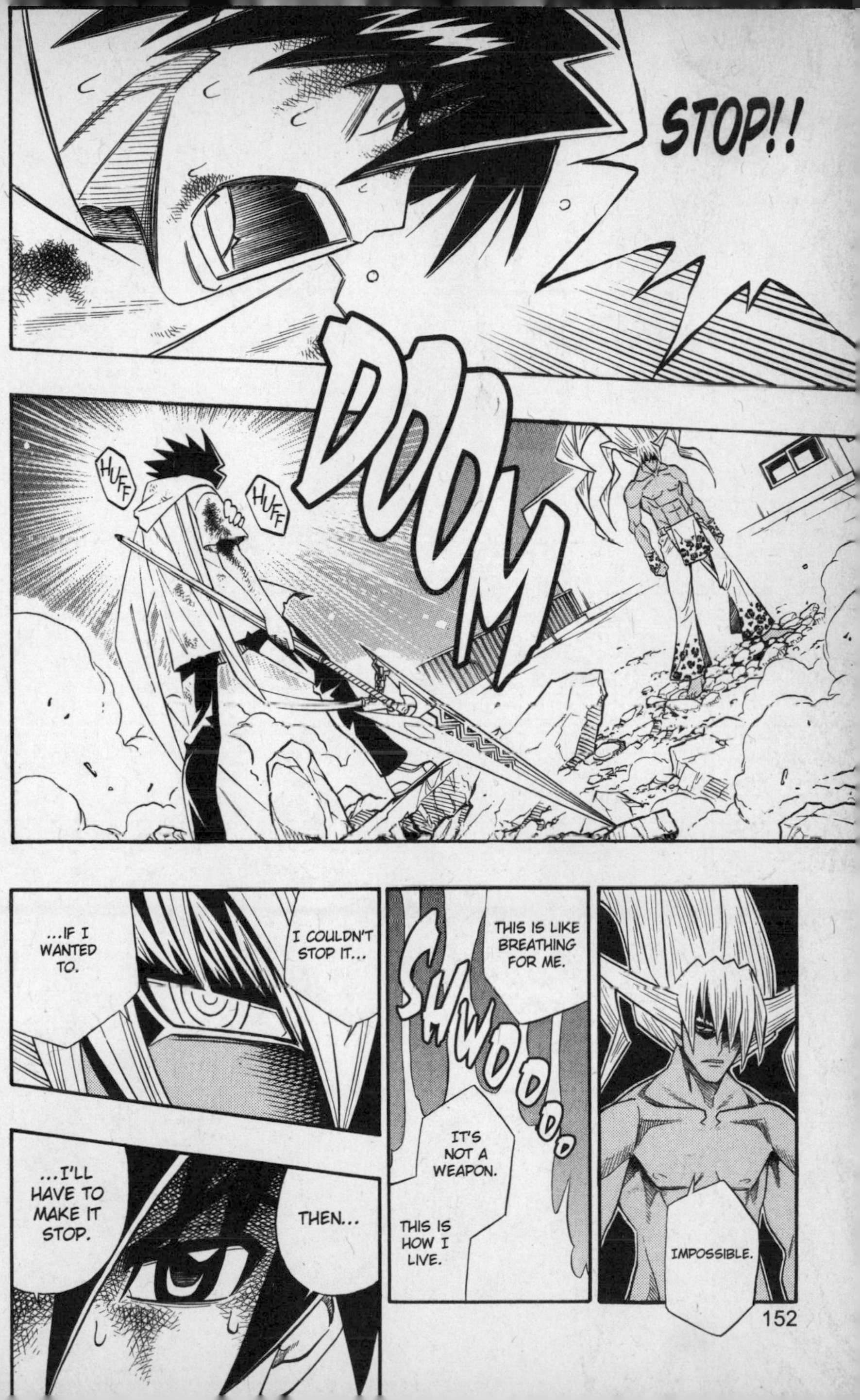
STOP!!
DOOM
HUFF
HUFF
IMPOSSIBLE.
THIS IS LIKE BREATHING FOR ME.
SHWOOOO
IT'S NOT A WEAPON.
THIS IS HOW I LIVE.
I COULDN'T STOP IT...
...IF I WANTED TO.
THEN...
...I'LL HAVE TO MAKE IT STOP.

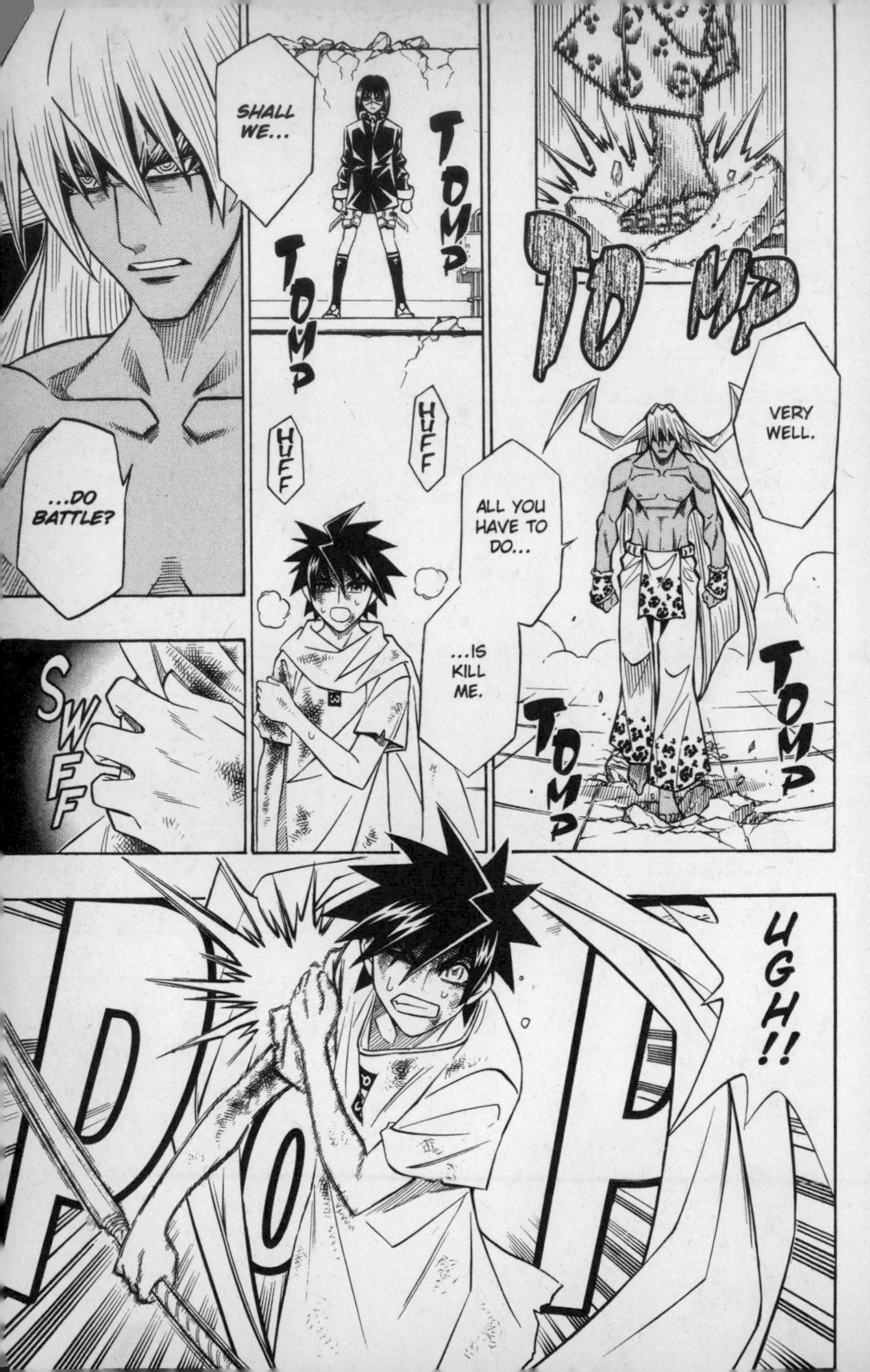
TOMP
VERY WELL.
TOMP
TOMP
SHALL WE...
TOMP
TOMP
HUFF
HUFF
ALL YOU HAVE TO DO...
...IS KILL ME.
...DO BATTLE?
SWFF
UGH!!
DOP

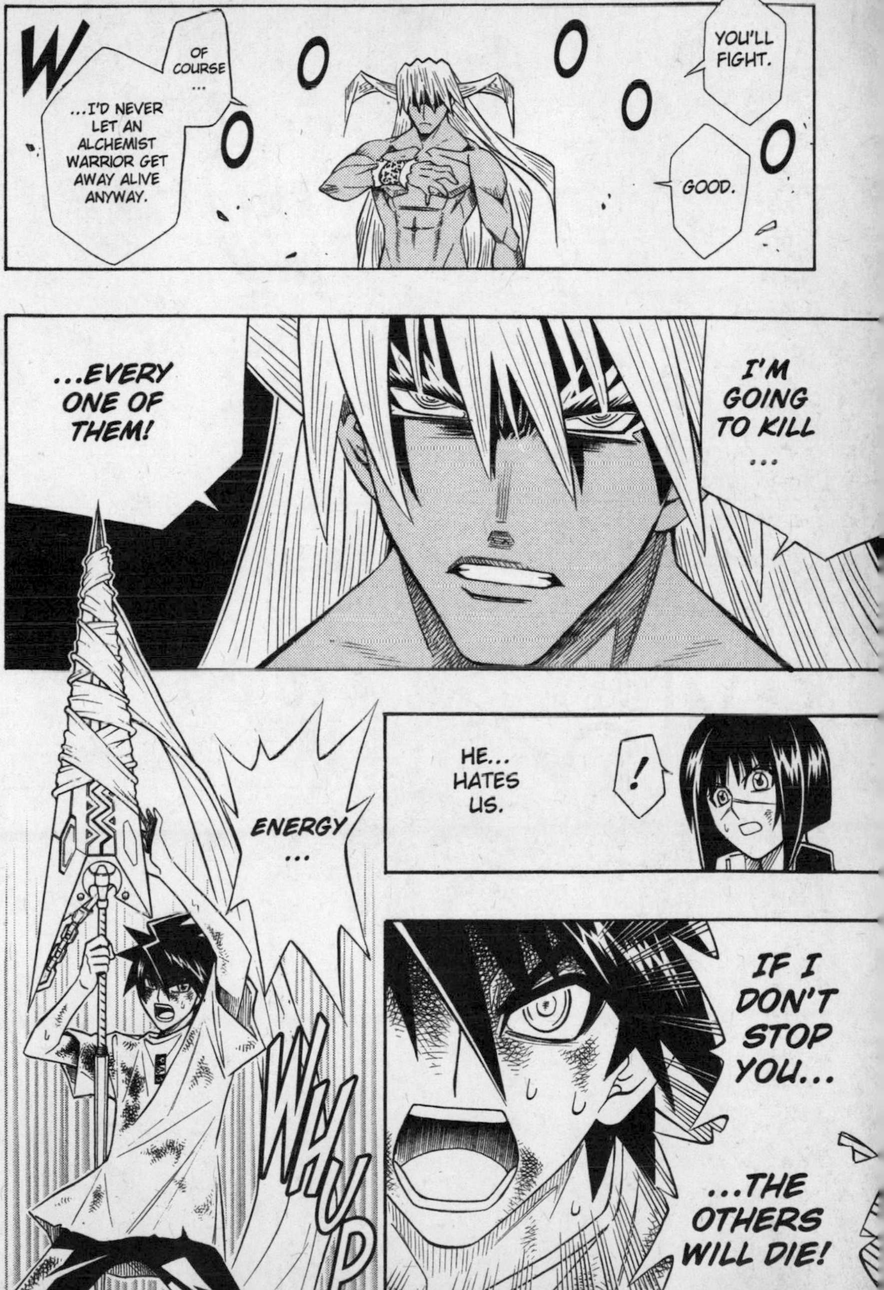
YOU'LL FIGHT.
GOOD.
OF COURSE...
...I'D NEVER LET AN ALCHEMIST WARRIOR GET AWAY ALIVE ANYWAY.
WOOOOO
I'M GOING TO KILL...
...EVERY ONE OF THEM!
!
HE... HATES US.
IF I DON'T STOP YOU...
...THE OTHERS WILL DIE!
ENERGY...
WHUP

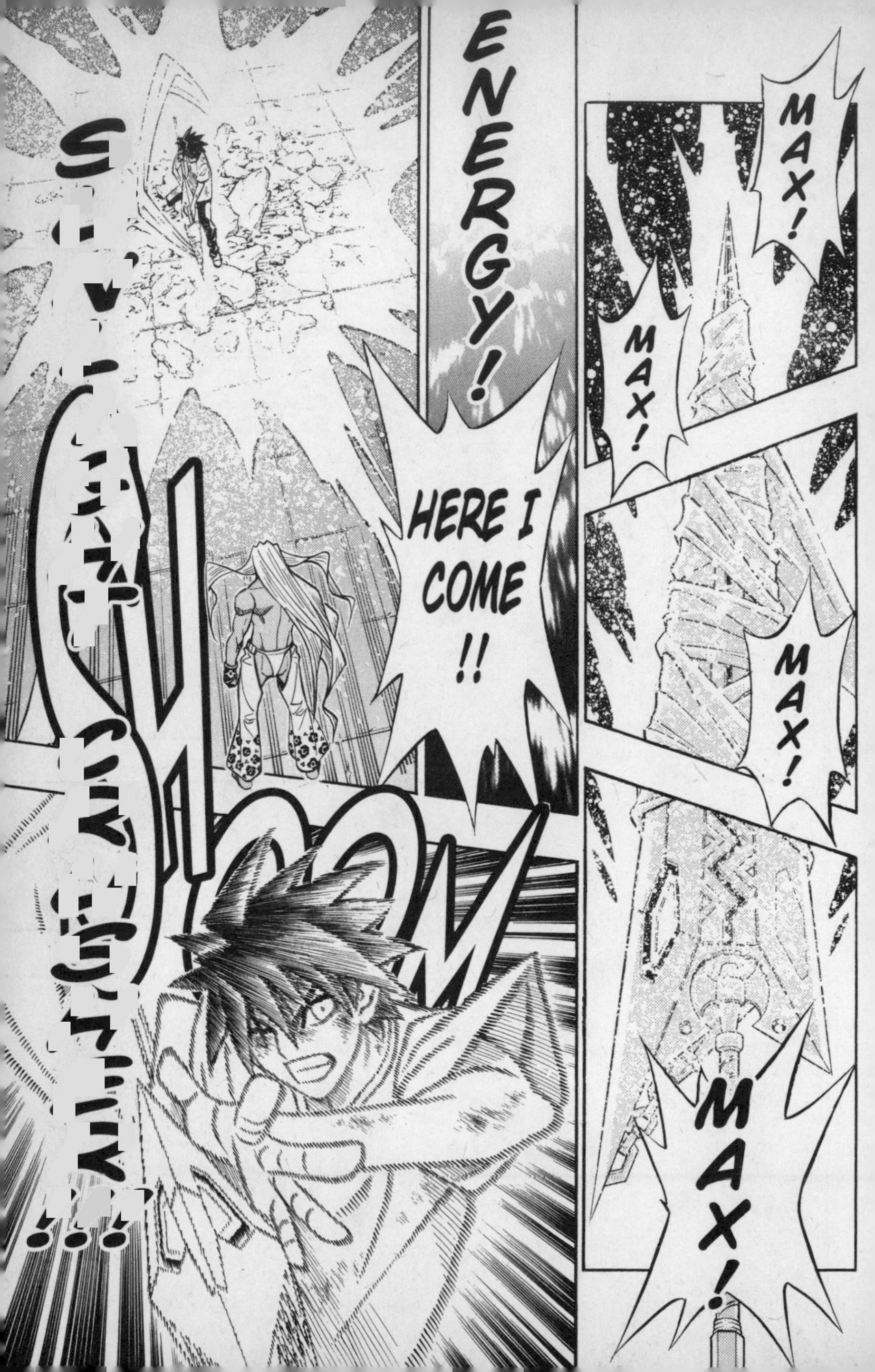
MAX!
MAX!
MAX!
MAX!
ENERGY!
HERE I COME!!

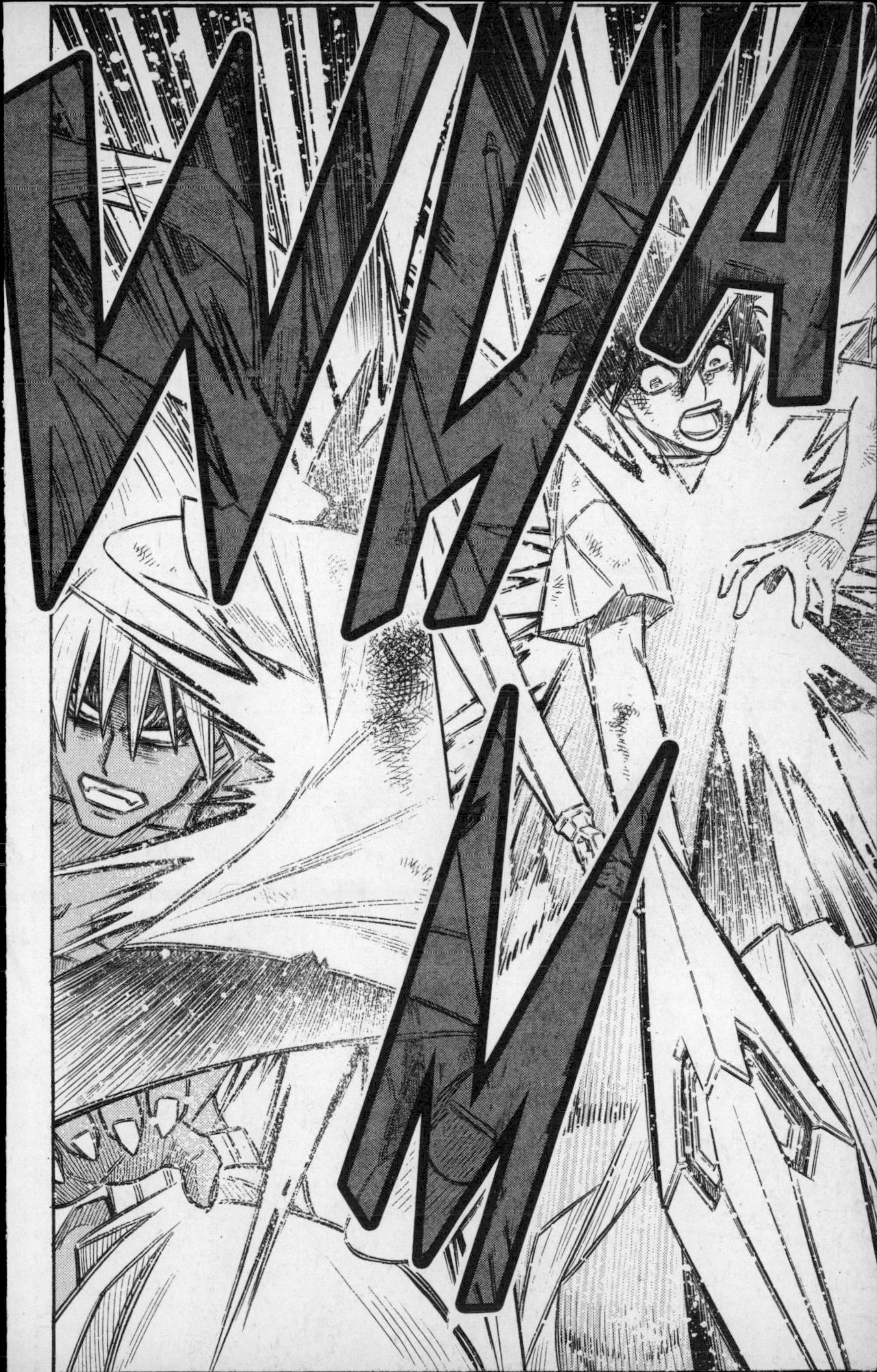
WHAM

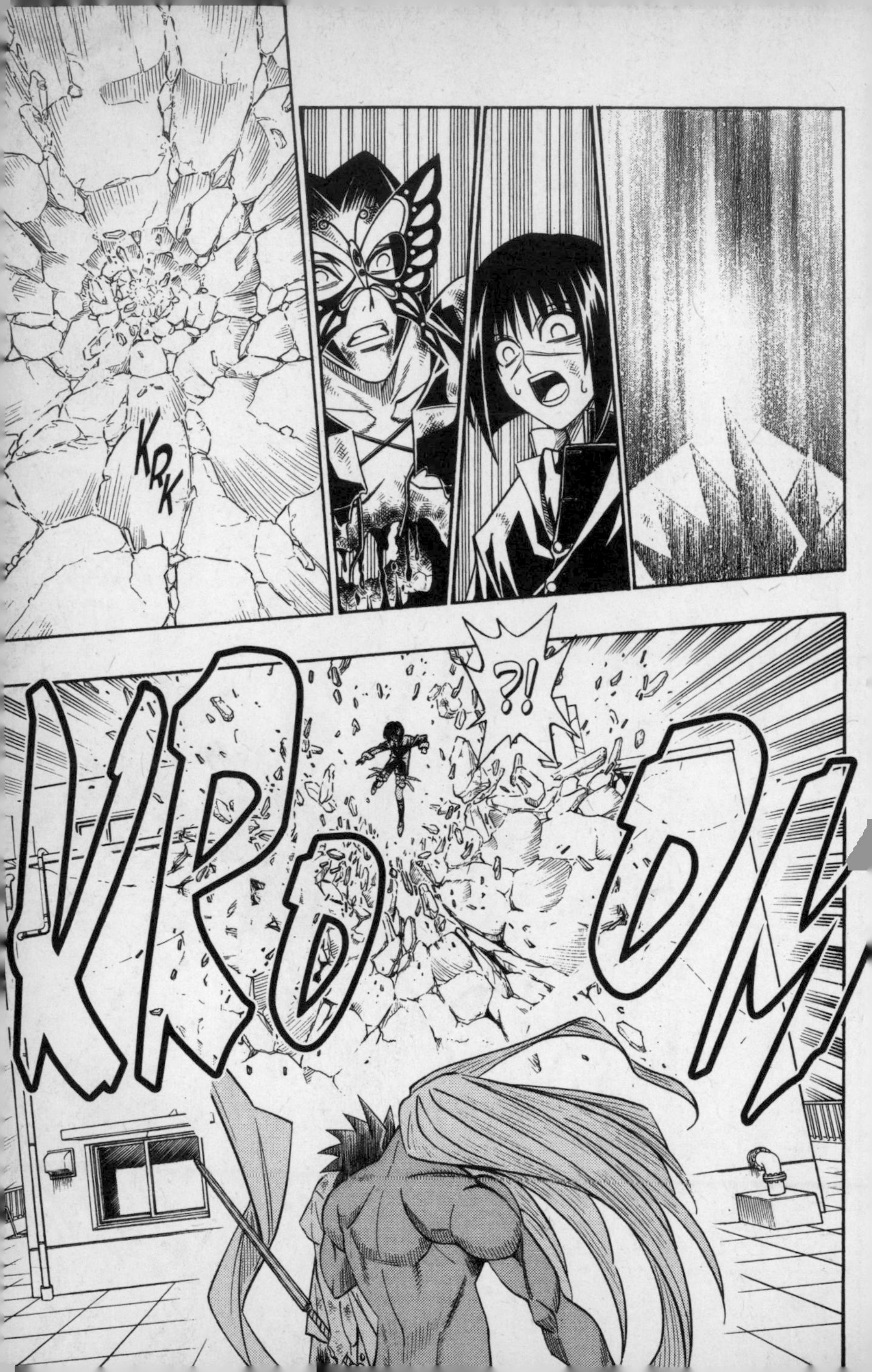
KRK
?!
KRBOOM

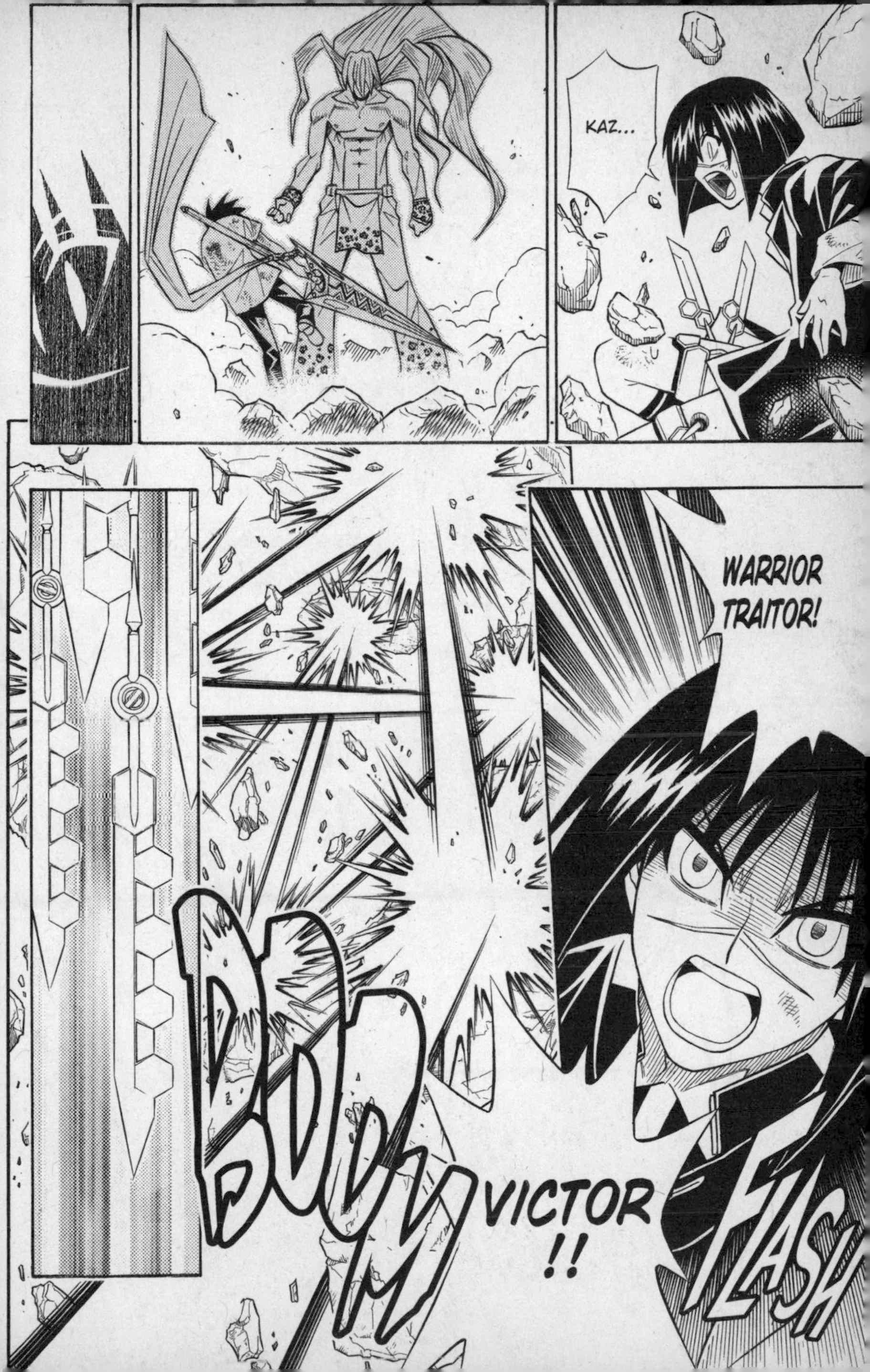
KAZ...
WARRIOR TRAITOR!
FLASH
VICTOR !!
BOOM

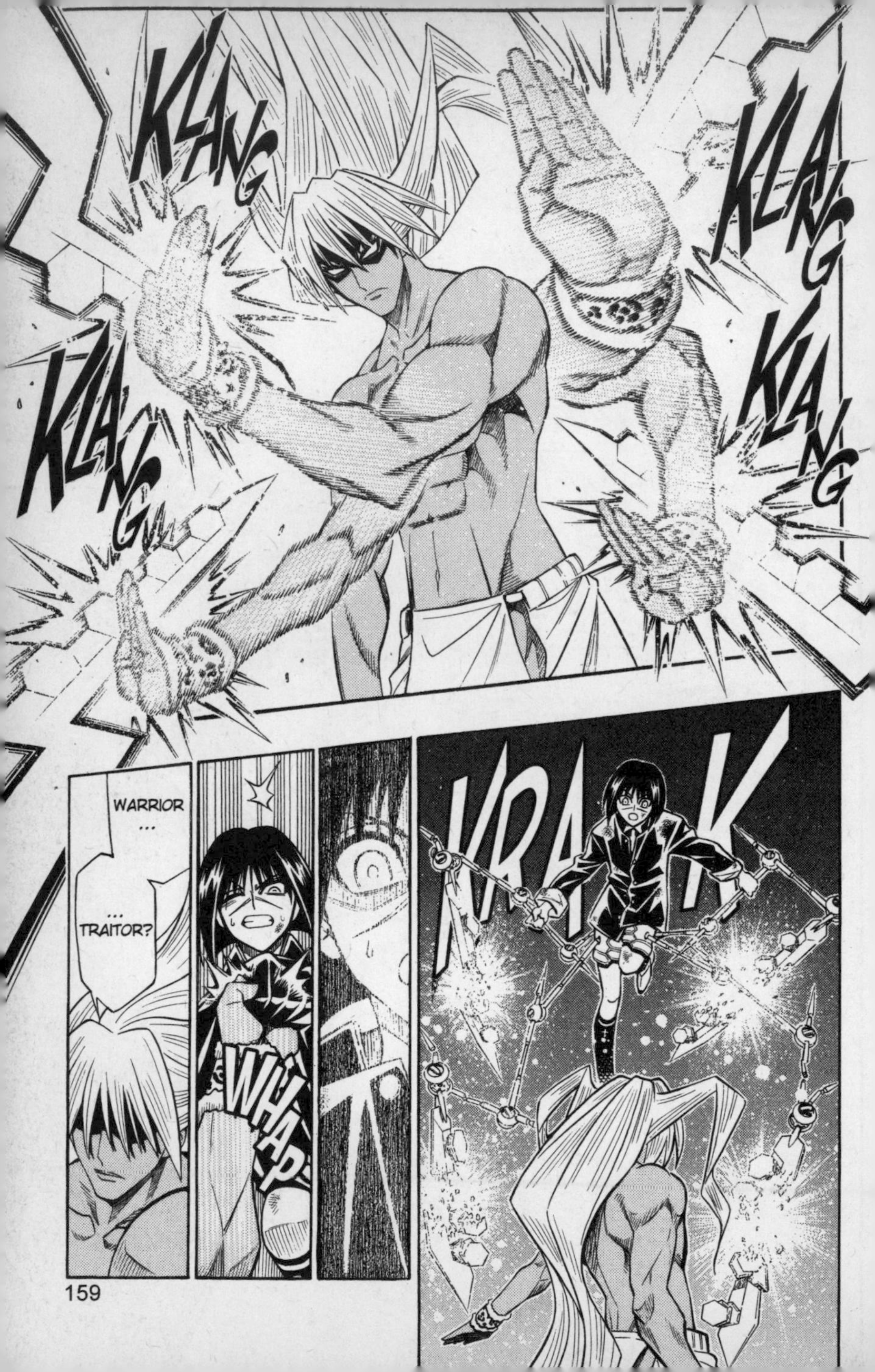
KLANG
KLANG
KLANG
KLANG
KRAK
WHAP
WARRIOR ...
... TRAITOR?

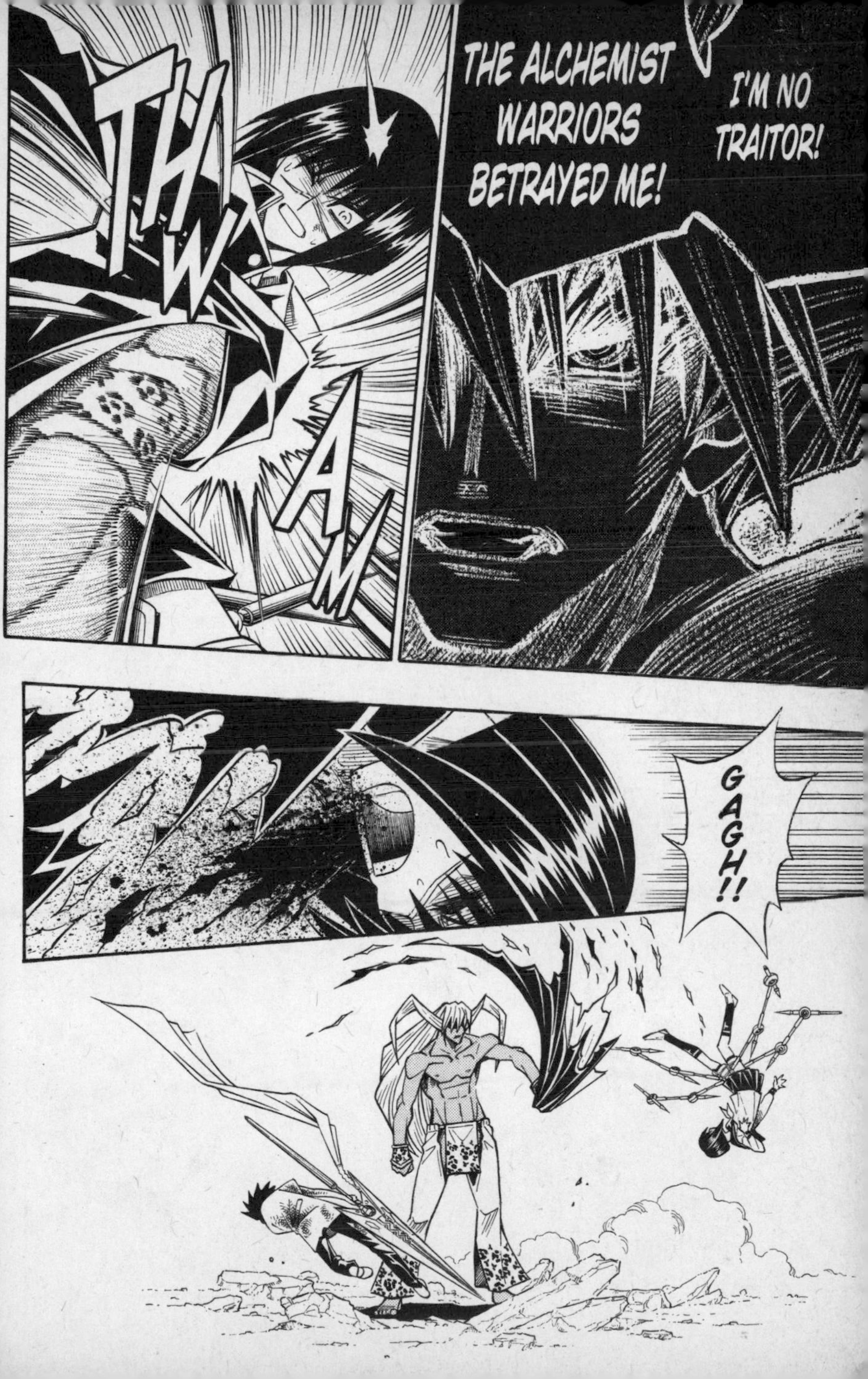
I'M NO TRAITOR!
THE ALCHEMIST WARRIORS BETRAYED ME!
THWAM
GAGH!!

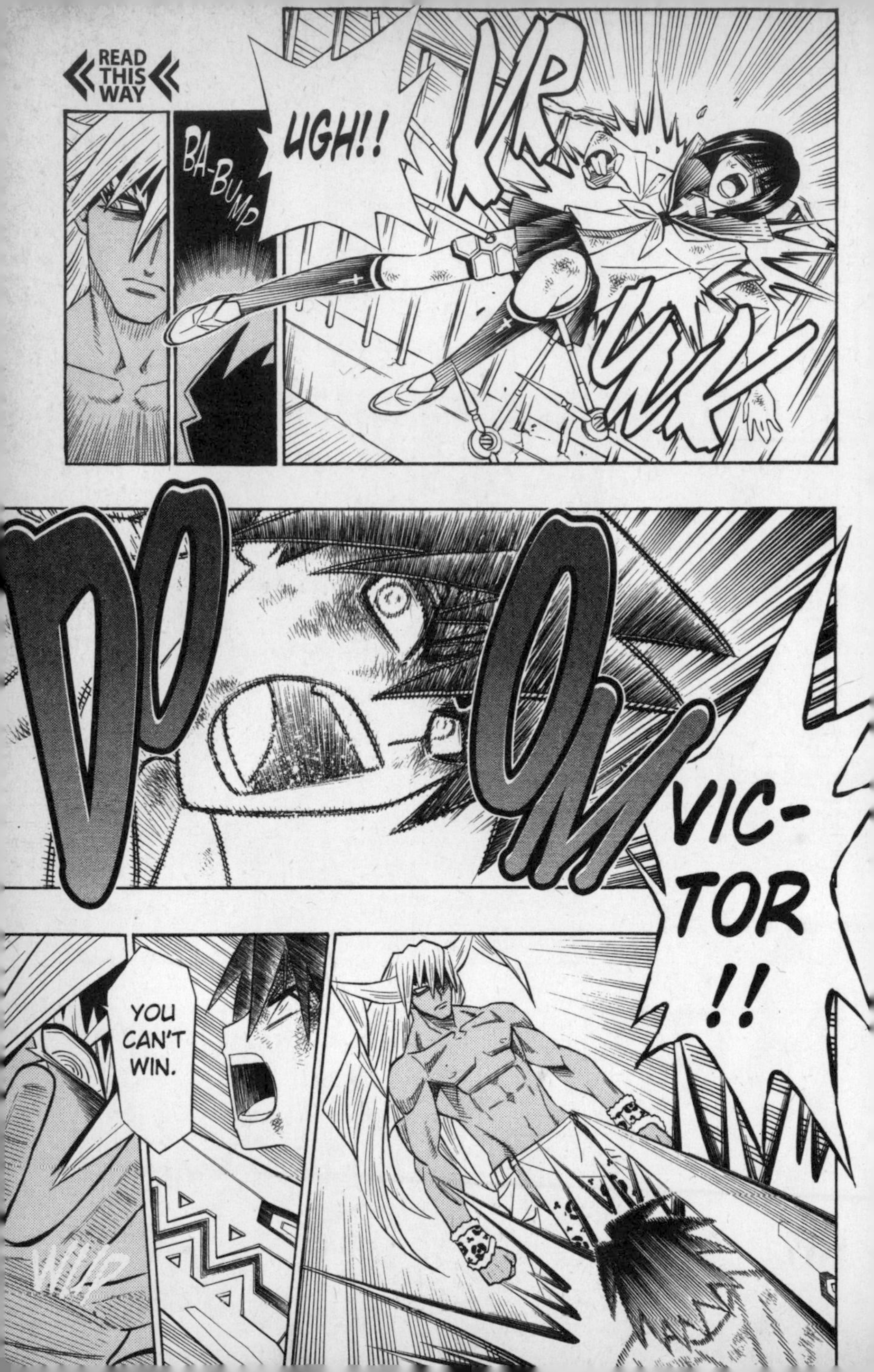
READ THIS WAY
UGH!!
VRUNK
BA-BUMP
DOOM
VICTOR!!
YOU CAN'T WIN.

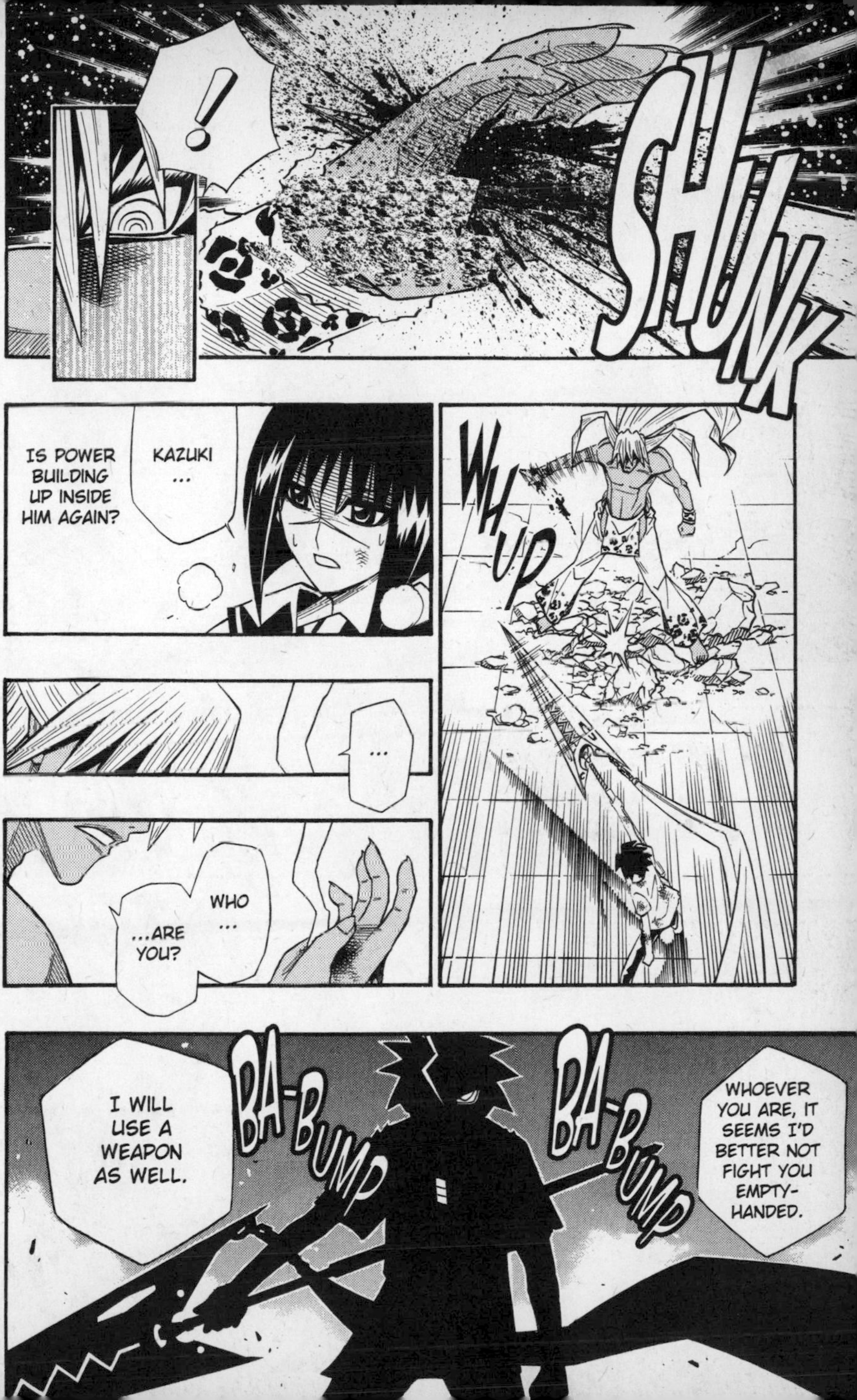
SHUNK
!
WHUP
KAZUKI ...
IS POWER BUILDING UP INSIDE HIM AGAIN?
...
WHO ...
...ARE YOU?
WHOEVER YOU ARE, IT SEEMS I'D BETTER NOT FIGHT YOU EMPTY-HANDED.
BA-BUMP
BA-BUMP
I WILL USE A WEAPON AS WELL.

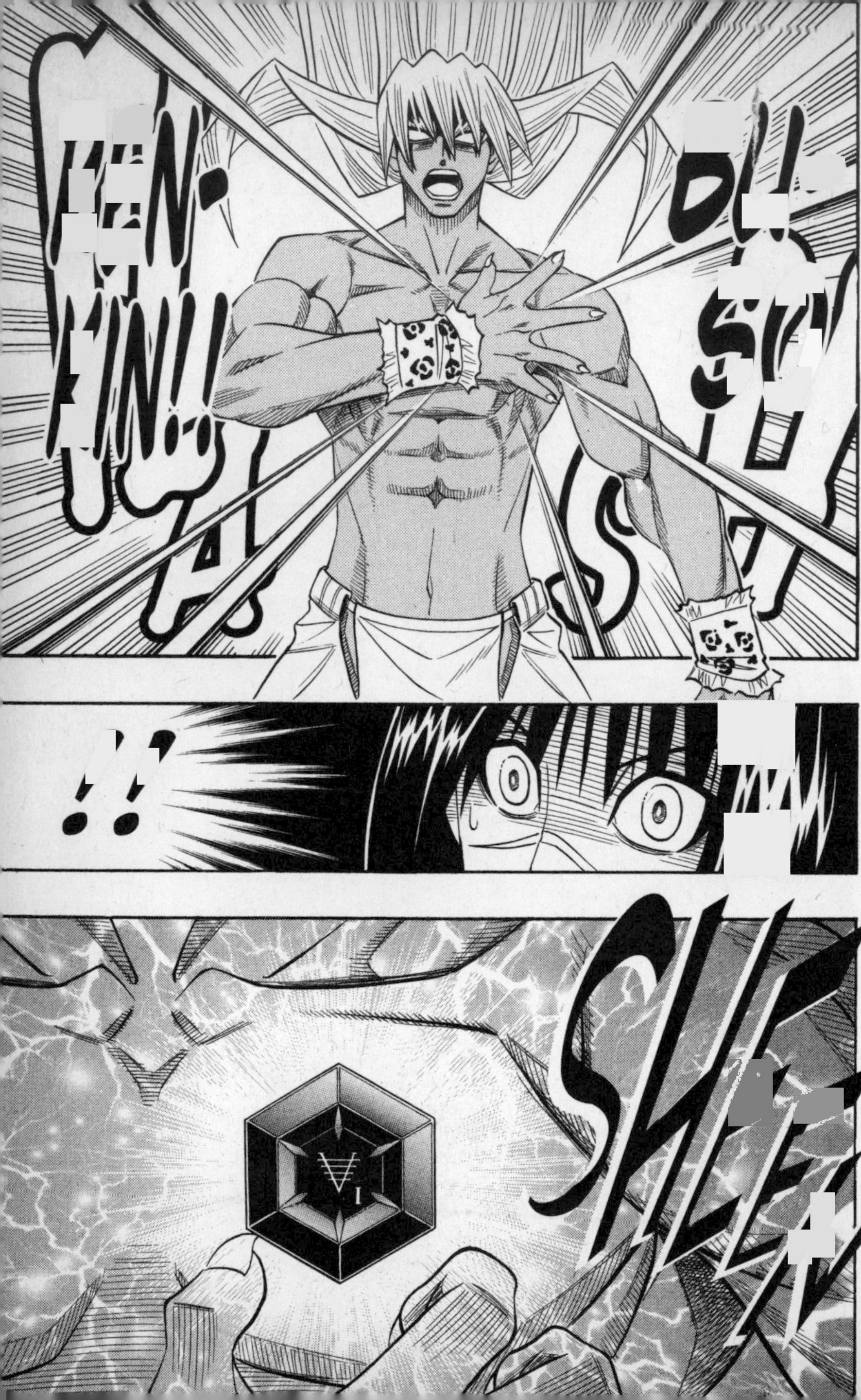
!!

Obey the commands of my whip!

Buso Renkin File No. 5

ノイズィハーメルン

NOISY HAMELIN

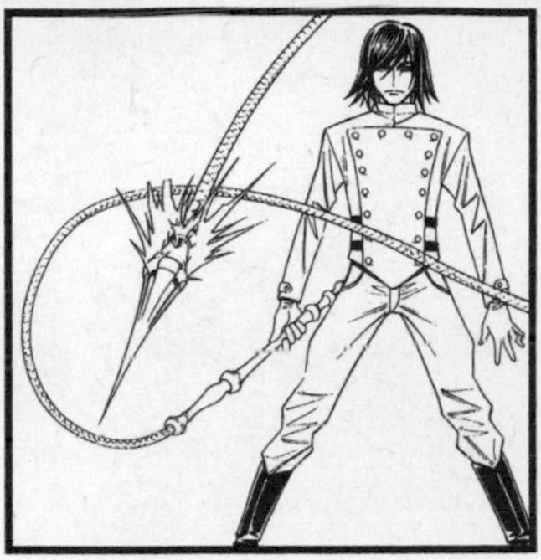

- Kakugane Serial Number: LXI (61)
- Creator: Homunculus Jinnai
- Form: Steel Whip
- Main Color: Copper
- Special Abilities: · The high-frequency sound this whip produces allows its wielder to control people hypnotically.
- Special Traits: · The effective range of the special ability is about 100 yards. There is no limit to the number of people it can control, but the greater the number, the weaker the effect.
  · Amplifies faint sound waves to enable its wielder to eavesdrop at a distance.
  · It can be used as a whip too, but does no more damage than a normal whip.

- Author's Notes:
  · I wanted a special weapon for the attack on the dormitory story and came up with this. It's based on a lion tamer's whip.
  · In terms of design, I used a picture I found in a book on weapons and added a nozzle to the tip.
  · My favorite thing about this weapon was that it gave me the chance to draw Mahiro in a hypnotic state.

NOISY HAMELIN

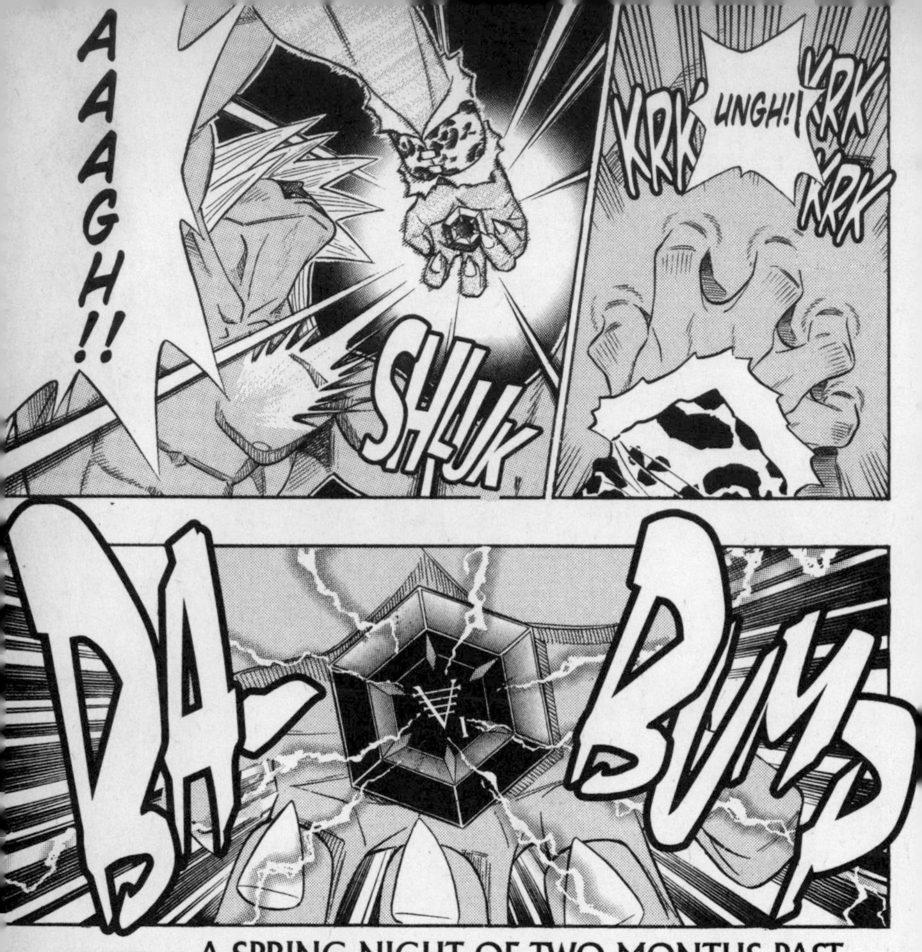
KRK
UNGH!
KRK
KRK
AAAAGH!!
SHLUK
DA-
BUMP

CHAPTER 45: A SPRING NIGHT OF TWO MONTHS PAST

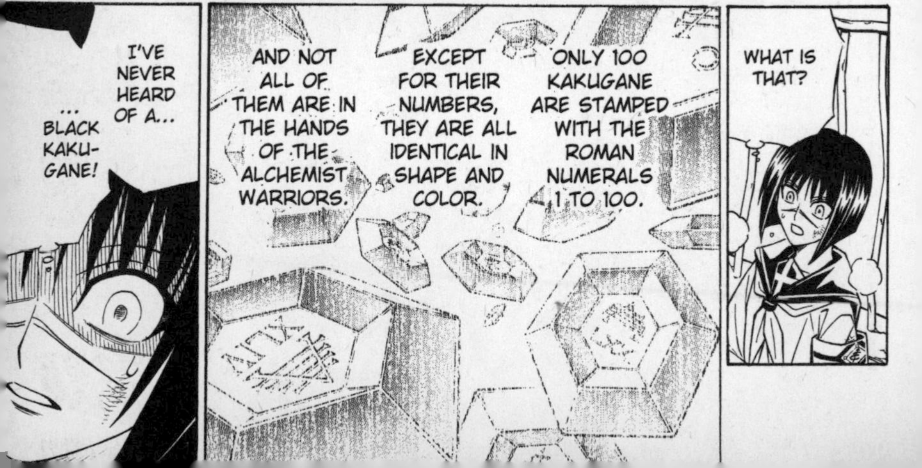
WHAT IS THAT?
ONLY 100 KAKUGANE ARE STAMPED WITH THE ROMAN NUMERALS 1 TO 100.
EXCEPT FOR THEIR NUMBERS, THEY ARE ALL IDENTICAL IN SHAPE AND COLOR.
AND NOT ALL OF THEM ARE IN THE HANDS OF THE ALCHEMIST WARRIORS.
I'VE NEVER HEARD OF A...
...BLACK KAKUGANE!

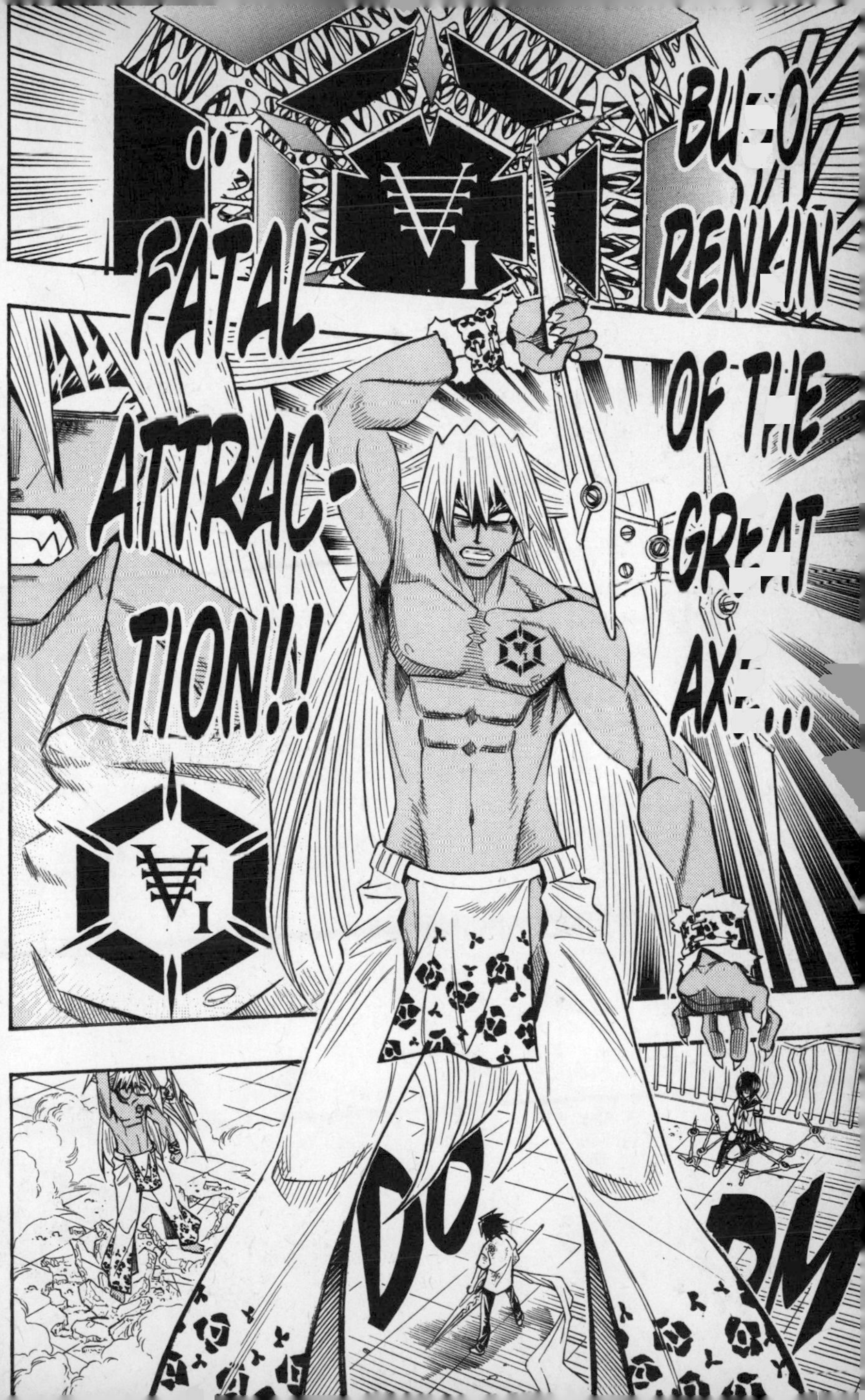
BUSO RENKIN OF THE GREAT AXE...
FATAL ATTRAC-TION!!
DOOM

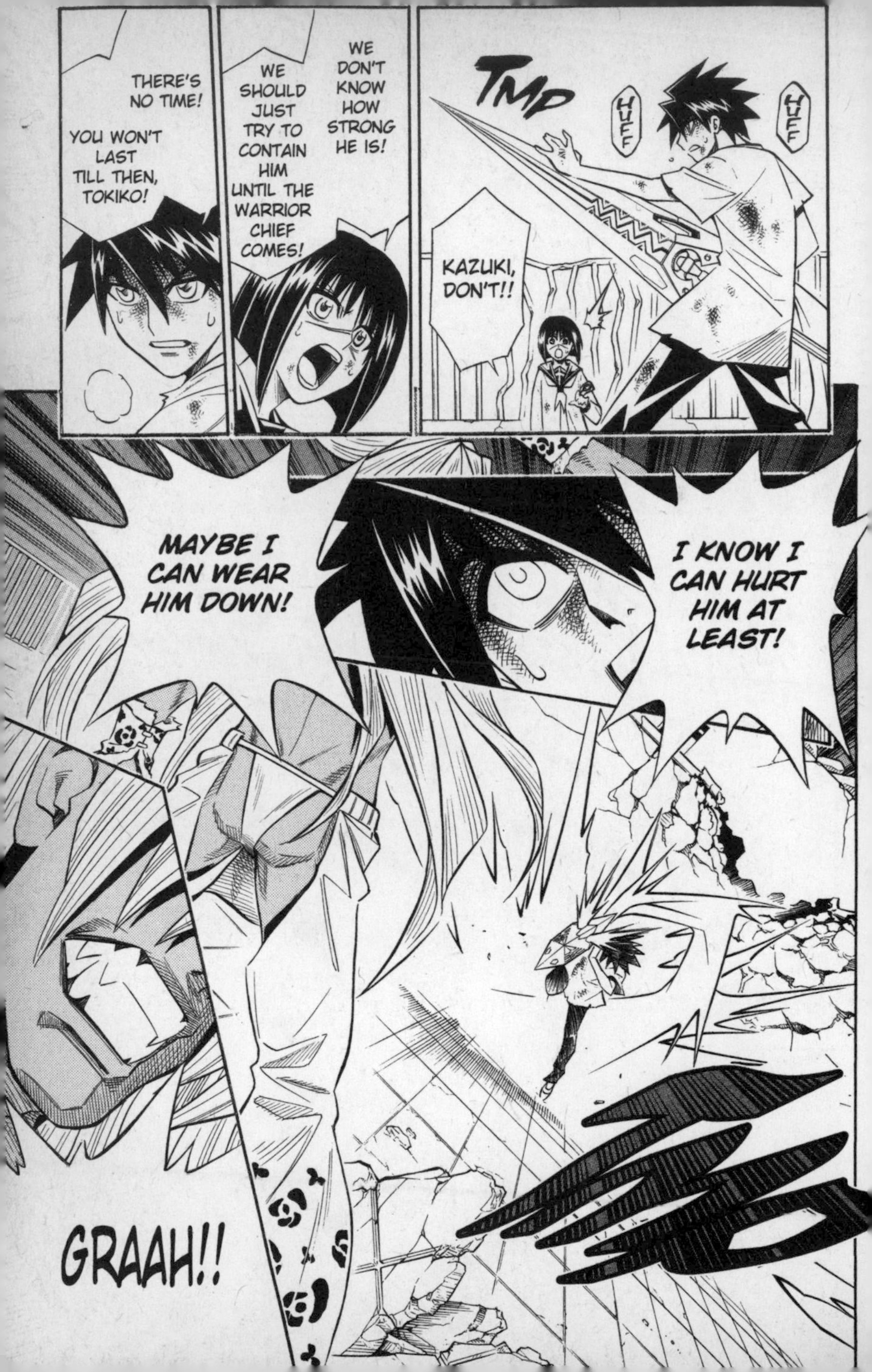
HUFF
TMP
HUFF
KAZUKI, DON'T!!
WE DON'T KNOW HOW STRONG HE IS!
WE SHOULD JUST TRY TO CONTAIN HIM UNTIL THE WARRIOR CHIEF COMES!
THERE'S NO TIME!
YOU WON'T LAST TILL THEN, TOKIKO!
I KNOW I CAN HURT HIM AT LEAST!
MAYBE I CAN WEAR HIM DOWN!
GRAAH!!

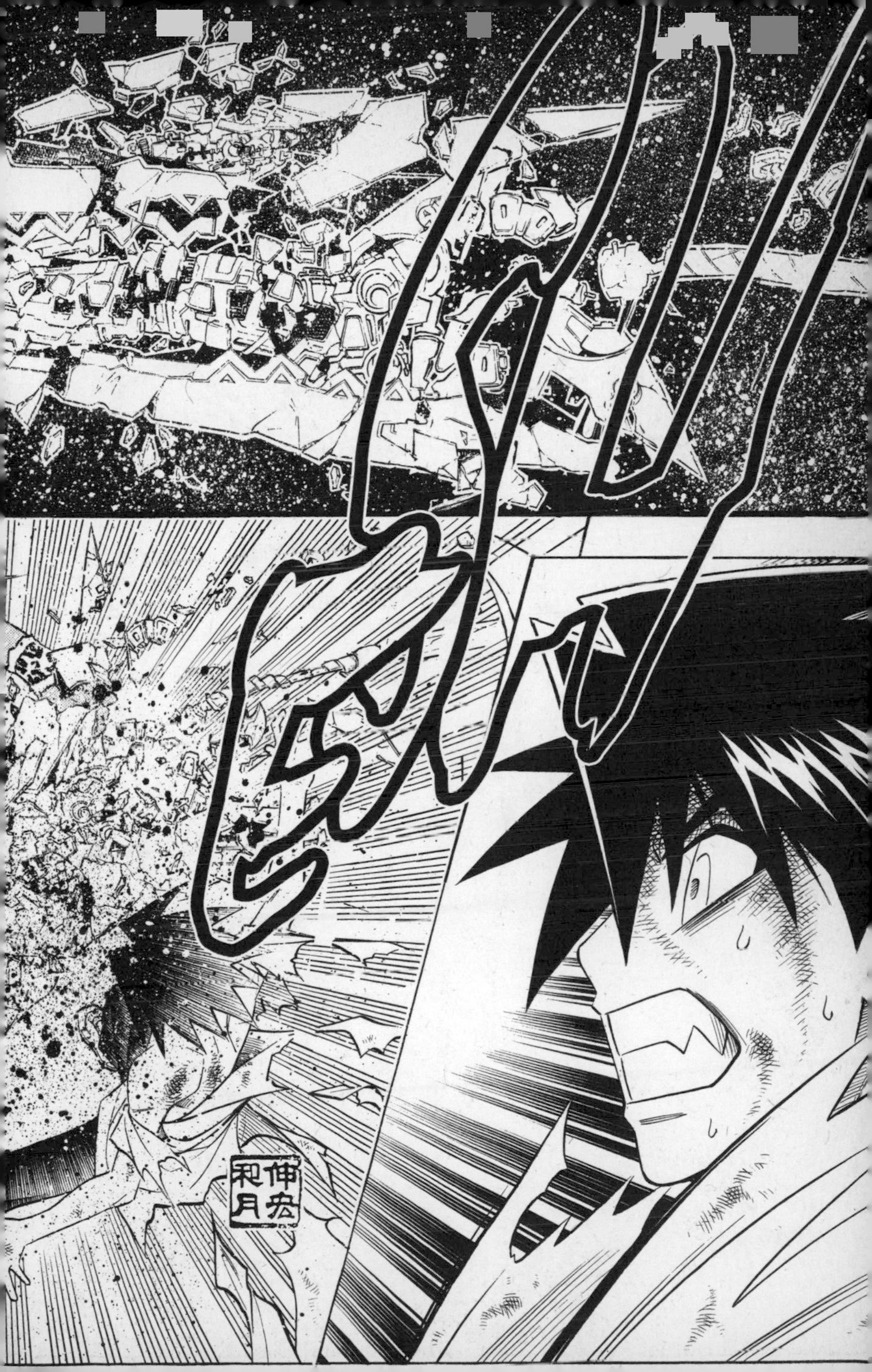
伸宏和月

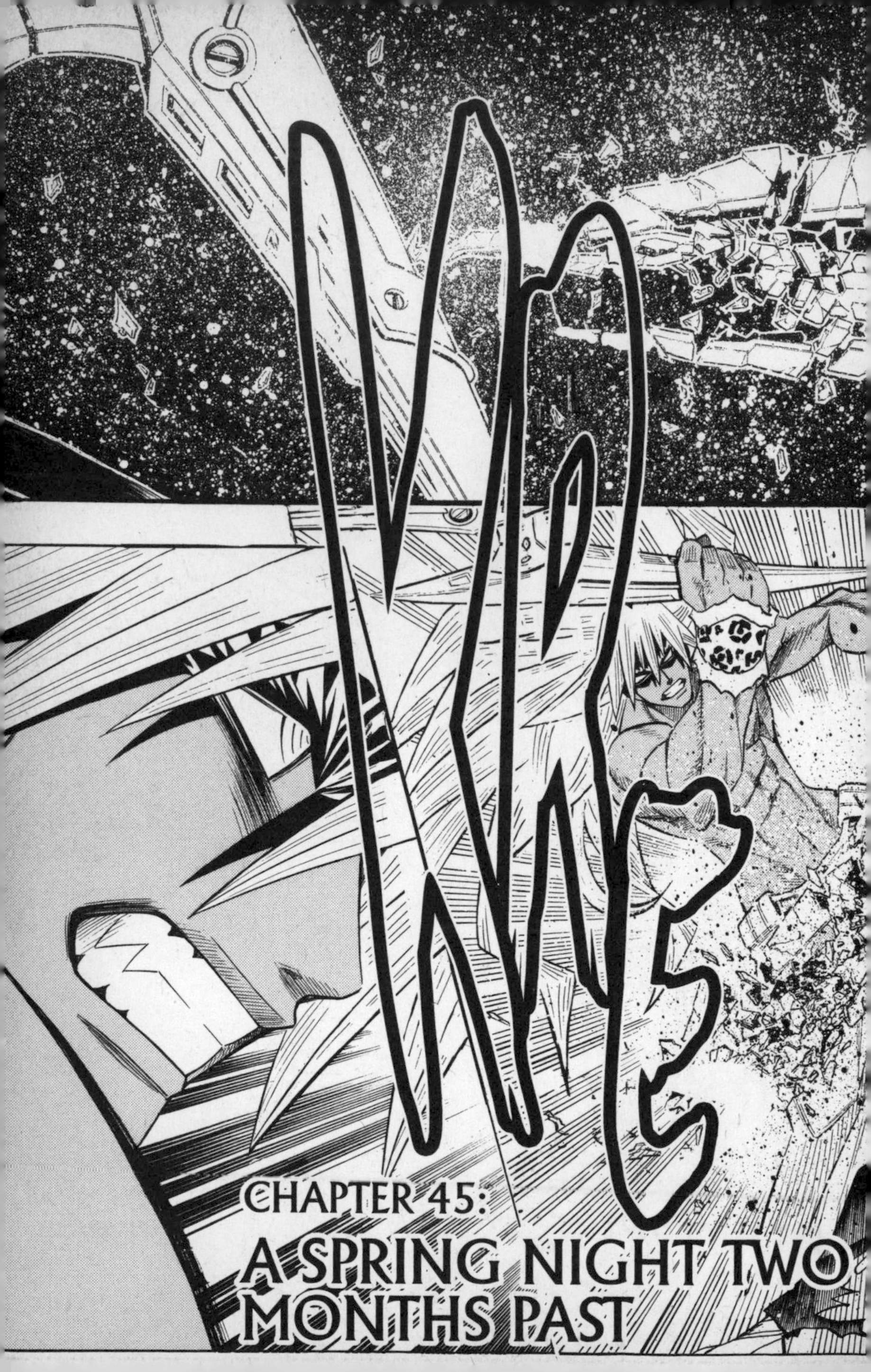
CHAPTER 45:
A SPRING NIGHT TWO MONTHS PAST

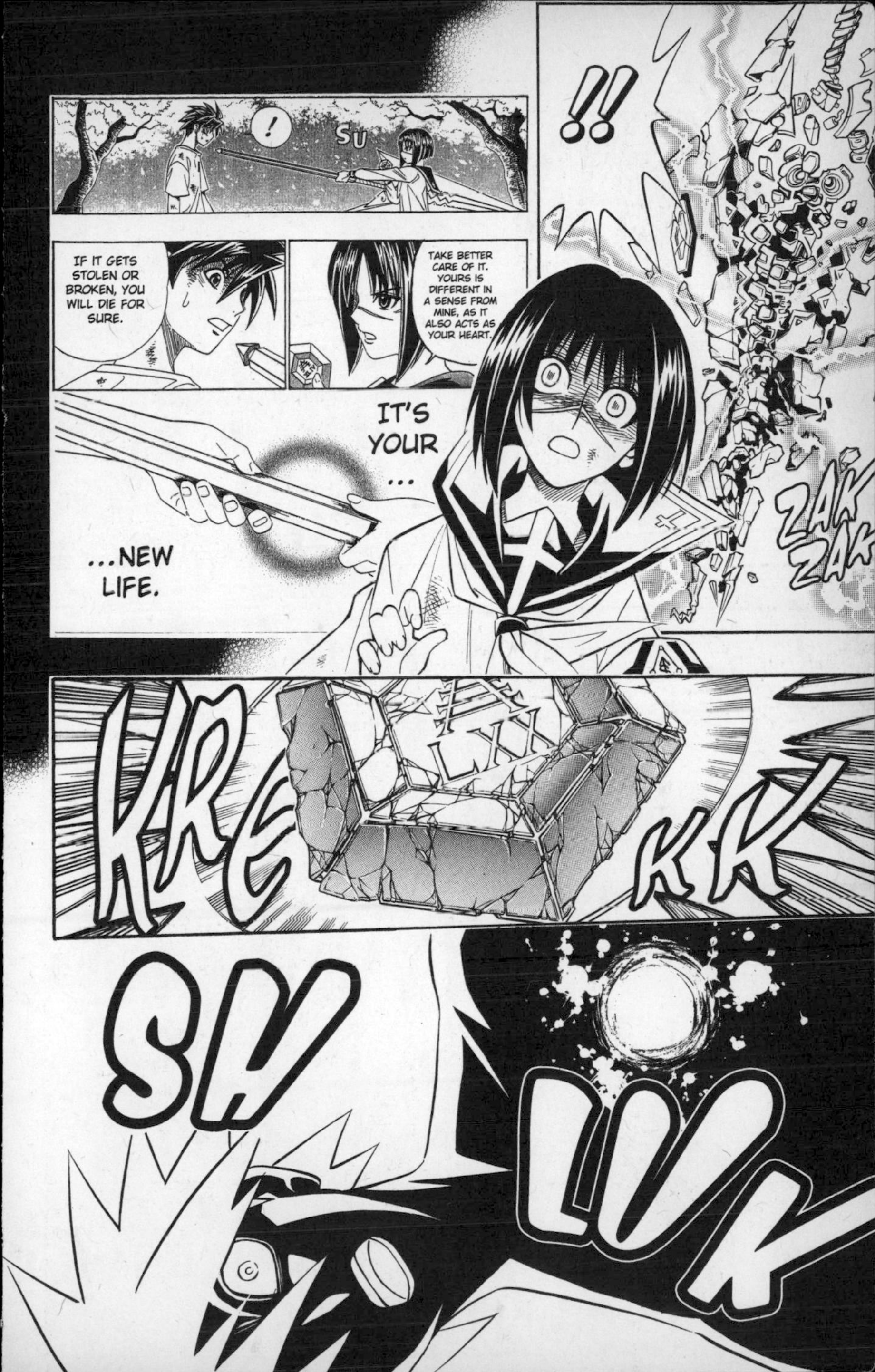
!!
ZAK ZAK
!
SU
TAKE BETTER CARE OF IT. YOURS IS DIFFERENT IN A SENSE FROM MINE, AS IT ALSO ACTS AS YOUR HEART.
IF IT GETS STOLEN OR BROKEN, YOU WILL DIE FOR SURE.
IT'S YOUR ...
...NEW LIFE.
KRE
KK
SH
LUK

READ THIS WAY

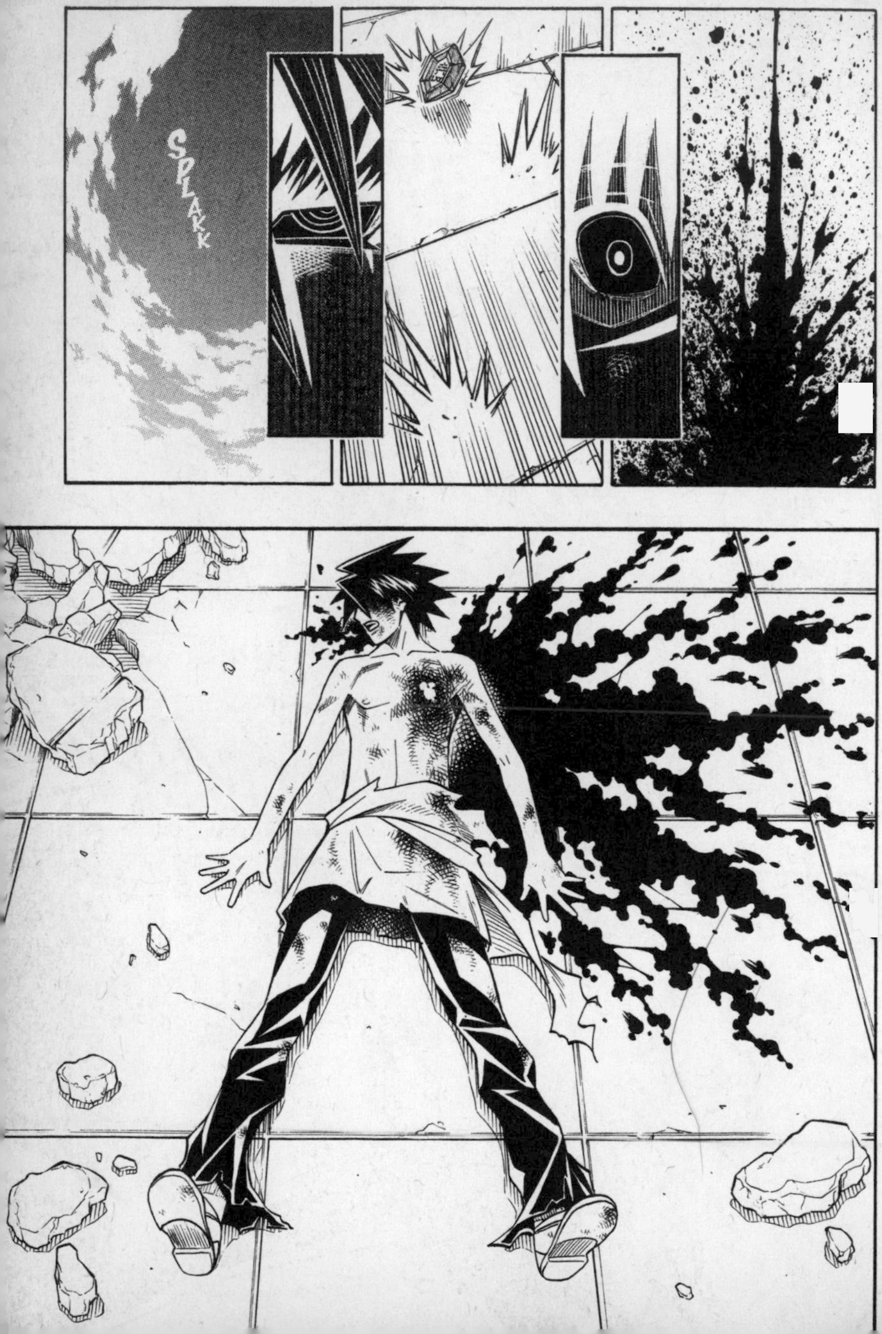
SPLAKK

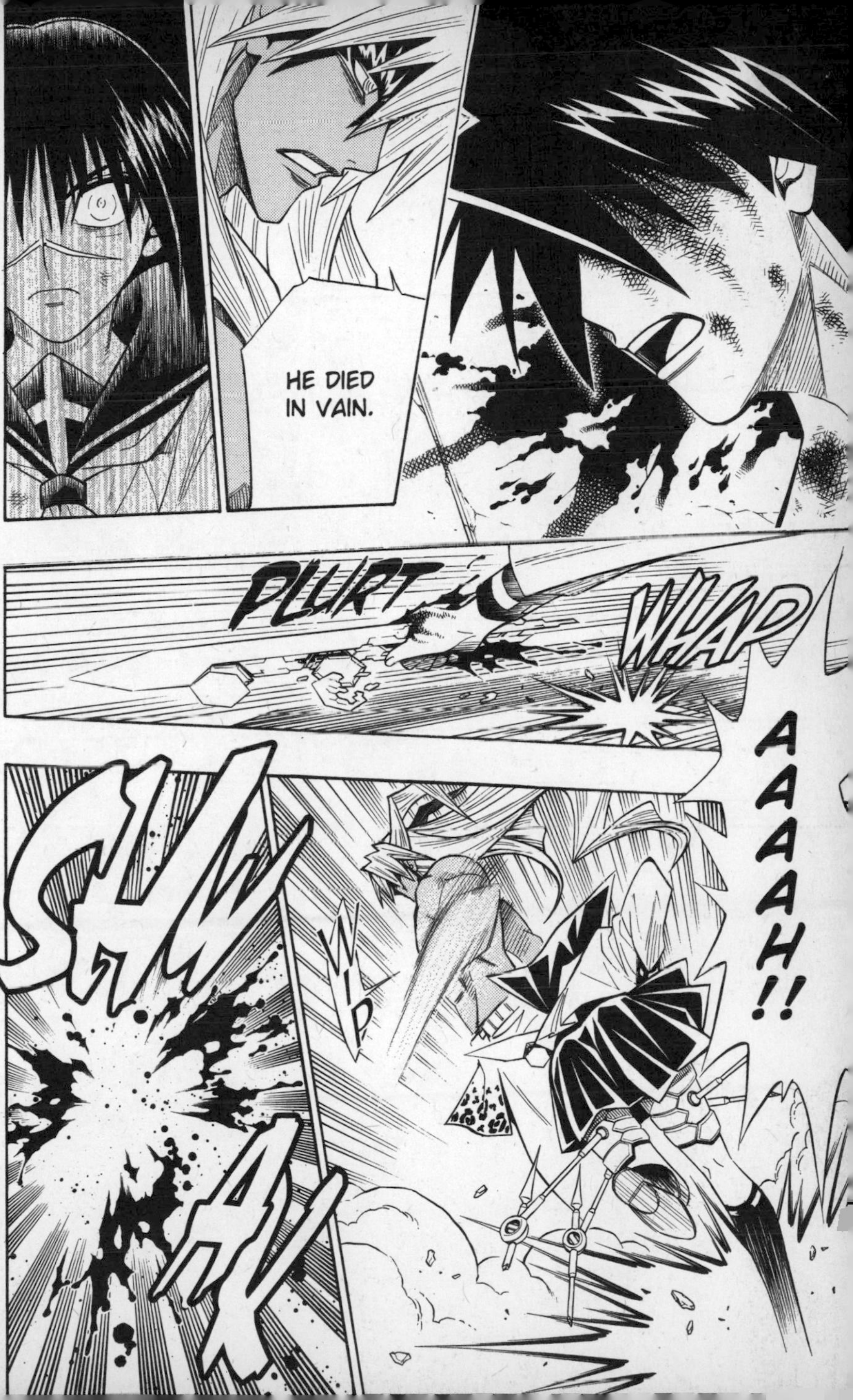
HE DIED IN VAIN.
WHAP
PLURT
AAAAAH!!
WIP
SHAA

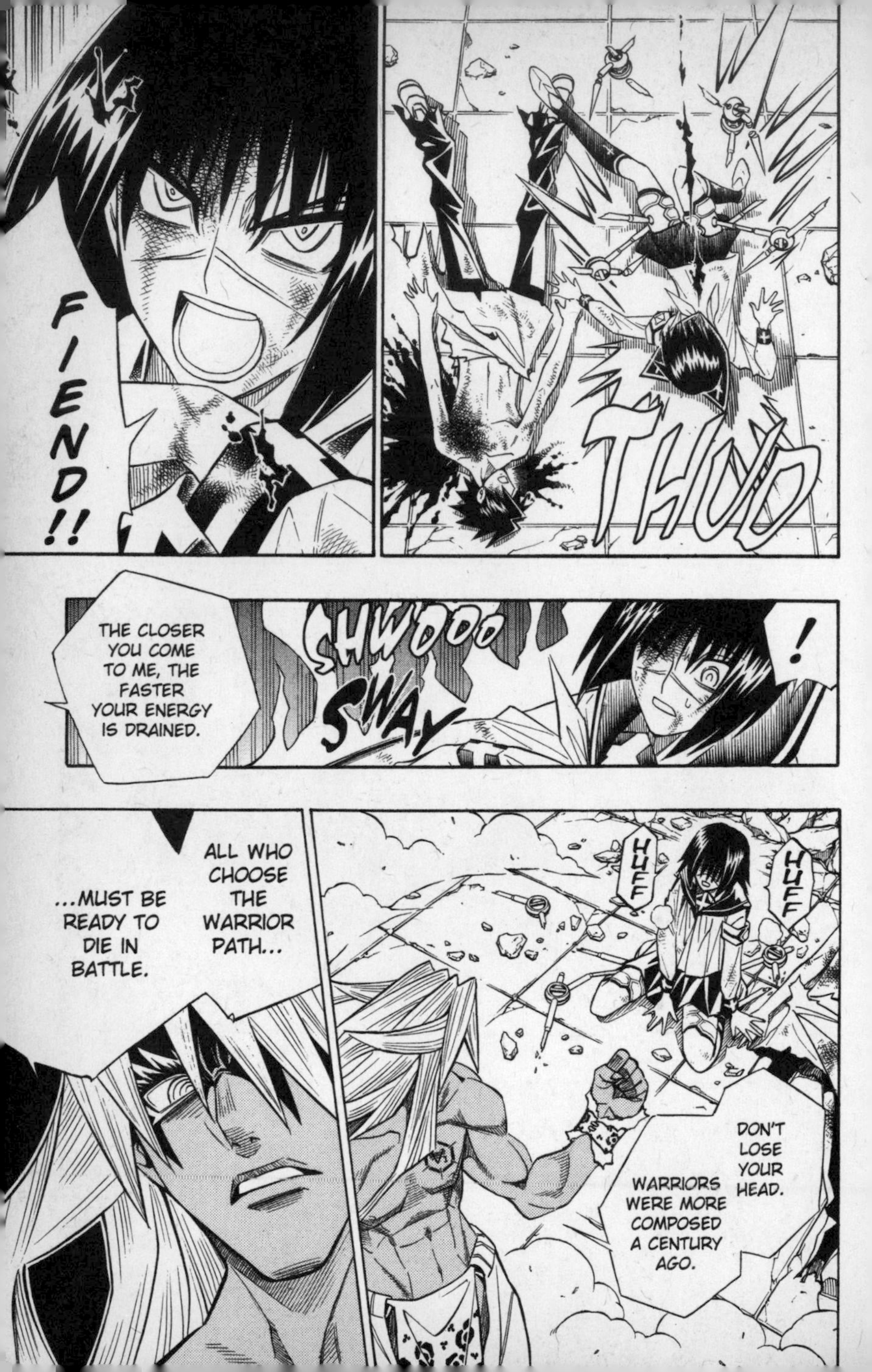
THUD
FIEND!!
!
SHWOOO
SWAY
THE CLOSER YOU COME TO ME, THE FASTER YOUR ENERGY IS DRAINED.
HUFF
HUFF
DON'T LOSE YOUR HEAD.
WARRIORS WERE MORE COMPOSED A CENTURY AGO.
ALL WHO CHOOSE THE WARRIOR PATH...
...MUST BE READY TO DIE IN BATTLE.

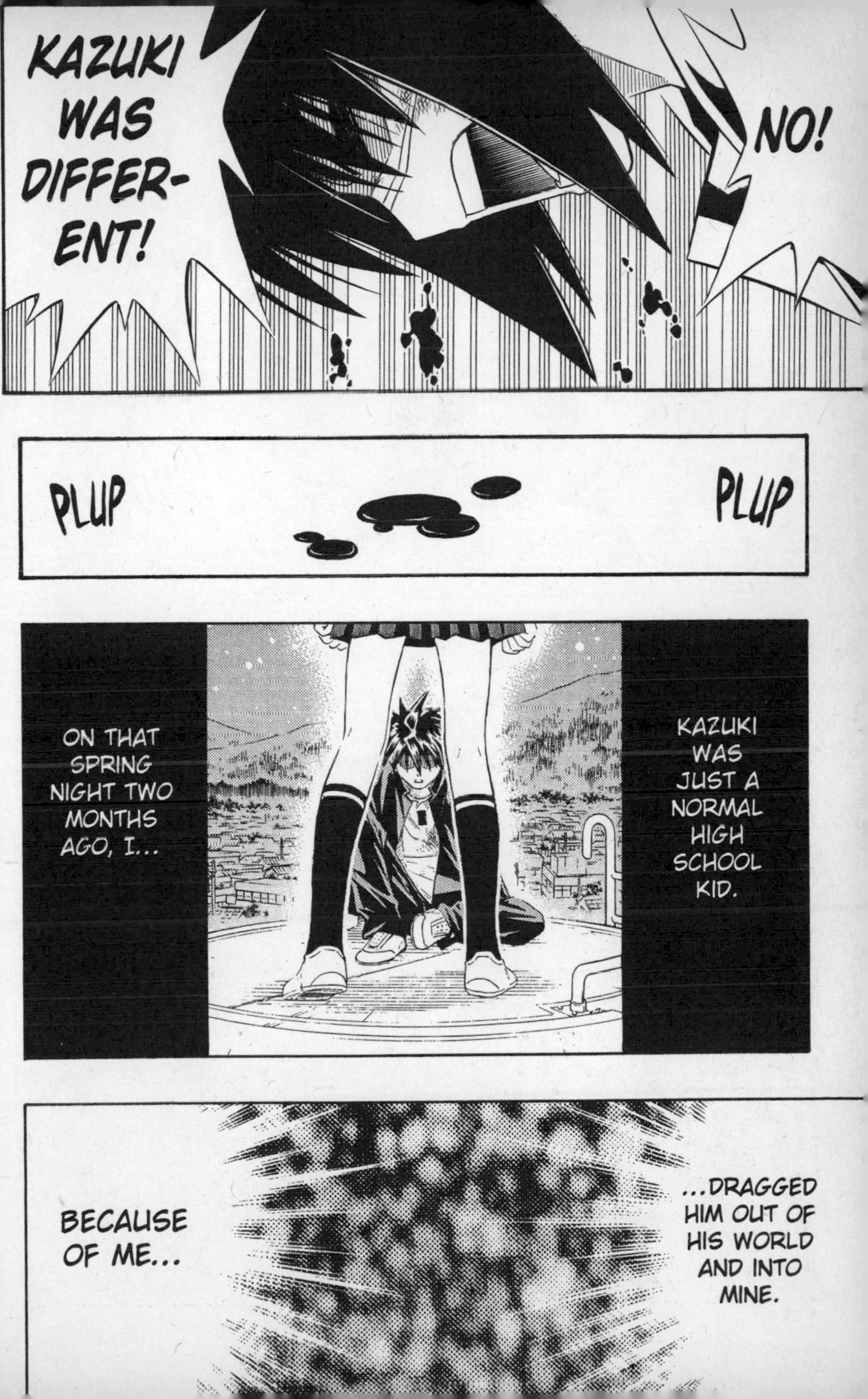
NO!
KAZUKI WAS DIFFER-ENT!
PLUP
PLUP
KAZUKI WAS JUST A NORMAL HIGH SCHOOL KID.
ON THAT SPRING NIGHT TWO MONTHS AGO, I...
...DRAGGED HIM OUT OF HIS WORLD AND INTO MINE.
BECAUSE OF ME...

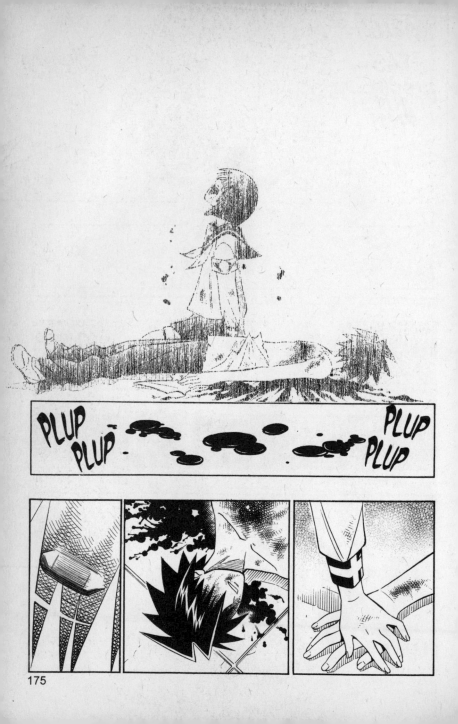

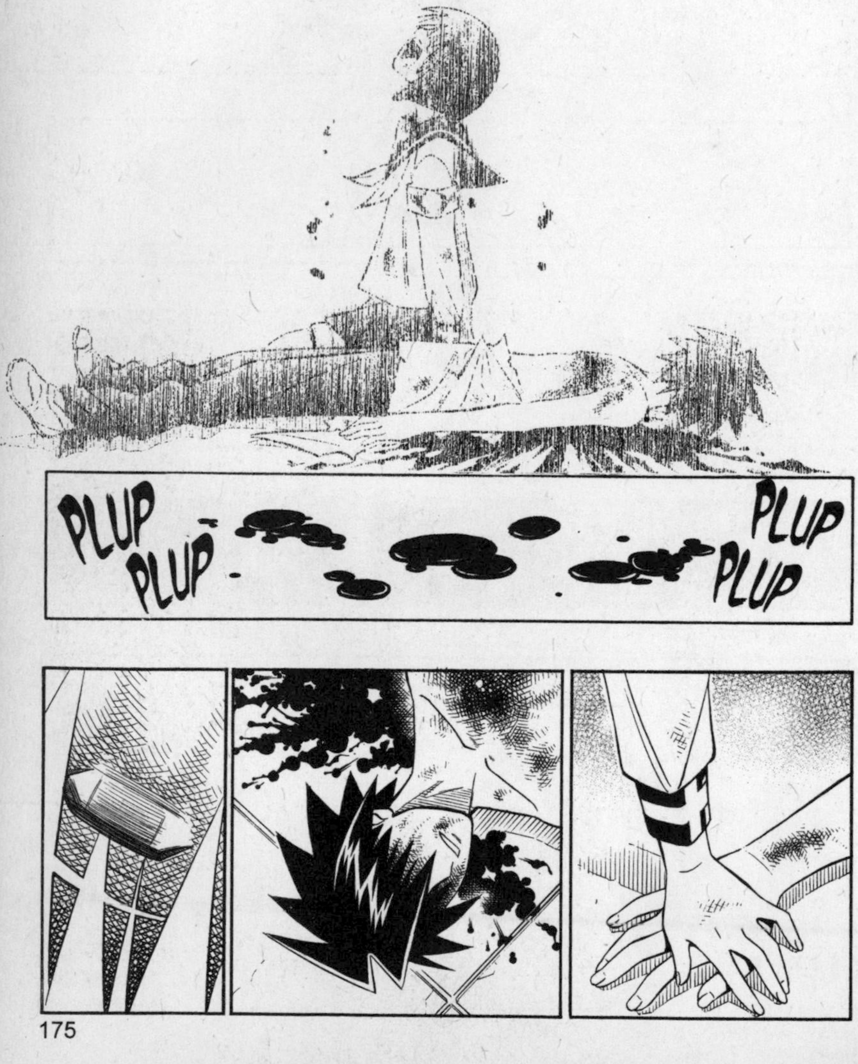
PLUP
PLUP
PLUP
PLUP

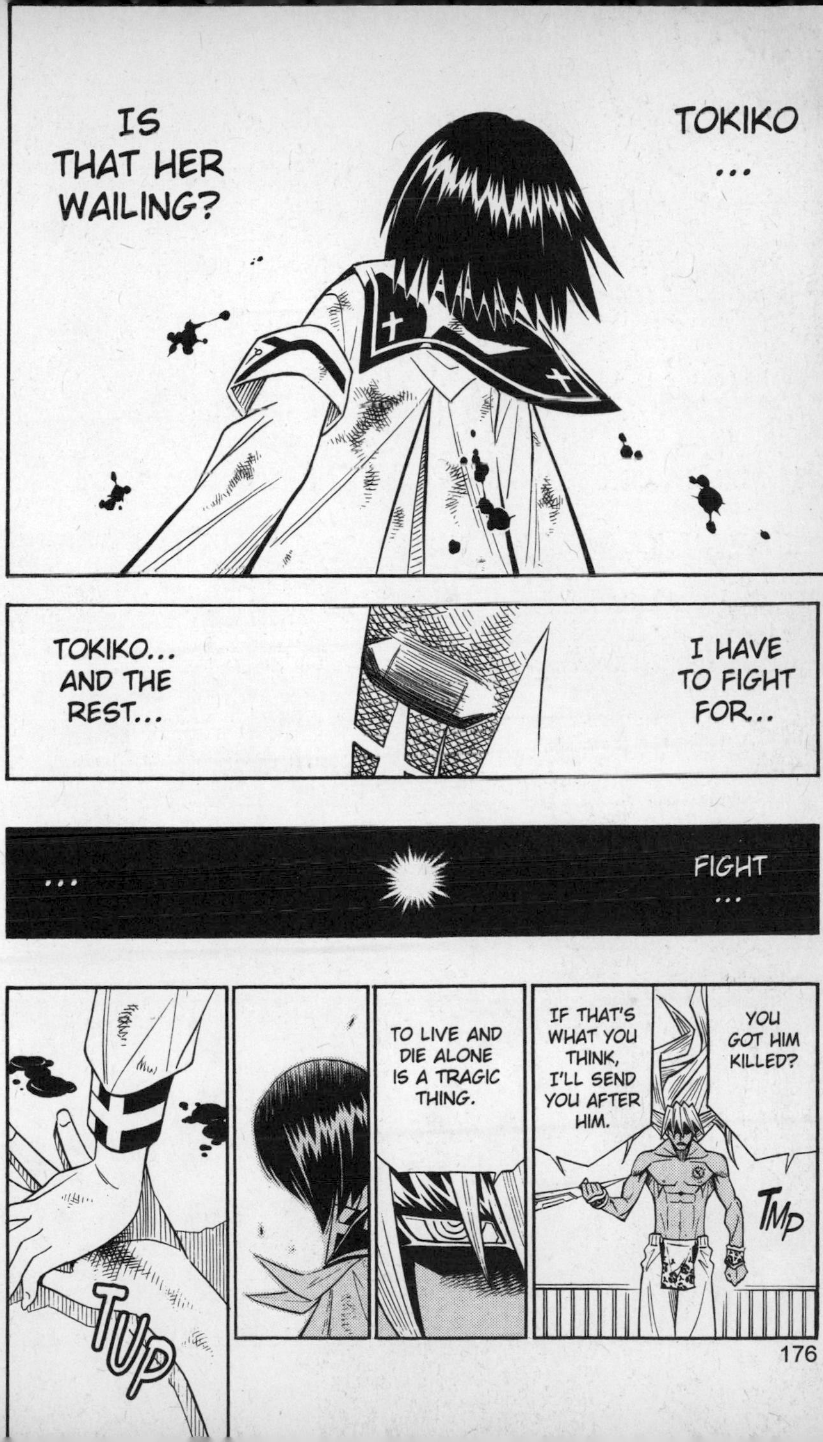
TOKIKO ...
IS THAT HER WAILING?
I HAVE TO FIGHT FOR...
TOKIKO... AND THE REST...
FIGHT ...
...
YOU GOT HIM KILLED?
IF THAT'S WHAT YOU THINK, I'LL SEND YOU AFTER HIM.
TMP
TO LIVE AND DIE ALONE IS A TRAGIC THING.
TUP

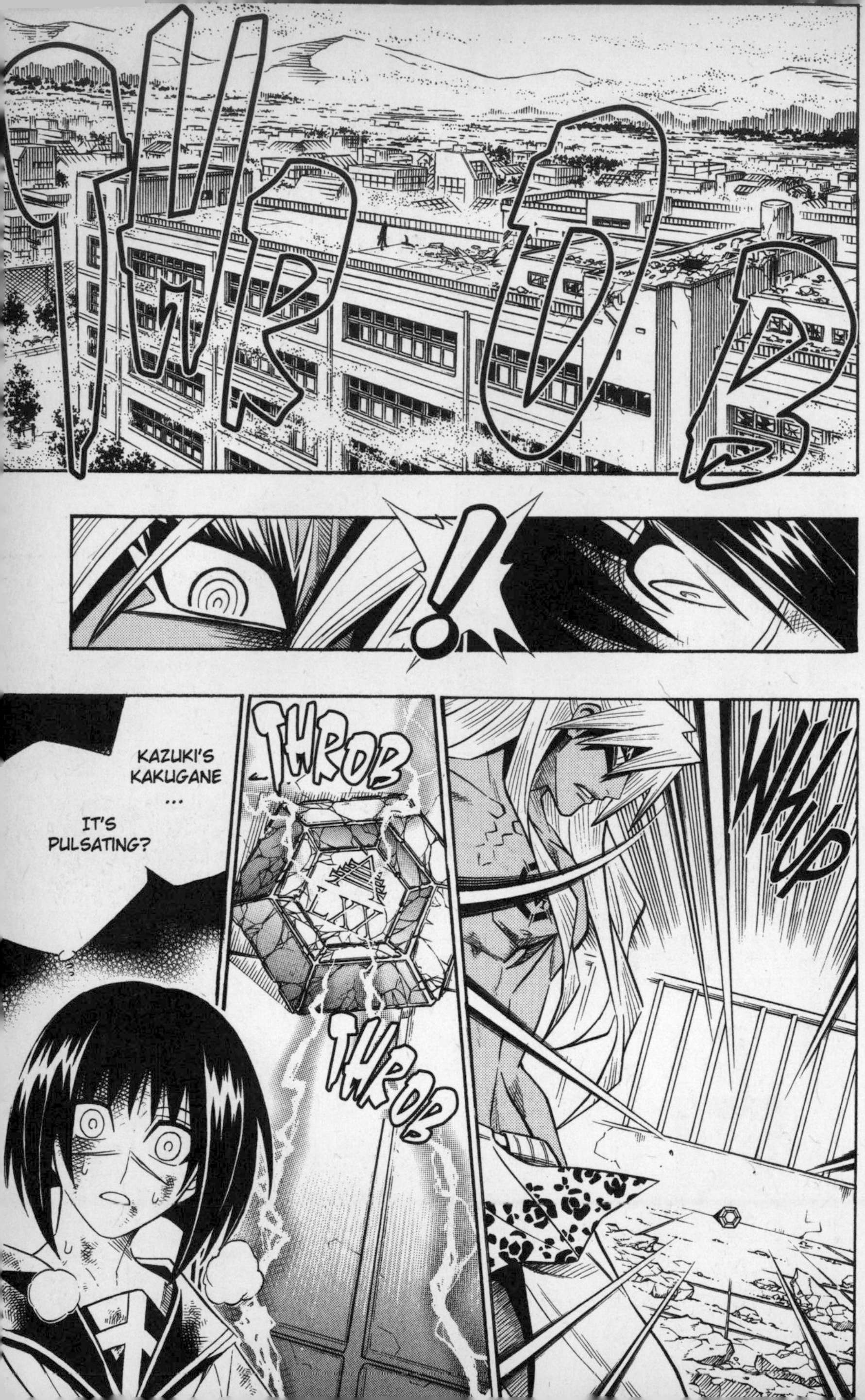
THROB
!
WHIP
THROB
KAZUKI'S KAKUGANE ...
IT'S PULSATING?
THROB

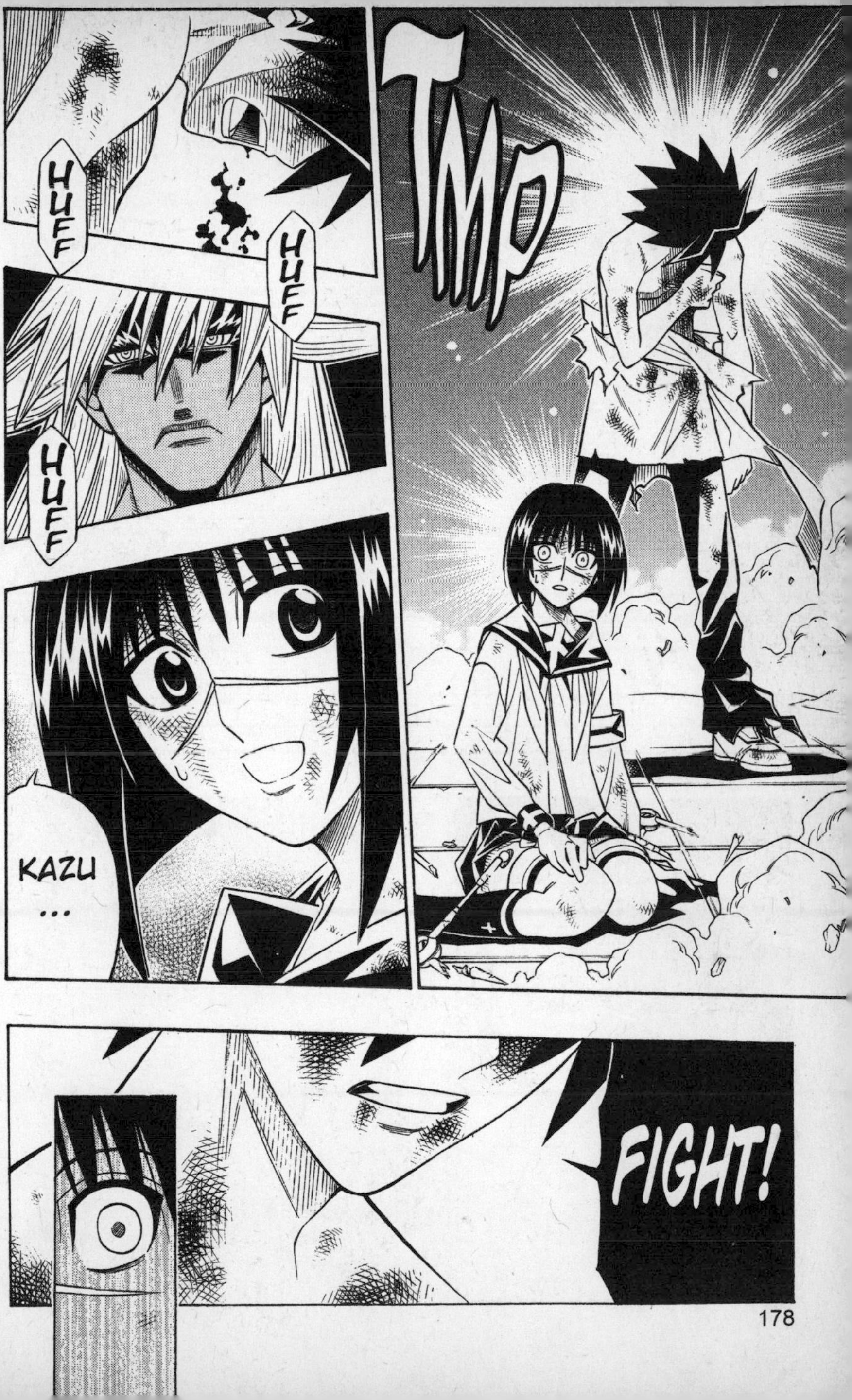
TMP
HUFF
HUFF
HUFF
KAZU ...
FIGHT!

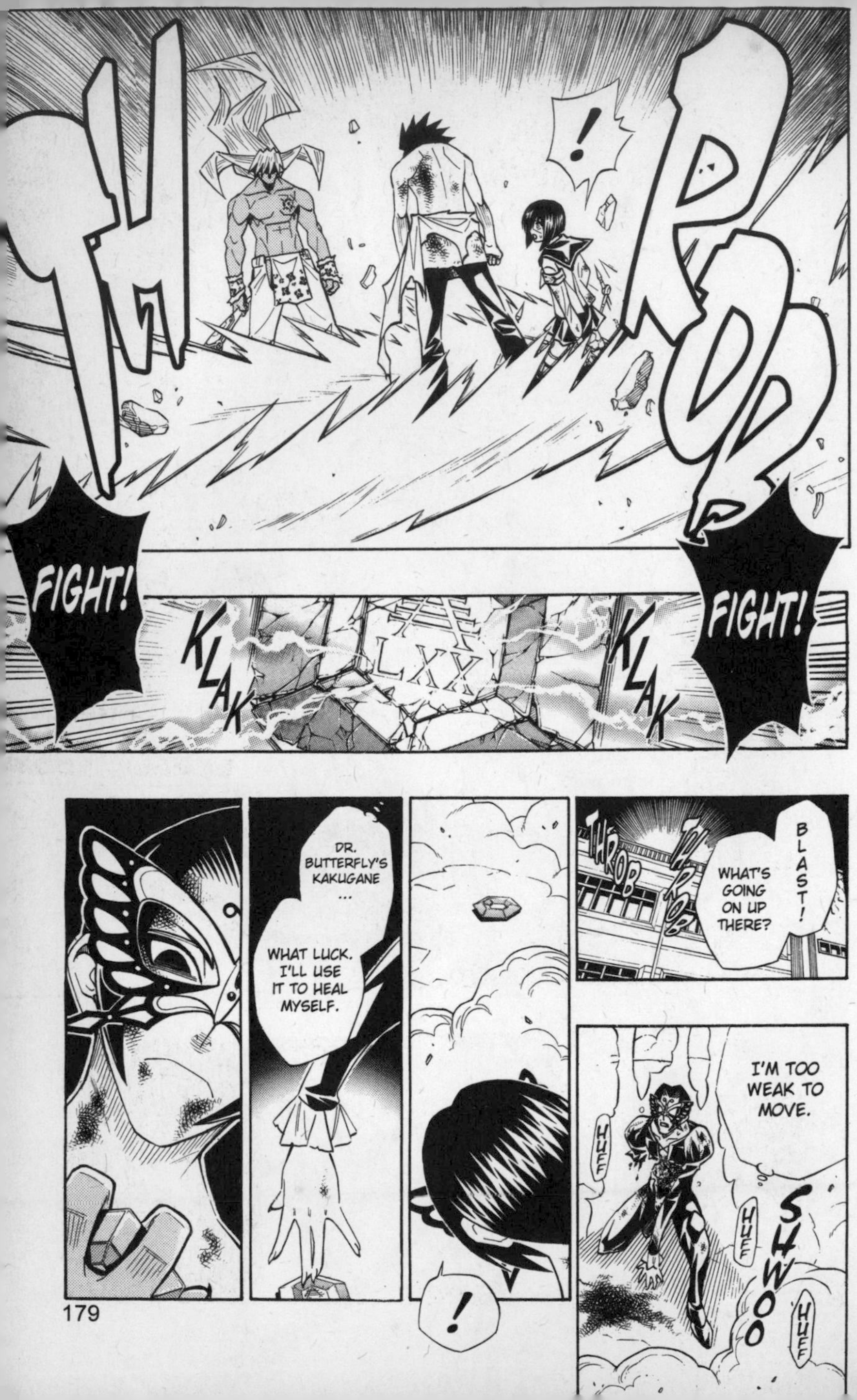
!
FIGHT!
FIGHT!
KLAK
KLAK
LXX
THROB
THROB
BLAST!
WHAT'S GOING ON UP THERE?
I'M TOO WEAK TO MOVE.
HUFF
HUFF
HUFF
SHWOO
!
DR. BUTTERFLY'S KAKUGANE ...
WHAT LUCK. I'LL USE IT TO HEAL MYSELF.

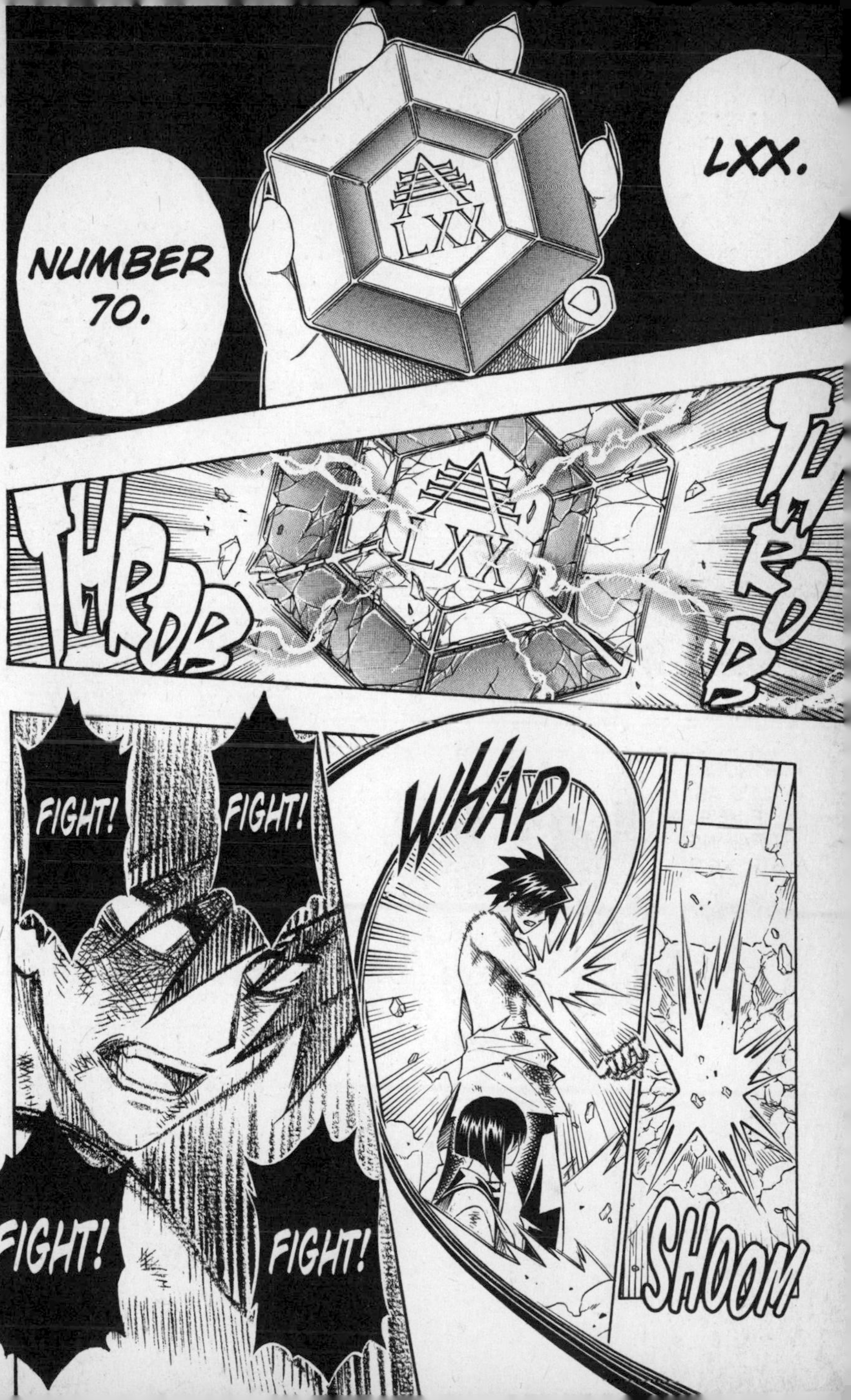
LXX.
NUMBER 70.
THROB
THROB
WHAP
SHOOM
FIGHT!
FIGHT!
FIGHT!
FIGHT!

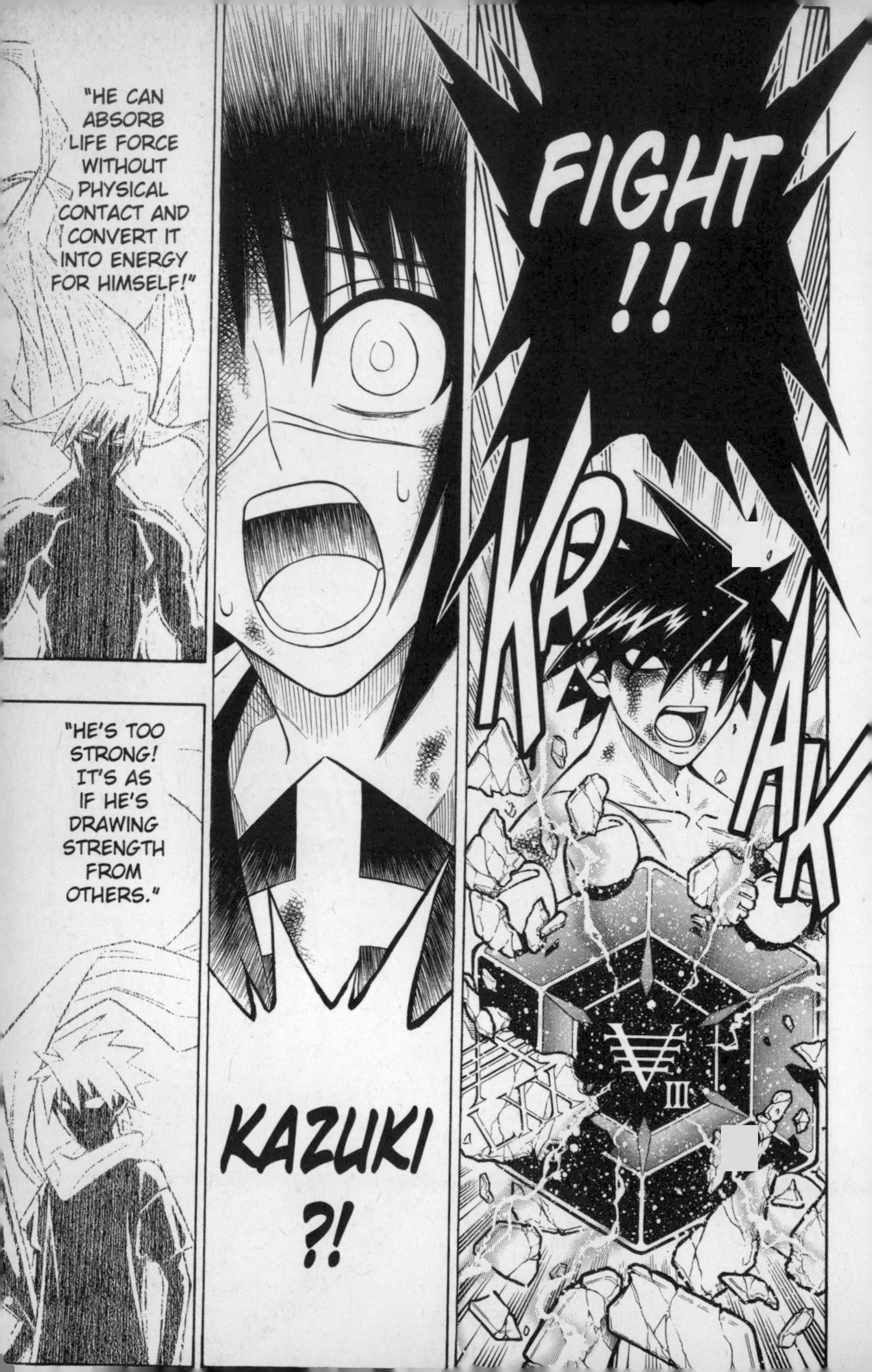
FIGHT!!
KRAK
KAZUKI ?!
"HE CAN ABSORB LIFE FORCE WITHOUT PHYSICAL CONTACT AND CONVERT IT INTO ENERGY FOR HIMSELF!"
"HE'S TOO STRONG! IT'S AS IF HE'S DRAWING STRENGTH FROM OTHERS."

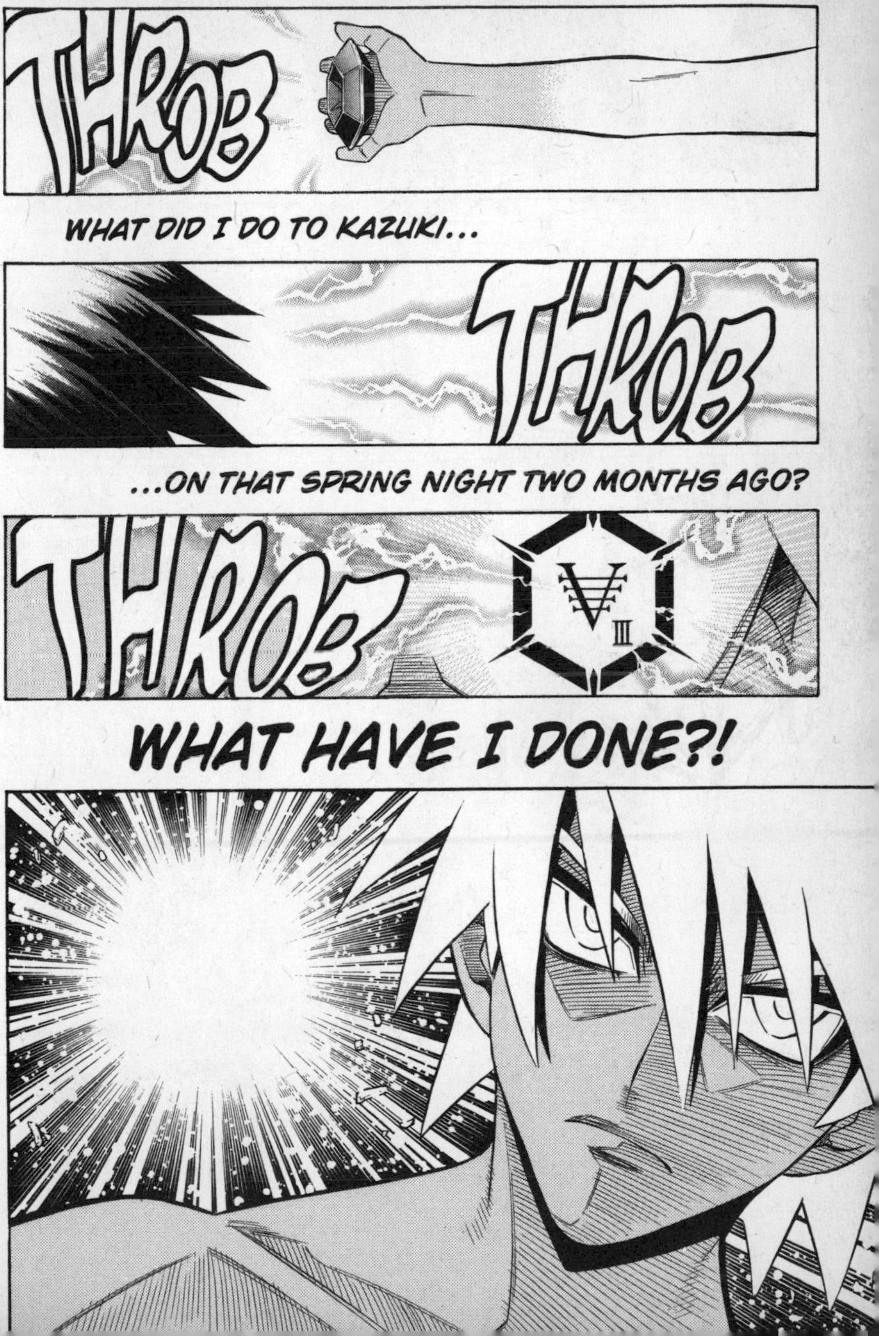
THROB
WHAT DID I DO TO KAZUKI...
THROB
...ON THAT SPRING NIGHT TWO MONTHS AGO?
THROB
WHAT HAVE I DONE?!

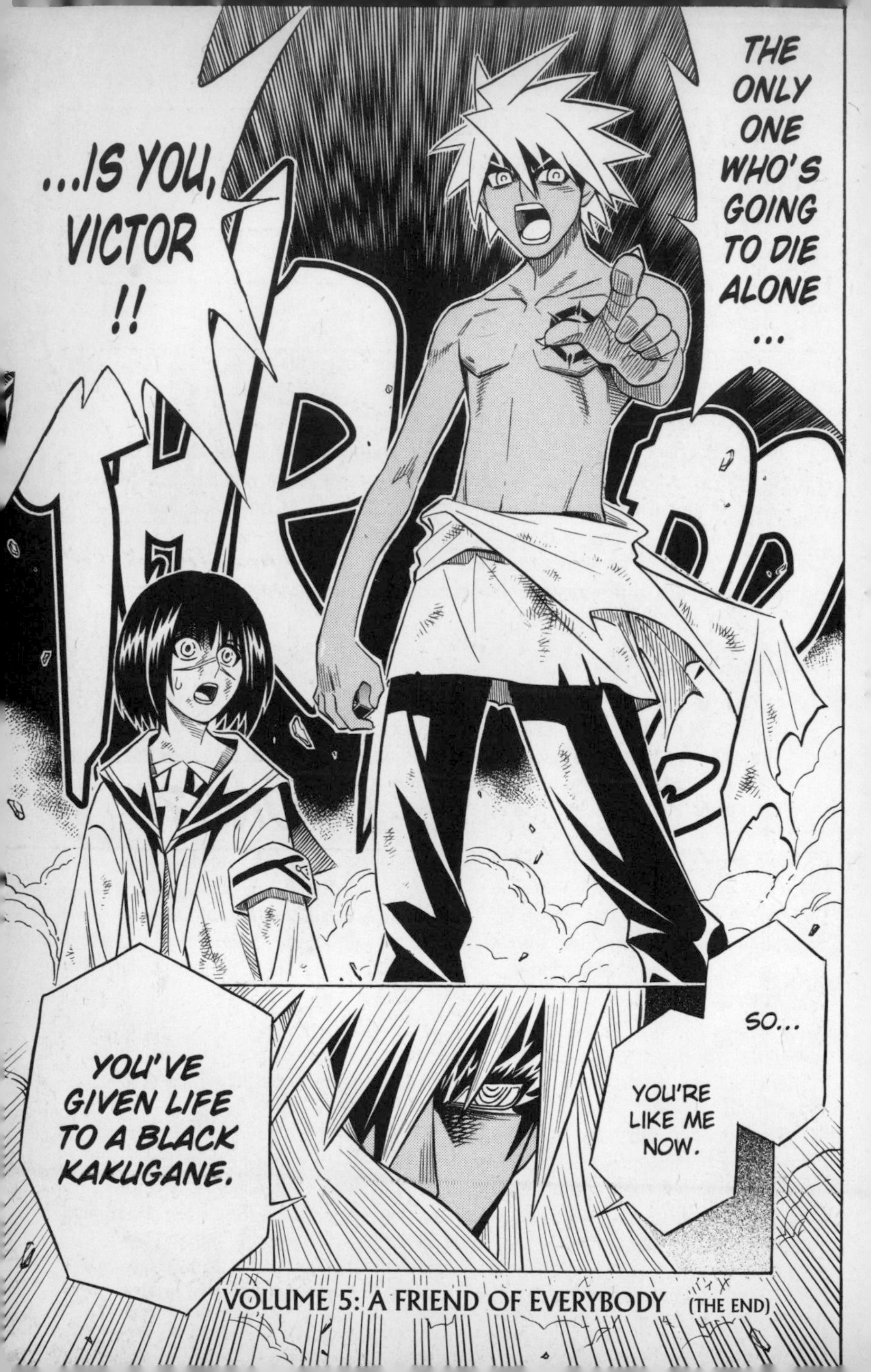
THE ONLY ONE WHO'S GOING TO DIE ALONE...
...IS YOU, VICTOR!!
SO...
YOU'RE LIKE ME NOW.
YOU'VE GIVEN LIFE TO A BLACK KAKUGANE.

VOLUME 5: A FRIEND OF EVERYBODY (THE END)

· Let's start with the homework from the previous volume, the origin of the word "Carnival." Here are three possibilities:

1) The Latin *carnem levare* (to take away the meat)
   · From a traditional festival like Lent.
2) The Latin *carnem vale* (farewell to meat)
   · From a traditional festival like Lent.
3) The Latin *caro vale* (farewell to meat)
   · Related to the practice of abstaining from eating meat.

These are some possible origins of the word that I've found. Kurosaki spent time in Brazil where she learned the third etymology. She says that in Catholic countries there's a holiday during which they don't eat any meat, but before it begins, they have a big party and eat lots of meat. In any case, the word "carnival" has nothing to do with cannibalism. But this is manga so I can claim the license to fictionalize things to make the story more interesting. But it doesn't excuse the mistake. Please accept my apology.

Chapter 37: In the Same Category

· I'm very pleased that the fog turned out so well without the use of tone. I'm using a lot more tone than I did in my earlier manga, but I have to admit I don't like using it very much. (I even removed the tone from Kazuki and Tokiko's school uniforms because I didn't like the way it looked.) I want to learn to use tone as little as possible but use it effectively when I do.
· Like Kamen Rider and Cyborg 009, a true hero needs a scarf! That's why Kazuki wrapped that cloth around his face like that. It was a lot of fun to draw.
· I like the way a boy's school jacket looks on a girl. That's why Tokiko puts on Kazuki's jacket to disguise her school uniform. Actually, the hem of her skirt should have shown under the jacket, but I thought it looked better if you couldn't see it. Of course, that started a whole new controversy. She's wearing a skirt, I promise!

Chapter 38: A Friend of Everybody

· The title is in English, but I really wanted the meaning to be "ally" rather than "friend."
· I crammed as much as I could into a single chapter. I put so much into it that I dreamt my first editor was scolding me for it. It's kind of like drinking CalPico concentrate without water. Readers complain that my stories are hard to follow sometimes. I guess I need to work on making them so they'll go down smoothly with a nice finish like properly diluted CalPico.
· The Idiot Trio has their moment in the spotlight. They symbolize Kazuki's normal life and don't usually fight. But they'll fight too if they have to. Up to now, it's been [continued]

suggested several times that the trio become Warriors themselves, but I always said no. Anyone can fight if they have to, but not just anybody can be a hero. The publisher doesn't like this theme, but I'm sticking to it.

Chapter 39: Overflowing Power
· The two-page spread in this chapter is, at least for me, the climax of the first part of Buso Renkin. It's good to have made it this far.
· Class B-2 comes to the rescue. They ran away at the beginning, but I wanted to show that all of Kazuki's classmates were good people, so I added these panels.
· The growing pile of blurred-out Homunculi. Now that I think about it, this was a pretty risky move. I never thought that my editor's comment, "Don't you think the mosaics make it seem even worse than it is?" would come back to haunt me.

Chapter 40: A Sign of Death
· Moonface's replications were an homage to Agent Smith from the Matrix, but he just looks really freaky with all those different heads. Then again, this is Moonface we're talking about.
· The Silver Skin AT (Alternate Type) is modeled on a navy uniform from the Age of Discovery.
· Papillon with butterfly wings just doesn't seem right. But then again, I'm okay with it. This is Papillon after all; what other kind of wings could he have?

Chapter 41: Papillon vs. Butterfly, Part I
· The freak's forefather is also a freak, so Dr. Butterfly proclaims himself "Lord" Butterfly and dons a nifty new cape to commemorate it. I have to say that the Butterfly Suit and cape work really well together…really.
· The characters in the hallucination may have been a little confusing for any new readers out there. I regret that a little. Still, I really enjoyed showing Papillon chasing his mask as it flutters away. But then, he's always fun to draw.

Chapter 41: Papillon vs. Butterfly, Part II
· I wanted to show how those two would try to outsmart each other, but it required too much exposition and slowed the tempo too much. I should've worked it out better in the scripting stage.
· Papillon announces that he wants to fly even higher as a butterfly. Since Papillon is the bad guy of this manga, I plan to expand on this in the future. He's not just an ordinary freak, you know?

Chapter 43: Who Are You?

· For three chapters straight, starting with this chapter, I was hit by a Jet Stream Attack* of toothache, headache, and stomach ache and was on the verge of passing out when I did this work. I think the content and the artwork show the effects. I'm very disappointed in myself.

* Jet Stream Attack--a three-pronged attack from the original *Gundam* anime.

· In the first half of this chapter there's a recap of Victor's origin. I was afraid that the readers would need the background, but I'm not sure it worked or was even necessary.

· The scene where Kazuki bursts upward through the floors and destroys the tank is one of my favorites. In this battle, Kazuki was the one who caused the most property damage. Does this disqualify him as a hero?

· Victor appears. I did his work at the peak of my toothache and, looking back at it now, the artwork lacks impact.

Chapter 44: The Pulse Quickens

· My headache was at its worse during this chapter. I wasn't sure whether to make Victor more intelligent or wilder. In the end, I couldn't make up my mind because my head hurt so much.

· Victor's half-exposed behind was a topic of debate. Some liked it and others hated it. I think the fundoshi looks really cool. And to clarify, the pattern on his fundoshi and leggings is leopard spots, not roses! Although an assistant did make that mistake at one point…

· Dr. Butterfly uses the last of his strength (he's only a mustache at this point) to talk to Victor. Here "good morning" and "good night" refer to birth and death.

Chapter 45: A Spring Night Two Months Past

· This was the most difficult chapter in the entire volume. Kazuki became like Victor. My editors asked me, "Don't you think the main character of a boy's comic should have special powers?" After months of working it out, I've come to the conclusion that strength gained by means of special powers is superficial strength. In a comic, it's more important how a character uses his or her strength. From this point on, Kazuki will have to fight for himself instead of for others. But Kazuki will always be Kazuki, no matter what. My original goals and themes for this title won't change either.

· Tokiko wails when she thinks Kazuki has been killed. This is no time for Tokiko to cry and show her tears. But I did wonder about not having her cry in this situation. So instead of "cry" I went with "wail." I think that's how Tokiko should be.

· And so →   To be continued.

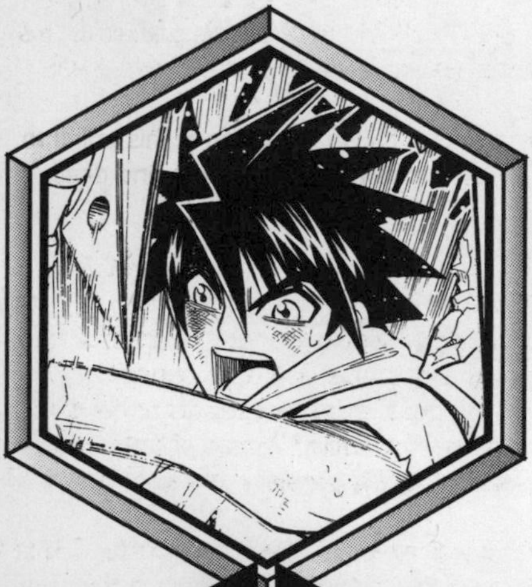

Buso Renkin

ブソウレンキン

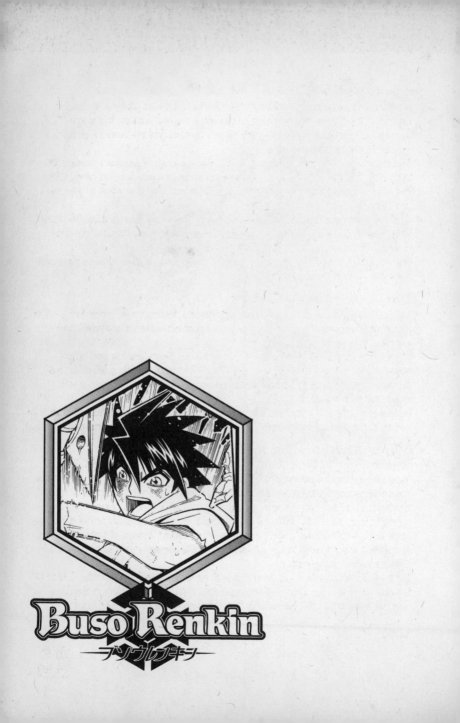

Coming Next Volume

Kazuki's black kakugane is growing more and more
deadly, and it will soon advance to the point where it
begins to drain life from others around him. Trying to
avoid this he goes on a secret mission with Tokiko to try
and find a way to stop this from happening. They soon
run into trouble when an elite group of Alchemist Warriors comes after them!

Available in June 2007!

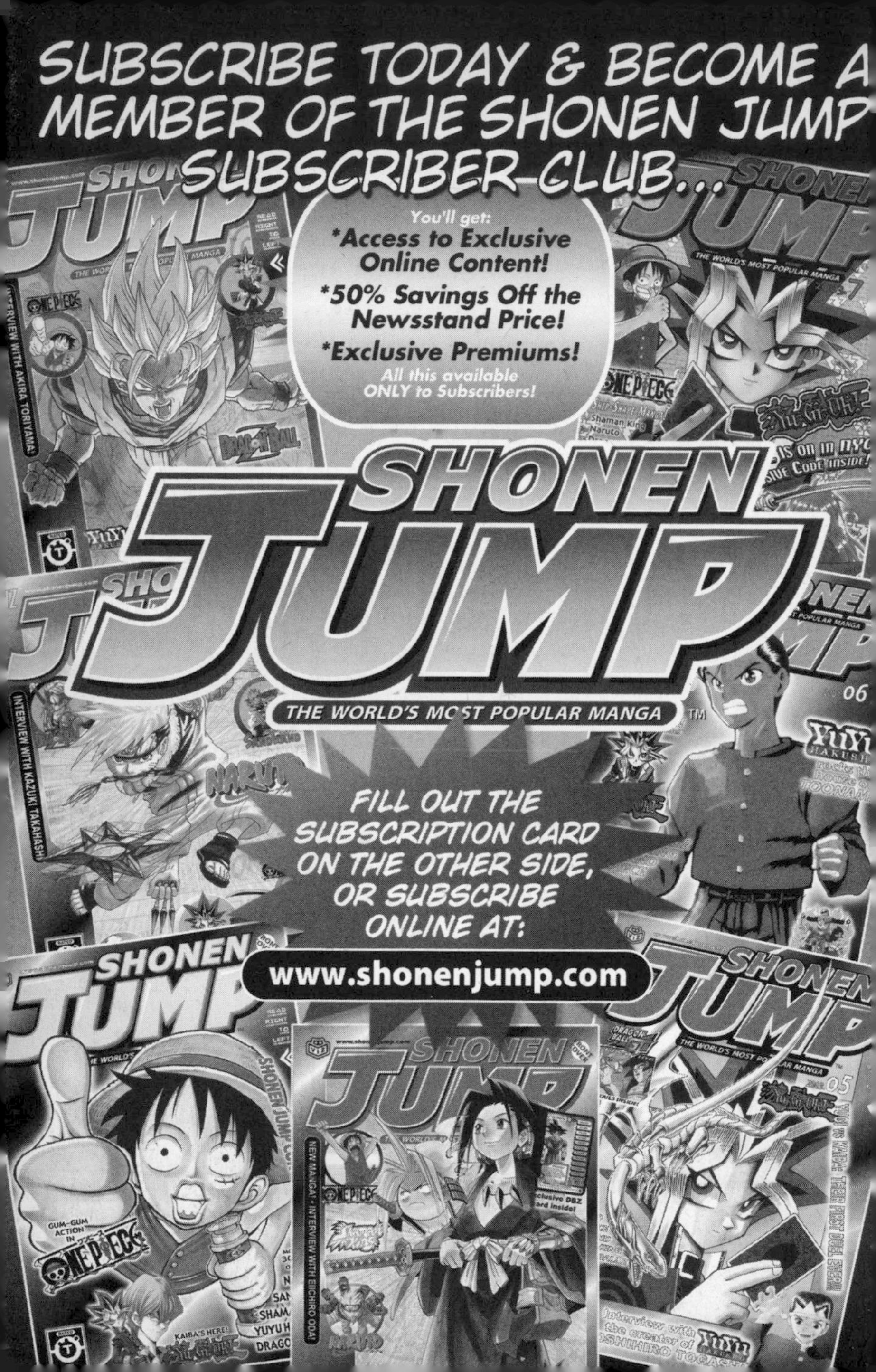